Culture and Group Processes

FRONTIERS OF CULTURE AND PSYCHOLOGY

Series Editors
Chi-yue Chiu
Ying-yi Hong
Michele J. Gelfand

Books in the Series

Culture and Group Processes
Edited by Masaki Yuki and Marilynn B. Brewer

Culture and Group Processes

EDITED BY MASAKI YUKI

AND

MARILYNN B. BREWER

Oxford University Press is a department of the University of Oxford.
It furthers the University's objective of excellence in research, scholarship,
and education by publishing worldwide.

Oxford New York
Auckland Cape Town Dar es Salaam Hong Kong Karachi
Kuala Lumpur Madrid Melbourne Mexico City Nairobi
New Delhi Shanghai Taipei Toronto

With offices in
Argentina Austria Brazil Chile Czech Republic France Greece
Guatemala Hungary Italy Japan Poland Portugal Singapore
South Korea Switzerland Thailand Turkey Ukraine Vietnam

Published in the United States of America by
Oxford University Press
198 Madison Avenue, New York, NY 10016

Library of Congress Cataloging-in-Publication Data
Culture and group processes / edited by Masaki Yuki and Marilynn B. Brewer.
pages cm
Includes bibliographical references and index.
ISBN 978-0-19-998547-0 (pbk : alk.paper) — ISBN 978-0-19-998546-3 (hardback : alk.paper)
1. Intergroup relations. 2. Social groups. 3. Culture. 4. Culture—Psychological aspects.
I. Yuki, Masaki, 1967- II. Brewer, Marilynn B., 1942-
HM716.C855 2013
302—dc23
2013017332

9 8 7 6 5 4 3 2 1

Printed in the United States of America
on acid-free paper

CONTENTS

PART THREE **Culture and Intergroup Processes**

SERIES PREFACE

Frontiers of Culture and Psychology is a new series of books that aims to bring together the very latest research in the field of culture and psychology, which is a broad and thriving discipline that spans all areas of psychology and has linkages to anthropology, communication, and sociology, among other disciplines. Each volume in the *Frontiers* series focuses on a specific key area of research in culture and psychology and provides a comprehensive and up-to-date review and integration of the latest empirical, theoretical, and practical issues in that area. Thus, in response to the field's growing needs, each volume is like a handbook covering a particular subarea of culture and psychology, yet it provides more focus and detail than is normally possible in traditional handbooks covering the whole of the discipline. As a result of improved communication, personal contacts, and extensive collaboration between laboratories, culture and psychology is now a truly international enterprise. The *Frontiers* volumes reflect this by covering relevant research activities carried out by scholars the world over. The volume editors and contributors are all internationally renowned scholars, whose work is at the cutting edge of research.

The idea of launching of the *Frontiers* series originated at a conference that Robert Wyer organized at the Hong Kong University of Science and Technology in December 2006. During the conference, we personally witnessed "the flowering of culture in behavioral research," an expression Marshall Segall, Walt Lonner, and John Berry—three forerunners of the field—used to characterize the state of the art in cross-cultural and cultural psychology. After a zealous conversation over a coffee break, we embraced the idea of starting a new book series as a milestone to mark the distance the field has traveled.

We are delighted that Masaki Yuki and Marilynn Brewer, two renowned scholars in culture and group research, agreed enthusiastically to edit a *Frontiers* volume on *Culture and Group Processes.* This volume, which features state-of-the-art research on the cultural dimension of group psychology, is a milestone volume in two senses: It is both the inaugural volume of the series as well as the first edited volume on this research topic. The 10 chapters included in this volume, all contributed by distinguished scientists in the field, systematically reveal the role of culture in group perceptions, group dynamics, identity negotiation, teamwork, intergroup relations, and intergroup communication, as well as the joint effect of cultural and group processes in interpersonal trust and creativity. While each chapter presents an incisive review of a focal research topic in culture and group processes, the volume as a whole showcases how researchers have harnessed innovative theoretical insights through creative synthesis of research in cross-cultural, cultural, social, and group psychology.

The launching of the *Frontiers* series has benefitted tremendously from the dedication of the competent editorial team at Oxford University Press. To them, we extend our sincere gratitude. We are particularly grateful to Lori Handelman and Abby Gross for their incessant support. We also thank our respective institutions, Nanyang Technological University and the University of Maryland, for their support. Last but not least, we thank the editors and the authors of this volume for their marvelous contributions.

Chi-yue Chiu
Singapore
Ying-yi Hong
Singapore
Michele J. Gelfand
College Park, Maryland

Culture and Group Processes

1

Culture and Group Processes

Defining the Interface

MARILYNN B. BREWER AND MASAKI YUKI

Although research on group structure, group process, and intergroup relations spans the social and behavioral sciences, and there is now a burgeoning literature on cultural psychology, the interface between these two areas of social science knowledge has yet to receive much attention. The growth of multinational corporations and cultural diversity in the workplace has spawned theory and empirical research on multicultural teams within the field of organizational behavior (e.g., Chen, 2006). However, the relationship between culture and group process goes well beyond what happens when individuals from different cultural backgrounds happen to come together in a group context.

Cultural influences pervade all aspects of group cognition and behavior both within and across cultural boundaries, including group identity, group norms, intragroup interaction and communication, cooperation and trust, and intergroup relations. The present volume was conceived and developed to expand our understanding of the mutual relationship between culture and group process across this broad array of group-related topics from the social psychological and organizational behavior literatures. To this end, we have recruited experts from cultural psychology and group research whose own work spans these two domains with the hope of illustrating the potential richness of ideas and insights to be gained by building bridges between theory of culture and theory of groups.

HUMANS AND GROUPS

Most behavioral scientists today accept the basic premise that human beings are adapted for group living. Even a cursory review of the physical endowments of our species—weakness, hairlessness, and extended infancy—makes it clear that we are not suited for survival as lone individuals, or even as small family units. Many of the evolved characteristics that have permitted humans to adapt to a wide range of physical environments create dependence on collective knowledge and cooperative information sharing (Kameda & Nakanishi, 2003). As a consequence, human beings are characterized by *obligatory interdependence* (Brewer & Caporael, 2006), and much of human activity is characterized by living and working in groups. Participation in groups serves a wide range of adaptive functions for individuals, including both material benefits of mutual aid and collective action, and subjective psychological benefits of affiliation and social identity. Thus, understanding how groups form and function is crucial to our understanding of social psychological processes more broadly.

Culture and Group Theory

How does bringing a cultural perspective to the study of group processes influence theory and research in this domain? Do cultural differences make a difference and, if so, at what level of theory must cultural factors be taken into account? At one extreme, some might contend that cultural differences run so deep that social theory must be culture specific, essentially developed from scratch in each new cultural context. At the other extreme, cultural differences may be viewed as superficial variations in behavioral practices that can easily be accommodated within existing theoretical perspectives. Somewhere between these extremes is the position that cultural differences do have a profound effect on cognition, values, and behavior, but that there are fundamental principles of social interaction and decision making that provide a substrate for illuminating, understanding, and managing cultural variation.

The chapters in this volume either explicitly or implicitly adopt this middle ground in approaching the issue of culture and its impact on group process. It is our contention that incorporating cultural factors not only informs but modifies and enriches theories of social behavior by forcing researchers to cope with the expanded variability generated by cultural differences in values, beliefs, and social arrangements.

CONCEPTUALIZING CULTURE IN RELATION TO GROUP PROCESS

Broadly defined, culture is a system of shared meanings and understandings, together with a set of practices that enact and reinforce the shared worldviews (Triandis, 1972). A critical element in this definition is that culture involves *shared* understandings among people who see themselves as part of a meaningful collective with some sense of shared identity, temporal continuity, and social interdependence. Cultures provide group members with answers to fundamental questions, including questions of self and identity (i.e., Who am I? or Who are we?), questions about how the physical and social world works and how things are interrelated (i.e., beliefs), and questions about how things should be and what is the right course of behavior (i.e., values) (Brewer & Chen, 2007).

Conceptualized as a system of shared meaning, symbols, values, and practice, culture exists at multiple levels of social organization. Large complex societies are often characterized as multicultural, differentiated into multiple (and often cross-cutting) subcultures based on significant ethnic, religious, economic, and political groupings. We also speak of "organizational culture" and, at yet a lower level of aggregation, of "work group culture" or even "team culture." Thinking of culture at each of these levels retains essential elements of culture as an emergent group property and a basis for distinctive group identity. Nonetheless, throughout this volume we focus almost exclusively on *national* culture as the level of social organization at which culture is embodied in formal and informal institutions, laws, and communication media that all members of the society are exposed to.

Culture and Social Identity

As noted in our treatment of the definition of culture, social groups are the locus of culture, and such groups are also sources of social identity for group members. Thus, it is not surprising that cultural identity and social identity are often represented as somewhat interchangeable constructs—as two sides of the same coin, so to speak. It is certainly true that the development of shared meanings, norms, and symbols (i.e., culture) contributes significantly to identity building in groups. Conversely, the existence of shared group identity greatly facilitates communication and emergence of shared culture (Brewer, 2001). Nonetheless, we argue that it is important to recognize that group culture and social identity are distinct constructs with different implications for interpersonal processes in groups (cf. Wan & Yu, Chapter 4, this volume).

Social identity is the explicit cognitive representation of the group as a social entity and the self as a component member of that entity, together with emotional attachment and loyalty to the group and its members. Individuals see themselves as having a common social identity by virtue of shared membership in a social network or social category per se. Cultural identity, on the other hand, derives from shared knowledge, values, and worldviews, together with endorsement of those understandings as one's personal views. As defined by Wan and Yu in Chapter 4, cultural identity starts with a type of metacognition—"intersubjective cultural representations," the shared beliefs that individuals of a cultural group have about the culture as a shared knowledge system. When individuals identify with a culture, they internalize the intersubjective cultural representations in their self definition. Thus, social identity and cultural identity represent different routes to group attachment and group loyalty, the former based on loyalty to the group as an entity, the latter based on adherence to collectively shared beliefs, values, and practices. Although these two forms of group identity can be mutually reinforcing, they are not necessarily perfectly aligned.

Situated Culture

In defining culture as a *system* of meanings, we are explicitly rejecting a view of culture as a static entity in favor of a more dynamic constructivist understanding of culture (Hong, Morris, Chiu, & Benet-Martinez, 2000). The constructivist perspective views culture not as a highly integrated general knowledge structure but more like a loose network of situation-specific knowledge structures such as schemas, categories, and implicit theories (Hong et al., 2000; Kitayama, 2002). In this view, members of a cultural group hold a repertory of ideas, values, and schemas—some even contradictory—with only some of these elements activated or brought to mind at any one time as a function of situational contingencies or recent experience. Culture, in other words, is situated cognition. The influence of culture on cognitive processes and behavior is dynamic rather than deterministic, the product of situation–knowledge interactions.

From a dynamic, situated perspective on culture, cultural differences need to be understood in terms of *cultural affordances*. As described by Kitayama (2002), "the notion of cultural affordances implies that different psychological tendencies are constantly fostered and primed by myriad elements of the attendant cultural context" (p. 94). From this perspective, cultures differ not just in central tendency (the average level of certain psychological characteristics such as connectedness) but, more important, "in terms of the contingency by which these responses are associated with other features of culture, such as type of situation" (Kitayama, 2002, p. 95).

A situated view of culture is particularly important for understanding the relationship between culture and group process because social interactions in the group context constitute specific social situations. Across the life space, individuals engage with many different types of groups—family groups, friendship groups, recreational groups, work groups, large organizations, national groups, and so on—that differ significantly in size, structure, purpose, and temporal extension. These group features constitute situational cues that activate cultural knowledge structures appropriate to that particular social context (see Zellmer-Bruhn & Gibson, Chapter 8, this volume). Thus, we cannot simply assume that individuals from a particular cultural background bring a single, fixed set of beliefs and values to all group encounters. Rather, to understand the interface between culture and group process, we need to know what cultural meanings are brought to bear in groups that vary in form and function.

Individualism-Collectivism and Group Process

Among the challenges that any stable society must meet is resolving potential conflicts between individual self-interest and collective welfare by defining the rights and obligations that group members hold vis-à-vis other group members. This aspect of national culture has been captured succinctly in the distinction between *individualism* and *collectivism* as broad cultural orientations (Hofstede, 1980; Triandis, 1995). Although this dimension has been defined in different ways by different theorists, there is a general consensus that it refers to variations across cultures in whether individuals are viewed as separate and autonomous entities or as interconnected and embedded in interdependent social relationships, along with normative prescriptions and values about the priority to be given to individual and group interests (Oyserman, Coon, & Kemmelmeier, 2002). As an aspect of culture, the individualism-collectivism dimension addresses questions regarding how individuals define themselves and their relationships to others within the social system, including self-representations, beliefs about independence and interdependence, and the relative value placed on self-fulfillment, relationships, and group welfare (Brewer & Chen, 2007).

Not surprisingly, this aspect of culture is seen as central to questions of how culture influences group processes. But the study of group process also reveals that the individualism-collectivism distinction itself may be oversimplified and in need of modification. As Yuki and Takamura (Chapter 3, this volume) point out, interdependence in groups (and the connections between individuals and others) may be conceptualized in at least two different ways. On the one hand, groups may be conceived as networks of *interpersonal* relationships, with mutual obligations and responsibilities specified at the dyadic level. On the other hand, groups may be conceived as collective entities with interests that supercede those of individual group members or relational ties, with obligations to others defined at the level of the welfare of the group as a whole. For this reason, Brewer and Chen (2007) have argued that the simple distinction between individualism and collectivism is inadequate and needs to be expanded to recognize the differentiation between relational and group-centered social connectedness. Across all societies, individuals maintain close personal relationships, small-group interpersonal networks, and membership in large, symbolic groups. But cultural systems rely more or less heavily on these different forms of social connection as the primary locus for defining the social self and exercising social control over individual behavior. What differs among people across cultures is the salience and priority of these different forms of social embeddedness.

Groups are clearly the locus of interpersonal relationships as well as collective entities. Furthermore, group members are often faced with the necessity of resolving conflicts between relational interests and group interests. Interpersonal harmony is not always compatible with achievement of other group goals, and reciprocal obligations to benefit particular others (friends and family) may not work to the benefit of the group as a whole. Thus, understanding cultural differences in the priority assigned to individual interests, maintenance of relational ties, or group welfare across different social contexts has important implications for predicting how culture will influence group process and outcomes.

Culture and Groups: A Mutual Relationship

The preceding discussion of the individualism-collectivism distinction illustrates a major theme that runs throughout the present volume: There is a mutual relationship between understanding culture and understanding group process. On the one side, groups exist *in* cultures—theories of group process must take into account the cultural context in which groups are defined and intragroup and intergroup behavior is regulated. On the other side, culture arises *in* groups—culture is a group product, an emergent property of the interdependent social exchange and mutual influence that constitutes group process. Social groups are the context in which culture is both created and enacted. The content of this volume systematically explores both sides of this bidirectional relationship.

GROUPS IN CULTURE

One way to define the interface between culture and group process is to recognize that groups form and develop in a cultural context. The most common approach to work on the influence of culture on groups is based on the assumption that cultural values (most specifically, individualism-collectivism) determine how individuals relate to social groups and the degree to which they either attach or detach themselves from their group memberships. However, recent developments in the field turn attention to how culture also affects the nature of groups themselves—how individuals conceptualize groups, the way they interact within groups, and the nature of intergroup behavior.

Culture and Cognition About Groups

One important aspect of cultural knowledge is shared understandings about how social groups are conceptualized in the first place. What constitutes a meaningful social group? What properties and capabilities are attributed to groups? What expectations do we hold about those who share common group membership? The answers provided to these questions of group cognition within different cultural traditions constitute an extremely important cultural context within which group processes play out.

Several chapters in the first section of this volume illustrate how group cognition is embedded in cultural knowledge systems. The concepts of *essentialism* and *entitativity* discussed in Chapter 2 by Haslam, Holland, and Karasawa refer to two aspects of culture-based understandings of what makes a group a group. Essentialism is the extent to which members of a given social group or social category are perceived to have some immutable underlying characteristics ("essence") in common that defines their group membership. Although all groups involve some form of perceived similarity among group members (e.g., similarity of traits, appearance, goals, experiences), perceptions of different groups vary in terms of whether these properties are essentialized. Importantly, cultural knowledge includes shared understandings of the nature of essentialism and which groups (including human beings) are seen as having essential characteristics. In reviewing the limited work that has been done thus far exploring cultural differences in this dimension of group cognition, Haslam, Holland, and Karasawa conclude that there is initial evidence for potentially important differences in the prevalence of essentialist beliefs across cultures, as well as differences in the structure and form of essentialist thinking (i.e., different "kinds" of essence).

Entitativity (a term coined by Campbell, 1958) is a second dimension of group cognition that refers to the extent to which a particular social group is perceived to be a meaningful, cohesive collective entity (as opposed to a loose aggregate of individuals). Entitativity and essentialism are distinct concepts, though related in that one basis for perceiving groups as an entity is similarity of member characteristics. However, judgments of entitativity go beyond mere similarity and reflect the extent to which group members interact, coordinate their actions, and behave as an organized unit. Thus, entitativity entails the perception of groups as dynamic social actors, with intentions, motivations, and effectance.

As with essentialism, there is as yet relatively little empirical research on differences across cultures in perceived entitativity of social groups. But what research there is suggests that, whereas essentialized thinking is more prevalent in Western cultures than in East Asia, Asians perceive a wider range of groups as high in entitativity (Kashima et al., 2005). Furthermore, the concept of entitativity is closely related to the perception of group *agency*, the extent to which groups are attributed with causal influence on events and on the behavior of group members. There is an extensive body of empirical work documenting that East Asians perceive groups as higher in agency than do individuals from Western cultures (Kashima et al., 2005; Morris, Menon, & Ames, 2001), which is consistent with the conclusion that groups are imbued with greater entitativity in Eastern cultures.

Learning more about cultural differences in perceptions of essentialism and entitativity is important because both of these cognitive constructs carry implications for other aspects of group perception, intragroup process, and behavior toward group members. Both essentialization and entitativity promote generalization processes—attributing group stereotypes to individual members and, conversely, inferring group characteristics from behaviors of individual members. Perceiving groups as agentic social actors has important implications for the attribution of collective responsibility for group member behavior, which in turn contributes to collective guilt and retribution (see Lee, Gelfand, & Shteynberg, Chapter 11, this volume). Group agency can also be linked to cultural differences in the bases for trust and why group membership can function as a cue for trust behavior (see Kwan & Hong, Chapter 5, this volume).

Beyond the cognition of groups qua groups, Chapter 3 by Yuki and Takemura deals with fundamental cultural differences in the bases of group formation and social identification with one's own groups. One form of group identity is the collective self as represented in the theoretical tradition of social identity theory and self-categorization theory (Tajfel & Turner, 1979; Turner et al. 1987). The other form of ingroup identity (relational self) is based on interpersonal connections and relational ties among group members. One defining distinction between these two social selves is that relational groups are *personalized*, incorporating dyadic relationships between the self and particular close others and with networks of interpersonal connections via the extension of these dyadic relationships. By contrast, collective social identity involves *depersonalized* relationships with others by virtue of common membership in a symbolic group. Collective identities do not require interpersonal knowledge or interaction but rely on shared symbols and cognitive representations of the group as a unit independent of personal relationships within the group.

Yuki and Takemura go on to discuss the important implications of this distinction between two forms of group identity for both intragroup and intergroup cognition and behavior. Importantly, they contend that persons from individualistic cultures are more likely to define their ingroups as depersonalized collective identities (with an associated orientation toward intergroup comparisons), whereas persons in collectivistic cultures represent their ingroups as relational networks (with an associated orientation toward intragroup relations and harmony).

The Role of Social Ecology and Institutions

After discussing cultural differences in the nature of social identity, Yuki and Takemura go on to draw a link between the concepts of relational and collective group identities and societal differences in *relational mobility*. Relational mobility is a social ecological construct that refers to the extent to which relational connections are freely chosen and disposable rather than ascribed, committed, and long lasting. According to this socio-ecological perspective, low relational mobility discourages individualistic notions of autonomy and self-efficacy because these are disruptive to maintenance of harmonious social relationships. When groups are not easily entered or exited, maintaining intragroup harmony is essential and attendance to intragroup relational ties is paramount. In high relational mobility societies, by contrast, individuals are more free to choose their group memberships based on similarity or functional value to the self, and monitoring the relative value or status of one's current ingroup compared to other groups is of more importance. Interestingly, this view is consistent with the findings from cross-cultural studies of perceived entitativity that suggest that people from Western (individualistic) societies are more likely to define group cohesion in terms of similarity of traits and characteristics, whereas East Asian (collectivistic) society members are more likely to perceive group entity in terms of relational structure and interdependence.

The relative importance placed on maintaining harmony and positive interpersonal relations within group contexts also has consequences for understanding the nature of ingroup trust, and this is the subject of Chapter 5 by Kwan and Hong. These authors argue that formal and informal institutions provide the cultural context for decisions about whether to trust another individual. In cultures characterized by reliance on relational networks and interpersonal connections, social behavior is closely monitored by members of the network, and behavior (such as violations of trust) that would disrupt harmony is negatively sanctioned by other ingroup members. In such a context, the knowledge that another individual shares network membership serves as a cue for expectation of trustworthiness, and trust decisions are heavily influenced by whether the trustee has relational ties with the trustor. In cultures where relational connections are less important as informal mechanisms of social control, trust is more likely to be person based or grounded in formal institutions. Thus, the formation of trust relationships that is essential for group coordination and cooperation may derive from very different sources, depending on cultural understandings about the nature of groups and group behavior.

CULTURE IN GROUPS

Culturally shared understandings of what it means to be a group and a good group member provide the backdrop for culture-based norms and expectations about how members will behave within specific types of groups. In the preceding section we have highlighted contents of this volume that illustrate how cultural knowledge, norms, and values influence how group processes are played out. The flip side of this perspective on the relation between culture and group process is to consider groups as a context in which culture is played out or enacted.

Group Process as Cultural Enactment

As we have already emphasized, culture is the product of group interaction. Culture, as defined previously, is a system of shared meaning and practices that emerges from social interaction; the need for coordination, structure, and common understanding among individuals within an interdependent social group is what gives rise to shared culture. Of course, not all groups develop a unique culture, but the emergence of culture as a function of social interaction over an extended period in the context of cooperative interdependence appears to be a universal feature of human social life (Chiu & Hong, 2006).

Groups also provide a situational context that cues relevant cultural knowledge and norms for appropriate behavior. A number of the chapters in the present volume deal with specific examples of how groups instantiate and enact cultural understandings. Consistent with the situated view of culture, Sanchez-Burks and Uhlmann (Chapter 6) draw a distinction between the cultural norms and values that are brought to bear in workplace contexts and those that might apply to non-work-related social contexts. They call attention in particular to aspects of US culture, derived from historical influences of Protestant ideology and beliefs, which draw a sharp distinction between relational values within versus outside of the workplace.

In what they designate as the "Protestant relational ideology," Sanchez-Burks and Uhlmann claim that US work culture is unique in deeming affective displays and a focus on social relationships as inappropriate in the workplace. Outside of work contexts, North Americans show just as much sensitivity to emotional cues and interpersonal concerns as most non-Americans, but are less relationally attentive at work. This depersonalization of work culture impinges on many aspects of group process in the work context, including reduced expression of emotion, direct rather than indirect communication style, and underestimation of the effects of relational conflict. By contrast, in societies where relational ties are an integral part of the workplace culture, group members are more sensitive to emotional cues, communication is more likely to be indirect (face saving), and there is greater concern with avoiding or resolving interpersonal conflicts within the work setting. Thus, a cultural understanding about the nature of work is reflected in workgroup practices and interaction behavior, with important implications for problems that might be encountered when individuals from different cultural backgrounds are brought together in work group settings.

How the enactment of cultural norms and understandings influences group performance is the subject of Chapter 7 by Li, Kwan, Liou, and Chiu, which explores the role of cultural factors in group creativity. The authors argue that creativity is inherently a social and cultural process and that the creative output of work teams or other groups is shaped by culture through intervening group processes. According to their model, a creative product is one that is both novel and valued. Thus, group production of a creative product entails not only *generating* novel ideas but also *selecting* ideas for further development and *accepting* them for final adoption. Of particular interest is the difference between generating and editing/selecting processes in terms of relevant criteria and related cognitive and social processes. Cultural norms and values can influence either of these stages of creative production but in different ways. With respect to Western versus East Asian cultural influences, the authors contend that there is little basis for claiming cultural differences in the capacity for generating novel or original ideas in groups. Rather, cultural differences surface at the idea selection stage where debates about the relevant importance of novelty and usefulness as selection criteria are engaged. It is at this juncture that groups in Western cultures appear to adopt more novel ideas than groups from Asian cultures. The authors speculate that this difference in outcome stems from perceived cultural norms of creativity that dictate the relative value placed on novelty versus functionality. Thus, the selection of ideas represents an expression of shared understandings of what is culturally valued.

Just as group decision making is an expression of cultural norms and values, the style of verbal and nonverbal communication in groups is also a form of cultural expression. The relationship between communication style and cultural identity is the subject of Chapter 10 by Noels, who notes that culture and communication are intimately connected in that "communication constitutes the practices by which culture is constructed and maintained, transmitted and transformed." Drawing on ethnolinguistic identity theory, Noels discusses communication both within and between groups as an identity negotiation process influenced by situated cultural norms and practices. Culturally shared understanding of what is appropriate language behavior across different everyday interactions is what makes communication relatively easy within ethnolinguistic communities. Particular attention is given to the effect of relational collectivistic (interdependent) compared to individualistic cultural influences on communication patterns, including direct versus indirect communication styles and the extent to which language styles shift depending on whether communicators are part of the same relational ingroup.

Multicultural Groups

Attention to cultural expression in groups inevitably raises questions about what happens when cultures mix—when individuals from different cultural backgrounds come together in a single group. As Noels points out Chapter 10, communication between members of different cultural groups highlights the intimate relationship between use of language and communication style and cultural identity. Intergroup communication can be characterized by unilateral or mutual accommodation (convergence) or linguistic distancing, depending on the goals of the interaction, identity motives, and relative status of the ethnolinguistic communities. In intergroup settings, interactants may adjust their communication style to correspond with the style of those with whom they interact in order to achieve a variety of goals, including information exchange and relationship building. On the other hand, if cultural identity motives are strongly activated by the intergroup context, interactants may be motivated to accentuate linguistic differences as symbols of ethnic distinctiveness and ingroup solidarity. In such cases, identity needs may interfere with accommodative processes that are essential to achieving the kind of shared understandings that make group coordination and goal achievement possible.

The role of mutual accommodation for effective group performance is particularly salient in the case of multicultural work teams. Several chapters in this volume deal with the special challenges associated with emergence of shared understandings and norms in multicultural teams where the normal processes of developing a common model of group task and process is complicated by the variability in cultural background and prior assumptions among team members. To be effective, work groups must resolve potentially conflicting culture-based norms and values through development of a shared understanding of the values and norms that guide team members when working together. In Chapter 9, Adair and Ganai refer to such shared schemas within multicultural teams as "third cultures" and go on to identity four different models by which diverse cultural elements may be combined to generate a unique team culture. Third cultures may be created from some combination of preexisting elements from the national cultures of team members, but of particular interest is the concept of an *emergent* third culture that contains novel elements not traceable to any of the parent cultures represented by group members, perhaps generated by the need to negotiate differences in values, perceptions, and expectations not typically encountered in monocultural team development.

The idea of emergent third cultures highlights the potential for cultural diversity in work groups to generate cognitive complexity and creativity. As Li, Kwan, Liou, and Chiu point out in Chapter 7, when group members with diverse backgrounds present ideas from their own cultural perspectives, other members become aware of the alternative approaches to solving the same problem, and synthesis of seemingly incompatible ideas can result in valuable innovation. Thus, when diverse cultural understandings can be successfully capitalized on, enhanced creativity is one of the potential benefits of intercultural exchange. However, as Li et al. discuss, whether this benefit of cultural diversity can be realized depends on whether cultural differences create a "fault line" within the group that impedes accommodation and group performance. Specifically, when team members are aware of group differences and are motivated by their identity needs to defend the purity and vitality of their culture, they may refuse to learn from and cooperate with members from other cultures. In contrast, when team members are aware of group differences and are motivated to learn from other cultures, they would engage culturally dissimilar members differently and be stimulated rather than threatened by differences in perspective.

In a related vein, Chapter 8 by Zellmer-Bruhn and Gibson in this volume tackles the question of whether and when cultural differences will be problematic for the performance of multicultural teams. As they point out, individual group members bring multiple sources of identity to team work, including role identities, social identities (e.g., gender, age), and cultural identities, and which identities are salient and acted upon depends on the context of interaction. The authors conceptualize culturally diverse work groups in terms of "intercultural interaction space," which may vary in physical (e.g., location in real or virtual space), cognitive (team purpose, role expectations, strategy), and affective aspects. These aspects of the interaction space in turn determine whether cultural identity of group members is salient, what cultural scripts are activated, and how much flexibility the group members have in adapting these cultural scripts to the particular task and role demands of the work group. This perspective is consistent with a dynamic situated view that sees culture not as a fixed worldview that individuals bring to an intercultural exchange but rather as a repertory of cultural elements that are activated and enacted in interaction with situational demands and constraints associated with group process.

FUTURE DIRECTIONS

As we indicated at the outset, this volume was developed to provide a sampling of the innumerable points of interface between the study of culture and the study of social groups. Across the diverse chapters, the contents of the volume illustrate the mutual relationship between culture and group process in terms of how groups are conceptualized, how intragroup and intergroup processes unfold, and how cultural differences are represented and resolved. Because empirical research on these issues is in its infancy, each chapter provides both a theoretical perspective and an agenda for future research.

Beyond East-West

One of the first things that strikes a reader of a volume such as this is that national culture is almost always operationalized in terms of differences between Western

European (primarily the United States) and East Asian (primarily China and Japan) cultures. Given the current geographic centers of the global economy, this focus on East-West differences may have practical as well as historical justification. But the increasing globalization of commerce and economic exchange and the expansion of multinational corporations across the world call for a more geographically diversified program of research on national culture and cultural differences. Expanding the range of geographical regions represented in studies of cultural influences may help overcome rather simplistic dichotomous or bipolar views of cultural differences. A good example of this is provided in the present volume in Chapter 11 by Lee, Gelfand, and Shteynberg. Drawing on research conducted in several countries in the Middle East, these authors suggest that differentiation along a vertical versus horizontal dimension among so-called collectivistic cultures gives rise to significant cultural differences in the spread of group-based retaliation and the effects of apology. Richer understanding of the variety of cultural forms across regions of the globe will be necessary to fully integrate theories of culture with theories of group process and intergroup relations.

Beyond Group Process

Contemporary research on culture and group process tends to focus on individual and interpersonal cognition, emotion, or behavior during the course of group interaction. For research and theory on cultural influences in groups to have greater applied impact, more attention should be paid to group *products* and performance. In the present volume, Chapter 7 by Li, Kwan, Liou, and Chiu on creativity in groups provides a stellar example of how cultural influences on group process and group norms have consequences for the creative products produced by work teams. Greater attention to these downstream consequences of cultural influences for group performance and longevity will be important if the study of the interface between culture and group process is to have practical implications for managing groups and improving team performance.

Culture, Group Process, and Social Change

Finally, future theory must deal with how changes in social structure associated with rapid globalization of the economy, geographical mobility, and communication technology such as social networking systems impact on both culture and group psychology. Interaction in multicultural teams and the emergence of "third cultures" in those group contexts (cf. Adair & Ganai, Chapter 9, this volume) is in itself a source of cultural change related to changes in our socio-structural environment. A social ecological approach, which makes it possible to analyze relationships between the structure of the external social environment and human psychological functioning (cf. Yuki & Takemura, Chapter 3, this volume), should provide a framework for future research and theory on the culture–group process interface.

It is our hope that the contents of the present volume both highlight the benefits of studying group process with a cultural lens and also advance an agenda for a fully integrated theory of culture and group process in the future.

REFERENCES

Brewer, M. B. (2001). Social identities and social representations: A question of priority? In K. Deaux & G. Philogene (Eds.), *Representations of the social* (pp. 306–311). Oxford, UK: Blackwell.

Brewer, M. B., & Caporael, L. R. (2006). An evolutionary perspective on social identity: Revisiting groups. In M. Schaller, J. Simpson, & D. Kenrick (Eds.), *Evolution and social psychology* (pp. 143–161). New York: Psychology Press.

Brewer, M. B., & Chen, Y. (2007). Where (who) are collectives in collectivism: Toward a conceptual clarification of individualism and collectivism. *Psychological Review, 114*, 133–151.

Campbell, D. T. (1958). Common fate, similarity, and other indices of the status of aggregates of persons as social entities. *Behavioral Science, 3*, 14–25.

Chen, Y. (Ed.). (2006). *National culture and groups*. Oxford, UK: Elsevier JAI.

Chiu, C-y., & Hong, Y. (2006). *Social psychology of culture*. New York: Psychology Press.

Hofstede, G. (1980). *Culture's consequences: International differences in work-related values*. Beverly Hills, CA: Sage.

Hong, Y.-Y., Morris, M. W., Chiu, C.-Y., & Benet-Martinez, V. (2000). Multicultural minds: A dynamic constructivist approach to culture and cognition. *American Psychologist, 55*, 709–720.

Kameda, T., & Nakanishi, D. (2003). Does social/cultural learning increase human adaptability? Rogers's question revisited. *Evolution and Human Behavior, 24*, 242–260.

Kashima, Y., Kashima, E., Chiu, C. Y., Farsides, T., Gelfand, M., Hong, Y. Y., . . . Yzerbyt, V. (2005). Culture, essentialism, and agency: Are individuals universally believed to be more real entities than groups? *European Journal of Social Psychology, 35*, 147–169.

Kitayama, S. (2002). Cultural and basic psychological processes—Toward a system view of culture: Comment on Oyserman et al. (2002). *Psychological Bulletin, 128*, 189–196.

Morris, M., Menon, T., & Ames, D. (2001). Culturally conferred conceptions of agency: A key to social perception of persons, groups, and other actors. *Personality and Social Psychology Review, 5*, 169–187.

Oyserman, D., Coon, H. M., & Kemmelmeier, M. (2002). Rethinking individualism and collectivism: Evaluation of theoretical assumptions and meta-analyses. *Psychological Bulletin, 128*, 3–72.

Tajfel, H., & Turner. J. C. (1979). An integrative theory of intergroup conflict. In W. Austin & S. Worchel (Eds.), *Social psychology of intergroup relations* (pp. 33–47). Chicago: Nelson.

Triandis, H. C. (1972). *The analysis of subjective culture*. New York: Wiley.

Triandis, H. C. (1995). *Individualism and collectivism*. Boulder, CO: Westview.

Turner, J. C., Hogg, M., Oakes, P., Reicher, S., & Wetherell, M. (1987). *Rediscovering the social group: A self-categorization theory*. Oxford, UK: Basil Blackwell.

PART ONE

Culture and Basic Group Processes

2

Essentialism and Entitativity Across Cultures

NICK HASLAM, ELISE HOLLAND, AND MINORU KARASAWA ■

Social psychologists have always been interested in groups and how people perceive them. Like visual perception, social perception is vulnerable to a variety of biases, illusions, and disorders. Social perceivers sometimes see things that are not there (illusory correlation). Sometimes they fail to see things that are blatantly obvious (discounting). They sometimes see only what they want to see (biased assimilation). They may be myopic, seeing only what is right in front of their noses and ignoring what is less salient (availability). The analogy between the perception of objects and the perception of groups can be labored too much, but it is a useful one nonetheless.

When we look upon the world, our visual system allows us to differentiate objects and to see them as solid entities. This is a truly remarkable constructive exercise: A two-dimensional array of stimulation within the individual body is transformed into a compellingly real, three-dimensional vision that is projected into a shared and objective outside world. Something similar takes place when we construct a representation of our social world. Based on our fragmentary experience with individual social actors, we piece together an image of society that is populated by differentiated, solid, and objectively existing social groups. Groups come to be seen as fundamentally real, factual, and natural. Just as we encounter diverse animals and without further thought take them to be instances of deeply different types of creature, so do we come to perceive varied individuals as examples of fundamentally different human types. Group perception, like visual perception, takes us from phenomenal experience to an ontological conviction that certain things are real.

This chapter explores the ways in which our social perception leads us to perceive certain social groups as fundamentally distinct entities or types. Research and theory on psychological essentialism teaches us that we tend to see some groups as having a deep-seated, unchanging essence that is shared by all group members and defines who they are. Research and theory on entitativity teaches the closely related lesson that groups differ in the extent to which they are seen as thing-like: the extent to which they are perceived as unified and coherent. Essentialism and entitativity are indispensable concepts for making sense of group perception because they allow us to think about how groups—some more than others—are seen as solid, three-dimensional, real, and meaningful.

Expressing the analogy between vision and group perception in this way may make it sound as if the latter is a hard-wired universal capacity, like much of our visual system. However, as we shall see, these aspects of group perception depend in many interesting ways on culture. Different cultures perceive groups and their members in quite different ways, and essentialize them to varying degrees and in varying manners. This might seem to destroy our analogy, except that increasingly cultural psychologists are showing how apparently basic aspects of vision are also penetrated by culture (e.g., Masuda & Nisbett, 2001). Both vision and group perception depend on what we desire, value, and care about, and construct representations of the world on that basis. To the degree that our concerns are shaped by our cultures, we would expect there to be important variations in how people from different cultures make sense of the essential nature of their social groups. After reviewing research and theory on essentialism and entitativity, we shall explore some of these variations. Throughout the chapter our emphasis is primarily on essentialism, reflecting the greater quantity of work on the concept.

SOCIAL PSYCHOLOGY RESEARCH ON ESSENTIALISM AND ENTITATIVITY

Social psychological study of essentialist thinking began in earnest with a theoretical paper by Rothbart and Taylor (1992), although Gordon Allport's seminal book *The Nature of Prejudice* (1954) alluded to beliefs in group essence several decades earlier. Rothbart and Taylor referred to recent investigations of psychological essentialism in relation to conceptual structure, notably the work of cognitive psychologists such as Medin and Ortony (1989). They extended this work from investigations of concepts in general to beliefs about kinds of person in particular. Forcefully expressing the constructionist view that all social categories are shaped by history, society, and culture, Rothbart and Taylor argued that viewing social categories as essence-based natural kinds is a serious ontological error. Whenever people believe or intuit that there is a deep-seated and shared essence of a social group, they fail to recognize the extent to which the category is contingent and constructed. In particular, they mistakenly infer that the category is inalterable and inductively potent: Social groupings are mistakenly seen as fixed and unchangeable, and as powerful sources of judgments about category members. Whenever a category is essentialized, that is, people believe that its members share countless hidden similarities, and that the category is highly informative about them.

Rothbart and Taylor (1992) were not content simply to identify a cognitive error and argued that this error had important social consequences. Essentialist thinking is not merely wrong but dangerous. It leads people to overvalue superficial perceptual cues such as skin color in social judgment, believing that they reveal fundamental biological differences between people, and it leads them to accentuate differences between categories. When we think in an essentialist manner, that is, we exaggerate the similarities among those who share the putative essence, and also the differences between those who have putatively different essences. Essentialist thinking therefore creates a social world in which groups of people are seen as divided into discrete and deep-seated types.

Following the original theoretical work of Rothbart and Taylor, empirical research on essentialist thinking about social categories developed in several directions. Some of these were pioneered by psychological anthropologists. Boyer (1993) explored misconceptions of social categories as "pseudo-natural kinds" in his African fieldwork. Hirschfeld (1996) conducted experimental studies with children on the development of essentialist views of race, arguing that children come into the world cognitively prepared to find distinct human kinds, and that essentialism is a general mode of thought that can be recruited by our social cognition of human diversity. Gil-White (2001) conducted field studies of essentialist thinking about ethnicity in Mongolia, arguing against Hirschfeld that essentialist thinking in the social domain represents an analogical borrowing of our folk-biological intuitions about species. Just as members of a biological taxon mate with one another and produce new members of their species, members of ethnic groups marry endogamously and produce fledgling members of the group. The research of these scholars was diverse theoretically, geographically, and methodologically, but it contributed substantially to the emerging literature with its seriousness about the role of culture and its focus on development.

Some lines of empirical research also grew out of social psychology rather than psychological anthropology. Yzerbyt and his colleagues (Yzerbyt, Rocher, & Schadron, 1997) examined "subjective essentialism" in relation to stereotyping processes, proposing that belief in a shared essence served as an explanation for a group's stereotypic properties, as well as serving the function of justifying the group's position in relation to other groups. Belief in a fixed, intrinsic essence serves to naturalize social inequality, so essentialist thinking plays a key role in system justification. Where Yzerbyt and colleagues focused on essentialism's functions, research by Haslam, Rothschild, and Ernst (2000) focused on its structure. Comparing the extent to which diverse social categories were essentialized, and examining several proposed facets of essentialist thinking, they found two underlying dimensions of essentialist beliefs that aligned with the theoretical dimensions of inalterability and inductive potential proposed by Rothbart and Taylor (1992). Categories varied in the extent to which they were seen more as natural kinds, judged to have discrete category boundaries, to have immutable category membership, to have defining properties, to exist unchanged through history, and to be in some respect "natural." Independently, they varied in how coherent, reified, or "entitative" they were perceived to be, with some categories seen as more homogeneous, informative, deep-seated, and person-defining than others. Consistent with the dire view of essentialist thinking advanced by Rothbart and

Taylor, categories that were of lower social status tended to be more essentialized than others.

The contributions surveyed in the last two paragraphs were all published in the decade following Rothbart and Taylor's classic work, and they can be held jointly responsible for the significant flowering of social psychological research on essentialism carried out in the decade since. That research has been tremendously varied, now including substantial contributions from developmental psychologists with interests in understandings of social categories (e.g., Gelman, 2003), and it is too large to review thoroughly. Even so, several trends in that body of recent research deserve mention as background for the discussions of essentialism and culture that follow. There has been growth in the range of psychological processes that essentialist thinking has been used to explain, in the range of social categories and attributes that the research has investigated, in the theories to which essentialism has been linked, and in the ways in which cultural phenomena have been related to it.

To begin with processes, early research and theory proposed that essentialist social thinking was implicated in stereotyping and prejudice but did not investigate these possibilities because their goal was to document the nature and structure of essentialist beliefs. More recent research has begun to deliver on these theoretical promises. The evidence to date strongly supports the view that essentialist thinking promotes stereotype endorsement and attention to stereotype-consistent information (Bastian & Haslam, 2006, 2007), as well as increasing self-stereotyping (Coleman & Hong, 2008) and related stereotype threat phenomena (Dar-Nimrod & Heine, 2006). Evidence for a relationship between essentialism and prejudice has been more mixed, with many studies showing a positive relationship between endorsement of essentialist beliefs and derogatory attitudes about ethnic and racial groups (e.g., Keller, 2005; Jayaratne et al., 2006; Roets & Van Hiel, 2011) and others drawing mixed conclusions (e.g., Haslam, Rothschild, & Ernst, 2002). In particular, some dimensions of essentialist thinking may be associated with lesser prejudice, as when beliefs that homosexuality is inborn, biologically based, immutable, and historically universal are found to be associated with more pro-gay attitudes (Haslam & Levy, 2006).

Recent research has also expanded the range of human diversity that is examined in essentialism research. Although early studies took racial and ethnic groups as their paradigm cases (e.g., Gil-White, 2001; Hirschfeld, 1996; Rothbart & Taylor, 1992), the past decade has seen important research on essentialist thinking about gender (e.g., Prentice & Miller, 2006), sexual orientation (Hegarty & Pratto, 2001), mental disorder (e.g., Ahn, Flanagan, Marsh, & Sanislow, 2006; Haslam, 2011), social class and caste (Mahalingam, 2003), and religious identities (Toosi & Ambady, 2011). Research has also moved beyond beliefs about recognized social categories to beliefs about forms of diversity usually considered to be personal attributes, such as personality traits (Gelman, Heyman, & Legare, 2007; Giles, Legare, & Samson, 2008; Haslam, Bastian, & Bissett, 2004).

The theoretical affinities of essentialism research have similarly undergone some broadening over time. Early writers such as Hirschfeld and Gil-White primarily linked research on psychological essentialism to nativist accounts of cognition, but more recent writers have been quick to explore other conceptual and theoretical links. Some writers have joined essentialist thinking to accounts of psychological motives and epistemic needs (e.g., Keller, 2005; Roets & Van Hiel, 2011). Others have explored common ground between essentialist thinking and the productive line of research on implicit person theories (Hong, Levy, & Chiu, 2001), recasting these beliefs in the fixity of human attributes as but one facet of a broader syndrome of essentialist beliefs (Haslam, Bastian, Bain, & Kashima, 2006). A series of papers by Mahalingam (e.g., 2003) explore essentialist thinking from the standpoint of critical social theory. In short, writers with diverse theoretical commitments and preferences have adopted essentialism as part of their conceptual equipment.

Research on entitativity has followed a somewhat different trajectory from research on essentialism. The concept was introduced by Campbell (1958), who coined the term to refer to the degree to which a social aggregate is seen as coherent, unified, and meaningful. It has sometimes been glossed as the "groupness" of groups. Campbell theorized that entitativity was based on Gestalt perceptual principles such as similarity, proximity, and common fate, but he left empirical work up to others. After several decades of neglect, that challenge was eventually taken up almost simultaneously by many scholars in the 1990s (e.g., Brewer & Harasty, 1996; Dasgupta, Banaji, & Abelson, 1999; Hamilton & Sherman, 1996; McConnell, Sherman, & Hamilton, 1997; McGarty, Haslam, Hutchinson, & Grace, 1995). These researchers linked entitativity to perceived group homogeneity and consistency, and also to the perception of a group as a dynamic social actor (Brewer, Hong, & Li, 2004). Other researchers have reported that perceived entitativity differs for different group types (Lickel et al., 2000), and established that it promotes the drawing of dispositional inferences about group members (Yzerbyt, Rogier, & Fiske, 1998). A valuable early volume (Yzerbyt, Judd, & Corneille, 2004) contains contributions by many key scholars on the concept and its relationship to essentialism.

Entitativity has cemented its place as a valuable concept for understanding group perception since these early contributions. Researchers have examined it in relation to group coherence and group agency, and extended it to studies of attitudes toward a wide variety of groups. Recent research has investigated how group entitativity promotes the perception of collective intentionality and responsibility (Hioki & Karasawa, 2010), how it is associated with prejudice toward outgroups (Newheiser, Tausch, Dovidio, & Hewstone, 2009), and how it is a desired property of ingroups, promoting identification with them (Sacchi, Castano, & Brauer, 2009). In consequence, entitativity has become a staple of research in intergroup relations and group dynamics.

The two lines of research on essentialism and entitativity have been approached from different theoretical perspectives. The study on essentialism, particularly on the perceived "naturalness" of social categories, has revealed the role of lay beliefs in the ontological basis of certain social groups. On the other hand, the study of entitativity has mainly analyzed factors that underlie the Gestalt perception by which a group is seen as a coherent, animated entity rather than a mere aggregate of individuals. In other words, the former line of research has examined the process through which lay perceivers presuppose and seek the latent entity that brings the group into existence, whereas the latter line of research, relatively speaking, has been more interested in the conditions under which a collection of parts reifies a whole in the view of perceivers. Conceptually orthogonal as they may appear, the two processes are integral parts of the psychological formation of groups, and evidence certainly indicates that lay people intuitively understand that social groups exist in their mind on the bases of a combination of these different components (Haslam et al., 2000).

THE PLACE OF CULTURE

Culture has not been a major preoccupation of scholars with an interest in essentialism and entitativity until quite recently. Much of the early research in social psychology involved documenting the structure and implications of beliefs about social categories and the determinants of perceived group cohesion within a single cultural context. The early developmentalists investigated age differences in essentialist thinking with little thought for cultural considerations. Similarly, most of the early anthropological work delved intensively into essentialist thinking within a particular culture in familiar ethnographic style. It is only recently that researchers have begun to conduct systematic cross-cultural comparisons of essentialism thinking and perceived entitativity, and to turn their attention to the implications of these phenomena for cultural phenomena beyond the immediate particularities of the study context. In this respect, the global expansion of social psychology, and the field's serious reckoning with the importance of culture, have both been tremendous blessings for this body of research.

In this section of the chapter we review a diverse body of research on the cultural dimensions of essentialism and entitativity. Our emphasis on the former mirrors the greater quantity of relevant research. The studies that we review were primarily conducted by social psychologists, but we also make reference to work carried out by developmental psychologists when they address beliefs about human categories and attributes, and by anthropologists when their work has a psychological flavor. We have organized the review into separate sections on essentialism and entitativity, and divided each section in distinct ways that capture the main distinctions and dynamics of each topic as we see them.

CULTURE AND ESSENTIALISM

Our investigation of the cultural dimensions of essentialism begins by examining several ways in which essentialist thinking might differ across cultural groups. First, it is possible that in some cultural settings differences between people—social categories or personal attributes such as traits and abilities—are essentialized to a greater degree than in other settings. That is, essentialist social thinking might differ quantitatively as a function of culture. Second, essentialist thinking might differ qualitatively as well. The nature of the essences believed to underpin social differences might vary across cultures in systematic ways, so that although one group might favor a biological idiom, such as DNA or "blood," another might construe essences as disembodied spiritual phenomena. A third and related form of cultural diversity in essentialist thinking relates to its structure, as the distinct conceptual elements that compose essentialist thinking—beliefs about immutability and inductive potential, for example—might covary in culturally specific ways. Finally, we will review research indicating that in addition to cultural differences in the degree, form, and structure of essentialist thinking, there might be differences in its social implications. Essentialist thinking might have different consequences for prejudice, for example, in different cultural settings and for people occupying cultural minority and majority positions within society.

Rather than focusing exclusively on cultural differences, we also review work that reveals equally striking and important commonalities. These include similar ways of understanding the ontology of race and ethnicity in very different cultural contexts, near-identical ways in which people from very different cultures construe the essential attributes of human nature, and deep resemblances in how people think essentialistically about individuals versus groups. It is only when the cross-cultural convergences and divergences are seen together that we can obtain a clear picture of the degree of cultural variability in essentialist thinking, and the degree to which strong relativist and universalist or nativist positions are challenged by the evidence.

The section of our review on entitativity is relatively brief and follows a somewhat stripped-down version of the organization of the preceding section. We first survey research on cross-cultural differences in perceived entitativity, examining possible differences in the degree to which social groups are seen as meaningful and coherent and then examining possible differences in the basis on which group coherence is perceived. In an extension of these quantitative and qualitative forms of cultural variation, we then review research on the cultural divergences in how individual and group targets are perceived as entitative. Finally, we attempt to place this evidence of cultural divergence in context by examining the body of work showing substantial cross-cultural similarities in perceived entitativity and the processes that give rise to it. We close the chapter with some concluding speculations and thoughts about the future of this field of research.

CULTURE AND DIFFERENCES IN DEGREE OF ESSENTIALIST THINKING

The most basic way in which essentialist thinking might be associated with culture is that it might vary by degree across cultures. Very few studies have made direct cross-cultural comparisons of this sort, but their findings indicate that differences in degree are readily obtained. Lockhart, Nakashima, Inagaki, and Keil

(2008) examined beliefs about the temporal stability and origins of traits among children and college students in Japan and the United States and found that in general Japanese participants held less essentialist intuitions. They tended to view traits as more malleable, were more optimistic about positive trait change, and in particular endorsed effort as a basis for change to a greater extent than the American participants. Lockhart and colleagues propose that a more incremental, nonessentialist view of traits is more prevalent in interdependent cultures and may have important implications for achievement motivation.

The lower level of attention to stable traits in East Asian culture is also suggested by the study of spontaneous trait inference. When people living in a Western culture (the United States in particular) are presented with behavioral episodes of an individual person, they typically draw inferences about the trait of the actor. The inferences seem to take place instantly, often automatically, and most important, without any special intention to do so (Winter & Uleman, 1984). However, spontaneous trait inference is markedly attenuated among people in cultures that emphasize interdependence and collectivism such as in East Asia (e.g., Korea; see Rhee, Uleman, Lee, & Roman, 1995) and in Hispanic communities (Zarate, Uleman, & Volis, 2001). In a similar vein, Maass, Karasawa, Politi, and Suga (2006) demonstrated that Japanese tend to represent acts by individuals and groups in more context-dependent terms (i.e., verbs), both in their open-ended descriptions and in their distorted memory, whereas Italians were more inclined to use trait terms (i.e., adjectives) in those representations. Kashima, Kashima, Kim, and Gelfand (2006) found exactly the same pattern of difference in a comparison between Koreans and Australians. Taken together, people in the Euro-American cultures show a greater tendency to account for a behavioral observation with underlying essences such as traits than do those in East Asian cultures. This potential difference across cultures seems to play a central role in the difference between the so-called analytic versus holistic cognition (Nisbett, 1998).

The view that essentialist thinking might be more prominent in independent or individualist cultures is somewhat challenged by the findings of a second study by Giles et al. (2008), who compared beliefs about aggression among South African and African American children. The South African children, whose culture was arguably more collectivist, believed aggression to be more inborn, more stable over time, and less malleable than the American children. The authors propose that the greater essentialism in South Africa might represent a legacy of the apartheid system's rigid social classifications—perhaps a questionable claim given the intrapersonal rather than intergroup nature of the beliefs they assessed—or a consequence of the children's greater exposure to violence. In either case, the study implies that cultural variations in essentialist thinking may reflect differences in culture and in social ecology.

Other evidence for cultural differences in the degree of essentialist thinking has examined groups within a single nation, defined by ethnicity. Jayaratne et al. (2009) found that African American participants were less likely to favor genetic explanations of physical and psychological traits than White Americans. Chandler (2001) compared the ways in which indigenous and nonindigenous young Canadians made sense of their personal continuity, and they showed that nonindigenous youth were more likely to hold an essentialist view that something in their personal identity "situated at some more or less subterranean level of internality" (p. 211) persisted through time. Indigenous youth tended to adopt a more narrative view in which their self-continuity "is guaranteed by the fact that there is always some story (often multiply authored) that succeeds in gluing together the distinctive time-slices of their lives" (p. 1999). Chandler argues that neither basis for self-continuity is superior, but that the lack of such a basis can lead to suicide, and a narrative sense of continuity is vulnerable when the collective cultural narratives of aboriginal people have been disrupted.

The studies reviewed in this section so far have all related to traits and other personal qualities rather than to group identities. Surprisingly, given the focus of much essentialism research on groups, there have been few truly cross-cultural examinations of essentialist beliefs about social categories. Pereira, Estramiana, and Gallo (2010) found a general tendency for English participants to essentialize social categories less than participants from Spain and Brazil, using a thought experiment methodology involving brain transplants between people of different groups. Explanations for this broad cultural difference were not examined. Two other studies have examined cultural comparisons within one nation. Birnbaum, Deeb, Segall, Ben-Eliyahu, and Diesendruck (2010) compared the degree to which Israel children from (Muslim) Arab and secular and religious Jewish backgrounds perceived a variety of social categories as inductively potent. Their primary finding was that religious Jewish children were especially likely to essentialize ethnic categories (i.e., Jews and Arabs), but only when these categories were verbally labeled. The authors speculate that this effect may reflect greater chronic labeling of ethnic categories and use of generics in religious Jewish households in Israel. Consistent with earlier work (Diesendruck & Haber, 2009), it may also show that religiosity is associated with more essentialist beliefs about social categories. Another study compared cultural contexts within the American Midwest (Rhodes & Gelman, 2009) and showed that older rural children and adolescents were more likely than their urban counterparts to essentialize racial and gender categories. As they aged, the rural children developed more naturalized views of racial categories and retained their naturalized views of gender, whereas the urban children developed more conventionalized views of gender and race in ways that were linked to the political views of their parents.

Comparing across different studies also allows us to examine differences in the essentializing of social categories between discrete cultures rather than merely between demographically distinct contexts within one culture. Gil-White (2001), for example, found evidence that Mongol and Kazakh participants essentialized their ethnic identities in thought experiments about infants adopted at birth by parents of the other ethnicity. Most participants believed that these infants would retain attributes of their birth parents' ethnicity despite being reared as members of another. However, Astuti, Solomon, and Carey (2004) found little evidence for such an essentialist view of group identity in similar studies among the Vezo of Madagascar. Vezo adults did not view differences between their ethnicity and others to be due to birth origins and biological inheritance, and tended to view their own identity in "performative" terms, emphasizing customs and beliefs rather than blood. Thus, the view that people invariably or by default naturalize or essentialize ethnic identity appears to be incorrect.

CULTURE AND DIFFERENCES IN KIND OF ESSENTIALIST THINKING

One aspect of essentialist thinking that was discussed by Medin and Ortony (1989) is that people frequently lack a well-grounded understanding of the nature of the essences that they believe in. People may instead hold the view, implicitly at least, that an unobservable category essence exists but that what it is cannot be known or can only be known by experts. The essence itself may be represented by an empty "essence placeholder." Given that the essence is seen as real but indeterminate, guesses about its nature are likely to reflect the kinds of explanatory forces that are salient within a culture. We should therefore not be surprised to find some cultural variability in views on the nature of essences.

There has been little empirical work on this possibility, but there is strong evidence that cultures may have different essence idioms. The centrality of genetic forms of essentialism in developed nations (Dar-Nimrod & Heine, 2011; Haslam, 2011; Keller, 2005) is obvious, as DNA has become the metaphor of choice for labeling the supposed essences of everything from mental disorders to commercial enterprises. In places where genetic science has yet to penetrate culturally, this essence idiom will of course not be available and alternatives will take their place. The one well-developed account in the literature is Boyer's (1993) investigation of essentialist thinking about religious healers among the Fang of West Africa. These healers, or at least the genuinely gifted ones, are seen as possessing an essence-like hidden property know as *evur*, which does not appear to be understood in a biological fashion but simply as an invisible causal power.

The range of possible kinds of explanatory factor that might qualify as essences in people's essentialist thinking about social groups clearly extends beyond scientific biology, although this may tend to be where essences of embodied social groups, such as those based on race, ethnicity, gender, disease, and disability, will tend to be located, at least in developed societies. Recent research has suggested that essentialist thinking might sometimes invoke social (Rangel & Keller, 2011) and symbolic essences (Whelan, Kashima, Haslam, & Benson, unpublished data). Whelan et al., for example, argued that national groups may be essentialized, but those that lack a simple ethnic basis for nationality, such as ethnically diverse immigrant nations, may base that essence on emotional attachment to national symbols. Although this attachment is seen as learned rather than inborn, it is learned early and deeply rather than simply reflecting a factual awareness of the nation's values and history. Supporting this possibility, Whelan and colleagues found that Australians perceived their national essence in primarily symbolic terms, whereas people from the more ethnically homogeneous Irish Republic primarily viewed their national essence in biological terms. More research is needed to examine the diversity of kinds of essence and their distribution across cultures.

CULTURE AND DIFFERENCES IN THE STRUCTURE OF ESSENTIALIST THINKING

A third way in which cultural differences in essentialist thinking might manifest is in the structure of essentialist beliefs. These beliefs are multifaceted—for example, discreteness, immutability, biological basis, inductive potential, and so on—and there is some evidence that the organization of these facets may be somewhat loose and context dependent. For example, Haslam and colleagues have found that these facets cohere into two dimensions when relating to differences among social categories (Haslam et al., 2000) and individual differences in people's beliefs about race and gender (Haslam et al., 2002), but that three dimensions emerge in beliefs about homosexuality (Haslam & Levy, 2006) and only one in beliefs about the nature of personality traits (Haslam et al., 2004) and in individual differences in the tendency to essentialize human attributes (Bastian & Haslam, 2006). If the structure of essentialist beliefs is contingent in this manner, it might be expected to vary across cultures.

Evidence for this possibility is almost completely lacking. However, two studies make it plausible. First, Tsukamoto and Karasawa (unpublished data) found that Haslam and colleagues' eight essentialism facets did not yield the same two dimensions in a study of Japanese participants' beliefs about the Japanese ethnic category. Second, Jayaratne et al. (2009) found that genetic essentialist explanations for psychological and physical traits were differently related to other forms of explanation among White and African Americans. The former tended to judge genetic explanations to be antithetical to environmental explanations, but the latter did not. These two findings are only suggestive, but together they raise the likelihood that the structure or organization of essentialist thinking may display at least subtle variations in different cultural settings.

CULTURE AND DIFFERENCES IN THE IMPLICATIONS OF ESSENTIALIST THINKING

In principle, people from two different cultures might essentialize a particular group in similar ways and to similar degrees, but their essentialist thinking might nevertheless have different relationships with other aspects of group perception. The same beliefs might have different implications for their attitudes or behavior toward the group in question, for example. Two studies demonstrate examples of this possibility. In the first, Hegarty (2002) examined the relationship between anti-gay attitudes and essentialist beliefs about sexual orientation, specifically beliefs that heterosexuality and homosexuality are immutable and deeply dichotomous, in both the United States and in the United Kingdom. He found that the belief that sexual orientations are immutable was associated with tolerance in the former but not in the latter. A likely explanation of this difference is that US participants were more likely to believe that immutability beliefs imply tolerance. Hegarty's findings suggest that people endorse immutability beliefs at least in part because they think these beliefs express tolerance, not because the beliefs are intrinsically associated with more lesbian and gay affirmative attitudes. Thus, the attitudinal implications of essentialist thinking may depend on the symbolic meanings attached to those beliefs in a particular cultural setting.

The different implications of essentialist thinking as a function of cultural background are vividly displayed in a study of discourse about ethnicity among ethnic Dutch and ethnic minority members in the Netherlands. Verkuyten (2003) showed that both groups recruited essentialist ways of thinking, but for strikingly different purposes. Ethnic Dutch participants sometimes expressed essentialist beliefs to argue for the fundamental cultural incompatibility of minorities and to justify the need for distancing and segregation. Ethnic minority participants expressed similarly essentialist sentiments but as a way of resisting pressures to assimilate: By presenting culture as a deep-seated essence, they justified claims for the importance of cultural maintenance rather than adaptation. Although in one respect both uses of essentialist discourse can be said to promote ethnic separation, the social implications are in other respects starkly different. From the cultural majority perspective, essentialist thinking promotes "new racism," but from the minority perspective it promotes multiculturalism and cultural identity.

CULTURE AND SIMILARITIES IN ESSENTIALIST THINKING

The preceding review has emphasized the ways in which essentialist thinking may differ across cultural groups, but it is also important to remember that similarities may be as important as the differences. For example, despite finding differences between Americans and Japanese in beliefs about trait change, Lockhart et al. (2008) found no difference in essentialist beliefs about the origins of traits. Karasawa, Asai, and Hioki (unpublished data) tested a direct translation of the scale developed by Haslam et al. (2000) to a Japanese college sample and found that the two-factor structure of "naturalness" and "entitativity" was duplicated. Bastian and Haslam (2008) found that both immigrants and hosts who essentialized group differences tended to desire greater social distance from one another: Essentialist immigrants have less desire to acculturate and essentialist hosts do not welcome their integration. Gil-White (2001) demonstrated that Mongols and Kazakhs essentialized ethnic identity equally in his adoption-related thought experiments. Zagefka, Pehrson, Mole, and Chan (2010) showed that essentialism had direct positive and indirect negative associations with collective guilt for members of groups that had committed historical atrocities, finding the same pattern of associations among Russian speakers in Latvia contemplating the Russian oppression of ethnic Latvians and among Germans contemplating the Holocaust.

One particularly interesting example of cross-cultural similarity comes from recent research by Park, Haslam, and Kashima (2012), who examined beliefs about human nature in Australia, Japan, and South Korea. Although we might expect substantial variability in views of what is essentially human across cultures, there was very high agreement in the personality traits that were seen as most human. In addition, traits associated with the relational self—those that express and enable close relationships and belonging—were universally judged to define human nature. Most important for our purposes, across the three samples there was very high agreement in the traits that were essentialized, and in every culture human nature was essentialized.

As we have seen, the quantity of research on culture and essentialism is not vast, but it shows that there is some meaningful variability in essentialist thinking across cultural contexts and groups. There are significant differences in the extent to which different cultural groups essentialize personal attributes and social groups, in ways that may reflect broad cultural syndromes such as interdependence as well as more specific variations in social experience, ideology, language, and religion. These differences may emerge and diverge developmentally, and they sometimes challenge early claims that race and ethnicity are invariably naturalized and essentialized (Gil-White, 2001; Hirschfeld, 1996).

Subtler cultural variations in essentialist think are also evident, although supported by more modest quantities of empirical research. The nature of the essences that people from different cultural backgrounds invoke may differ, so that the dominance in the contemporary industrialized world of biological and specifically genetic essence idioms may not extend to other parts of the world. Social, symbolic, and spiritual essences may also be intuited. It remains for future research to determine how widespread these and potentially other essence types may be in essentialist thinking across cultures, and for theorists to decide how far the concept of "essence" can stretch to encompass such diverse kinds of explanatory factor. Besides these differences in essence types, there is also evidence that the structure and implications of essentialist thinking about human diversity may display cultural variations, although these variations are almost entirely unexplored as yet. Much remains to be done before an adequate understanding of the role of culture in essentialist social thinking can be developed.

In this connection we must also note that our review, with its focus on cultural differences and similarities, has omitted some important research and theory with an important cultural dimension that does not fit neatly into that schema. For example, one recent line of work (reviewed in Hong, Chao, & No, 2009) examines how essentialist views of race may have substantial implications for intercultural processes. One study (Chao, Chen, Roisman, & Hong, 2007) showed that Asian Americans who held a more essentialist view of race experienced more stress in navigating their bicultural identities and more difficulty switching between their two cultural frames. Seeing race as a deep and fundamental distinction makes it more difficult to bridge the cultural divisions within the self. Similarly, No et al. (2008) found that Asian Americans who thought more essentialistically about race perceived greater differences between Asian and White Americans and identified less strongly as Americans. By implication, essentialist thinking encouraged greater cultural separateness. The same implication flows from work by Wagner et al. (2010), who showed that essentialists tend to hold more negative views of ethnically mixed offspring, believing that this kind of hybridizing of supposedly incompatible cultures produces a loss of identity and sense of belonging, as well as "essence collapse." Work of this sort illustrates how essentialist thinking can have major ramifications for intercultural relations and cultural identity beyond the framework of cultural similarities and differences that we have adopted in this chapter.

CULTURE AND ENTITATIVITY

Considerably less research has been conducted on the role of culture in entitativity judgments, so our review will be necessarily brief compared to our treatment of essentialism. Nevertheless, there have been a few important studies which strongly suggest that these judgments show meaningful and consequential variations across cultures. Perhaps the most substantial study was carried out by Kashima and colleagues (2005), who investigated the extent to which four social targets (individuals, families, friendship groups, and society at large) were perceived as entitative by participants from eight cultures, three English-speaking, three East Asian, and two continental European. Acknowledging the concept's differing meanings, they assessed entitativity as group inalterability, consistency, and agency. The individual was generally perceived to be the most entitative of the four targets on all three measures, but culture interacted with target in some analyses. Most interestingly, all of the Western samples judged the individual to be more agentic than society, with families and friendship groups intermediate, but no such difference was observed in any East Asian sample. In short, East Asian participants were much more willing than Westerners to ascribe agentic mental states (beliefs, desires, and intentions) to society as a whole, but no more apt to do so for smaller and more intimate and interactive groups.

Evidence of stronger tendencies to perceive social groups as entitative in East Asian cultures than in the West has also been provided by Spencer-Rogers, Williams, Hamilton, Peng, and Wang (2007). Their work revealed that Chinese participants perceived a variety of groups as more entitative than Americans and ascribed more internally consistent dispositions to group members. This tendency may have significant implications for social judgment, as Spencer-Rogers et al. found that Chinese participants were also more likely to draw stereotypic inferences about members of fictitious groups on the basis of their group membership. A tendency to perceive groups as coherent and meaningful entities may therefore promote a tendency to stereotype group members.

More recent research has continued the focus on comparisons between Western and East Asian cultures. Kurebayashi, Hoffman, Ryan, and Murayama (2012) examined the factors that contributed to Japanese and American participants' judgments of group entitativity, focusing on similarities in traits versus shared goals and other dynamic properties. Both sets of properties predicted perceived entitativity of a variety of social categories (e.g., women), intimacy groups (e.g., families), and task groups (e.g., orchestra members) in both samples, but the more static attribute similarities were more strongly predictive in the United States and the dynamic properties more predictive in Japan. Japanese participants also perceived task groups as more entitative than intimacy groups, whereas the opposite pattern held among American participants, perhaps signifying a greater tendency for Japanese people to ascribe coherence to groups with clearly shared dynamic goals.

Kurebayashi et al.'s (2012) work is consistent with earlier research by Yuki (2003), which established that Japanese understandings of groups tend to focus on dynamic relational properties such as internal interconnections and cooperativeness, whereas American understandings place more emphasis on the existence of shared traits. Ingroup identification and loyalty were more associated with relational factors for Yuki's Japanese participants, whereas they were more associated with homogeneity of attributes among his US participants.

This body of research on culture and entitativity is rather limited in quantity, but its very limitations allow some tentative conclusions to be drawn. All of the studies have emphasized the East Asian versus Western distinction, and all have focused on relatively simple comparative questions. Their common thread is that East Asian cultures may be more prone to regard groups as entitative than Western cultures and to construe entitativity in more dynamic terms, perceiving it as more a matter of shared goals and relationships than shared essential properties. In this respect, these findings accord with some work suggesting higher levels of essentialist thinking in Western than East Asian samples (Lockhart et al., 2008).

Although we have seen that there are some cultural differences in the extent to which certain groups are perceived as entitative, and in the factors that influence these perceptions, it is also important to recognize that there are also important cross-cultural similarities. Kashima et al. (2005) showed that the individual was uniformly seen as more entitative than groups across their eight cultures. Similarly, Lickel et al. (2000) and Ip, Chiu, and Wan (2006) found no differences in the determinants of perceived group entitativity between American and Polish or Chinese samples, respectively. Thus, although research on culture and entitativity is as yet relatively undeveloped, it has shown some potentially important but nevertheless relatively subtle variations overall.

CONCLUSIONS

Our review of the rapidly growing literature on the role of culture in perceived essentialism and entitativity indicates that there are some intriguing variations in these phenomena. Although early research on these topics tended to ignore or bracket off culture in the interests of defining and establishing them, the past decade in particular has broadened in scope. In the process we have seen a marked increase in cross-cultural studies, in studies that compare across different cultural groups or contexts within nations, and in noncomparative work that explores the implications of beliefs about the nature of groups for cultural phenomena such as bicultural identity, acculturation, and majority-minority relations.

The bulk of this increase has been in studies of essentialist thinking. Studies on the role of culture in perceived entitativity have tended to focus more narrowly on East-West comparisons, on differences in levels of entitativity, and to a lesser extent on differences in its determinants. This work has yielded some relatively clear and important messages for students of group perception, but it is also less rich than the body of work on essentialism. That work has addressed perceptions of personal attributes as well as groups, has investigated a wider assortment of cultural comparisons, has ventured into developmental issues, and has examined a wider assortment of consequences of essentialist thinking. It has also asked a more varied set of research questions, including not just the comparison of levels of essentialist beliefs but also cultural variations in its form, structure, and implications. In this respect, investigation of the cultural dimensions of essentialist thinking is more advanced than the investigation of these dimensions of entitativity.

The role of culture in essentialist thinking is also less clear, however. The diversity of research questions, methods, cross-cultural comparisons, theoretical perspectives, and even understandings of what essentialism essentially *is* makes it difficult to draw straightforward conclusions. Evidently there are some cross-cultural differences in the degree to which certain social phenomena are essentialized, but these do not align along simple East-West cultural divides and probably vary according to whether personal attributes or social groups are the phenomena of interest. The factors that influence these differences of degree are also unavoidably diverse, ranging from broad cultural syndromes to highly particular religious beliefs, political ideologies, and linguistic practices. Similarly, there appear to be cultural differences in how essences are understood qualitatively—whether as biological, social, or spiritual elements—and in the structure and social implications of essentialist thinking. We are only beginning to understand these complexities, and the field is ripe for a new generation of culturally oriented social psychologists to take steps to resolve them.

REFERENCES

Ahn, W., Flanagan, E., Marsh, J. K., & Sanislow, C. (2006). Belief about essences and the reality of mental disorders. *Psychological Science, 17*, 759–766.

Allport, G. W. (1954). *The nature of prejudice*. Reading, MA: Addison-Wesley.

Astuti, R., Solomon, G. E. A., & Carey, S. (2004). Constraints on conceptual development: A case study of the acquisition of folkbiological and folksociological knowledge in Madagascar. *Monographs of the Society for Research in Child Development, 69*, 1–135.

Bastian, B., & Haslam, N. (2006). Psychological essentialism and stereotype endorsement. *Journal of Experimental Social Psychology, 42*, 228–235.

Bastian, B., & Haslam, N. (2007). Psychological essentialism and attention allocation: Preferences for stereotype consistent and inconsistent information. *Journal of Social Psychology, 147*, 531–541.

Bastian, B., & Haslam, N. (2008). Immigration from the perspective of hosts and immigrants: The roles of psychological essentialism and social identity. *Asian Journal of Social Psychology, 11*, 127–140.

Birnbaum, D., Deeb, I., Segall, G., Ben-Eliyahu, A., & Diesendruck, G. (2010). The development of social essentialism: The case of Israeli children's inferences about Jews and Arabs. *Child Development, 81*, 757–777.

Boyer, P. (1993). Pseudo-natural kinds. In P. Boyer (Ed.), *Cognitive aspects of religious symbolism* (pp.121–141). New York, NY: Cambridge University Press.

Brewer, M. B., & Harasty, A. S. (1996). Seeing groups as entities: The role of receiver motivation. In R. M. Sorrentino & E. T. Higgins (Eds.), *Handbook of motivation and cognition* (Vol. 3, pp. 347–370). New York, NY: Guilford Press.

Brewer, M. B., Hong, Y. Y., & Li, Q. (2004). Dynamic entitativity: Perceiving groups as actors. In V. Yzerbyt, C. M. Judd, & O. Corneille (Eds.), *The psychology of group perception: Perceived variability, entitativity, and essentialism* (pp. 25–38). New York, NY: Psychology Press.

Campbell, D. T. (1958). Common fate, similarity, and other indices of the status of aggregates of persons as social entities. *Behavioural Science, 3*, 14–25.

Chandler, M. (2001). The time of our lives: Self-continuity in native and non-native youth. *Advances in Child Development and Behavior, 28*, 175–221.

Chao, M., Chen, J., Roisman, G. I., & Hong, Y. Y. (2007). Essentializing race: Implications for bicultural individuals' cognition and physiological reactivity. *Psychological Science, 18*, 341–348.

Coleman, J. M., & Hong, Y. (2008). Beyond nature and nurture: The influence of lay gender theories on self-stereotyping. *Self and Identity, 7*, 34–53.

Dar-Nimrod, I., & Heine, S. J. (2006). Exposure to scientific theories affects women's math performance. *Science, 314*, 435.

Dar-Nimrod, I., & Heine, S. (2011). Genetic essentialism: On the deceptive determinism of DNA. *Psychological Bulletin, 137*, 800–818.

Dasgupta, N., Banaji, M. R., & Abelson, R. P. (1999). Group entitativity and group perception: Associations between physical features and psychological judgment. *Journal of Personality and Social Psychology, 77*, 991–1003.

Diesendruck, G., & Haber, L. (2009). God's categories: The effect of religiosity on children's teleological and essentialist beliefs about categories. *Cognition, 110*, 100–114.

Gelman, S. A. (2003). *The essential child: Origins of essentialism in everyday thought*. Oxford, UK: Oxford University Press.

Gelman, S. A., Heyman, G. D., & Legare, C. H. (2007). Developmental changes in the coherence of essentialist beliefs about psychological characteristics. *Child Development, 78*,757–774.

Giles, J. W., Legare, C., & Samson, J. E. (2008). Psychological essentialism and cultural variation: Children's beliefs about aggression in the United States and South Africa. *Infant and Child Development, 17*, 137–150.

Gil-White, F. (2001). Are ethnic groups biological species to the human brain? Essentialism in human cognition of some social groups. *Current Anthropology, 42,* 515–554.

Hamilton, D. L., & Sherman, S. J. (1996). Perceiving individuals and groups. *Psychological Review, 103,* 336–355.

Haslam, N. (2011). Genetic essentialism, neuroessentialism, and stigma: Comment on Dar-Nimrod & Heine (2011). *Psychological Bulletin, 137,* 819–824.

Haslam, N., Bastian, B., Bain, P. G., & Kashima, Y. (2006). Psychological essentialism, implicit theories, and intergroup relations. *Group Processes and Intergroup Relations, 9,* 63–76

Haslam, N., Bastian, B., & Bissett, M. (2004). Essentialist beliefs about personality and their implications. *Personality and Social Psychology Bulletin, 30,* 1661–1673.

Haslam, N., & Levy, S. (2006). Essentialist beliefs about homosexuality: Structure and implications for prejudice. *Personality and Social Psychology Bulletin, 32,* 471–485.

Haslam, N., Rothschild, L., & Ernst, D. (2000). Essentialist beliefs about social categories. *British Journal of Social Psychology, 39,* 113–127.

Haslam, N., Rothschild, L., & Ernst, D. (2002). Are essentialist beliefs associated with prejudice? *British Journal of Social Psychology, 41,* 87–100.

Hegarty, P. (2002). "It's not a choice, it's the way we're built": Symbolic beliefs about sexual orientation in the United States and in Britain. *Journal of Community and Applied Social Psychology, 12,* 153–166.

Hegarty, P., & Pratto, F. (2001). Sexual orientation beliefs: Their relationship to antigay attitudes and biological determinist arguments. *Journal of Homosexuality, 41,* 121–135.

Hioki, K., & Karasawa, M. (2010). *Shudan no jittaisei ga shugouteki ito to sekinin no handan ni oyobosu eikyou - Kigyou no ihoukoui wo meguru jikkenteki kenkyu* [Effects of group entitativity on the judgment of collective intentionality and responsibility]. *Japanese Journal of Psychology, 81,* 9–16.

Hirschfeld, L. A. (1996). *Race in the making: Cognition, culture, and the child's construction of human kinds.* Cambridge, MA: MIT Press.

Hong, Y-Y., Chao, M. M., & No, S. (2009). Dynamic interracial/intercultural processes: The role of lay theories of race. *Journal of Personality, 77,* 1283–1309.

Hong, Y., Levy, S. R., & Chiu, C. (2001). The contribution of the lay theories approach to the study of groups. *Personality and Social Psychology Review, 5,* 97–105.

Ip, G. W., Chiu, C., & Wan, C. (2006). Birds of a feather and birds flocking together: Physical versus behavioural cues may lead to trait- versus goal-based group perception. *Journal of Personality and Social Psychology, 90,* 368–381.

Jayaratne, T. E., Gelman, S. A., Feldbaum, M., Sheldon, J. P., Petty, E. M., & Kardia, S. L. R. (2009). The perennial debate: Nature, nurture, or choice? Black and White Americans' explanations for individual differences. *Review of General Psychology, 13,* 24–33.

Jayaratne, T., Ybarra, O., Sheldon, J. P., Brown, T. N., Feldbaum, M., Pfeffer, C. A., & Pett, E. M. (2006). White Americans' genetic lay theories of race differences and sexual orientation: Their relationship with prejudice toward blacks, and gay men and lesbians. *Group Processes and Intergroup Relations, 9,* 77–94.

Kashima, Y., Kashima, E., Chiu, C. Y., Farsides, T., Gelfand, M., Hong, Y. Y., . . . Yzerbyt, V. (2005). Culture, essentialism, and agency: Are individuals universally believed to be more real entities than groups? *European Journal of Social Psychology, 35,* 147–169.

Kashima, Y., Kashima, E. S., Kim, U., & Gelfand, M. (2006). Describing the social world: How is a person, a group, and a relationship described in the East and West? *Journal of Experimental Social Psychology, 42*, 388–396.

Keller, J. (2005). In genes we trust: The biological component of psychological essentialism and its relationship to mechanisms of motivated social cognition. *Journal of Personality and Social Psychology, 88*, 686–702.

Kurebayashi, M. A., Hoffman, L. R., Ryan, C. S., & Murayama, A. (2012). Japanese and American perceptions of group entitativity and autonomy: A multilevel analysis. *Journal of Cross-Cultural Psychology, 43*, 349–365.

Lickel, B., Hamilton, D., Wieczorkowska, G., Lewis, A., Sherman, S. J., & Uhles, N. A. (2000). Varieties of groups and perception of group entitativity. *Journal of Personality and Social Psychology, 78*, 223–246.

Lockhart, K. L., Nakashima, N., Inagaki, K., & Keil, F. C. (2008). From ugly duckling to swan? Japanese and American beliefs about the stability and origins of traits. *Cognitive Development, 23*, 155–179.

Maass, A., Karasawa, M., Politi, F., & Suga, S. (2006). Do verbs and adjectives play different roles in different cultures? A cross-linguistic analysis of person representation. *Journal of Personality and Social Psychology, 90*, 734–750.

Mahalingam, R. (2003). Essentialism, culture, and power: Representations of social class. *Journal of Social Issues, 59*, 733–749.

Masuda, T., & Nisbett, R. E. (2001). Attending holistically versus analytically: Comparing the context sensitivity of Japanese and Americans. *Journal of Personality and Social Psychology, 81*, 922–934.

McConnell, A. R., Sherman, S. J., & Hamilton, D. L. (1997). Target entitativity: Implications for information processing about individual and group targets. *Journal of Personality and Social Psychology, 72*, 750–762.

McGarty, C., Haslam, S. A., Hutchinson, K. J., & Grace, D. M. (1995). Determinants of perceived consistency: The relationship between group entitativity and the meaningfulness of categories. *British Journal of Social Psychology, 34*, 237–256.

Medin, D., & Ortony, A. (1989). Psychological essentialism. In S. Vosniadou & A. Ortony (Eds.), *Similarity and analogical reasoning* (pp. 179–195). New York, NY: Cambridge University Press.

Newheiser, A. K., Tausch, N., Dovidio, J. F., & Hewstone, M. (2009). Entitativity and prejudice: Examining their relationship and the moderating effect of attitude certainty. *Journal of Experimental Social Psychology, 45*, 920–926.

Nisbett, R. E. (1998). Essence and accident. In J. M. Darley & J. Cooper (Eds.), *Attribution and social interaction: The legacy of Edward E. Jones* (pp. 171–200). Washington, DC: American Psychological Association.

No, S., Hong, Y., Liao, H., Lee, K., Wood, D., & Chao, M. M. (2008). Lay theory of race affects and moderates Asian Americans' responses towards American culture. *Journal of Personality and Social Psychology, 95*, 991–1004.

Park, J., Haslam, N., & Kashima, Y. (2012). Relational to the core: Beliefs about human nature in Japan, Korea, and Australia. *Journal of Cross-Cultural Psychology, 43*, 774–783.

Pereira, M. E., Estramiana, J. L. A., & Gallo, I. S. (2010). Essentialism and the expression of social stereotypes: A comparative study of Spain, Brasil and England. *Spanish Journal of Psychology, 13*, 808–817.

Prentice, D. A., & Miller, D. T. (2006). Essentializing differences between women and men. *Psychological Science, 17*, 129–135.

Rangel, U., & Keller, J. (2011). Essentialism goes social: Belief in social determinism as a component of psychological essentialism. *Journal of Personality and Social Psychology, 100*, 1056–1078.

Rhee, E., Uleman, J. S., Lee, H. K., & Roman, R. J. (1995). Spontaneous self-descriptions and ethnic identities in individualistic and collectivistic cultures. *Journal of Personality and Social Psychology, 69*, 142–152.

Rhodes, M., & Gelman, S. A. (2009). A developmental examination of the conceptual structure of animal, artifact, and human social categories across two cultural contexts. *Cognitive Psychology, 59*, 244–274.

Roets, A., & Van Hiel, A. (2011). The role of need for closure in essentialist entitativity beliefs and prejudice: An epistemic needs approach to racial categorization. *British Journal of Social Psychology, 50*, 52–73.

Rothbart, M., & Taylor, M. (1992). Category labels and social reality: Do we view social categories as natural kinds? In G. R. Semin & K. Fiedler (Eds.), *Language and social cognition* (pp. 11–36). London, UK: Sage.

Sacchi, S., Castano, E., & Brauer, M. (2009). Perceiving one's nation: Entitativity, agency and security in the international arena. *International Journal of Psychology, 44*, 321–332.

Spencer-Rogers, J., Williams, M. J., Hamilton, D. L., Peng, K., & Wang, L. (2007). Culture and group perception: Dispositional and stereotypic inferences about novel and rational groups. *Journal of Personality and Social Psychology, 93*, 525–543.

Toosi, N., & Ambady, N. (2011). Ratings of essentialism for eight religious identities. *International Journal for the Psychology of Religion, 21*, 17–29.

Verkuyten, M. (2003). Discourses about ethnic group (de-)essentialism: Oppressive and progressive aspects. *British Journal of Social Psychology, 42*, 371–391.

Wagner, W., Kronberger, N., Nagata, M., Sen, R., Holtz, P., & Palacios, F. F. (2010). Essentialist theory of "hybrids": From animal kinds to ethnic categories and race. *Asian Journal of Social Psychology, 13*, 232–246.

Winter, L., & Uleman, J. S. (1984). When are social judgments made? Evidence for the spontaneousness of trait inferences. *Journal of Personality and Social Psychology, 47*, 237–252.

Yuki, M. (2003). Intergroup comparison versus intragroup relationship: A cross-cultural examination of social identity theory in North American and East Asian cultural contexts. *Social Psychology Quarterly, 66*, 166–183.

Yzerbyt, V., Judd, C. M., & Corneille, O. (Eds.). (2004). *The psychology of group perception: Perceived variability, entitativity, and essentialism*. New York, NY: Psychology Press.

Yzerbyt, V., Rocher, S., & Schadron, G. (1997). Stereotypes as explanations: A subjective essentialistic view of group perception. In R. Spears, P. J. Oakes, N. Ellemers, & S. A. Haslam (Eds.), *The social psychology of stereotyping and group life* (pp. 20–50). Cambridge, UK: Blackwell.

Yzerbyt, V., Rogier, A., & Fiske, S. T. (1998). Group entitativity and social attribution: On translating situational constraints into stereotypes. *Personality and Social Psychology Bulletin, 24*, 1089–1103.

Zagefka, H., Pehrson, S., Mole, R. C. M., & Chan, E. (2010). The effect of essentialism is settings of historic intergroup atrocities. *European Journal of Social Psychology, 40,* 718–732.

Zárate, M. A., Uleman, J. S., & Voils, C. I. (2001). Effects of culture and processing goals on the activation and binding of trait concepts. *Social Cognition, 19,* 295–323.

3

Intergroup Comparison and Intragroup Relationships

Group Processes in the Cultures of Individualism and Collectivism

MASAKI YUKI AND KOSUKE TAKEMURA

Groups are ubiquitous. As a distinctively "ultrasocial" animal (Campbell, 1983), we humans cannot live without groups. Throughout our ancestry history, we have created and utilized groups collectively for survival, reproduction, and for better living. While there are other social species who form and depend on groups for their survival, no other primate species is capable of creating and utilizing groups that are greater in size and complexity than are humans (Brewer & Caporael, 2006; Dunbar, 1996). There also is a great diversity in human groups, ranging from families, clans, local communities, work and interest groups, hobby and religious groups, nations, and network communities. Groups are crucial "tools" for human adaptation.

Given the indispensability and ubiquity of social groups, however, there seems to have emerged variations across societies in how individuals relate to groups. In this chapter we deal with cross-cultural differences in group processes, or how people in different societies differentially relate to, that is, see, think about, and behave in, their groups. We will particularly focus on the differences in group processes between the cultures of individualism and collectivism, which have been the primary target of investigations in contemporary cultural psychology. First, we will review theory and research on individualism and collectivism, which assumed a simple distinction between cultures characterized by independence and autonomy versus interdependence and group centeredness, and then a challenge that the theory faced. Second, we will describe our own attempt to tackle this problem: a new theory to propose that people in individualistic cultures do not necessarily detach themselves from groups but instead are involved in groups in a way that is different from people in collectivist cultures. We specifically propose that people in individualistic cultures are intergroup oriented; that is, they identify themselves with the ingroup as an abstract social category and look at the ingroup as a monolithic social category comprised of members who share similar attributes in the comparative context with outgroups. On the other hand, people in collectivistic cultures are intragroup oriented; that is, they perceive the self to be connected with other ingroup members via relational ties and the ingroup to be a bounded network of such ties. Third, we review empirical evidence in support of the theory. Finally, we will attempt to provide a new theoretical framework using a socio-ecological approach to integrate the traditional individualism-collectivism framework and the theory of cultural differences in group processes.

INDIVIDUALISM AND COLLECTIVISM: A BRIEF HISTORY AND CHALLENGE

Traditional research on group processes in cultural and cross-cultural psychologies has primarily focused on how people in different societies differ in their level of group centeredness, as contrasted with individual centeredness. That is, most research is devoted to identifying and distinguishing between societies where individuals are fundamentally embedded in social groups and societies where individuals are free from constraints by groups. Hofstede (1980) first empirically examined how different societies across the world distribute on this cultural dimension. Based on the work-value survey from more than 115,000 employees of an international firm from 53 countries and regions across the globe, Hofstede identified four principal cultural dimensions—power-distance, uncertainty avoidance, individualism, and masculinity. Individualism, as contrasted with collectivism at the opposite pole of the dimension, has attracted the most attention and stimulated the greatest number of subsequent investigations (see Triandis, 1995 for a review). While both individualism and collectivism are now seen as multidimensional constructs, theorists largely agree that the principal distinction between the two lies in differences in the degree of ingroup identity and loyalty (Triandis, Bontempo, Villareal, Asai, & Lucca, 1988; Yamaguchi, 1994). The core theme of individualism is the conception of individuals as autonomous beings who are separate from groups, while the central theme of collectivism is the conception of individuals as parts of groups or collectives. Individuals in individualistic cultures are expected to show less ingroup loyalty, giving priority to personal goals over the goals of collectives. In contrast, individuals in collectivistic cultures either make no distinction between personal and collective goals, or if they do so, they subordinate their personal goals to collective goals (Triandis, 1995).

Among a number of countries and regions, North America (the United States and Canada) and East Asia (such as Japan, China, and Korea) have been treated, respectively, as prototypic representatives of individualistic and collectivist cultures. As such, most empirical investigations into these constructs have compared samples from these two geographical areas. Numerous attempts have been made to uncover psychological and behavioral differences in such phenomena as self-concepts, emotions, social judgment, communication styles, sense of justice, and so on, and these differences have been interpreted as manifestations of the differences in the levels of individualism and collectivism (see Fiske, Kitayama, Markus, & Nisbett, 1998; Kim, Triandis, Kagitchbasi, Choi, & Yoon, 1994; Smith & Bond, 1999, for reviews).

A Challenge

After rigorous investigation flourished over 20 years, however, a stunning fact has been uncovered: People in so-called individualistic cultures are actually highly group oriented. A groundbreaking meta-analytic paper by Oyserman, Coon, and Kemmelmeier (2002) has revealed that North Americans, while being confirmed to be more individualistic than people in almost any other part of the world, are simultaneously very high on the collectivism dimension. Their level of collectivism was higher than Japanese, did not differ significantly from Koreans, and was sometimes higher than Chinese, depending on the scale content used in the studies (see also Takano & Osaka, 1999).

There have been various reactions to this striking finding. Some insisted that cross-cultural differences in individualism versus collectivism actually did not exist or, at least, were not empirically warranted (Matsumoto, 1999; Takano & Osaka, 1999). Other researchers who were in favor of the theory pointed out a lack of validity of the reviewed findings, since the studies primarily relied on Likert scales, which are vulnerable to biases such as cross-cultural differences in response sets (Chen, Lee, & Stevenson, 1995) and the reference group used when making judgments (Heine, Lehman, Peng, & Greenholtz, 2002), and thus one should not rely on the results.

There is, nonetheless, another possibility that was generally overlooked. Namely, while groups are universally important for all human beings, the type of psychological and behavioral processes that operate in group contexts may vary between cultures. In other words, there can be multiple *kinds* of group orientation, in which group identification and behaviors might differ *qualitatively* rather than *quantitatively* between cultures. In the next section, we introduce our model of type of group orientation and how this differs between individualistic and collectivistic cultures (Brewer & Yuki, 2007; Yuki, 2003, 2011).

CROSS-CULTURAL DIFFERENCES IN PSYCHOLOGICAL UNDERPINNINGS OF GROUP PROCESSES

Before going into the theory itself, however, we need to make explicit two critical assumptions to the theory. First, group processes are not uniform; there are qualitatively diverse ways for individuals to relate to groups. As will be discussed in detail, individuals can focus on similarities and differences between the self and groups, or on interpersonal relationships within a group. The second and more theoretically complex assumption is that individualism does not prescribe social isolation but is a kind of social orientation. It prescribes how human beings, which are ultrasocial animals, ought to associate with each other but in a way that is different from individuals in the culture of collectivism. As stated earlier, Oyserman et al.'s (2002) meta-analysis, which uncovered high collectivism among North Americans, simultaneously confirmed that North Americans were highly individualistic, to the degree that was higher than people in other parts of the world. But how can individualism, which prescribes independence from social contexts at least on the surface, coexist with a strong group orientation? The current chapter also attempts to solve this question after showing how cultures vary in the type of predominant group processes.

Social Identity Theory and Group Process in Individualistic Cultures

Social identity theory, along with self-categorization theory, has been accepted in Western social psychology as the single comprehensive theory of psychological underpinnings of an array of intergroup and group phenomena (Tajfel & Turner, 1986; Turner, Hogg, Oakes, Reicher, & Wetherell, 1987). The basic tenet is that all group behaviors ultimately derive from the phenomenon called depersonalization of self-representation. This occurs when a cognitive representation of the self is defined in terms of membership in a shared social category, and in effect there is no subjective distinction between the self and the group as a whole. When social identity is made salient, individuals "come to perceive themselves more as the interchangeable exemplars of a social category than as unique personalities defined by their individual differences from others" (Turner et al., 1987, p. 50). In other words, it is when cognitive representation of the self shifts from the personal self to the collective self (Hogg & Abrams, 1988).

This form of depersonalization occurs in a comparative context between the ingroup and outgroup. That is, a categorization of the self as a group member is more likely to occur when the perceived differences between the self and other ingroup members are smaller than the differences between ingroup and outgroup members. In other words, an ingroup cannot be defined without an outgroup, and intergroup comparison is crucial. Because social identity necessitates the self to be defined at the ingroup level, the value of the self is derived from the value of the ingroup. This leads to the expectation that individuals will focus on intergroup status differences and be motivated to achieve positive intergroup distinctiveness.

In this comparative context, features shared by ingroup members that distinguish them from the outgroup lead to the development of a group "prototype." Perceptions of the self and other ingroup members are then assimilated to this ingroup prototype. Ingroup members are perceived as similar to one another, and the ingroup as a whole becomes perceived to be homogeneous (Hogg & Turner, 1987). Some later developments of social identity theory have focused on differences in prototypicality among group members, with relative prototypicality being associated with differential influence and marginalization within the group

(Hogg, 2001). In any case, social identity implies a depersonalized perception of the ingroup, by viewing group members either as interchangeable or as differing in terms of their prototype-based position in the group.

Intragroup Relationships as the Bases of Group Processes in Collectivistic Cultures

Yuki and colleagues have proposed that an alternative model is necessary to describe the predominant characteristics of group cognition and behaviors among people in collectivistic cultures (Brewer & Yuki, 2007; Yuki, 2003, 2011). Social identity theory, which is widely accepted in Western social psychology, is a primarily intergroup-focused theory, meaning that it views intergroup comparison as a key source of ingroup identification. This model does not accurately capture predominant mechanisms underlying group behaviors in collectivistic cultures. The first discrepancy is that, in contrast to social identity theory, group behaviors among people in collectivistic cultures are intragroup rather than intergroup phenomena. For instance, Confucianism, which has exerted a profound influence on East Asian societies for more than 2,000 years, focuses almost exclusively on intragroup, rather than intergroup, relationships (Kim & Lee, 1994; King & Bond, 1985).

In line with this, people in collectivistic cultures are found to have strong motivation to maintain harmonious and reciprocal intragroup relationships. For instance, research has shown that people in collectivistic cultures tend to prefer the principle of equality over equity in reward allocation within the ingroup (Bond, Leung, & Wan, 1982; Hui, Triandis, & Yee, 1991; Kashima, Siegal, Tanaka, & Isaka, 1988; Kim, Park, & Suzuki, 1990; Leung & Bond, 1982; Leung & Park, 1986; Mann, Radford, & Kanagawa, 1985), to discern and understand other members' personal thoughts and feelings (Azuma, 1994; Choi, Kim, & Choi, 1993), and to prioritize animosity reduction in conflict resolution (Kirkbride, Tang, & Westwood, 1991; Leung, 1987; Leung, Au, Fernandez-Dols, & Iwawaki, 1992; Leung & Lind, 1986; Ohbuchi & Takahashi, 1994). Also, in order to maintain social harmony within the ingroup, they must constantly pay attention to the structure of complex relationships between ingroup members, both horizontally and vertically, and understand where in the network they are located. For instance, anthropologists point out that East Asians are particularly attentive to ascribed status differences between ingroup members (Nakane, 1970). To act appropriately, individuals should begin social interactions by assessing the role relationship between oneself and others (Hwang, 1999).

In line with this argument, Abrams, Ando, and Hinkle (1998) found that both British and Japanese workers' intentions to quit their jobs were affected by level of identification with their company as a whole. Japanese workers' turnover intention, however, was also predicted by a subjective norm—their perception of whether people who are close to them want them to continue working for the company. These results indicate that a relational factor is more influential in group loyalty of people in collectivistic than individualistic cultures.

Furthermore, there has been virtually no empirical support for the widely held expectation that people in collectivistic cultures will be more ingroup serving than people in individualistic cultures. Evidence rather suggests that discrimination against outgroups is actually more pronounced in individualistic cultures. We will discuss cross-cultural differences in intergroup discrimination in more detail later.

Self-Concept: Relational Rather Than Collective

The second aspect that differs between the *inter*group-focused and *intra*group-focused models of group orientation is how the self is purported to be represented cognitively in the minds of individuals. Since the early days of research on the self, theorists have hypothesized that the self involves multiple components (Cooley, 1902; Loevinger, 1976; Mead, 1934). The primary distinction is between the personal or individual self and the social or group self. More recent research has explored various implications of this view, and more attention has been given to multiple forms of the social self. Although different distinctions among types of social selves have been made (e.g., Breckler & Greenwald, 1986; Deaux, 1993), the distinction most relevant to the present argument is the one by Brewer and Gardner (1996) between the *collective* and the *relational* selves (see also Kashima & Hardie, 2000; Kashima et al., 1995). The collective self is the self defined in terms of prototypical properties that are shared among depersonalized members of a common ingroup (Brewer, 1991). The relational self, on the other hand, is the self defined in terms of connections and role relationships with significant others (Cross & Madson, 1997; Gilligan, 1982; Markus & Kitayama, 1991; McGuire & McGuire, 1982). The relational self generally is associated with a psychological tendency to emphasize interpersonal relatedness, intimacy, and interdependence (Baumeister & Leary, 1995).

Although collectivistic values focus on interpersonal relationships, the term *collectivism* is sometimes used as if it were equivalent to the concept of collective self as defined by Brewer and Gardner (1996) and others. Other scholars, however, who apply more indigenous theoretical perspectives, have defined the predominant form of the self among people in collectivistic cultures more in terms of its relational aspect (Choi et al., 1993; Hamaguchi, 1977; Lebra, 1976; Markus & Kitayama, 1991). Among many such terms, the best known is the interdependent self, proposed by Markus and Kitayama (1991). These authors state that Asian cultures "are organized according to meanings and practices that promote the fundamental connectedness among individuals within a significant relationship (e.g., family, workplace, and classroom)" and that "the self is made meaningful primarily in reference to those social relations of which the self is a participating part" (Kitayama, Markus, Matsumoto, & Norasakkunkit, 1997, p. 1247). Both *jen*, a concept of person in China, and *jibun*, a notion of self in Japan, imply that the self is located in social relations (Hamaguchi, 1977; Hsu, 1981; Lebra, 1976). In the Confucian paradigm, individuals see themselves situated symbolically in the web of a relational network through which they define themselves (King & Bond, 1985) (see Brewer & Chen, 2007, for a more extensive argument on the confusion between relational and collective selves in the traditional individualism-collectivism literature).

Although this idea is often misunderstood, maintaining an "interdependent" self is not only different from the self-representation at the category level (Turner et al., 1987) but also from the phenomenon known as "self-extension," to include significant others as part of the self (Aron, Aron, & Smollan, 1992). Consistent with this view, research found that emotional closeness and identity overlap with one's friendship group was quite weak among Japanese, as compared with Euro-Americans and Dutch (Uleman, Rhee, Bardoliwalla, & Semin, 2000). Instead, people with an interdependent self believe that individuals, including themselves, are distinct personalities who are mutually connected via stable and visible relational ties (Hamaguchi, 1977; Ho & Chiu, 1994; Vignoles, Chryssochoou, & Breakwell, 2000). In the words of Fiske, Kitayama, Markus, and Nisbett (1998), "[L]iving interdependently does not mean the loss of self, the fusion of self with other, or the absence of self-interests. What it does mean is that attention, cognition, affect, and motivation are organized with respect to relationship and norms" (p. 925). Although the self among people in collectivistic cultures is embedded in social relations, it is attributed to "the capacity to do right or wrong, and, ultimately, the individual alone is responsible for what he is" (King & Bond, 1985, p. 31).

Ingroup Representation: Bounded Network Rather Than Homogenous Entity

The prevalence of the relational self, rather than collective self, among people in collectivistic cultures does not imply that they downplay the ingroup as a meaningful social unit. In fact, they do impose boundaries between ingroups and outgroups (Gudykunst, 1988; Smith & Bond, 1999). The critical difference, nonetheless, is that those in collectivistic cultures do not depict individuals' perceptions of their ingroups as depersonalized entities, as social identity theory would predict, but as complex networks of interrelated individual members (Choi et al., 1993; Hamaguchi, 1977; Ho, 1993; Kim & Lee, 1994; Lebra, 1976; Nakane, 1970). This relational view of groups was evident even in the teachings of Confucius, who conceptualized a family as a network consisting of three of the "Five Cardinal Relations": between father and son, elder brother and younger brother, and husband and wife. This relationship-based representation is also the basis for the conception of larger groups. Confucius considered the ideal society as a "massive and complicated role system" (King & Bond, 1985, p. 30). Even today, people often use the metaphor of a family when they speak of other kinds of groups, in which vertical and horizontal roles are clearly differentiated (Chang, Lee, & Koh, 1996; Nakane, 1970).

The East Asian way of perceiving the ingroup as a network can be described in more theoretical terms, congruent with an alternative form of perceived group entitativity. The term *entitativity* was coined by Donald Campbell (1958) to denote the degree to which a social collective is viewed as a single unit or entity. Among factors that determine entitativity, perceived similarity or homogeneity has attracted the greatest attention in subsequent research (e.g., Brewer & Harasty, 1996; McGarty, Haslam, Hutchinson, & Grace, 1995). However, later theorization also focused on organization and structure, or dynamic properties, as alternative bases for entitativity, such as a hierarchical structure within the group, as a differentiation of roles and functions among the members, as a purposive integration of activity, and/or as clear differences in leadership, power, status, and responsibility (Hamilton, Sherman, & Lickel, 1998; Lickel, Hamilton, & Sherman, 2001). What can be predicted from the current argument is that the predominant basis of group entitativity may differ between individualistic and collectivistic cultures. In line with this, Kurebayashi, Hoffman, Ryan, and Murayama's (2012) cross-cultural study showed that trait similarity among group members predicted entitativity among Americans, whereas for Japanese shared goals and dynamic properties were more strongly associated with entitativity (see Haslam, Holland, & Karasawa, Chapter 2, this volume, for a more detailed review of culture and group entitativity).

The contrast between the depersonalized and the network view of ingroups is also consistent with the distinction between *common-identity* and *common-bond* groups (Prentice, Miller, & Lightdale, 1994). In common-identity groups, members are attached more strongly to the group per se than to fellow group members. In common-bond groups, members are attached to individual members of the group; their ingroup identification and their evaluation of individual members are closely correlated. Evidence suggests that attachment to and identification with the ingroup as a whole and to individual ingroup members are empirically independent from each other (Hogg, 1993; Karasawa, 1991; Prentice et al., 1994). The common-identity group is similar to social identity theory's view of ingroups as undifferentiated and depersonalized, whereas the common-bond group may be consistent with the view of ingroups by people in collectivistic cultures as composed of cognitively differentiated members.

EMPIRICAL EVIDENCE FOR CROSS-CULTURAL DIFFERENCES IN GROUP PROCESSES

The hypothesized cross-cultural differences in group processes—intergroup comparison focus in individualistic cultures, and intragroup relationship orientation in collectivistic cultures—has a number of implications for various social psychological phenomena pertaining to the issues of self and identity, attention and motivation, intragroup behavior, and intergroup behavior. Evidence relevant to these implied differences is reviewed in the following sections.

Ingroup Identities

Traditionally, theorists on individualism and collectivism simply assumed that the self-representations of people in individualistic cultures will consist primarily of idiocentric traits and attributes, whereas members of collectivist cultures will incorporate more social references, including allocentric, relational constructs and group memberships (Triandis, 1989). But comparative research on the spontaneous self-concept of respondents in different cultures has not consistently supported this simple relationship between culture and content of representations of the self (see Brewer & Chen, 2007 for an extensive review). Some studies comparing self-descriptions of participants from collectivistic societies (including Kenya, Malaysia, India, Japan, China, and Korea) and individualistic societies (United States, Britain, and Australia) have found support for the contention that collectivists generate a larger proportion of social identity references (Dhawan, Roseman, Naidu, & Rettek, 1995; Ma & Schoeneman, 1997; Ross, Xun, & Wilson, 2002; Trafimow, Triandis, & Goto, 1991; Triandis, McCusker, & Hui, 1990). On the other hand, some studies have found that US respondents used an equal, or sometimes even greater, proportion of social descriptors in their spontaneous self-concepts than respondents from Japan, China, or Korea (Bond & Cheung, 1983; Cousins, 1989; Rhee, Uleman, Lee, & Roman, 1995).

The picture becomes drastically different when one incorporates the distinction between relationship-based and category-based social identities proposed by Brewer and Gardner (1996) and looks more closely at different types of responses obtained in these studies. In general, participants from collectivist cultures generate more references to social relationships and role identities in their spontaneous self-descriptions, but respondents in individualistic cultures are equal or greater in their references to social group or social category memberships. In a particularly comprehensive cross-cultural test, Watkins et al. (1998) obtained responses from a large number of university students from four different individualistic cultures (Australia, Canada, New Zealand, and Whites in South Africa) and five collectivist cultures (China, Ethiopia, Philippines, Turkey, and Blacks in South Africa). They classified self-descriptions obtained with the Twenty Statements Test (Kuhn & McPartland, 1954) into four categories: idiocentric (e.g., personal qualities, traits, attitudes), allocentric (relational constructs such as sociable, good friend, etc.), small group memberships (e.g., family relationships), and large group memberships (e.g., I am a student; I am Chinese). The results showed that, while members of individualistic cultures and of collectivistic cultures generated approximately the same proportion of idiocentric self-descriptions, the two groups differed in the *type* of social reference that appeared most frequently. Respondents from collectivistic countries tend to generate greater number of self-descriptions pertaining to *allocentric* or *small group memberships*, whereas those from individualistic countries generated more references to *large group* memberships.

In a more direct test of cultural differences in the meaning of ingroup in social identification processes, Yuki (2003) compared predictors of the strength of ingroup identity and loyalty between Japan and the United States. He asked both American and Japanese university students to report how they perceived two kinds of ingroups of different sizes—their country and a small social group to which they belonged (such as sports teams or activity groups). One set of measures pertained to features of the ingroup as a social category, such as perceived intragroup homogeneity and perceived status differences between ingroup and outgroups. Another set of measures included perceived relational connections with the ingroup, such as knowledge about individual differences and relationships among group members and the sense of personal connectedness between the self and other group members. It was found that for Japanese, ingroup identification and loyalty were determined solely by the relational factors, with no significant correlation with the categorical factors. In contrast, Americans' identity and loyalty were associated significantly with both the relational factors and the categorical factors.

Kashima, Hardie, Wakimoto, and Kashima (2011) tested the influence of social contexts that make social identities salient. They primed Australians and Asians in Australia with four contextual primes: individual, relational, collective, and control (nonsocial). The results showed that the relational context gave rise to increased social self-descriptions (relational and collective jointly) among Asians, whereas the collective context increased it among Australians. These patterns are consistent with Yuki and colleagues' model of cultural difference in the meaning and cognitive representation of social selves.

Attention to Group Characteristics

The aforementioned results are consistent with the idea that people in individualistic and collectivistic cultures have different foci in group contexts. However, this conclusion is weakened by a reliance on Likert scales, since, as discussed earlier, they are vulnerable to various confounding factors (Chen et al., 1995; Heine et al., 2002). It is thus crucial to examine the hypothesized cultural differences through other methods, such as by assessing online responses or mental responses spontaneously produced as people behave in actual social settings (Kitayama, 2002).

Takemura, Yuki, and Ohtsubo (2010) compared spontaneous attention to intergroup status differences and intragroup relationships between Americans and Japanese. In a study represented ostensibly as an "impression formation study," participants were asked to read three scenarios. Each scenario depicted a daily situation involving three groups, one of which was described as the participants' ingroup. Every scenario included several pieces of information regarding status differences between the three groups (intergroup comparison information), as well as relationships between three ingroup members and their cooperativeness (intragroup relationship information). After a few filler questions, participants were asked to complete a surprise memory test. For each scenario, participants were asked to indicate whether information presented, either pertaining to intragroup relationship and intergroup comparisons, accurately described what had been written in the scenarios they had read previously. The results showed, as predicted, that compared to Japanese participants, memory performance among US participants was biased toward intergroup status difference information over intragroup relationship information. Americans, who are more likely to hold a collective and depersonalized conceptualization of the self within the intergroup context, are more receptive to information pertaining to status differences between groups than are Japanese, whose relational social identity is more focused on the connections of distinct individuals within the group.

Intragroup Behaviors

The distinction between the intergroup comparison and intragroup relational orientations has a number of implications for people's behaviors in intragroup contexts. A volume of evidence supports Yuki and colleagues' expectation that predominant patterns of group behaviors will differ between collectivists and individualists. For instance, a leadership study showed that collectivist values were associated with perceived effectiveness of personalized, as opposed to depersonalized, leadership style (Hogg et al., 2005). In the following, we particularly focus on how this theoretical dimension affects the process underlying trust toward a stranger (see also Kwan & Hong, Chapter 5, this volume, for an intensive review of research on culture and trust).

Trust has been a central psychological construct in the social sciences (Kramer, 1999; Ostrom & Walker, 2003; Putnam, 2000; Yamagishi, 2011). While definitions of trust vary greatly across different research traditions, what we deal with here pertains to an expectation of beneficent treatment from others in uncertain or risky situations (Foddy, Platow, & Yamagishi, 2009). More specifically, trust reflects a belief that others will act in a way that will benefit (or not harm) oneself, *before* one knows the outcome of others' behaviors (Dasgupta, 1988). Trust is typically called for in situations where another person has the potential to gain at one's expense but can choose *not* to do so (Yamagishi & Yamagishi, 1994).

Of particular interest here is the role of trust in contexts where participants must decide whether to rely on others with whom they have little or no personal knowledge or history of an interpersonal relationship (Cook, 2001; Foddy et al., 2009; Kramer, 1999; Ostrom, 1998; Tyler, 2001; Yamagishi & Yamagishi, 1994). Although it is generally difficult to establish trust in strangers, such impersonal trust is essential for the creation and maintenance of many forms of economic exchange, organizations, and social and political institutions.

A common solution to the problem of trusting strangers is to rely on social distance: "trust neighbors, but not outsiders" (Macy & Skvoretz, 1998, p. 651) or trusting ingroup while distrusting outgroup others. In contrast to the popular view that collectivists should be more trustful than individualists to the ingroup, however, evidence suggests that people from individualist cultures and individuals with individualistic orientations often show greater ingroup bias in trust than people from collectivistic cultures and collectivistic individuals (e.g., Buchan, Croson, & Dawes, 2002; Buchan, Johnson, & Croson, 2006; Yamagishi et al., 2005). For instance, Buchan et al. (2002) found that, in an investment game involving indirect exchange situation, participants with individualistic cultural orientations increased their levels of trust in unknown others (in terms of amount of monetary investment) when shared identity of an arbitrary social category with the target person was made salient. Participants with a collectivist orientation, on the contrary, did not alter the level of trust regardless of whether a category identity was salient. Using a similar procedure in a subsequent study, Buchan, Croson, and Johnson (2006) compared trust behaviors between US and Chinese participants. They found that US participants showed a clear ingroup bias in trust, whereas Chinese did not show such a tendency. Likewise, Yamagishi et al. (2005) found that sharing of group membership (e.g., same country, same university) was sufficient to generate higher trust in ingroup members for Australians, but not for Japanese.

These counterintuitive findings regarding the relationship between collectivist cultural values and group-based trust can be understood if one recognizes that there are two distinct bases for the trust for a stranger in the ingroup. The first is a shared social category, which gives a basis for a *depersonalized trust* (Brewer, 1981). When a shared social categorization is made salient, cognitive representations of fellow ingroup members and that of the self overlap. This change in the level of self-concept, in line with social identity theory, leads individuals to expect ingroup members to allocate resources fairly than selfishly (Foddy et al., 2009), to conserve resources for the sake of the ingroup (Brewer & Kramer, 1986), and to contribute more to the public good without knowing whether other ingroup members are also contributing their shares (Wit & Kerr, 2002). In the second basis for trust, individuals can trust others when they (believe that they) are directly or indirectly connected to each other through interpersonal ties (Coleman, 1990). A shared network of interpersonal relationships provides a mechanism for extending *personalized* trust to unknown others who are part of the social network. If we incorporate the aforementioned discussion on the qualitative differences in group processes across cultures, it is possible that the former, category-based version of trust may be more predominant in individualistic cultures, whereas the latter, interpersonal connection-based version may be more predominant in collectivistic cultures.

Based on this reasoning, Yuki, Maddux, Brewer, and Takemura (2005) conducted a series of experiments to test whether the basis for trust toward strangers may differ between cultures, in accordance with the meaning of ingroups. They hypothesized that Americans' trust toward a stranger would be based on categorical distinctions between ingroups and outgroups; they would trust someone who shares the same social category with the self and show less trust toward those who do not share categories. By contrast, Japanese trust in a stranger would be determined by whether the person is likely to share an indirect personal relationship with the self, regardless of category boundaries. Shared ingroup membership may provide one basis for inferring relational connections to an unknown other, but potential network ties across category boundaries should be equally likely to elicit trust. In other words, the researchers predicted that if it is likely that an unknown outgroup member shares an indirect interpersonal connection with the self (through a personal acquaintance), this cross-group relationship link should generate trust for an outgroup member in Japan but not in the United States.

Results from two experiments, one vignette study using hypothetical scenarios and one laboratory study that involved real monetary stakes, supported the hypothesis. Across both studies, Americans' trust was based on categorical distinctions; they trusted a stranger (someone they had not met before) in the ingroup more than strangers in outgroups. Presence or absence of an acquaintance in the outgroup did not affect the levels of trust. On the other hand, trust for Japanese participants depended more on the likelihood that they had direct or indirect relationship links with the targets. In particular, the participants' expectation that they might have indirect interpersonal connections (because they had an acquaintance in that group) affected outgroup trust for Japanese. Overall, evidence supports Yuki and colleagues' general theoretical framework that the psychological underpinnings of intragroup behaviors differ between individualistic and collectivistic cultures.

Intergroup Discrimination

Discrimination is found in all human societies (Sumner, 1906). Ingroup-outgroup discrimination refers to preferential treatments directed toward ingroup over outgroup members. The question here is whether differences in the predominant group processes between individualistic and collectivistic cultures will affect the type of intergroup behaviors that people in those cultures engage in.

Traditionally, the literature on individualism and collectivism simply assumed that the latter culture prescribes sharper ingroup-outgroup distinctions, and thus expected that people in collectivist cultures would show greater intergroup discrimination (Triandis, 1995). As Iyengar, Lepper, and Ross (1999) put it, "as the self-other boundary becomes less distinct, the distinction between ingroup members and outgroups members assumes greater significance... assimilating ingroup members to self may lead individuals to contrast ingroup and outgroup members more sharply, making them relatively more susceptible to different cognitive, perceptual, and motivational biases" (p. 279). This logic is congruent with that of social identity theory.

In fact, results from a number of comparative studies seem to be in line with the idea that collectivist values are associated with a greater ingroup-outgroup differentiation. For instance, an experiment on the effects of cultural cues on social behavior showed that a priming with Chinese (vs. American or culture-neutral) symbols made college students from Hong Kong (who are expected to be biculturals) to be more cooperative in the Prisoner's Dilemma game with their friends. However, the priming did not affect these biculturals' cooperative choices when they played the game with strangers (Wong & Hong, 2005). In other words, Chinese symbols, as compared to American symbols, lead to greater ingroup bias in cooperation. Second, a study on communication showed that Korean and Japanese students tend to think that communication with classmates is more intimate, smooth, and less difficult than communication with strangers. These differences were not found among American participants (Gudykunst, Yoon,

& Nishida, 1987). Third, studies on distributive justice have shown that people from collectivist cultures tend to support the use of different reward allocation norms to ingroup (equality) and outgroup (equity). Such differentials are less evident among American participants (Leung & Bond, 1984; Mahler, Greenberg, & Hayashi, 1981). Finally, a comparative study on conflict resolution showed that culture and target interactively affect how individuals deal with interpersonal disputes. Hong Kong Chinese college students were, in comparison with their American counterparts, less likely to pursue a conflict with an ingroup disputant (close friend) but more likely to pursue a conflict with an outgroup disputant (stranger) (Leung, 1988). It must be noted, nonetheless, that none of these findings indicate that people in collectivistic cultures are motivated toward maximizing ingroup-outgroup differences (as predicted by social identity theory), but simply that they relate differently to ingroups and outgroups.

If one takes into consideration the present argument that there are cultural differences in predominant group processes, the psychological underpinnings behind intergroup discrimination should differ between cultures. That is, the source of intergroup discrimination and distinction among people in collectivistic cultures will not be based on the orientation toward active comparison and differentiation between groups, as social identity theory depicts, but instead will be a necessary consequence of their motivation for the maintenance of harmonious and reciprocal relationships within the ingroup. Much evidence is available to support this expectation. First, research indicates that evaluative ingroup bias is greater in individualistic than in collectivistic cultures, particularly when the targets of evaluation are category-based ingroups and outgroups. For instance, Bond and Hewstone (1988) found that Chinese students in Hong Kong had fewer positive images of the ingroup than did British students. Heine and Lehman (1997) found that Japanese students rated their own universities less positively than did students from rival universities; this pattern was not found among Canadian students. Snibbe, Kitayama, Markus, and Suzuki (2003) found significantly less ingroup favoritism among Japanese football fans compared with their American counterparts, athough the two groups did not differ in the magnitude of ingroup identification. Finally, Rose (1985) found that Americans had more positive views of their country than did Japanese.

Conversely, research indicates that not only people in individualistic cultures but also in collectivistic cultures engage in evaluative ingroup bias when the groups are defined in terms of relational connections (Endo, Heine, & Lehman, 2000). Even their self-critical attitudes have been interpreted as a strategy to maintain harmonious relationships with others (Heine & Lehman, 1997; Kitayama et al., 1997). The importance of maintaining harmonious relationships in collectivistic cultures is further indicated by findings that relationship harmony is more strongly associated with subjective well-being in Hong Kong than in the United States (Kurman & Sriram, 1997; Kwan, Bond, & Singelis, 1997).

Evidence reviewed thus far pertained to intergroup bias in evaluation, but behaviors in intergroup contexts are also expected to differ between cultures. In the literature on social identity theory, intergroup discrimination in allocation of rewards has been well documented in experimental research using the minimal intergroup paradigm (Brewer, 1979; Diehl, 1990; Tajfel, 1970; Tajfel, Billig, Bundy, & Flament, 1971). In the typical minimal group studies, ingroups are defined as genuinely categorical, in the sense that they are determined based on arbitrary bases, such as by lottery, dot estimation tendency (overestimator vs. underestimator), and artistic preference, and, more important, there is no substantial interdependence among members. An implication from Yuki and colleagues' theory is that ingroup bias based on such abstract categorical distinctions will be more pronounced among Westerners than Asians. In fact, Wetherell (1982) found that the magnitude of ingroup bias in the minimal group paradigm was smaller among children with Polynesian compared to European cultural background; Polynesian children rather attempted to benefit both ingroup and outgroup members. In the study on trust by Buchan et al. (2006), which we cited earlier, half of the participants were asked to play the role of "responders" who were to decide whether they should return a portion of the money received (with trust) from the "senders," who were either in the (minimal) ingroup or outgroup. The results showed that American participants exhibited significant ingroup bias, returning a greater amount of money to the ingroup than to outgroup senders, whereas Chinese showed the opposite tendency. Moreover, this cultural difference was explained by cultural orientation of individualism-collectivism. That is, the effect of culture ceased to be significant when individual difference in individualism-collectivism was statistically controlled, with individualists showing greater ingroup bias than collectivists within both countries.

Intergroup discrimination in collectivistic cultures is more a function of interdependence within a group. Congruent with this reasoning, a series of studies by Yamagishi and colleagues with Japanese participants (Jin, Yamagishi, & Kiyonari, 1996; Karp, Jin, Yamagishi, & Shinotsuka, 1993) showed that presence or absence of interdependence among ingroup members greatly affected whether participants engaged in ingroup bias. In the experiments, participants were asked to perform a reward allocation task between one ingroup and one outgroup member. In one condition, which is consistent with the standard procedure of minimal group experiments (e.g., Tajfel et al., 1971), participants were told that every participant, including themselves, was to perform the allocation task. In another condition, however, they were asked to draw a lottery and were told that they were chosen to be the only participant within the ingroup who was to perform the reward allocation task. A critical difference between the two conditions is that whereas the former involves the structure of mutual fate control within a group, the latter did not have such a structure of interdependence. The results indicate that the presence of intragroup interdependence is requisite for Japanese to privilege ingroups over outgroups. Together with the results of similar studies conducted in North America and Australia, which consistently found a significant ingroup discrimination even when reciprocal interdependence within groups was eliminated (e.g., Perreault & Bourhis, 1998; Platow, McClintock, & Liebrand, 1990; but see also Yamagishi, Mifune, Liu, & Pauling, 2008), it seems fair to conclude that the motivational basis for intergroup discrimination differs between cultures: creating maximum positive intergroup distinctiveness in the culture of individualism but maintaining reciprocal intragroup relationships in the culture of collectivism.

INDIVIDUALISM AND INTERGROUP COMPARISON: A SOCIO-ECOLOGICAL ACCOUNT

Evidence reviewed thus far supports the claim by Yuki and colleagues (Brewer & Yuki, 2007; Yuki, 2003, 2011) that there are cross-cultural differences in the *kinds*, but not the *levels*, of predominant group orientations. Specifically, in so-called individualist societies such as North America, people are oriented toward intergroup comparison; they tend to define social groups in terms of shared features among group members, to have a depersonalized view of the self as a prototypical exemplar of the ingroup, and to be motivated to achieve higher intergroup status. On the other hand, in societies that have been traditionally viewed as collectivistic such as East Asia, individuals are oriented toward intragroup relationships; they define groups in terms of shared and bounded interpersonal networks among group members, perceive the self as a distinctive but constitutive part of the network, and are motivated to maintain harmonious and reciprocal relationships between the members. There is, however, one critical question that remains unanswered: From where do these differences originate? Especially puzzling is why North Americans, who have been proved to be more individualistic than people in other parts of the world (Oyserman et al., 2002), are simultaneously concerned about comparing between groups. In this final section, we attempt to answer this intriguing question by incorporating the socio-ecological perspective (Nisbett & Cohen, 1996; Oishi & Graham, 2010; Yuki & Schug, 2012).

There is one critical point that needs to be understood in order to make sense of why people in individualistic cultures are oriented toward intergroup comparisons; that is, individualism is not an isolation or alienation from the society but is a form of *social* orientation. Evidence actually indicates that people living in individualistic societies are often more socially oriented than those in collectivistic cultures. For instance, people in more individualistic states in the United States, when compared with those in less individualistic states, are found to have greater inclination for charitable giving and volunteerism (Kemmelmeier, Jambor, & Letner, 2006) and to have greater social capital (represented by such tendencies as higher interpersonal trust and more frequent engagement in social and political activities) (Allik & Realo, 2004).

The main goal of the socio-ecological perspective is to delineate how the mind and behavior of individuals are related to the natural and social habitats that surround them, such as climate, economic, political, educational, societal, and organizational reward systems, as well as more intermediate structures such as the characteristics of cities, towns, and neighborhoods, housing, and family and kin relationships. This approach actually has a long history in psychology (Barker, 1968; Berry, 1979) but is regaining popularity in various fields of social and cultural sciences (Henrich et al., 2005; Nisbett & Cohen, 1996; Üskül, Kitayama, &

Nisbett, 2008). Although this approach may sound akin to that of ecological biologists who primarily study animals' behaviors in relation to their natural habitats, the important distinction is that it also deals with the recursive process in which human mind and behavior affect and create social habitats (see Oishi & Graham, 2010, for an extensive review of this approach).

One socio-ecological factor that has recently received extensive focus is the level of interpersonal or intergroup *mobility* (Adams, 2005; Chen, Chiu, & Chan, 2009; Oishi, 2010; Yamagishi & Yamagishi, 1994; Yuki & Schug, 2012). We particularly focus on a factor called *relational mobility*, defined as the degree to which there is an availability of options in a given society or social context regarding interpersonal relationships, such as opportunities to acquire new, maintain current, and sever old relationships (Yuki & Schug, 2012; Yuki et al., 2007). Societies low in relational mobility are those where people collectively create and maintain long-standing relationships and groups. Maintaining committed and long-standing relationships with specific others helps reduce social uncertainty such as risks of being cheated (Yamagishi, Jin, & Kiyonari, 1999). Societies high in relational mobility, on the other hand, provide people with an abundance of opportunities to meet strangers and create new relationships, in order for people to utilize opportunities (Yamagishi & Yamagishi, 1994). This concept, as well as other factors that may be closely tied to relational mobility, has proven useful in explaining various differences in psychological and behavioral tendencies between peoples in individualistic and collectivistic cultures, such as differences in the level of trust in strangers (Yamagishi & Yamagishi, 1994; Yuki et al., 2007), self-enhancement (Falk, Heine, Yuki, & Takemura, 2009), determinants of happiness (Yuki, Sato, Takemura, & Oishi, 2013), pursuit of uniqueness (Yamagishi, Hashimoto, & Schug, 2008), self-disclosure (Schug, Yuki, & Maddux, 2010), reward and punishment toward cooperators and defectors (Wang & Leung, 2010), and proneness to shame (Sznycer et al., 2012).

Of particular interest here is that studies have revealed that high relational mobility in a society leads to psychological tendencies that have been traditionally thought of as "individualistic." For instance, Falk et al. (2009) showed that the difference in the level of self-enhancement between European Canadians and Japanese was mediated statistically by perceived level of relational mobility in the local environment. They argue that unrealistically high confidence about one's own ability encourages one to approach someone that has high social status, which is only possible in societies high in relational mobility, such as North America. In societies with low relational mobility, on the other hand, such an unrealistic confidence would be rather socially detrimental, since it may disrupt harmony in long-standing relationships with people around them (Falk et al., 2009). Similarly, Debies-Carl and Huggins (2009) have found that individuals living in urban areas, where people tend to have more opportunities to select interaction partners (Fischer, 1975), tend to have greater self-efficacy. Also, Akaeda (2010) reported that unconventional attitudes were found to be higher in more populated areas and residentially mobile (thus presumably relationally mobile) areas (see also Oishi, 2010).

Relational Mobility and Group Processes

Now, how do different levels of relational mobility in a society lead to different types of group processes? High relational mobility societies afford individuals with greater freedom to choose which group(s) they should join. A necessary consequence from this freedom of choice is that individuals should attempt to join groups that have higher rather than lower status, because the membership in the former will generally provide them with larger resources. This leads individuals to monitor intergroup status differences and attempt to associate with groups of higher status. Consistent with this idea, studies have found that people in more residentially mobile societies, as well as individuals with larger personal residential mobility, more opportunistically change their ingroup identity (i.e., depending on the success or failure of the ingroup) than those who are in less residentially mobile societies and those who move less (Oishi, Ishii, & Lun, 2009).

Also, relative freedom of choice afforded by high relational mobility leads individuals to form groups around similarities and common interests, because these features should facilitate coordinated action and collective goal pursuit. Consistent with this idea, it has been shown that a reason why American friends are more similar to each other than Japanese friends is higher relational mobility in the former. Although people in both cultures prefer similar to dissimilar others as friends, the opportunities to find and make friends with similar others are fewer in Japan, a society low in relational mobility (Schug, Yuki, Horikawa, & Takemura, 2009).

On the other hand, in a society with low relational mobility, group memberships tend to be ascribed and predetermined. It is difficult for individuals to leave groups even if they find the groups to be either unsatisfactory (i.e., low status) or incompatible with their own attitudes and goals. It is therefore of critical importance for them to maintain harmonious and reciprocal relationships with fellow ingroup members, by recognizing and accommodating individual differences. Behind this is social groups being constructed so that members can monitor each other's behavior, and high visibility of individual members may serve as a mechanism for inhibiting potential freeriding (Miller & Kanazawa, 2000; Yamagishi, Jin, & Miller, 1998). Congruent with this idea, cross-cultural experiments showed that Japanese became less cooperative and less trusting toward the ingroup when there was no system of ingroup monitoring and sanctioning, whereas Americans did not change their level of cooperation and trust as a function of the presence or absence of a monitoring and sanctioning system (Yamagishi, 1988a, 1988b) (see also Kwan & Hong, Chapter 5, this volume).

Moreover, to be successful in a society with low relational mobility, individuals must also navigate friction between other ingroup members, requiring great attention to the ingroup's complex relational networks. Indirectly supporting this claim, an experiment conducted in Japan showed that participants who were better at judging good and bad relationships within ingroups possessed characteristics that were considered adaptive in stable interpersonal relations; such stability is characteristic of collectivistic societies (Yamagishi & Kosugi, 1999).

An implication from this consideration is that what groups mean for individuals may differ between societies, depending on socio-ecological conditions. In societies with low relational mobility, groups are what individuals take for granted. They are afforded with specific groups and must live there for a long time even if they personally do not prefer to. Such longevity of groups and social relationships, however, helps to reduce social uncertainty and serves as the foundation for effective and routinized social exchange and mutual cooperation. What individuals then seek is how to improve their lives in relation with given others and circumstances while avoiding risks of being ostracized.

In societies with high relational mobility, on the other hand, groups are what individuals opportunistically create and select in order to achieve their personal goals. Here is where the anomaly posed in Oyserman et al. (2002) is solved: why North Americans are high both on individualism and collectivism dimensions. That is, North American intergroup comparison orientation is an "individualists' collectivism," among those who are afforded with "freedom of choice" at the societal level. On the contrary, East Asian intragroup relationship orientation is a "collectivists' collectivism," who have little choice and are bounded in the existing ingroup. While groups have always been a universal "tool" for human adaptation, a great diversity has emerged with regard to its specific forms and how individuals relate to it, according to the structure of the society that they have collectively created.

CONCLUSION

In this chapter, we have discussed how predominant group processes differ between the cultures of individualism and collectivism. Also, we attempted to explain the source of this difference from the perspective of a socio-ecological approach. The socio-ecological perspective provides a novel explanation for why individualism that is prevalent in Western societies, on the one hand, is associated with depersonalized and symbolic collective identities and behaviors to seek positive intergroup distinctiveness, which has been depicted by social identity theory, on the other. It suggests that high relational mobility, or the degree of freedom in choosing relational partners and social groups to which one belongs, provides incentives for individuals to promote oneself as an individual, as well as membership in a group with higher status and greater similarity. It is expected that an application of the socio-ecological perspective will enrich our understanding of the more fundamental bases for human group behaviors, and thus help to make it a genuinely *social* psychological theory of group processes.

REFERENCES

Abrams, D., Ando, K., & Hinkle, S. (1998). Psychological attachment to the group: Cross-cultural differences in organizational identification and subjective norms as predictors of workers' turnover intentions. *Personality and Social Psychology Bulletin, 24*(10), 1027–1039.

Adams, G. (2005). The cultural grounding of personal relationship: Enemyship in North American and West African worlds. *Journal of Personality and Social Psychology, 88*(6), 948–968.

Akaeda, N. (2010). A re-examination of urban effects: Multilevel analysis of unconventionality. *The Annals of Japan Association for Urban Sociology, 28*, 237–252.

Allik, J., & Realo, A. (2004). Individualism-collectivism and social capital. *Journal of Cross-Cultural Psychology, 35*(1), 29–49.

Aron, A., Aron, E., & Smollan, D. (1992). Inclusion of other in the Self Scale and the structure of interpersonal closeness. *Journal of Personality and Social Psychology, 63*(4), 596–612.

Azuma, H. (1994). *Nihonjin no shitsuke to kyoiku: Hattatsu no nichibei hikaku ni motoduite*. Tokyo, Japan: Tokyo Daigaku Shuppankai.

Barker, R. G. (1968). *Ecological psychology: Concepts and methods for studying the environment of human behavior*. Stanford, CA: Stanford University Press.

Baumeister, R. F., & Leary, M. R. (1995). The need to belong: Desire for interpersonal attachments as a fundamental human motivation. *Psychological Bulletin, 117*(3), 497–529.

Berry, J. W. (1979). A cultural ecology of social behavior. In L. Berkowitz (Ed.), *Advances in experimental social psychology* (Vol. 12, pp. 177–207). New York, NY: Academic Press.

Bond, M. H., & Cheung, T-S. (1983). College students' spontaneous self-concept. *Journal of Cross-Cultural Psychology, 14*(2), 153–171.

Bond, M. H., & Hewstone, M. (1988). Social identity theory and the perception of intergroup relations in Hong Kong. *International Journal of Intercultural Relations, 12*(2), 153–170.

Bond, M. H., Leung, K., & Wan, K-C. (1982). The social impact of self-effacing attributions: The Chinese case. *Journal of Social Psychology, 118*(2), 157–166.

Breckler, S. J., & Greenwald, A. G. (1986). Motivational facets of the self. In R. M. Sorrentino & E. T. Higgins (Eds.), *Handbook of motivation and cognition: Foundations of social behavior* (pp. 145–164). New York, NY: Guilford Press.

Brewer, M. B. (1979). In-group bias in the minimal intergroup situation: A cognitive-motivational analysis. *Psychological Bulletin, 86*(2), 307–324.

Brewer, M. B. (1981). Ethnocentrism and its role in interpersonal trust. In M. B. Brewer & B. Collins (Eds.), *Scientific inquiry and the social sciences: A volume in honor of Donald T. Campbell* (pp. 345–360). San Francisco, CA: Jossey-Bass.

Brewer, M. B. (1991). The social self: On being the same and different at the same time. *Personality and Social Psychology Bulletin, 17*(5), 475–482.

Brewer, M. B., & Caporael, L. R. (2006). An evolutionary perspective on social identity: Revisiting groups. In M. Schaller, J. A. Simpson & D. T. Kenrick (Eds.), *Evolution and social psychology* (pp. 143–161). Madison, CT: Psychosocial Press.

Brewer, M. B., & Chen, Y-R. (2007). Where (Who) are collectives in collectivism? Toward conceptual clarification of individualism and collectivism. *Psychological Review, 114*(1), 133–151.

Brewer, M. B., & Gardner, W. (1996). Who is this "we?" Levels of collective identity and self representations. *Journal of Personality and Social Psychology, 71*(1), 83–93.

Brewer, M. B., & Harasty, A. S. (1996). Seeing groups as entities: The role of perceiver motivation. In R. M. Sorrentino & E. T. Higgins (Eds.), *Handbook of motivation and cognition, Vol. 3. The interpersonal context* (pp. 347–370). New York, NY: Guilford Press.

Brewer, M. B., & Kramer, R. M. (1986). Choice behavior in social dilemmas: Effects of social identity, group size, and decision framing. *Journal of Personality and Social Psychology, 50*(3), 543–549.

Brewer, M. B., & Yuki, M. (2007). Culture and social identity. In S. Kitayama & D. Cohen (Eds.), *Handbook of cultural psychology* (pp. 307–322). New York, NY: Guilford Press.

Buchan, N. R., Croson, R. T. A., & Dawes, R. M. (2002). Swift neighbors and persistent strangers: A cross-cultural investigation of trust and reciprocity in social exchange. *American Journal of Sociology, 108*(1), 168–206.

Buchan, N. R., Johnson, E. J., & Croson, R. T. A. (2006). Let's get personal: An international examination of the influence of communication, culture and social distance on other regarding preferences. *Journal of Economic Behavior and Organization, 60*(3), 373–398.

Campbell, D. T. (1958). Common fate, similarity, and other indices of the status of aggregates of persons as social entities. *Behavioral Science, 3*(1), 14–25.

Campbell, D. T. (1983). The two distinct routes beyond kin selection to ultrasociality: Implications for the humanities and social sciences. In D. Bridgeman (Ed.), *The nature of prosocial development: Theories and strategies* (pp. 11–39). New York, NY: Academic Press.

Chang, W. C., Lee, L., & Koh, S. (1996, June 27-29). *The concept of self in a modern Chinese context.* Paper presented at the 50th Anniversary Conference of the Korean Psychological Association, Seoul, Korea.

Chen, C., Lee, S-Y., & Stevenson, H. W. (1995). Response style and cross-cultural comparisons of rating scales among East Asian and North American students. *Psychological Science, 6*(3), 170–175.

Chen, J., Chiu, C-Y., & Chan, S. (2009). The cultural effects of job mobility and the belief in a fixed world: Evidence from performance forecast. *Journal of Personality and Social Psychology, 97*(5), 851–865.

Choi, S. C., Kim, U., & Choi, S. H. (1993). Indigenous analysis of collective representations: A Korean perspective. In U. Kim, & J. W. Berry (Eds.), *Indigenous psychologies: Research and experiences in cultural context* (pp. 193–210). Newbury Park, CA: Sage.

Coleman, J. S. (1990). *Foundations of social theory.* Cambridge, MA: Harvard University Press.

Cook, K. S. (2001). *Trust in society.* New York, NY: Russell Sage Foundation.

Cooley, C. H. (1902). *Human nature and the social order.* New York, NY: Scribner's.

Cousins, S. D. (1989). Culture and self-perception in Japan and the United States. *Journal of Personality and Social Psychology, 56*(1), 124–131.

Cross, S. E., & Madson, L. (1997). Models of the self: Self-construals and gender. *Psychological Bulletin, 122*(1), 5–37.

Dasgupta, P. S. (1988). Trust as a commodity. In D. Gambetta, (Ed.). *Trust: Making and breaking cooperative relations* (pp. 49–72). Oxford, England: Blackwell.

Deaux, K. (1993). Reconstructing social identity. *Personality and Social Psychology Bulletin, 19*(1), 4–12.

Debies-Carl, J. S., & Huggins, C. M. (2009). "City air makes free": A multi-level, cross-national analysis of self-efficacy. *Social Psychology Quarterly, 72*(4), 343–364.

Dhawan, N., Roseman, I. J., Naidu, R., & Rettek, S. (1995). Self-concepts across two cultures: India and the United States. *Journal of Cross-Cultural Psychology, 26*(6), 606–621.

Diehl, M. (1990). The minimal group paradigm: Theoretical explanations and empirical findings. *European Review of Social Psychology, 1*(1), 263–292.

Dunbar, R. I. M. (1996). *Grooming, gossip, and the evolution of language*. London, UK: Faber & Faber.

Endo, Y., Heine, S. J., & Lehman, D. R. (2000). Culture and positive illusions in close relationships: How my relationships are better than yours. *Personality and Social Psychology Bulletin, 26*(12), 1571–1586.

Falk, C. F., Heine, S. J., Yuki, M., & Takemura, K. (2009). Why do Westerners self-enhance more than East Asians? *European Journal of Personality, 23*(3), 183–203.

Fischer, C. S. (1975). Toward a subcultural theory of urbanism. *American Journal of Sociology, 80*(6), 1319–1341.

Fiske, A. P., Kitayama, S., Markus, H. R., & Nisbett, R. E. (1998). The cultural matrix of social psychology. In D. Gilbert, S. Fiske, & G. Lindzey (Eds.), *The handbook of social psychology* (4th ed., Vol. 2, pp. 915–981). San Francisco, CA: McGraw Hill.

Foddy, M., Platow, M. J., & Yamagishi, T. (2009). Group-based trust in strangers: The role of stereotypes and expectations. *Psychological Science, 20*(4), 419–422.

Gilligan, C. (1982). *In a different voice: Psychological theory and women's development*. Cambridge, MA: Harvard University Press.

Gudykunst, W. B. (1988). Culture and intergroup processes. In M. H. Bond (Ed.), *The cross-cultural challenge to social psychology* (pp. 165–181). Thousand Oakes, CA: Sage.

Gudykunst, W. B., Yoon, Y-C., & Nishida, T. (1987). The influence of individualism-collectivism on perceptions of communication in ingroup and out-group relationships. *Communication Monographs, 54*(3), 295–306.

Hamaguchi, E. (1977). *"Nihon rashisa" no saihakken*. Tokyo, Japan: Nihon Keizai Shinbunsha.

Hamilton, D. L., Sherman, S. J., & Lickel, B. (1998). Perceiving social groups: The importance of the entitativity continuum. In C. Sedikides, J. Schopler, & C. A. Insko (Eds.), *Intergroup cognition and intergroup behavior* (pp. 47–74). Mahwah, NJ: Erlbaum.

Heine, S. J., & Lehman, D. R. (1997). The cultural construction of self-enhancement: An examination of group-serving biases. *Journal of Personality and Social Psychology, 72*(6), 1268–1283.

Heine, S. J., Lehman, D. R., Peng, K., & Greenholtz, J. (2002). What's wrong with cross-cultural comparisons of subjective Likert scales? The reference-group effect. *Journal of Personality and Social Psychology, 82*(6), 903–918.

Henrich, J., Boyd, R., Bowles, S., Camerer, C., Fehr, E., Gintis, H., . . . Tracer, D. (2005). "Economic man" in cross-cultural perspective: Behavioral experiments in 15 small-scale societies. *Behavioral and Brain Sciences, 28*(6), 795–855.

Ho, D. Y. F. (1993). Relational orientation in Asian social psychology. In U. Kim & J. W. Berry (Eds.), *Indigenous psychologies: Research and experience in cultural context* (pp. 240–259). Newbury Park, CA: Sage.

Ho, D. Y. F., & Chiu, C-Y. (1994). Component ideas of individualism, collectivism, and social organization: An application in the study of Chinese culture. In U. Kim, H. C. Triandis, C. Kagitcibasi, S-C. Choi, & G. Yoon (Eds.), *Individualism and collectivism: Theory, method, and applications* (pp. 137–156). Thousand Oaks, CA: Sage.

Hofstede, G. (1980). *Culture's consequences: International differences in work-related values*. Beverly Hills, CA: Sage.

Hogg, M. A. (1993). Group cohesiveness: A critical review and some new directions. *European Review of Social Psychology, 4*(1), 85–111.

Hogg, M. A. (2001). A social identity theory of leadership. *Personality and Social Psychology Review, 5*(3), 184–200.

Hogg, M. A., & Abrams, D. (1988). *Social identifications: A social psychology of intergroup relations and group processes.* Florence, KY: Taylor & Frances/Routledge.

Hogg, M. A., Martin, R., Epitropaki, O., Mankad, A., Svensson, A., & Weeden, K. (2005). Effective leadership in salient groups: Revisiting leader-member exchange theory from the perspective of the social identity theory of leadership. *Personality and Social Psychology Bulletin, 31*(7), 991–1004.

Hogg, M. A., & Turner, J. C. (1987). Intergroup behaviour, self-stereotyping and the salience of social categories. *British Journal of Social Psychology, 26*(4), 325–340.

Hsu, F. L. K. (1981). *Americans and Chinese: Passage to differences* (3rd ed.). Honolulu: University of Hawaii Press.

Hui, C., Triandis, H. C., & Yee, C. (1991). Cultural differences in reward allocation: Is collectivism the explanation? *British Journal of Social Psychology, 30*(2), 145–157.

Hwang, K. K. (1999). Filial piety and loyalty: Two types of social identification in Confucianism. *Asian Journal of Social Psychology, 2*(1), 163–183.

Iyengar, S. S., Lepper, M. R., & Ross, L. (1999). Independence from whom? Interdependence with whom? Cultural perspectives on ingroups versus outgroups. In D. A. Prentice & D. T. Miller (Eds.), *Cultural divides: Understanding and overcoming group conflict* (pp. 273–301). New York, NY: Russell Sage Foundation.

Jin, N., Yamagishi, T., & Kiyonari, T. (1996). Bilateral dependency and the minimal group paradigm. *Japanese Journal of Psychology, 67*(2), 77–85.

Karasawa, M. (1991). Toward an assessment of social identity: The structure of group identification and its effects on in-group evaluations. *British Journal of Social Psychology, 30*(4), 293–307.

Karp, D., Jin, N., Yamagishi, T., & Shinotsuka, H. (1993). Rising the minimum in the minimal group paradigm. *Japanese Journal of Experimental Social Psychology, 32*(3), 231–240.

Kashima, E. S., & Hardie, E. A. (2000). The development and validation of the Relational, Individual, and Collective self-aspects (RIC) Scale. *Asian Journal of Social Psychology, 3*(1), 19–48.

Kashima, E. S., Hardie, E. A., Wakimoto, R., & Kashima, Y. (2011). Culture- and gender-specific implications of relational and collective contexts on spontaneous self-descriptions. *Journal of Cross-Cultural Psychology, 42*(5), 740–758.

Kashima, Y., Siegal, M., Tanaka, K., & Isaka, H. (1988). Universalism in lay conceptions of distributive justice: A cross-cultural examination. *International Journal of Psychology, 23*, 51–64.

Kashima, Y., Yamaguchi, S., Kim, U., Choi, S-C., Gelfand, M. J., & Yuki, M. (1995). Culture, gender, and self: A perspective from individualism-collectivism research. *Journal of Personality and Social Psychology, 69*(5), 925–937.

Kemmelmeier, M., Jambor, E. E., & Letner, J. (2006). Individualism and good works: Cultural variation in giving and volunteering across the United States. *Journal of Cross-Cultural Psychology, 37*(3), 327–344.

Kim, K. I., Park, H. J., & Suzuki, N. (1990). Reward allocations in the United States, Japan, and Korea: A comparison of individualistic and collectivistic cultures. *Academy of Management Journal, 33*(1), 188–198.

Kim, U., & Lee, S. H. (1994, June 23). *The Confucian model of morality, justice, selfhood and society: Implications for modern society.* Paper presented at the Eighth International Conference on Korean Studies.

Kim, U., Triandis, H. C., Kagitcibasi, C., Choi, S. C., & Yoon, G. (1994). *Individualism and collectivism: Theory, method, and applications.* Newbury Park, CA: Sage.

King, A. Y. C., & Bond, M. H. (1985). The Confucian paradigm of man: A sociological view. In W-S. Tseng & D. Y. H. Wu (Eds.), *Chinese culture and mental health* (pp. 29–46). New York, NY: Academic Press.

Kirkbride, P. S., Tang, S. F., & Westwood, R. I. (1991). Chinese conflict preferences and negotiating behaviour: Cultural and psychological influences. *Organization Studies, 12*(3), 365–386.

Kitayama, S. (2002). Culture and basic psychological processes—Toward a system view of culture: Comment on Oyserman et al. (2002). *Psychological Bulletin, 128*(1), 89–96.

Kitayama, S., Markus, H. R., Matsumoto, H., & Norasakkunkit, V. (1997). Individual and collective processes in the construction of the self: Self enhancement in the United States and self-criticism in Japan. *Journal of Personality and Social Psychology, 72*(6), 1245–1267.

Kramer, R. M. (1999). Trust and distrust in organizations: Emerging perspectives, enduring questions. *Annual Review of Psychology, 50*, 569–598.

Kuhn, M. H., & McPartland, T. S. (1954). An empirical investigation of self-attitudes. *American Sociological Review, 19*(1), 68–76.

Kurebayashi, K., Hoffman, L., Ryan, C. S., & Murayama, A. (2012). Japanese and American perceptions of group entitativity and autonomy: A multilevel analysis. *Journal of Cross-Cultural Psychology, 43*(2), 349–364.

Kurman, J., & Sriram, N. (1997). Self-enhancement, generality of self-evaluation, and affectivity in Israel and Singapore. *Journal of Cross-Cultural Psychology, 28*(4), 421–441.

Kwan, V. S. Y., Bond, M. H., & Singelis, T. M. (1997). Pancultural explanations for life satisfaction: Adding relationship harmony to self-esteem. *Journal of Personality and Social Psychology, 73*(5), 1038–1051.

Lebra, T. S. (1976). *Japanese patterns of behavior.* Honolulu: University of Hawaii Press.

Leung, K. (1987). Some determinants of reactions to procedural models for conflict resolution: A cross-national study. *Journal of Personality and Social Psychology, 53*(5), 898–908.

Leung, K. (1988). Some determinants of conflict avoidance. *Journal of Cross-Cultural Psychology, 19*(1), 125–136.

Leung, K., Au, Y-F., Fernandez-Dols, J. M., & Iwawaki, S. (1992). Preference for methods of conflict processing in two collectivist cultures. *International Journal of Psychology, 27*(2), 195–209.

Leung, K., & Bond, M. H. (1982). How Chinese and Americans reward task-related contributions: A preliminary study. *Psychologia: An International Journal of Psychology in the Orient, 25*(1), 32–39.

Leung, K., & Bond, M. H. (1984). The impact of cultural collectivism on reward allocation. *Journal of Personality and Social Psychology, 47*(4), 793–804.

Leung, K., & Lind, E. A. (1986). Procedural justice and culture: Effects of culture, gender, and investigator status on procedural preferences. *Journal of Personality and Social Psychology, 50*(6), 1134–1140.

Leung, K., & Park, H-J. (1986). Effects of interactional goal on choice of allocation rule: A cross-national study. *Organizational Behavior and Human Decision Processes, 37*(1), 111–120.

Lickel, B., Hamilton, D. L., & Sherman, S. J. (2001). Elements of a lay theory of groups: Types of groups, relationship styles, and the perception of group entitativity. *Personality and Social Psychology Review, 5*(2), 129–140.

Loevinger, J. (1976). *Ego development: Conceptions and theories.* San Francisco, CA: Jossey-Bass.

Ma, V., & Schoeneman, T. J. (1997). Individualism versus collectivism: A comparison of Kenyan and American self-concepts. *Basic and Applied Social Psychology, 19*(2), 261–273.

Macy, M. W., & Skvoretz, J. (1998). The evolution of trust and cooperation between strangers: A computational model. *American Sociological Review, 63*(5), 638–660.

Mahler, I., Greenberg, L., & Hayashi, H. (1981). A comparative study of rules of justice: Japanese versus American. *Psychologia: An International Journal of Psychology in the Orient, 24*(1), 1–8.

Mann, L., Radford, M., & Kanagawa, C. (1985). Cross-cultural differences in children's use of decision rules: A comparison between Japan and Australia. *Journal of Personality and Social Psychology, 49*(6), 1557–1564.

Markus, H. R., & Kitayama, S. (1991). Culture and the self: Implications for cognition, emotion, and motivation. *Psychological Review, 98*(2), 224–253.

Matsumoto, D. (1999). Culture and self: An empirical assessment of Markus and Kitayama's theory of independent and interdependent self-construals. *Asian Journal of Social Psychology, 2*(3), 289–310.

McGarty, C., Haslam, S. A., Hutchinson, K. J., & Grace, D. M. (1995). Determinants of perceived consistency: The relationship between group entitativity and the meaningfulness of categories. *British Journal of Social Psychology, 34*(3), 237–256.

McGuire, W. J., & McGuire, C. V. (1982). Significant others in self space: Sex differences and developmental trends in social self. In J. Suls (Ed.), *Psychological perspectives on the self* (Vol. 1, pp. 71–96). Hillsdale, NJ: Erlbaum.

Mead, G. H. (1934). *Mind, self, and society.* Chicago, IL: University of Chicago Press.

Miller, A. S., & Kanazawa, S. (2000). *Order by accident: The origin and consequences of conformity in contemporary Japan.* Boulder, CO: Westview.

Nakane, C. (1970). *Japanese society.* Berkeley: University of California Press.

Nisbett, R. E., & Cohen, D. (1996). *Culture of honor: The psychology of violence in the South.* Boulder, CO: Westview Press.

Ohbuchi, K., & Takahashi, Y. (1994). Cultural styles of conflict management in Japanese and Americans: Passivity, covertness, and effectiveness of strategies. *Journal of Applied Social Psychology, 24*(15), 1345–1366.

Oishi, S. (2010). The psychology of residential mobility: Implications for the self, social relationships, and well-being. *Perspectives on Psychological Science, 5*(1), 5–21.

Oishi, S., & Graham, J. (2010). Social ecology: Lost and found in psychological science. *Perspectives on Psychological Science, 5*(4), 356–377.

Oishi, S., Ishii, K., & Lun, J. (2009). Residential mobility and conditionality of group identification. *Journal of Experimental Social Psychology, 45*(4), 913–919.

Ostrom, E. (1998). A behavioral approach to the rational choice theory of collective action: Presidential address, American Political Science Association, 1997. *American Political Science Review, 92*(1), 1–22.

Ostrom, E., & Walker, J. (Eds.). (2003). *Trust and reciprocity: Interdisciplinary lessons from experimental research*. New York, NY: Russell Sage Foundation.

Oyserman, D., Coon, H. M., & Kemmelmeier, M. (2002). Rethinking individualism and collectivism: Evaluation of theoretical assumptions and meta-analyses. *Psychological Bulletin, 128*(1), 3–72.

Perreault, S., & Bourhis, R. Y. (1998). Social identification, interdependence and discrimination. *Group Processes and Intergroup Relations, 1*(1), 49–66.

Platow, M. J., McClintock, C. G., & Liebrand, W. B. G. (1990). Predicting intergroup fairness and ingroup bias in the minimal group paradigm. *European Journal of Social Psychology, 20*(3), 221–239.

Prentice, D. A., Miller, D. T., & Lightdale, J. R. (1994). Asymmetries in attachments to groups and to their members: Distinguishing between common-identity and common-bond groups. *Personality and Social Psychology Bulletin, 20*(5), 484–493.

Putnam, R. D. (2000). *Bowling alone: The collapse and revival of American community*. New York, NY: Touchstone Books/Simon & Schuster.

Rhee, E., Uleman, J. S., Lee, H. K., & Roman, R. J. (1995). Spontaneous self-descriptions and ethnic identities in individualistic and collectivistic cultures. *Journal of Personality and Social Psychology, 69*(1), 142–152.

Ross, M., Xun, W. Q. E., & Wilson, A. E. (2002). Language and the bicultural self. *Personality and Social Psychology Bulletin, 28*(8), 1040–1050.

Schug, J., Yuki, M., Horikawa, H., & Takemura, K. (2009). Similarity attraction and actually selecting similar others: How cross-societal differences in relational mobility affect interpersonal similarity in Japan and the USA. *Asian Journal of Social Psychology, 12*(2), 95–103.

Schug, J., Yuki, M., & Maddux, W. (2010). Relational mobility explains between- and within-culture differences in self-disclosure to close friends. *Psychological Science, 21*(10), 1471–1478.

Smith, P. B., & Bond, M. H. (1999). *Social psychology across cultures* (2nd ed.). Boston, MA: Allyn and Bacon.

Snibbe, A. C., Kitayama, S., Markus, H. R., & Suzuki, T. (2003). They saw a game: A Japanese and American (football)field study. *Journal of Cross-Cultural Psychology, 34*(5), 581–595.

Sumner, W. G. (1906). *Folkways: A study of the sociological importance of usages, manners, customs, mores, and morals*. Boston, MA: Ginn.

Sznycer, D., Takemura, K., Delton, A. W., Sato, K., Robertson, T., Cosmides, L., & Tooby, J. (2012). Cross-cultural differences and similarities in proneness to shame: An adaptationist and ecological approach. *Evolutionary Psychology, 10*(2), 352–370.

Tajfel, H. (1970). Experiments in intergroup discrimination. *Scientific American, 223*(5), 96–102.

Tajfel, H., Billig, M. G., Bundy, R. P., & Flament, C. (1971). Social categorisation and intergroup behavior. *European Journal of Social Psychology, 1*(2), 149–177.

Tajfel, H., & Turner, J. C. (1986). The social identity theory of intergroup behavior. In S. Worchel & W. G. Austin (Eds.), *Psychology of intergroup relations* (pp. 276–293). Chicago, IL: Nelson-Hall.

Takano, Y., & Osaka, E. (1999). An unsupported common view: Comparing Japan and the U.S. on individualism/collectivism. *Asian Journal of Social Psychology, 2*(3), 311–341.

Takemura, K., Yuki, M., & Ohtsubo, Y. (2010). Attending inside or outside: A Japanese-US comparison of spontaneous memory of group information. *Asian Journal of Social Psychology, 13*(4), 303–307.

Trafimow, D., Triandis, H. C., & Goto, S. G. (1991). Some tests of the distinction between the private self and the collective self. *Journal of Personality and Social Psychology, 60*(5), 649–655.

Triandis, H. C. (1989). The self and social behavior in differing cultural contexts. *Psychological Review, 96*(3), 506–520.

Triandis, H. C. (1995). *Individualism and collectivism*. Boulder, CO: Westview.

Triandis, H. C., Bontempo, R., Villareal, M., Asai, M., & Lucca, N. (1988). Individualism-collectivism: Cross-cultural perspectives on self-ingroup relationships. *Journal of Personality and Social Psychology, 54*(2), 323–338.

Triandis, H. C., McCusker, C., & Hui, C. H. (1990). Multimethod probes of individualism and collectivism. *Journal of Personality and Social Psychology, 59*(5), 1006–1020.

Turner, J. C., Hogg, M. A., Oakes, P. J., Reicher, S. D., & Wetherell, M. S. (1987). *Rediscovering the social group: A self-categorization theory*. Oxford, UK: Blackwell.

Tyler, T. R. (2001). Why do people rely on others? Social identity and social aspects of trust. In K. S. Cook (Ed.), *Trust in society* (pp. 285–306). New York, NY: Russell Sage Foundation.

Uleman, J. S., Rhee, E., Bardoliwalla, N., & Semin, G. (2000). The relational self: Closeness to ingroups depends on who they are, culture, and the type of closeness. *Asian Journal of Social Psychology, 3*(1), 1–17.

Üskül, A. K., Kitayama, S., & Nisbett, R. E. (2008). Ecocultural basis of cognition: Farmers and fishermen are more holistic than herders. *Proceedings of the National Academy of Sciences USA, 105*(25), 8552–8556.

Vignoles, V. L., Chryssochoou, X., & Breakwell, G. M. (2000). The distinctiveness principle: Identity, meaning, and the bounds of cultural relativity. *Personality and Social Psychology Review, 4*(4), 337–354.

Wang, C. S., & Leung, A. K-Y. (2010). The cultural dynamics of rewarding honesty and punishing deception. *Personality and Social Psychology Bulletin, 36*(11), 1529–1542.

Watkins, D., Adair, J., Akande, A., Gerong, A., McInerney, D., Sunar, D., ... Wondimu, H. (1998). Individualism-collectivism, gender and the self-concept: A nine culture investigation. *Psychologia: An International Journal of Psychology in the Orient, 41*(4), 259–271.

Wetherell, M. (1982). Cross-cultural studies of minimal groups: Implications for the social identity theory of intergroup relations. In H. Tajfel (Ed.), *Social identity and intergroup relations* (pp. 207–240). Cambridge, UK: Cambridge University Press.

Wit, A. P., & Kerr, N. L. (2002). "Me versus just us versus us all": Categorization and cooperation in nested social dilemmas. *Journal of Personality and Social Psychology, 83*(3), 616–637.

Wong, R. Y-M., & Hong, Y-Y. (2005). Dynamic influences of culture on cooperation in the prisoner's dilemma. *Psychological Science, 16*(6), 429–434.

Yamagishi, T. (1988a). Exit from the group as an individualistic solution to the free rider problem in the United States and Japan. *Journal of Experimental Social Psychology, 24*(6), 530–542.

Yamagishi, T. (1988b). The provision of a sanctioning system in the United States and Japan. *Social Psychology Quarterly, 51*(3), 265–271.

Yamagishi, T. (2011). *Trust: The evolutionary game of mind and society*. New York, NY: Springer.

Yamagishi, T., Hashimoto, H., & Schug, J. (2008). Preferences versus strategies as explanations for culture-specific behavior. *Psychological Science, 19*(6), 579–584.

Yamagishi, T., Jin, N., & Kiyonari, T. (1999). Bounded generalized reciprocity: Ingroup favoritism and ingroup boasting. *Advances in Group Processes, 16*, 161–197.

Yamagishi, T., Jin, N., & Miller, A. S. (1998). In-group bias and culture of collectivism. *Asian Journal of Social Psychology, 1*(3), 315–328.

Yamagishi, T., & Kosugi, M. (1999). Character detection in social exchange. *Cognitive Studies, 6*(2), 179–190.

Yamagishi, T., Makimura, Y., Foddy, M., Matsuda, M., Kiyonari, T., & Platow, M. J. (2005). Comparisons of Australians and Japanese on group-based cooperation. *Asian Journal of Social Psychology, 8*(2), 173–190.

Yamagishi, T., Mifune, N., Liu, J. H., & Pauling, J. (2008). Exchanges of group-based favours: Ingroup bias in the prisoner's dilemma game with minimal groups in Japan and New Zealand. *Asian Journal of Social Psychology, 11*(3), 196–207.

Yamagishi, T., & Yamagishi, M. (1994). Trust and commitment in the United States and Japan. *Motivation and Emotion, 18*(2), 129–166.

Yamaguchi, S. (1994). Empirical evidence on collectivism among the Japanese. In U. Kim, H. C. Triandis, C. Kagitcibasi, S-C. Choi & G. Yoon (Eds.), *Individualism and collectivism: Theory, method, and applications* (pp. 175–188). Newbury Park, CA: Sage.

Yuki, M. (2003). Intergroup comparison versus intragroup relationships: A cross-cultural examination of social identity theory in North American and East Asian cultural contexts. *Social Psychology Quarterly, 66*(2), 166–183.

Yuki, M. (2011). Intragroup relationships and intergroup comparisons as two sources of group-based collectivism. In R. M. Kramer, G. J. Leonardelli, & R. W. Livingston (Eds.), *Social cognition, social identity, and intergroup relations: A Festschrift in honor of Marilynn Brewer* (pp. 247–266). New York, NY: Taylor & Francis.

Yuki, M., Maddux, W. W., Brewer, M. B., & Takemura, K. (2005). Cross-cultural differences in relationship- and group-based trust. *Personality and Social Psychology Bulletin, 31*(1), 48–62.

Yuki, M., Sato, K., Takemura, K., & Oishi, S. (2013). Social ecology moderates the association between self-esteem and happiness. *Journal of Experimental Social Psychology, 49*(4), 741–746.

Yuki, M., & Schug, J. (2012). Relational mobility: A socioecological approach to personal relationships. In O. Gillath, G. E. Adams, & A. D. Kunkel (Eds.), *Relationship science: Integrating evolutionary, neuroscience, and sociocultural approaches* (pp. 137–151). Washington, DC: American Psychological Association.

Yuki, M., Schug, J., Horikawa, H., Takemura, K., Sato, K., Yokota, K., & Kamaya, K. (2007). Development of a scale to measure perceptions of relational mobility in society. *CERSS Working Paper #75*. Retrieved May 2013, from http://lynx.let.hokudai.ac.jp/cerss/english/workingpaper/index.cgi?year=2007

4

A Knowledge-Based Account of Cultural Identification

The Role of Intersubjective Representations

CHING WAN AND JIA YU

As an American born and raised in the United States, Jill has had much exposure to American culture. She shares with other Americans some common beliefs about the values, goals, practices, and norms that are considered to be central in defining American culture. Jill could identify with American culture because of her categorical membership as an American. She could also identify with American culture because of her personal endorsement of the representations of American culture that she shares with other Americans.

Alvin lives in Singapore. He is a hip-hop enthusiast. He was exposed to hip-hop culture through varied information sources such as his hip-hop dance class, hip-hop music channels on the Internet, and online forums of hip-hop enthusiasts. Through these information exchange channels, Alvin comes to hold a set of common beliefs as shared with other hip-hop enthusiasts on what the hip-hop culture is about. Although there is no clear categorical membership into hip-hop culture, Alvin's knowledge of the shared beliefs of the culture provides the basis of his hip-hop cultural identification.

Despite the different circumstances of cultural identification in the two examples, both involve the collectively shared cultural knowledge that individuals hold in understanding their cultural identification. The collectively shared knowledge about a culture can be referred to as *intersubjective cultural representations* (Chiu, Gelfand, Yamagishi, Shteynberg, & Wan, 2010; Wan & Chiu, 2009). These representations inform individuals of the socially validated shared reality that not only guides social judgments and behaviors (e.g., Heine, Buchtel, & Norenzayan, 2008; Shteynberg, Gelfand, & Kim, 2009; Zou et al., 2009) but also serves as the basis for identification with the culture (e.g., Wan, Chiu, Peng, & Tam, 2007; Wan, Chiu, Tam, Lee, Lau, & Peng, 2007). In this chapter, we focus on the role of intersubjective cultural representations in cultural identification. We first introduce the concept of intersubjective cultural representation in cultural psychology research. Then, we examine characteristics of cultural identification from the perspective of intersubjective cultural representation. Specifically, we make the distinction between category-based cultural identification and knowledge-based cultural identification. Category-based cultural identification refers to identification based on categorical membership to a cultural group, whereas knowledge-based cultural identification refers to identification based on intersubjective cultural representations. This distinction raises new research questions and has important implications for research on intragroup and intergroup processes.

INTERSUBJECTIVE REPRESENTATIONS AS SHARED CULTURAL KNOWLEDGE

Intersubjective cultural representations refer to the common beliefs that individuals of a cultural collective have about the shared knowledge traditions of a culture (Chiu, Gelfand, Yamagishi, Shteynberg, & Wan, 2010; Wan & Chiu, 2009). The construct draws from the theoretical discussion of culture as shared symbolic meanings (Geertz, 1973; Keesing, 1974; Romney, Boyd, Moore, Batchelder, & Brazill, 1996). It refers to a part of culture that is based on cultural members' common understandings of the cultural meanings that are characteristic of the culture's beliefs, values, norms, and practices. These shared meanings are perpetuated in a cultural collective via communication at the interpersonal and collective level so that most members of the culture would have similar representations of the most central cultural characteristics. The shared meanings are also likely to be embodied in external cultural carriers such as literature, music, and advertisements (Morling & Lamoreaux, 2008). As such, individuals of American culture are likely to have some common understanding of what beliefs, values, norms, and practices would define American culture. These shared American cultural meanings are likely to be conveyed in such external cultural carriers as the literary writings by American authors and the advertisements of iconic American brands.

When intersubjective cultural representation is used to identify a culture's defining characteristics, the focus is not on the personal characteristics of individuals in the culture, but on what individuals know of the symbolic meanings that are being widely shared and transmitted as knowledge traditions in the culture. This requires a culture-referent method of measurement in which individuals are asked to report their understandings of a culture's central characteristics. For example, to identify characteristic American cultural values with the intersubjective cultural representations approach, one would seek American individuals' common understandings of what values are considered important to American culture (Wan, Chiu, Tam et al., 2007). This culture-referent method has been applied successfully in describing cross-cultural differences in cultural orientations (Shteynberg et al., 2009; Wan, Chiu, Tam et al., 2007) and in explaining culture's effects on social cognition and behaviors (Shteynberg et al., 2009; Wan, Tam, & Chiu, 2010; Zou et al., 2009).

Two premises of the intersubjective representations approach are especially relevant to research on cultural identification and group processes. First, the representations are shared among individuals experiencing the same culture rather than being idiosyncratic subjective representations of single individuals. Second, an individual's possession of shared knowledge on certain cultural characteristics is separate from and does not entail the individual's endorsement of the characteristics as personal characteristics.

On the first premise, when most individuals in a cultural collective as a whole share the same representation about the culture, then the representation has an intersubjective basis. The creation and perpetuation of widely and consensually shared representations of the culture rely on the dynamic meaning negotiations in which individuals are inevitably involved when they navigate the cultural milieu in their everyday life. The dynamic meaning negotiation process involves both individual-level interpersonal interactions and collective-level social discourse, where communication among members of the culture molds the consensual representation of the culture and selects the cultural knowledge representations to be transmitted in further communication (see Wan & Chiu, 2009 for more detailed discussion). In this process, pieces of knowledge are selectively retained in the cultural members' common representations. Also, the symbolic meanings of knowledge can potentially be altered in the process of transmission. Yet knowledge representations concerning the most central characteristics of the culture are often the least transformed and the most frequently transmitted (Sperber, 1996), thus constituting the most widely distributed knowledge traditions of a culture (Barth, 2002).

The intersubjectivity of a piece of knowledge provides an indication of the degree of collective validation of the piece of knowledge. Much research in social psychology has acknowledged the importance of consensual beliefs in providing individuals with a sense of validated reality. When individuals are uncertain of the true state of the matter, they seek information from social others to serve as their guides (e.g., Festinger, 1954; Sherif, 1936; Sherif & Sherif, 1964). When people have a high need for epistemic certainty, they are especially likely to seek the maintenance of consensus in their ingroup (Kruglanski, Pierro, Mannetti, & De Grada, 2006) and follow the consensually validated cultural norms (Fu et al., 2007). When individuals communicate with others, the establishment and use of a shared understanding of reality contributes to the success of the communication (Hardin & Higgins, 1996; Krauss & Fussell, 1991). With intersubjective cultural representations, what individuals know to be characteristic of their culture is no longer based on the individuals' idiosyncratic personal perceptions but based on the collectively validated perceptions about the culture. As such, these representations and the knowledge of their sharedness provide individuals with a perceived cultural reality that can be trusted and relied upon. This perception would in turn guide an individual's cultural identification and other psychological processes.

On the second premise, individuals' knowledge of a culture and their own personal characteristics are two distinct constructs. This is not to deny the influence of cultural knowledge on individuals' personal characteristics, especially when forces of cultural transmission foster the development of personal characteristics consistent with the central cultural characteristics (e.g., Miyamoto, Nisbett, & Masuda, 2006; Savani, Morris, Naidu, Kumar, & Berlia, 2011; Tam & Lee, 2010). However, whereas most individuals who have some experience with a culture would acquire the shared cultural knowledge about the culture, how the personal characteristics are affected by the possession of cultural knowledge is a separate, independent issue (Hong, Wan, No, & Chiu, 2007). This can be demonstrated by recent evidence showing that the widely shared representations of a culture are not necessarily correlated with the personal characteristics that members of the culture possess. In a study of cultural values, for example, the correlation between the intersubjectively represented importance of values to a culture and cultural members' personal endorsement of the values was far from perfect, with much individual difference in the direction and strength of the correlation (Wan, Chiu, Tam et al., 2007). Similarly, a multicountry study of personality found that cultural members' ratings of their country's personality traits and their self-reports of the personality traits were essentially unrelated (Terracciano et al., 2005).

Intersubjective cultural representations are knowledge built upon communicative processes. As long as individuals have some experience in a culture, they are likely to acquire knowledge of the widely shared representations of the culture. In contrast, personal characteristics are outcomes of multiple sources of influence ranging from genetics to immediate social relationships to cultural influences to idiosyncratic personal choice. Cultural knowledge is only one of the many factors that influence the development of individuals' personal characteristics. Given the different origins of cultural knowledge and individual personal characteristics, the dissociation between the two should not be surprising.

The potential dissociation between individuals' cultural knowledge and their personal characteristics allows for new questions to be addressed concerning cultural identification. Specifically, one could examine how the alignment between personal characteristics and the intersubjective cultural representations might contribute to an individual's identification with the culture. One could also examine how the selective use of intersubjective cultural representations might contribute to the active construction of a desired cultural identity. These questions cannot be addressed without the conceptual separation of cultural knowledge and the self.

TWO BASES OF CULTURAL IDENTIFICATION

Recent research has provided initial evidence linking intersubjective cultural representations with identification with a culture. These empirical studies have asked individuals to rate the importance of certain values to their culture. These culture-referent ratings allowed the researchers to identify core cultural values through intersubjective representations (values that members of a culture as a collective consider to be most important *to their culture*) and examine the effect of individuals' endorsement of the intersubjectively important cultural characteristics on their cultural identification. In an initial study, individuals who endorsed the intersubjectively important values of a culture were found to have developed stronger identification with the culture over time (Wan, Chiu, Tam, et al., 2007). The same method was applied to studying multicultural identities. Specifically, Wan, Chiu, Peng et al. (2007) asked multicultural individuals to provide culture-referent ratings of each of their multiple cultures. These ratings were then used to identify values intersubjectively represented to differentiate the cultures, that is, those values that the participants perceived to be much more important to one culture than to another culture. Results of the study found that individuals who personally endorsed these values were more likely to have differential identification with the cultures. Finally, the cultural identification resulting from self-intersubjective representation alignment could affect individuals' culture-related judgments and behaviors. For example, American voters' personal endorsement of social attitudes intersubjectively represented to define a political party displayed more identification with the party, which in turn resulted in actual voting behavior in support of the party's candidate (Wan, Tam, & Chiu, 2010).

To fully appreciate the contribution of intersubjective cultural representations in understanding cultural identification, we consider it important to differentiate two aspects of identification with a culture—identification with culture as a social category (category-based cultural identification) and identification with culture as shared knowledge (knowledge-based cultural identification). Whereas the former is closely related to the typical social psychological account of collective identity, the latter points to a new way of conceptualizing cultural identification that could lead to unique research questions not addressed by the current literature.

Category-based cultural identification refers to identification with the culture as a social category. This kind of identification is based on the categorization of the self as part of a social collective, often with delineated boundaries, such as membership in national groups and political parties. When a person's identification with a culture is based on categorical membership, one would expect such identification to follow principles governing collective identities as discussed in social identity theories. For example, the salience of a collective identity depends on whether the contextual intergroup contrast directs individuals' attention to the collective identity (Tajfel & Turner, 1979; Turner, Hogg, Oakes, Reicher, & Wetherell, 1987). Also, the need for positive distinctiveness of one's ingroup would lead to the display of intergroup bias, favoring the ingroup over the outgroup (Tajfel & Turner, 1979). This display of intergroup bias is especially likely when individuals perceive the outgroup as a threat to the ingroup (Riek, Mania, & Gaertner, 2006).

Social identity theories predict that when a social identity is salient, individuals would see the self as an interchangeable member of the collective and self-stereotype with the prototypic characteristics of the ingroup (Hogg & Turner, 1987). Although the utilization of the content of group characteristics in self-perception is a potential consequence, knowledge of the ingroup's shared characteristics is not a necessary prerequisite for category-based identification to develop in the first place. In fact, identification with a social category can be activated by situational intergroup contrast, even when group members do not share much common history and knowledge base. This can be illustrated by early social identity research using the minimal group paradigm, where group membership is randomly assigned to different groups based on arbitrary criteria with minimal psychological meaning (Tajfel, Billig, Bundy, & Flament, 1971; Turner et al., 1987). Even with such arbitrary group membership, individuals have shown ingroup favoritism in their intergroup attitudes and behaviors (e.g., Grieve & Hogg, 1999; Lemyre & Smith, 1985).

When it comes to category-based cultural identification, the development of the categorical membership does not necessarily require common interest, social interaction, and previous life history among cultural members. In fact, some categorical cultural group memberships are of an ascribed nature, in which categorization of individuals into the cultural membership is determined by such preexisting criteria as birthplace and ancestry. As long as individuals fulfill the entry categorization criteria, they would possess a category-based cultural identity that does not depend on their experience with the culture of the collective.

Knowledge-based cultural identification, in contrast, refers to identification with the shared knowledge traditions of a culture. These knowledge traditions are not the historical, traditional practices of a culture's past. Rather, they are the shared knowledge that has been distributed within a culture and considered by most members of the culture to be central in defining the culture. In other words, they have an established sharedness in the culture based on intersubjective representations in the cultural collective. When individuals identify with a culture's shared knowledge tradition, they internalize the intersubjective cultural representations of the culture in the definition of the self (Hong et al., 2007; Wan, Chiu, Tam et al., 2007). The liking and positive attachment to a culture is based on the individual's personal endorsement of the characteristics of the culture that are widely considered to be important to the culture. In this process, having knowledge of a culture is the prerequisite for knowledge-based cultural identification. To have strong cultural identification, individuals would first need to possess certain knowledge that is widespread within a culture. Such perception of culture, including beliefs and values, requires individuals to share certain common history and collective memories with other members of the culture. Individuals cannot identify with a culture's shared knowledge traditions if they do not have some idea of what the shared knowledge traditions are.

Knowledge-based cultural identification is distinct from category-based cultural identification as the two types of cultural identification are founded on different bases. However, it is important to note that there is a certain level of overlap between the two types of identification in real-life cultural groups. The intersubjective representations of a culture can serve as basis of the prototypic characteristics of the cultural group. People who personally endorse the intersubjective representations of a culture (strong knowledge-based cultural identification) are also likely to be more strongly attached to their categorical membership in the cultural group (strong category-based cultural identification). However, it is also possible that a person who feels strong emotional attachment to a cultural group does not necessarily personally agree with the intersubjective cultural representations being shared in the group. The American who feels strong loyalty to American culture but often criticizes the widely shared values of the culture would be one who has strong category-based American identification but weak knowledge-based American identification. On the contrary, the American whose personal values are aligned with Japanese cultural knowledge traditions but is not categorically classified as a Japanese is an example of an individual with strong knowledge-based but weak category-based Japanese identification.

CHARACTERISTICS OF KNOWLEDGE-BASED CULTURAL IDENTIFICATION

A knowledge-based account of cultural identification has certain characteristics that would make significant contribution to furthering the field's understanding of cultural identification. First, it directs attention to a definition of culture more fitting of the nature of culture as shared knowledge representations that transcend the limit of categorical boundaries. Second, it allows for the examination of the varied ways in which individuals connect with the shared knowledge representations in constructing their cultural identity. Intersubjective representations provide the shared normative reality of what the culture is about (Wan, Torelli, & Chiu, 2010). Thus, it guides individuals' interpretations of the central symbolic meanings of a culture and bounds the range of possibilities in cultural identity construction. Individuals then can utilize these shared cultural representations in constructing their cultural identity.

Redefined Cultural Boundary

Most extant research on culture has examined cultural groups with relatively clear and identifiable boundaries such as nationality and ethnic ancestry. Similarly, discussions of cultural identification have often focused on membership in cultures with clear boundaries. However, as advocated by Cohen (2009), there are many kinds of culture beyond nationality and ethnicity, such as religion and social class. More important, these cultures often reach beyond the confines of clear group boundaries. One useful way of understanding such cultures and their cultural identity implications would be to consider the intersubjective representations of these cultures. Culture defined from an intersubjective representations perspective is not restricted to the shared knowledge traditions of groups delineated by clear physical boundary or categorical membership. Individuals in cultures with demarcated population and those in cultures with less clear boundaries are equally likely to have common representations of their culture. As an example, although hip-hop culture is often strongly associated with African American communities, the culture has spread globally, with individuals from other ethnicities within the United States and from other countries around the world holding the values and participating in the lifestyles of hip-hop culture (e.g., Bennett, 2001; Harkness, 2011). The global spread of the culture and the diversity of individuals participating in the culture mean that it cannot be easily defined by group boundaries.

The lack of clear group boundary does not detract the psychological meaning of the culture in individuals' lives. Recent research on cultural differences has started to move beyond nationality or ethnic ancestry to consider new types of culture such as social class and religion. Although these studies did not examine intersubjective representations of the cultures, they provide evidence demonstrating that experiences with cultures that lack distinct boundaries exert influence on individuals' psychological processes just like nationality and ethnic ancestry do. For example, Stephens, Markus, and Townsend (2007) studied the effect of social class within the United States on agency beliefs and choice. They found that middle-class and working-class individuals tended to experience different sociocultural environments that fostered the development of independent and interdependent preference of agency, respectively. Again going beyond demarcated cultural boundary, Hommel and colleagues (Hommel, Colzato, Scorolli, Borghi, & van den Wildenberg, 2011) compared Italian Roman Catholics to Italian secular individuals and Dutch Calvinists to Dutch atheists. They found that religion affected individuals' performance on cognition-driven action control tasks.

With intersubjective cultural representations as the foundation, in knowledge-based cultural identification, the boundary of cultural membership is drawn by whether an individual shares the common representations about a culture with the majority of individuals in the culture rather than by categorical membership. To the extent that the individual has knowledge of the intersubjective representations of the culture, identification with the culture is possible. The redefinition of cultural boundary in cultural identification not only allows for the study of new types of cultural identification such as religious identity but also allows for cultural identification research that is more suited for an increasingly mobile and connected world. When cultural boundary is no longer drawn around demarcated populations, individuals' identification with cultural knowledge traditions is not limited to physical locations and categorical membership. Examples abound when one considers information flow in an interconnected and globalized world. With the global information flow, individuals are no longer limited to the cultural knowledge of their home culture. They also have access to the shared knowledge traditions of cultural groups that are often not their own. Hip-hop culture has spread beyond the African American communities in the United States to around the world with increasing ease through the advancement of mass telecommunication technology. Teenagers in China are exposed to the values and practices of Western culture via culturally iconic brands such as Nike and Starbucks, Hollywood movies, and the Internet, while teenagers in the United States are exposed to Japanese anime and Chinese martial arts movies. Empirical research has found that European Americans who have not had direct exposure to East Asia can now be primed with East Asian cultural icons to display decision-making responses akin to East Asians (Alter & Kwan, 2009). With access comes potential internalization of the shared knowledge traditions of a culture.

Although an individual may not be categorized as belonging to a particular culture by members of the culture and even the individual's own self, it becomes increasingly possible for this individual to demonstrate strong knowledge-based cultural identification with the culture. This phenomenon can only be examined with a conceptualization of cultural identification as based on shared cultural knowledge.

Intersubjective Representations as Identity Guide

Intersubjective cultural representations provide a collective basis for cultural identification. The representations guide how individuals understand the meaning of the culture that they are identifying with via the shared perceptions of a cultural collective. Collective cultural meaning negotiation processes result in the transmission of intersubjective representations to individuals. As long as an individual has some degree of experience of a culture, this individual can be expected to possess knowledge about the most widely shared knowledge representations about the culture. This can be seen in children's display of competence in their own culture as socialization agents such as parents and other caretakers often focus on the transmission of important cultural knowledge in their socialization practices (e.g., Cho, Sandel, Miller, & Wang, 2005; Friedlmeier, Corapci, & Cole, 2011; Tam & Lee, 2010). Also, new members of a culture acquire sociocultural competence as they gain knowledge of the host culture after living in the host culture for a duration of time (Ward & Kennedy, 1994). Although individuals differ in their exact cultural experience and as a result, the degree of their cultural competence, it is likely that most individuals who have had some experience with the culture would be able to discern the central characteristics of a culture that are often the most widely distributed in the culture. Sharing such basic knowledge about the intersubjective representations of a culture allows individuals the competence required to successfully navigate the cultural milieu according to the cultural demands of daily situations. More important, as individuals' understandings of a culture are based on the intersubjective cultural representations, their identification with the culture would also likely utilize these intersubjective representations.

For individuals who belong to distinct subgroups within a culture, the intersubjective representations of the culture that guide their cultural identification could be the result of collective meaning contention and reconstruction within their own subgroup. Subgroups such as ethnic groups and groups with different political ideologies within a culture often face different sociocultural and economic realities. They also tend to be motivated to maintain their ingroup interests, which might be in conflict with the interests of other subgroups. These different realities and group interests could lead to differential representations of the common culture. For example, when subgroups within a culture are in contention over the interpretation of a common history, they often generate highly different representations of the common history. In New Zealand, even though New Zealanders of European descent and those of Maori descent have considerable consensus on what constitutes the most important historical event in New Zealand, the two groups also showed different interpretations of the common history (Liu, Wilson, McClure, & Higgins, 1999). As a consequence, members of different subgroups could identify with the same culture based on different intersubjective representations of the culture.

Finally, for multicultural individuals, the intersubjective representations that they are exposed to not only define each of their multiple cultures but also include comparisons and contrasts of the cultures. Research on multiculturalism has discussed how exposure to multiple cultures creates potential tensions within individuals as the knowledge traditions of the cultures may pose incompatible demands on the individual (Benet-Martínez & Haritatos, 2005; Padilla, 1994; Phinney, 1999). However, these perceptions are not based solely on the individuals' personal experiences with the multiple cultures. Rather, the intercultural discourse and the real and perceived competitions among cultural groups within a society could shape the common representations of how the multiple cultures relate to one another and their compatibility. These representations could in turn provide boundaries to the possibilities of individuals engaging knowledge representations of the two cultures simultaneously in their cultural identification. For example, in a society that endorses a melting pot ideology (Berry, 2001) in handling the existence of multicultural groups in the society, where minority groups are encouraged to assimilate to the mainstream culture rather than maintaining their heritage culture, the intersubjective representations might involve incompatibility between the mainstream culture and the minority culture. Such representation could hinder the possibility of simultaneously strong identification with both cultures, even when the individual can claim categorical membership in both cultures. In contrast, when a society endorses a pluralism ideology (Berry, 2001) and multiple cultural groups are in fact able to coexist harmoniously, then the intersubjective representations could be about the compatibility of the cultures and thus allow for simultaneously strong identification with the cultures.

Agentic Choice

Although acquisition of cultural knowledge is quite inevitable, possession of cultural knowledge does not necessitate strong cultural identification (Hong et al., 2007). Intersubjective cultural representations constrain the possibilities of cultural identification; at the same time, knowledge-based identification with a culture is also partly an individual's agentic choice. In fact, empirical evidence showed much within-culture variability in the degree to which individuals personally endorse the intersubjectively represented important characteristics of a culture (Wan, Chiu, Tam et al., 2007). Whereas some individuals show a strong alignment between their personal characteristics and the intersubjectively represented cultural characteristics, other individuals display a much weaker alignment. Such variation in the alignment between personal characteristics and intersubjectively represented cultural characteristics has been shown to predict identification with the culture and the development of strong identification over time. That is, identification with a culture becomes stronger when the intersubjectively represented characteristics of a culture are aligned with the personal characteristics of the individual (Wan et al., 2010; Wan, Chiu, Tam et al., 2007; Zhang & Chiu, 2011). Thus, current evidence suggests that the choice to identify with a particular culture is a matter of the match between an individual's personal characteristics and the intersubjective representations of the culture's most important characteristics.

Also taking an agentic view, identity researchers working outside of the perspective of social identity theories have argued that individuals can choose to utilize aspects of the social representations to construct their own identification with the collective in order to fulfill their identity needs (e.g., Breakwell, 2001; Hammack, 2008; Palmer, 2007). Consistent with this perspective, discussion of the identity negotiation strategies that multicultural individuals might engage in reflects the different possible ways in which multicultural individuals might choose to mix and merge the intersubjective representations of the multiple cultures involved. Hong and colleagues (2007) summarized three possibilities. First, individuals might consider the similarities between the multiple cultural representations and be able to blend and integrate the representations into one coherent representation, thus providing the basis for an integrated multicultural identity (e.g., Miramontez, Benet-Martínez, & Nguyen, 2008; Phinney & Devich-Navarro, 1997). Second, individuals may focus on the differences and incompatibilities between representations of the multiple cultures. These individuals may keep the multiple cultures separate and shift between the cultures according to situational demands (Benet-Martínez & Haritatos, 2005). This separation in the representation of the multiple cultures would then support the existence of multiple cultural identities that are kept apart within an individual. Third, individuals could employ elements of each of the multiple cultures in generating a new set of cultural knowledge traditions that goes beyond the simple addition of the original cultural representations. This in turn would support the creation of a new personal multicultural identity that is uniquely different from cultural identities based on the contributing origin cultures.

The agentic choice possibility does not mean that individuals have complete control in whether to internalize the intersubjective representations of a culture and in how they would utilize the intersubjective representations to construct the cultural identity. Certain aspects of the cultural transmission process do favor the internalization of cultural knowledge. Socialization goals in child development often imply an expectation of internalization (Kuczynski & Navara, 2006). Interpersonal communication that relies on the shared reality between communicator and the audience has been found to change the communicator's personal attitudes (Higgins & Rholes, 1978). Also, individuals are likely to be exposed to situations that would foster the development of personal tendencies that are consistent with the most important values of the culture (e.g., Kitayama, Markus, Matsumoto, & Norasakkunkit, 1997; Savani et al., 2011). With repeated exposure to situations that reinforce certain intersubjective cultural representations, individuals who grew up in a particular cultural context could have internalized the intersubjective representations of the culture. And for multicultural individuals, whether they are able to engage in the strategy of cultural identity negotiation of their choice would be limited by the intersubjective representations of the multiple cultures and their relations in the larger society where they reside.

However, socialization is neither unidirectional nor deterministic in that individuals exert their agency in influencing the socialization process and deciding what they would eventually internalize (Kuczynski & Navara, 2006). Communication based on shared reality would result in a change in personal attitudes only when the communicator has the goal of establishing shared reality with the audience but not when the goal is unrelated to shared reality, such as an entertainment goal and a compliance goal (Echterhoff, Higgins, Kopietz, & Groll, 2008). Finally, the fact that individuals sometimes display culturally appropriate psychological tendencies in situations that foster such tendencies could be a result of conformity rather than internalization. Conformity does not always imply private acceptance (Cialdini, Kallgren, & Reno, 1991; Deutsch & Gerard, 1955). This possibility would partially explain the lack of consistent cross-cultural differences in self-reported individualism-collectivism based on qualitative and quantitative reviews (Oyserman, Coon, & Kemmelmeier, 2002; Takano & Osaka, 1999). Therefore, despite exposure to intersubjective cultural representations facilitating potential internalization of the specific representations, individuals could still hold a certain level of independence from cultural influence and be able to exert their agency in their choice of cultural identification.

To summarize, knowledge-based cultural identification builds upon the dynamic social construction of intersubjective cultural representations. Individuals' participation in the negotiation of shared meanings in a cultural collective both shapes the intersubjective cultural representations coming out of the negotiation process and provides individuals with information on the shared representations in the collective. The established intersubjective representations bound the possibility of identification with a culture by providing the consensually represented definitions of a particular culture, and in multicultural contexts, the relations among the multiple cultures. At the same time, as agentic actors, individuals selectively utilize existing representations to construct their cultural identity. Within the limits set by the intersubjective representations, individuals can choose to align the self with the intersubjective representations of the culture or distance the self from the representations. Such process allows an individual to achieve a desired cultural identity, even when the cultural group membership is ascribed, and when there is no clear cultural group categorization. When an individual is categorized as a member of a cultural group by birth or legal rights, the individual has the choice to identify, disidentify, or partially identify with the shared knowledge traditions of the culture. When there is no clear cultural group categorization, as long as there exists intersubjective representations of a culture's knowledge tradition, individuals can utilize such shared knowledge in cultural identification processes.

IMPLICATIONS FOR GROUP PROCESSES

Considering cultural identification from an intersubjective representations perspective provides insights for understanding intragroup and intergroup processes of cultural collectives. In the following, we discuss how knowledge-based cultural identity could affect the judgment of who a genuine member of a cultural group should be and the acceptance of new members into a cultural group. We will also examine the implications of defining culture with intersubjective representations for research on individuals' reactions to and resolution of intergroup conflict.

Cultural Authenticity

A more globalized world brings more movement of individuals across cultural boundaries and more blurred definitions of cultural group membership. One of the results of such global change is often an increase in diversity of population composition within cultural groups. With the increase in diversity also comes the contention of cultural authenticity, which involves the question of who the true members of a culture are. The issue of cultural authenticity not only affects the psychological well-being of individuals whose cultural authenticity is being questioned but also creates points of contention and discord within a cultural group. Past evidence has shown that individuals vary in the characteristics that they focus on when discussing the quality of someone who is a true member of a culture (Palmer, 2007; Park-Taylor et al., 2008; Rodriguez, Schwartz, & Whitbourne, 2010). It is possible that category-based cultural identity and knowledge-based cultural identity would direct individuals' focus to different criteria of cultural authenticity. The different foci in turn would have different implications in the consideration of a culture's flexibility in accepting cultural deviants and new members.

A focus on category-based cultural identity would prescribe the use of categorical membership as the criterion for cultural authenticity judgment. Such judgment of categorical membership is often based on whether an individual possesses the prototypic physical characteristics or ancestral background that would allow him or her to be categorized easily as part of the cultural group. This judgment criterion is akin to the ethnic definition of nationalism discussed in the social science literature. An ethnic definition of nationalism defines nationality by an idea of ethnicity that is ascribed and inherited by blood and ancestry (Ignatieff, 1994; Pehrson & Green, 2010). Such a definition has implications for how visible minorities are perceived. Visible minorities, who are often perceived to be different from the majority group on some inherited characteristics such as skin color, could be perceived as less representative members of a cultural group than members of the majority group. For example, in the United States, African Americans and Asian Americans are found to be less implicitly associated with America than White Americans, with the association difference especially prominent for White Americans who have strong American identification (Devos & Banaji, 2005). If these visible minorities are considered less representative categorical members of the group, they could also be considered as less authentic members of the culture of the group.

A focus on knowledge-based cultural identity, on the other hand, would prescribe the possession of shared knowledge representations of the culture to determine an individual's cultural authenticity. Thus, an individual would need to possess knowledge about certain values, ideology, beliefs, and practices that are widely shared in the culture and personally endorse such shared knowledge to be considered an authentic member of the culture. This conceptualization of cultural authenticity is akin to the civic definition of nationalism, in which nationality is defined by achievable qualities such as sharing the defining values and ideologies of the nation (Ignatieff, 1994; Pehrson & Green, 2010). With this conceptualization, categorical membership is no longer the critical criterion for cultural authenticity judgment. An individual's lack of categorical membership in the cultural group does not detract from the individual's cultural authenticity as long as the individual shares the intersubjective representations. Thus, it is possible for individuals of any ethnic heritage to become American as long as the individuals share the intersubjective representations of American culture. Also, categorically belonging to the cultural group could still result in inauthenticity judgment if the individual does not share the intersubjective representations of the culture. Thus, in the United States, ethnic minorities sometimes engage in contentious discourse on the authenticity of the ethnic heritage identity because of variations in knowledge and endorsement of the practices, values, and beliefs of the ethnic culture (e.g., Palmer, 2007).

The two foci of cultural authenticity have different potential consequences for intragroup cohesion in a cultural collective. Research related to a category-based definition of cultural membership has found that the more that individuals use this definition in their judgment of cultural membership, the less willing they are to accept categorical diversity in their group. When individuals and their conationals endorse an ethnic definition of nationalism, strong national identification would predict a more exclusive view toward national membership, and thus stronger anti-immigrant sentiments (Pehrson & Green, 2010). Individuals who hold an essentialist view of national group membership believe that nationality is based on fixed, immutable attributes such as ancestry and blood (Haslam, Bastain, Bain, & Kashima, 2006; Pehrson, Brown, & Zagefka, 2009). When these individuals strongly identify with a nation, they tend to be less receptive of categorical diversity within the nation (Li & Brewer, 2004; Pehrson et al., 2009). Similarly, Yogeeswaran and Dasgupta (2010) found that individuals who had stronger implicit beliefs that true Americans were White were less receptive of Asian Americans in contexts related to national security. These findings suggest that a focus on a category-based cultural identity could lead to more exclusion of individuals from being a member of the cultural group based on fixed characteristics of individuals such as skin color and birthplace, even when the individual is technically considered to be a member of the cultural group. The category-based rule combined with strong identification with the cultural group would result in more stringent criteria for categorical cultural authenticity judgment.

In contrast, a knowledge-based focus of cultural authenticity might result in higher receptiveness toward categorical diversity in a cultural group. A recent study provides support for this proposition. Wakefield and colleagues (2011) manipulated Scottish participants' criteria for judgment of Scottish national identity. The participants were induced to endorse either criteria based on ancestry or criteria based on cultural participation. Then, the researchers measured the participants' attitudes toward a target of Chinese heritage who displayed strong personal association with Scotland. Participants who were induced to use cultural participation as criteria judged the target to be higher in Scottishness, were more likely to provide help to the target, and were more willing to accept the target's criticisms of Scotland. Although cultural participation is not entirely the same as possession of intersubjective knowledge, it is reasonable to infer that judgments based on achievable acquisition of cultural knowledge rather than relatively fixed category membership would result in similar acceptance of diversity.

The existence of a knowledge-based cultural identity allows individuals a route for seeking belongingness to a culture and demonstrating cultural authenticity when their category-based cultural identity is in doubt. This is demonstrated by the effect of identity denial on minority group's endorsement of intersubjectively shared representations of the mainstream culture. Research has shown that although Asian Americans do not differ from White Americans in their strength of American identification, Asian Americans are consistently perceived as less American than White Americans (Cheryan & Monin, 2005; Devos & Banaji, 2005). More important, in Cheryan and Monin's (2005) study, when Asian Americans were denied of their American identity, they spent more effort in demonstrating their knowledge of American culture and expressing stronger endorsement of characteristic American practices. Note that participants in the study considered themselves as Americans and considered American culture to be an important part of their identity. Thus, endorsement of cultural knowledge could be used as a means to reaffirm the American identity when the identity cannot be affirmed via categorical membership. It is likely that if the individuals did not view the cultural knowledge as an important part of their cultural identity, then an identity denial would not lead to stronger endorsement of the widely shared cultural knowledge.

A knowledge-based focus of cultural authenticity does not always lead to more tolerance. When the shared knowledge is the center of contention concerning the true meaning of the culture, a knowledge-based focus of cultural authenticity judgment might actually generate more discord within the cultural collective than a category-based focus. Different subgroups within a culture are exposed to somewhat different socioeconomic circumstances in a culture, with sometimes conflicting group interests. These different circumstances could lead to the perpetuation of different intersubjective representations of the culture. For example, whereas European Americans perceive American culture more in abstract, ideological terms, Asian Americans are more likely to perceive American culture in terms of cultural behaviors and customs (Tsai, Mortensen, Wong, & Hess, 2002). Differences in intersubjective representations exist not only between majority and minority groups and between dominant and subordinate groups but also between groups vying for dominance in shaping the discourse on cultural authenticity. In politics, supporters of opposing political parties not only hold different political ideologies but also criticize the opposition as holding values that can be construed as deviating from the core representations of the culture. Regardless of whether such discourse is created by politicians more to achieve self-serving ends, the public is inevitably engaged in the negotiation of the content of cultural authenticity.

One interesting question to ask is when category-based cultural identity focus or knowledge-based cultural identity focus would dominate in judgments of cultural authenticity. It is conceivable that for certain cultural identities that are often determined at birth, such as gender, Jewish, and Muslim identities, judgment of cultural authenticity is more influenced by category-based focus than by knowledge-based focus. In contrast, for cultural identities that are often considered to be achieved, such as political and Protestant identities, judgment of cultural authenticity would be more strongly influenced by knowledge-based focus. It is also likely that the individual's own nature of cultural identification would direct the individual to use the criteria that are consistent with the self's cultural identification. Therefore, individuals who identify with a culture based on cultural knowledge endorsement might also judge others' cultural membership on the same criterion. Empirical research would be needed to provide answers on this issue.

Acculturation of New Members

Acculturation is the process of change due to intercultural contact (Berry, 2001). For individuals who leave their heritage culture to settle in a new host culture with the intention of long-term stay, crossing the cultural boundary results in multiple psychological changes. Sociocultural adaptation involves the individual's gain of cultural competence in knowing the normative expectations of appropriate behaviors for navigating the new culture, whereas psychological adjustment involves the change in the individual's well-being and satisfaction (Searle & Ward, 1990). In addition, individuals may experience a change in their cultural identity with the addition of new cultural identity with respect to the host culture and either change or abandonment of existing heritage cultural identity (Berry, 2001). Acquisition of shared cultural knowledge is necessary for the new member to gain cultural competence in the new culture. At the same time, the new member's cultural identity development is simultaneously dependent on the individual's personal characteristics, the shared knowledge traditions of the heritage culture, and that of the host culture.

Successful sociocultural adaptation requires the new members to acquire the necessary knowledge about the host culture to competently navigate the physical and social environments in the host culture. This requires the acquisition of not only objective knowledge such as language skills and social customs but also accurate knowledge of the intersubjective representations of the culture and accurate estimates of the degree of sharedness of the cultural knowledge. The perpetuation of intersubjective cultural representations in a collective relies much on the influence that social others have on individuals as individuals establish and reinforce shared reality in communication (Hardin & Higgins, 1996), with proximal others having stronger influence on an individual's representations (Nowak, Szamrej, & Latané, 1990). The implication is that a new member's representations of the host culture are likely to be affected by the collective of individuals surrounding the new member. If the newcomer is surrounded by others who come from the same heritage culture with limited contact with the mainstream culture, then knowledge about the mainstream culture would likely remain limited to the potentially biased representations shared among the group of individuals from the heritage culture rather than acquiring the mainstream representations. On the contrary, if the newcomer is surrounded by individuals from the host culture, then the individual is more likely to acquire more accurate knowledge of the intersubjective representations of the host culture at a faster rate. The individuals from the host culture could also exert social pressure on the newcomers to acquire the necessary knowledge to fit into the host society, thus providing an even stronger push for the newcomer to learn the appropriate intersubjective representations.

Empirical research on the effect of social network on new members' acculturation has provided some evidence for the differential effects of source of social ties in affecting sociocultural and psychological adjustment. Social support from others of the same heritage culture provides buffers against acculturative stress and is related to increased experience of psychological well-being (e.g., Garcia, Ramirez, & Jariego, 2002; Lee, Koeske, & Sales, 2004). Contact with host nationals, on the other hand, has positive effects on the new member's acquisition of appropriate sociocultural skills (e.g., Kashima & Loh, 2006; Ward & Kennedy, 1993). Kosic, Kruglanski, Pierro, and Mannetti (2004) found that the effect of the initial social ties that new cultural members had depended on the individuals' need for cognitive closure. Specifically, for individuals with a high need for cognitive closure, those who had initial ties mostly with others from the same heritage culture tended to prefer to maintain exclusive contact with the heritage culture and avoid contact with the host culture, whereas those who had initial ties mostly with others from the host culture preferred to take up the host culture and avoid contact with the heritage culture. This effect of initial social ties was not found for individuals with a low need for cognitive closure. As the consensual knowledge representations held by social others provide epistemic certainty (Kruglanski & Webster, 1996), under situations of ambiguity and uncertainty, the intersubjective cultural representations held in the social network surrounding the new member could provide the much needed knowledge and certainty for the individual to navigate the cultural environment and, in the process, shapes the individual's own representations of the culture.

The content of intersubjective cultural representations that the new member initially acquires has consequences for the individual's negotiation between the existing heritage cultural identity and the new host cultural identity. New members to a culture often bring with them representations of their heritage culture and preconceptions of the host culture. The perceived distance between the heritage culture and the host culture not only poses difficulty in a new member's adjustment to the host culture (Galchenko & van de Vijver, 2007; Ward & Searle, 1991) but also affects how the individual might identify with the two cultures. When the individual perceives high compatibility between the host culture and the heritage culture, the individual would be likely to consider the compatibility between the two cultural identities and be able to identify with both cultures simultaneously (Benet-Martínez & Haritatos, 2005; Miramontez et al., 2008). However, the two cultures could also be perceived to be incompatible. This perceived incompatibility could be a discrepancy between the new members' preferred acculturation strategy and their representations of the host culture's preferred acculturation strategies of them (e.g., Mähönen, Jasinskaja-Lahti, & Liebkind, 2011). The discrepancy could also be about new members' representations of the widely shared values of the heritage culture and the widely shared values of the host culture (Benet-Martínez & Haritatos, 2005). When the cultures are perceived to be incompatible, the individual would find it difficult to integrate the two cultural identities, which might result in the individual having to choose between the two identities instead of embracing both (Mähönen et al., 2011) or having to shift between the two cultural identities instead of integrating the two into one bicultural identity (Benet-Martínez & Haritatos, 2005).

Intergroup Relations

Negative attitudes toward outgroups and intergroup conflicts are often based on the perceived threats that the outgroup poses to the ingroup (Riek, Mania, & Gaertner, 2006). Intersubjective cultural representations pertain to a culture's shared value and belief systems. Therefore, threats to intergroup relations based on intersubjective cultural representations would be a threat toward these shared value and belief systems. This is similar to symbolic intergroup threat as discussed in the intergroup literature. Symbolic threat refers to the threat that an outgroup poses to the ingroup's value and belief systems when the outgroup is perceived to hold different worldviews from the ingroup (Stephan, Diaz-Loving, & Duran, 2000). Such perceived difference generates negative emotional reactions such as disgust and fear (Cottrell & Neuberg, 2005) and contributes to negative attitudes toward the outgroup (e.g., Riek et al., 2006; Stephan et al., 2000). Symbolic threat is perceived to be threatening to the ingroup rather than the individual's personal self to the extent that the threat is considered to violate the group's collective meaning system rather than an individual's personal values. Any threat to these widely shared central characteristics would result in a defense of the positivity of the ingroup culture (Wan, Torelli, & Chiu, 2010).

The implication of considering threats to intersubjective cultural representations is that a threat toward characteristics that are consensually shared to be central to a culture could be stronger, and in turn elicit stronger reactions, than a threat toward characteristics that are not shared. Social others provide validation for individuals' beliefs (Fazio, 1979; Festinger, 1954). In a collective, sharedness of a knowledge presentation provides legitimacy for the representations and signifies a collectively validated reality. Also, high perceived social consensus on an issue has been found to result in high certainty of the correctness of an individual's attitude on the issue, which leads to higher resistance toward attitude change (Petrocelli, Tormala, & Rucker, 2007). Similarly, as the intersubjective representations of a cultural group's central characteristics are based on the widely shared agreement among members of the culture, the representations are likely to be associated with more perceived collective support than representations that are only subjectively held by a single individual. Therefore, when individuals perceive an outgroup to be posing a threat to these intersubjectively represented cultural characteristics of the ingroup culture, the individuals are likely to perceive strong social support and legitimacy for their threat perception. The increase in perceived legitimacy could thus exacerbate the perception of threat from the outgroup, leading to more negative evaluations of the outgroup while the individuals hold stronger beliefs that the evaluation is justified.

Apart from the strength of intergroup conflict perception, intersubjective cultural representations have implications for the routes through which intergroup conflict can be resolved. Existing accounts on the reduction of intergroup conflict tend to focus on category-based group membership and how the categorization process generates favoritism for the ingroup in intergroup situations (Brewer, 2007). As intergroup conflict is considered to be the outcome of an ingroup-outgroup contrast, the solution to the conflict would be a redefinition of intergroup boundary. For example, the common ingroup identity model focuses on the recategorization of ingroup and outgroup members as part of a common, more inclusive higher level category (Gaertner, Dovidio, Nier, Ward, & Banker 1999). Also, more complex categorizations provide additional categorization alternatives so that individuals would not be focused on a single dimension for categorization. For example, in cross-categorization (Migdal, Hewstone, & Mullen, 1998), the salience of multiple ingroup identities allows individuals to recognize the same person as an outgroup member on one category dimension but an ingroup member on a different independent category dimension. By utilizing alternative categorization criteria, members of an outgroup can be recategorized as being part of an ingroup. This could lead to a reduction in conflict due to intergroup contrasts.

When intergroup conflict is based on the perceived differences in the widely shared values and beliefs of the groups in contact, then the reduction of conflict is likely to require a change in the representations of the differences and recast the intersubjective focus on similarities rather than differences between groups. This reduction of intergroup conflict might hinge on individuals taking the perspective of and acquiring more knowledge about the outgroup, which could result in either stronger representations of similarities rather than differences between the groups or reconsideration of differences between groups as being less threatening. One way to achieve the new intergroup representation is through intergroup contact (Allport, 1954; Pettigrew & Tropp, 2008). Similar to the acquisition of other knowledge representations, contact with an outgroup would facilitate the acquisition of more accurate and nuanced knowledge representations of the outgroup, which could in turn reduce intergroup bias. However, just like perceived social consensus could support stronger beliefs of outgroup threat to the ingroup, the shared nature of the intersubjective representations is likely to make the representations harder to change through intergroup contact. As stated earlier, the intersubjective nature of the knowledge representations provides epistemic certainty to the individuals. These representations are more likely to be considered to be the true and correct state of affairs. Just as attitudes with high certainty tend to be more resistant to change (Petrocelli et al., 2007), such certainty in intersubjective representations might pose difficulties in the change of representations about the outgroup in intergroup contact situations.

Other than intergroup contact, given the nature of intersubjective representations, we would expect communication processes within a group to potentially guide intergroup relations. Public discourse has an important role in shaping the nature of intergroup relations as the media and other channels of collective communication selectively focus on certain aspects of conflicts between cultures. The average individual is more likely to be exposed to such discourse rather than have direct experience with members of an outgroup. An average American is more likely to be exposed to public discourse about China and Russia than actually meeting an individual from these outgroups. When the public discourse focuses on intergroup conflicts, then individuals might have stronger beliefs on intergroup conflict. However, if public discourse can fuel intergroup conflict, then one interesting question to ask is whether a shift in the discourse content could reduce intergroup conflict. In a field experiment conducted in Rwanda, Paluck (2009) investigated the effect of a radio soap opera in reducing intergroup prejudice. For the duration of 1 year, communities of Rwandans were exposed to either a radio soap opera broadcast carrying messages of intergroup trust and harmony or a control radio soap opera on health. She found that the intergroup harmony broadcast changed individuals' perceived norms of intergroup relations as these individuals showed stronger beliefs of the social norm of reconciliation and openness toward groups in conflict. This change in normative belief was also accompanied by changes in individuals' behaviors regarding openness and cooperation in intergroup contact. Interestingly, the radio broadcast did not affect the personal beliefs of the individuals. This study offers evidence that the content of public discourse could shape individuals' representations of the shared norms in their culture. Further research on the role of intersubjective representations in the reduction of intergroup conflict would need to address the mechanism through which public discourse might contribute to change in intersubjective representations of the ingroup and outgroup, and the potential effects on individuals' personal beliefs and behaviors.

Extant research on intergroup relations has more of a focus on category-based group membership and its associated consequences for intergroup bias. As such, research on reduction of intergroup bias has focused much on changing the cognitive categorization of ingroup and outgroup members. However, intergroup relations could also be about the widely shared worldview systems, as illustrated by the many international conflicts framed as arising from ideological differences. Reduction in conflict based on intersubjective representations would likely require new strategies beyond redefining categorical boundaries.

CONCLUDING REMARKS

An intersubjective representations approach of cultural research examines culture and its influence on individuals via individuals' collectively shared representations of the culture. These representations are built upon interpersonal and collective communication processes that allow for dynamic negotiation of the symbolic meanings that are characteristic of a culture. Although individuals may not participate actively in the cultural meaning negotiation process, they are at the very least exposed to the meaning negotiation discourse through their interaction with the physical and sociocultural environment. Through such exposure, individuals come to share with other individuals in the cultural collective similar representations of the most central characteristics of the culture.

In this chapter, we have utilized the concept of intersubjective cultural representations to understand cultural identification. Intersubjective cultural representations separate the shared symbolic meanings of the culture that characterize the cultural collective from cultural collective as a social category. Our proposed distinction of category-based and knowledge-based cultural identification follows this separation, with the former referring to culture as social category and the latter referring to culture as shared meanings. The cultural and social psychology literature has ample empirical work on category-based cultural identification. In contrast, research that conceptualizes cultural identification as knowledge based is scarce. However, a consideration of knowledge-based cultural identification could generate new research predictions different from that of a category-based perspective. A cultural collective is not an empty, arbitrary category. The collectively shared content that defines the culture of the collective is equally important, if not more so, than the category label. A knowledge-based account of cultural identification would direct research focus to such collectively shared content.

REFERENCES

Allport, G. W. (1954). *The nature of prejudice*. Reading, MA: Addison-Wesley.

Alter, A. L., & Kwan, V. S. Y. (2009). Cultural sharing in a global village: Evidence for extracultural cognition in European Americans. *Journal of Personality and Social Psychology*, *96*, 742–760. doi: 10.1037/a0014036.

Barth, F. (2002). An anthropology of knowledge. *Current Anthropology*, *43*, 1–18. doi:10.1086/324131.

Benet-Martínez, V., & Haritatos, J. (2005). Bicultural identity integration (BII): Components and psychosocial antecedents. *Journal of Personality*, *73*, 1015–1050. doi: 10.1111/j.1467-6494.2005.00337.x.

Bennett, A. (2001). *Cultures of popular music*. Buckingham, UK: Open University Press.

Berry, J. W. (2001). A psychology of immigration. *Journal of Social Issues, 57*, 615–631. doi: 10.1111/0022-4537.00231.

Breakwell, G. M. (2001). Social representational constraints upon identity processes. In K. Deaux & G. Philogène (Eds.), *Representations of the social* (pp. 271–284). Malden, MA: Blackwell.

Brewer, M. B. (2007). The social psychology of intergroup relations: Social categorization, ingroup bias, and outgroup prejudice. In A. W. Kruglanski & E. T. Higgins (Eds.), *Social psychology: Handbook of basic principles* (2nd ed., pp. 695–715). New York, NY: Guilford Press.

Cheryan, S., & Monin, B. (2005). Where are you really from? Asian Americans and identity denial. *Journal of Personality and Social Psychology, 89*, 717–730. doi:10.1037/0022–3514.89.5.717.

Chiu, C., Gelfand, M. J., Yamagishi, T., Shteynberg, G., & Wan, C. (2010). Intersubjective culture: The role of intersubjective perceptions in cross-cultural research. *Perspectives on Psychological Science, 5*, 482–493. doi:10.1177/1745691610375562.

Cho, G. E., Sandel, T. L., Miller, P. J., & Wang, S. (2005). What do grandmothers think about self-esteem? American and Taiwanese folk theories revisited. *Social Development, 14*, 701–721. doi:10.1111/j.1467-9507.2005.00325.x\.

Cialdini, R. B., Kallgren, C. A., & Reno, R. R. (1991). A focus theory of normative conduct: A theoretical refinement and reevaluation of the role of norms in human behavior. In M. P. Zanna (Ed.), *Advances in experimental social psychology* (Vol. 24, pp. 201–234). San Diego, CA: Academic Press.

Cohen, A. B. (2009). Many forms of culture. *American Psychologist, 64*, 194–204. doi: 10.1037/a0015308.

Cottrell, C. A., & Neuberg, S. L. (2005). Different emotional reactions to different groups: A sociofunctional threat-based approach to "prejudice". *Journal of Personality and Social Psychology, 88*, 770–789. doi: 10.1037/0022-3514.88.5.770.

Devos, T., & Banaji, M. R. (2005). American = white? *Journal of Personality and Social Psychology, 88*, 447–466. doi: 10.1037/0022-3514.88.3.447.

Deutsch, M., & Gerard, H. B. (1955). A study of normative and informational social influences upon individual judgment. *Journal of Abnormal and Social Psychology, 51*, 629–636. doi: 10.1037/h0046408.

Echterhoff, G., Higgins, E. T., Kopietz, R., & Groll, S. (2008). How communication goals determine when audience tuning biases memory. *Journal of Experimental Psychology: General, 137*, 3–21. doi:10.1037/0096-3445.137.1.3.

Fazio. R. H. (1979). Motives for social comparison: The construction-validation distinction. *Journal of Personality and Social Psychology, 37*, 1683–1698. doi:10.1037/0022-3514.37.10.1683.

Festinger, L. (1954). A theory of social comparison processes. *Human Relations, 7*, 117–140.

Friedlmeier, W., Corapci, F., & Cole, P. M. (2011). Emotion socialization in cross-cultural perspective. *Social and Personality Psychology Compass, 5*, 410–427. doi: 10.1111/j.1751-9004.2011.00362.x.

Fu, J. H-Y., Morris, M. W., Lee, S.-L., Chao, M., Chiu, C.-Y., & Hong, Y.-Y. (2007). Epistemic motives and cultural conformity: Need for closure, culture, and context as determinants of conflict judgments. *Journal of Personality and Social Psychology, 92*, 191–207. doi: 10.1037/0022-3514.92.2.191.

Gaertner, S. L., Dovidio, J. F., Nier, J. A., Ward, C. M., & Banker, B. S. (1999). Across cultural divides: The value of a superordinate identity. In D. A. Prentice & D. T. Miller (Eds.), *Cultural divides: Understanding and overcoming group conflict* (pp. 173–212). New York, NY: Russell Sage Foundation.

Galchenko, I., & van de Vijver, F. J. R. (2007). The role of perceived cultural distance in the acculturation of exchange students in Russia. *International Journal of Intercultural Relations, 31*, 181–197. doi:10.1016/j.ijintrel.2006.03.004.

Garcia, M. F., Ramirez, M. G., & Jariego, I. M. (2002). Social support and locus of control as predictors of psychological well-being in Moroccan and Peruvian immigrant women in Spain. *International Journal of Intercultural Relations, 26*, 287–310.

Geertz, C. (1973). *The interpretation of cultures.* New York, NY: Basic Books.

Grieve, P. G., & Hogg, M. A. (1999). Subjective uncertainty and intergroup discrimination in the minimal group situation. *Personality and Social Psychology Bulletin, 25*, 926–940. doi: 10.1177/01461672992511002.

Hammack, P. L. (2008). Narrative and the cultural psychology of identity. *Personality and Social Psychology Review, 12*, 222–247. doi:10.1177/1088868308316892.

Hardin, C. D., & Higgins, E. T. (1996). Shared reality: How social verification makes the subjective objective. In R. M. Sorrentino & E. T. Higgins (Eds.), *Handbook of motivation and cognition, Vol. 3. The interpersonal context* (pp. 28–84). New York, NY: Guilford Press.

Harkness, G. (2011). Backpackers and gangstas: Chicago's white rappers strive for authenticity. *American Behavioral Scientist, 55*, 57–85. doi:10.1177/0002764210381729.

Haslam, N., Bastain, B., Bain, P., & Kashima, Y. (2006). Psychological essentialism, implicit theories, and intergroup relations. *Group Processes and Intergroup Relations, 9*, 63–76.

Heine, S. J., Buchtel, E. E., & Norenzayan, A. (2008). What do cross-national comparisons of personality traits tell us? The case of conscientiousness. *Psychological Science, 19*, 309–313. doi:10.1111/j.1467-9280.2008.02085.x.

Higgins, E., & Rholes, W. S. (1978). 'Saying is believing': Effects of message modification on memory and liking for the person described. *Journal of Experimental Social Psychology, 14*, 363–378. doi:10.1016/0022-1031(78)90032-X.

Hogg, M. A., & Turner, J. C. (1987). Intergroup behaviour, self-stereotyping and the salience of social categories. *British Journal of Social Psychology, 26*, 325–340. doi: 10.1111/j.2044-8309.1987.tb00795.x.

Hommel, B., Colzato, L. S., Scorolli, C., Borghi, A. M., & van den Wildenberg, W. P. M. (2011). Religion and action control: Faith-specific modulation of the Simon effect but not Stop-Signal performance. *Cognition, 120*, 177–85. doi:10.1016/j.cognition.2011.04.003.

Hong, Y., Wan, C., No, S., & Chiu, C. (2007). Multicultural identities. In S. Kitayama & D. Cohen (Eds.), *Handbook of cultural psychology* (pp. 323–345). New York, NY: Guilford Press.

Ignatieff, M. (1994). *Blood and belonging: Journeys into the new nationalism.* New York, NY: Farrar, Straus, and Giroux.

Kashima, E. S., & Loh, E. (2006). International students' acculturation: Effects of international, conational, and local ties and need for closure. *International Journal of Intercultural Relations, 30*, 471–485. doi: 10.1016/j.ijintrel.2005.12.003.

Keesing, R. M. (1974). Theories of culture. *Annual Review of Anthropology, 3*, 73–97. doi: 10.1146/annurev.an.03.100174.000445.

Kitayama, S., Markus, H., Matsumoto, H., & Norasakkunkit, V. (1997). Individual and collective processes in the construction of the self: Self-enhancement in the United States and self-criticism in Japan. *Journal of Personality and Social Psychology, 72*, 1245–1267. doi:10.1037/0022-3514.72.6.1245.

Kosic, A., Kruglanski, A., Pierro, A., & Mannetti, L. (2004). The social cognition of immigrants' acculturation: Effects of the need for closure and the reference group at entry. *Journal of Personality and Social Psychology, 86*, 796–813.

Krauss, R. M., & Fussell, S. R. (1991). Perspective-taking in communication: Representations of others' knowledge in reference. *Social Cognition, 9*, 2–24.

Kruglanski, A. W., Pierro, A., Mannetti, L., & De Grada, E. (2006). Groups as epistemic providers: Need for closure and the unfolding of group-centrism. *Psychological Review, 113*, 84–100. doi: 10.1037/0033-295X.113.1.84.

Kruglanski, A. W., & Webster, D. M. (1996). Motivated closing of the mind: "Seizing" and "freezing." *Psychological Review, 103*, 263–283. doi: 10.1037/0033-295X.103.2.263.

Kuczynski, L., & Navara, G. S. (2006). Sources of innovation and change in socialization, internalization and acculturation. In M. Killen & J. G. Smetana (Eds.), *Handbook of moral development* (pp. 299–327). Mahwah, NJ: Erlbaum.

Lee, J-S., Koeske, G. F., & Sales, E. (2004). Social support buffering of acculturative stress: A study of mental health symptoms among Korean international students. *International Journal of Intercultural Relations, 28*, 399–414. doi: 10.1016/j.ijintrel.2004.08.005.

Lemyre, L., & Smith, P. M. (1985). Intergroup discrimination and self-esteem in the minimal group paradigm. *Journal of Personality and Social Psychology, 49*, 660–670. doi: 10.1037/0022-3514.49.3.660.

Li, Q., & Brewer, M. B. (2004). What does it mean to be an American? Patriotism, nationalism, and American identity after 9/11. *Political Psychology, 25*, 727–739.

Liu, J. H., Wilson, M. S., McClure, J., & Higgins, T. R. (1999). Social identity and the perception of history: Cultural representations of Aotearoa/New Zealand. *European Journal of Social Psychology, 29*, 1021–1047. doi: 10.1002/(SICI)1099-0992(199912)29:8<1021::AID-EJSP975>3.0.CO;2-4.

Mähönen, T. A., Jasinskaja-Lahti, I., & Liebkind, K. (2011). Cultural discordance and the polarization of identities. *Group Processes and Intergroup Relations, 14*, 505–515. doi:10.1177/1368430210379006.

Migdal, M. J., Hewstone, M., & Mullen, B. (1998). The effects of crossed categorization on intergroup evaluations: A meta-analysis. *British Journal of Social Psychology, 37*, 303–324.

Miramontez, D., Benet-Martínez, V., & Nguyen, A.-M. (2008). Bicultural identity and self/group personality perceptions. *Self and Identity, 7*, 430–445. doi: 10.1080/15298860701833119.

Miyamoto, Y., Nisbett, R. E., & Masuda, T. (2006). Culture and the physical environment: Holistic versus analytic perceptual affordances. *Psychological Science, 17*, 113–119. doi:10.1111/j.1467-9280.2006.01673.x.

Morling, B., & Lamoreaux, M. (2008). Measuring culture outside the head: A meta-analysis of individualism-collectivism in cultural products. *Personality and Social Psychology Review, 12*, 199–221. doi:10.1177/1088868308318260.

Nowak, A., Szamrej, J., & Latané, B. (1990). From private attitude to public opinion: A dynamic theory of social impact. *Psychological Bulletin, 97*, 362–376. doi: 10.1037/0033-295X.97.3.362.

Oyserman, D., Coon, H. M., & Kemmelmeier, M. (2002). Rethinking individualism and collectivism: Evaluation of theoretical assumptions and meta-analyses. *Psychological Bulletin, 128*, 3–72. doi:10.1037/0033-2909.128.1.3.

Padilla, A. M. (1994). Bicultural development: A theoretical and empirical examination. In R. Malgady & O. Rodriguez (Eds.), *Theoretical and conceptual issues in Hispanic mental health* (pp. 20–51). Melbourne, FL: Krieger.

Palmer, J. D. (2007). Who is the authentic Korean American? Korean-born Korean American high school students' negotiations of ascribed and achieved identities. *Journal of Language, Identity, and Education, 6*, 277–298.

Paluck, E. (2009). Reducing intergroup prejudice and conflict using the media: A field experiment in Rwanda. *Journal of Personality and Social Psychology, 96*, 574–587. doi:10.1037/a0011989.

Park-Taylor, J., Ng, V., Ventura, A. B., Kang, A. E., Morris, C. R., Gilbert, T., . . . Androsiglio, R. A. (2008). What it means to be and feel like a "true" American: Perceptions and experiences of second-generation Americans. *Cultural Diversity and Ethnic Minority Psychology, 14*, 128–137.

Pehrson, S., Brown, R., & Zagefka, H. (2009). When does national identification lead to the rejection of immigrants? Cross-sectional and longitudinal evidence for the role of essentialist in-group definitions. *British Journal of Social Psychology, 48*, 61–76. doi: 10.1348/014466608X288827.

Pehrson, S., & Green, E. G. T. (2010). Who we are and who can join us: National identity content and entry criteria for new immigrants. *Journal of Social Issues, 66*, 695–716. doi: 10.1111/j.1540-4560.2010.01671.x.

Petrocelli, J. V., Tormala, Z. L., & Rucker, D. D. (2007). Unpacking attitude certainty: Attitude clarity and attitude correctness. *Journal of Personality and Social Psychology, 92*, 30–41. doi: 10.1037/0022-3514.92.1.30.

Pettigrew, T. F., & Tropp, L. R. (2008). How does intergroup contact reduce prejudice? Meta-analytic tests of three mediators. *European Journal of Social Psychology, 38*, 922–934. doi: 10.1002/ejsp.504.

Phinney, J. S. (1999). An intercultural approach in psychology: Cultural contact and identity. *Cross-Cultural Psychology Bulletin, 33*, 24–31.

Phinney, J. S., & Devich-Navarro, M. (1997). Variations in bicultural identification among African American and Mexican American adolescents. *Journal of Research on Adolescence, 7*, 3–32.

Riek, B. M., Mania, E. W., & Gaertner, S. L. (2006). Intergroup threat and outgroup attitudes: A meta-analytic review. *Personality and Social Psychology Review, 10*, 336–353. doi: 10.1207/s15327957pspr1004_4.

Rodriguez, L., Schwartz, S. J., & Whitbourne, S. K. (2010). American identity revisited: The relation between national, ethnic, and personal identity in a multiethnic sample of emerging adults. *Journal of Adolescent Research, 25*, 324–349.

Romney, A. K., Boyd, J. P., Moore, C. C., Batchelder, W. H., & Brazill, T. J. (1996). Culture as shared cognitive representations. *Proceedings of the National Academy of Sciences USA, 93*, 4699–4705.

Savani, K., Morris, M. W., Naidu, N. R., Kumar, S., & Berlia, N. V. (2011). Cultural conditioning: Understanding interpersonal accommodation in India and the United States in terms of the modal characteristics of interpersonal influence situations. *Journal of Personality and Social Psychology, 100*, 84–102. doi:10.1037/a0021083.

Searle, W., & Ward, C. (1990). The prediction of psychological and sociocultural adjustment during cross-cultural transitions. *International Journal of Intercultural Relations, 14*, 449–464. doi:10.1016/0147-1767(90)90030-Z.

Sherif, M. (1936). *The psychology of social norms*. New York, NY: Harper & Row.

Sherif, M., & Sherif, C. W. (1964). *Reference groups*. New York, NY: Harper & Row.

Shteynberg, G., Gelfand, M. J., & Kim, K. (2009). Peering into the 'magnum mysterium' of culture: The explanatory power of descriptive norms. *Journal of Cross-Cultural Psychology, 40*, 46–69. doi:10.1177/0022022108326196.

Sperber, D. (1996). *Explaining culture: A naturalistic approach*. Oxford, UK: Blackwell.

Stephan, W. G., Diaz-Loving, R., & Duran, A. (2000). Integrated threat theory and intercultural attitudes: Mexico and the United States. *Journal of Cross-Cultural Psychology, 31*, 240–249. doi:10.1177/0022022100031002006.

Stephens, N. M., Markus, H. R., & Townsend, S. S. M. (2007). Choice as an act of meaning: The case of social class. *Journal of Personality and Social Psychology, 93*, 814–830. doi: 10.1037/0022-3514.93.5.814.

Tajfel, H., Billig, M. G., Bundy, R. P., & Flament, C. (1971). Social categorization and intergroup behaviour. *European Journal of Social Psychology, 1*, 149–178. doi: 10.1002/ejsp.2420010202.

Tajfel, H., & Turner, J. C. (1979). An integrative theory of intergroup conflict. In W. G. Austin & S. Worchel (Eds.), *The social psychology of intergroup relations* (pp. 33–47). Monterey, CA: Brooks/Cole.

Takano, Y., & Osaka, E. (1999). An unsupported common view: Comparing Japan and the U.S. on individualism/collectivism. *Asian Journal of Social Psychology, 2*, 311–341. doi:10.1111/1467-839X.00043.

Tam, K., & Lee, S. (2010). What values do parents want to socialize in their children? The role of perceived normative values. *Journal of Cross-Cultural Psychology, 41*, 175–181. doi:10.1177/0022022109354379.

Terracciano, A. A., Abdel-Khalek, A. M., Ádám, N. N., Adamovová, L. L., Ahn, C. k., Ahn, H. N., . . . McCrae, R. R. (2005). National character does not reflect mean personality trait levels in 49 cultures. *Science, 310*(5745), 96–100. doi:10.1126/science.1117199.

Tsai, J. L., Mortensen, H., Wong, Y., & Hess, D. (2002). What does "being American" mean? A comparison of Asian American and European American young adults. *Cultural Diversity and Ethnic Minority Psychology, 8*, 257–273. doi: 10.1037/1099-9809.8.3.257.

Turner, J. C., Hogg, M. A., Oakes, P. J., Reicher, S. D., & Wetherell, M. S. (1987). *Rediscovering the social group: A self-categorization theory*. Oxford, UK: Blackwell.

Wakefield, J. R. H., Hopkins, N., Cockburn, C., Shek, K. M., Muirhead, A., Reicher, S., & van Rijswijk, W. (2011). The impact of adopting ethnic or civic conceptions of national belonging for others' treatment. *Personality and Social Psychology Bulletin, 37*, 1599–1610. doi:10.1177/0146167211416131.

Wan, C., & Chiu, C. (2009). An intersubjective consensus approach to culture: The role of intersubjective norms versus cultural self in cultural processes. In R. S. Wyer, C. Chiu, & Y. Hong (Eds.), *Understanding culture: Theory, research, and application* (pp. 79–91). New York, NY: Psychology Press.

Wan, C., Chiu, C., Peng, S., & Tam, K. (2007). Measuring cultures through intersubjective cultural norms: Implications for predicting relative identification with two or more cultures. *Journal of Cross-Cultural Psychology, 38*, 213–226. doi:10.1177/0022022106297300.

Wan, C., Chiu, C., Tam, K., Lee, S., Lau, I., & Peng, S. (2007). Perceived cultural importance and actual self-importance of values in cultural identification. *Journal of Personality and Social Psychology, 92*, 337–354. doi:10.1037/0022-3514.92.2.337.

Wan, C., Tam, K., & Chiu, C. (2010). Intersubjective cultural representations predicting behaviour: The case of political culture and voting. *Asian Journal of Social Psychology, 13*, 260–273. doi:10.1111/j.1467-839X.2010.01318.x.

Wan, C., Torelli, C. J., & Chiu, C. (2010). Intersubjective consensus and the maintenance of normative shared reality. *Social Cognition, 28*, 422–446. doi:10.1521/soco.2010.28.3.422.

Ward, C., & Kennedy, A. (1993). Where's the "culture" in cross-cultural transition? Comparative studies of sojourner adjustment. *Journal of Cross-Cultural Psychology, 24*, 221–249.

Ward, C., & Kennedy, A. (1994). Acculturation strategies, psychological adjustment, and sociocultural competence during cross-cultural transitions. *International Journal of Intercultural Relations, 18*, 329–343. doi:10.1016/0147-1767(94)90036-1.

Ward, C., & Searle, W. (1991). The impact of value discrepancies and cultural identity on psychological and sociocultural adjustment of sojourners. *International Journal of Intercultural Relations, 15*, 209–224. doi: 10.1016/0147-1767(91)90030-K.

Yogeeswaran, K., & Dasgupta, N. (2010). Will the "real" American please stand up? The effect of implicit national prototypes on discriminatory behavior and judgments. *Personality and Social Psychology Bulletin, 36*, 1332–1345. doi: 10.1177/0146167210380928.

Zhang, A. Y., & Chiu, C-Y. (2011). Goal commitment and alignment of personal goals predict group identification only when the goals are shared. *Group Processes and Intergroup Relations,15*, 425–437. doi: 10.1177/1368430211415440.

Zou, X., Tam, K., Morris, M. W., Lee, S., Lau, I., & Chiu, C. (2009). Culture as common sense: Perceived consensus versus personal beliefs as mechanisms of cultural influence. *Journal of Personality and Social Psychology, 97*, 579–597. doi: 10.1037/a0016399.

5

Culture, Group Processes, and Trust

LETTY Y-Y. KWAN AND YING-YI HONG

He who does not trust enough will not be trusted.

—Lao Tzu, *Tao Te Ching*, 600 BCE–531 BCE

It is impossible to go through life without trust: That is to be imprisoned in the worst cell of all, oneself.

—Graham Greene, *The Ministry of Fear*, 1943

Trust binds people together and contributes to successful interpersonal and intragroup relationships. In organizational settings, trust toward one's leaders promotes job satisfaction, lowers employee turnover rate, increases perceived fairness, and improves employees' efficacy (Dirks, 2000; Golembiewski & McConkie, 1975; Mayer, Davis, & Schoorman, 1995). Trust among employees promotes cooperation and improves team dynamics (Golembiewski & McConkie, 1975). In general, trust affects how individuals relate to each other, and almost all social relationships require trust (Arrow, 1974; Bromiley & Cummings, 1995).

Although trust is universally valued in social relationships, trust processes differ across cultures (Ferrin & Gillespie, 2010; Hofstede, 1980). To understand the cross-cultural differences in trust processes, we propose that culture, trust, and group processes influence each other. As shown in Figure 5.1, certain cultural lay beliefs and cultural norms support specific trust patterns within a culture, and these adaptive trust patterns evolve within the culture. Successful formation of intergroup and intragroup relationships using this culture-specific set of trust patterns reaffirms the validity of the cultural lay beliefs and reinforces culturally normative behaviors. That is, some of our beliefs or norms in the culture lead us to use certain cues to determine trust, and if that leads to a successful trust relationship, we will continue to use those cues in the future. The success in relationship development likely reaffirms the very belief we use to assess trust in the first place.

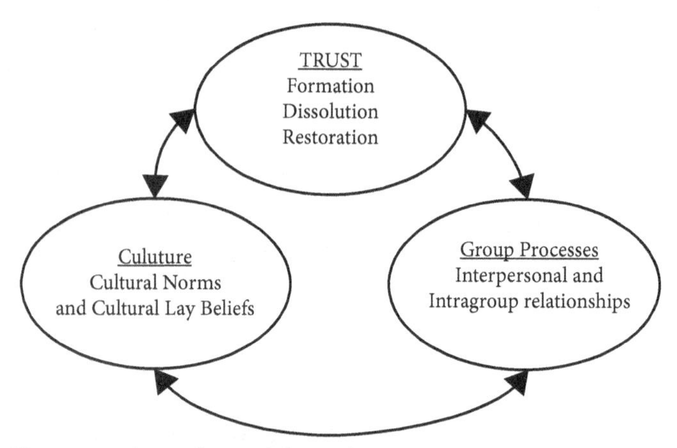

Figure 5.1. A circular model on culture, trust, and group processes.

This chapter will focus on understanding the role of trust in relationships across cultures, including trust development, trust dissolution, and trust restoration. Furthermore, the cultural lay beliefs that support specific trust and social interactive patterns will be discussed. We plan to achieve this objective by analyzing three determining factors of trust: (a) the characteristics of the trustor (e.g., the trustor's culture and its attendant worldview), (b) the characteristics of the trustee (e.g., the trustee's ability, competency, and integrity), and (c) the institutional processes (e.g., social structure wherein trust takes place). In the following sections, we will first define what trust is and explain how different definitions are contested under different cultural contexts. Next, we will introduce the initial trust formation model (McKnight, Cummings, & Chervany, 1998) and integrate it with the cultural theories to understand trust formation, trust dissolution, and trust restoration across different cultural ecologies. We will conclude by suggesting a model through which cultural norms and cultural lay beliefs can influence trust processes.

DEFINITION OF TRUST AND THE TRUST DECISION-MAKING PROCESS

Trust refers to the "[P]sychological state comprising the intention to accept vulnerability based upon positive expectations of the intentions or behaviors of another" (Rousseau, Sitkin, Burt, & Camerer, 1998, p. 395). It consists of three important elements: (1) the trustor's decision to trust, (2) the trustee' trustworthiness from the perspective of the trustor, and (3) the risk and uncertainty surrounding the trust decision (Mayer et al., 1995; McKnight et al., 1998; Rossouseu et al., 1998).

Trust is a broad concept, and researchers do not always agree on what trust means. For example, the *act* of trust by the trustor can be driven by the perceived trustworthiness of the trustee; but it can also be driven by the trustor's perception of how the external environment controls the trustee's action (e.g., the institutional control that is exerted on the trustee's actions). Some argue that in contexts where there is external control of the trustee's behavior (e.g., when the trustee's behavior is heavily sanctioned or reprimanded by others), trust is not needed. That being said, although external control mechanisms can reduce uncertainty and render trust less important, this type of assurance (i.e., institutional control mechanisms) does not completely eliminate uncertainty. For example, a recent study conducted by the authors showed that in a buying-selling context, trustors still indicate an above average level of risk and uncertainty with the transaction even when a tightly controlled institutional system is in place (Kwan & Hong, unpublished data). Likewise, trust research that was carried out in a culture where high institutional constraint is pervasive showed that individuals still relied on other cues to make trust decisions (e.g., Yamagishi, 2011). We contend that even in a society with a strong institutional system, trust is still needed to alleviate the impact of perceived risks in social exchanges.

Moreover, trust researchers routinely use trustor's "willingness to risk" (Mayer et al., 1995) as a proxy measure for behavioral trust (Kim, Ferrin, Cooper, & Dirks, 2004). Therefore, in the current chapter, the concept of trust will be defined as the *trusting behavioral act*—the act of relinquishing power over outcomes valuable to the self (Tanis & Postmes, 2005; e.g., buying a used bicycle on Craigslist from a seller) regardless of whether these trusting behaviors are driven by an intention to accept vulnerability based on positive expectations of the trustee or a perception of a tight formal or informal institutional control on the trustee's behaviors.

TRUST DEVELOPMENT

A trust relationship is influenced by the personal characteristics of the trustor, the characteristics of the trustee, and the reciprocal monitoring relationship between the trustor and the trustee. Understanding how individuals make initial trust decisions—the decision on whether to trust somebody initially, is important. Because such decisions often have a long-term impact on the relationship between the trustor and trustee. For example, when a buyer purchases a product on eBay, the buyer expects that the seller will deliver the product in good condition and the seller expects that the buyer will pay the agreed sales price of the product. After entering this agreement, if the buyer fails to pay for the goods after bidding for it, or if the seller fails to deliver the goods after the buyer has paid, trust is violated and a long-term trust relationship will not follow. Contrarily, if both sides carry out their agreement, the likelihood of repurchasing from the same seller will increase. In this example, both the seller and the buyer may experience a higher risk and uncertainty in the initial transaction, and thus are more vulnerable at the initial trust development stage than at a later stage.

To avoid being cheated, the trustor will determine the trustworthiness of the trustee using various trust cues. Successful transactions are marked by a "good fit" between the decision to trust and the actual trustworthiness of the trustee. Trusting others indiscriminately increases the trustor's risk (from the earlier example, if the buyer purchases from a seller with a poor selling record, the chances of the buyer not receiving the goods increases), while having too little trust in others also risks missing opportunities of social and economic gains (if the buyer is overly conservative in deciding who to buy from, he or she might lose out on bargain buys; Hardin, 2002). If the transaction is a success, the likelihood of repurchasing from the same seller will increase. Many trust researchers argue that initial trust formation decisions deserve the most attention because they have lasting effects on future interactions (Berscheid & Graziano, 1979). In the subsequent sections, we will introduce the initial trust formation model (McKnight et al., 1998) and review related cultural theories to understand how culture influences trust initiation and development.

A Model of Initial Trust Formation

The initial trust formation model (McKnight et al., 1998) is used to understand why, despite the lack of prior experiences with each other, individuals still engage in trusting behaviors. In the initial trust formation model, interpersonal trust is defined as the combination of trusting intentions and trusting beliefs. Trusting intentions refer to the trustor's willingness to allow the self to be vulnerable to potential loss through trusting the trustee. Trusting beliefs refer to the trustor's perceived characteristics of the trustee, such as the trustee's ability, integrity, predictability, and benevolence. The relative impacts of the trusting intentions and trusting beliefs on initial trust development depend on three major factors—(a) trustor's disposition to trust, (b) cognitive processes, and (c) institution-based trust (see Fig. 5. 2).

First, disposition to trust is a characteristic of the trustor; it refers to the trustor's propensity to trust general others in his or her surroundings (Rotter, 1971). Second, the cognitive processes that can affect initial trust development involve those that implicate social or reputation categorization. Social categorization refers to how one categorizes the relationship between the self and others. Ingroup categorization, or placing the trustee in one's own social group, can increase trust (Brewer, 1981; Lewis & Weigert, 1985; Mayer et al., 1995; McAllister, 1995;

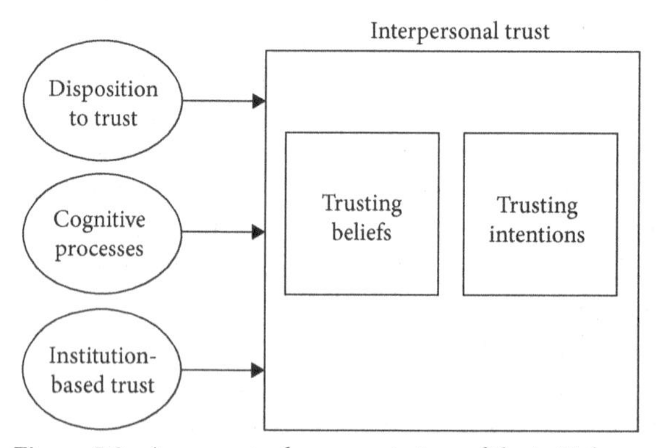

Figure 5.2. A conceptual representation of the initial trust model.

Meyerson, Weick, & Kramer, 1996). Reputation categorization refers to the use of a target's membership in a reputable group to infer high integrity, and thus trustworthiness of the target. For example, being a member of the Doctors Without Borders, a highly reputable group, would be deemed to have high integrity and thus trustworthiness. Aside from social membership of the trustees, personal characteristics of the trustees (benevolence, integrity, and ability) would affect formation of trust as well. Third, institution-based trust recognizes that the social structure or context where the trust decision takes place can influence trust development. For example, a society instituted with an efficient monitoring and sanctioning system for punishing transgressors can facilitate trusting behaviors (Lane & Bachmann, 1996; McKnight et al., 1998, McKnight & Chervany, 2002; Shapiro, 1987; Yamagishi, 1999; Yamagishi & Yamagishi, 1994; Zucker, 1986).

The initial trust formation model's prediction of the strength of interpersonal trust is contingent on the aforementioned three factors. Trust researchers have examined these three factors and their effects on trusting beliefs and intentions separately. In the following sections, we will review the research literature that focuses on these three factors and discuss how culture might influence each of them.

Trustors' Characteristics and Their Disposition to Trust

Being able to trust others is a hallmark of healthy personality development (Erikson, 1956); and early research by Rotter (1967, 1980) has identified several personal characteristics that are related to high versus low general trust. Some of the identified characteristics have been further examined in recent studies, including our brain chemistry (e.g., level of oxytocin; Kosfeld, Heinrichs, Zak, Fischbacher, & Fehr, 2005), personality traits (e.g., calmness or low levels of trait anxiety; Fahr & Irlenbusch, 2008), and emotions (e.g., gratitude; Dunn & Schweitzer, 2005).

Trustor attributes, such as emotion, can affect a trustor's beliefs about what trustee characteristics should be used to judge trustworthiness. For example, a trustor's specific trusting beliefs can change according to his or her emotional conditions. In one study, White (2005) found that when decisions are made under no emotional difficulties (i.e., when the consequences of the decision are small), individuals trust an expert's opinions (i.e., focusing on ability). However, when decisions are made under high emotional difficulties (when the consequences of the decision are large), people tend to trust the opinions of a benevolent person (i.e., focusing on benevolence).

Trusting beliefs also influence purchase intentions in e-commerce settings. Results from a consumer behavior study showed that purchase intentions increase when the Web site's trust characteristics match the consumer's (trustor's) expectations (Schlosser, White, & Llyod, 2006). Specifically, the researchers separated online consumers into two categories: the "searcher" and the "browser." Online consumers are considered "searchers" when they search for specific product information. Past research indicated that searchers have the highest visitor-to-buyer ratio. That is, they are goal oriented and are motivated to find answers in the most efficient manner (Schlosser et al, 2006). These searchers have the tendency to use the ability (the Web site investment, including the design of the Web store) of the trustee to gauge their trust decision. In contrast, online consumers who do not seek out specific product information (the browsers) are usually more concerned about whether the Web store can fulfill their benevolence expectation in a transaction. A Web store's (trustee's) ability does not influence the browsers' trust decisions as much as it influences the searcher's trust decision. Instead, the browsers rely on the Webstore's perceived benevolence (e.g., Webstore's emphasis on privacy and integrity of their store) when making their trust decision.

These findings illustrate the pronounce effects of the trustor's characteristics on trust decisions: Different motivations were linked to different sets of trusting beliefs. Trust occurs when a trustee possesses characteristics that match the trustor's trust beliefs.

A vast amount of research has shown that culture influences trust beliefs. The formation and development of trust differ across cultures (Ferrin & Gillespie, 2010; Hofstede, 1980). Americans report higher *general trust* than Japanese do. When Americans and Japanese were asked, "Do you think you can put your trust in most people, or do you think it is always best to be on your guard?" over 47% of Americans agreed that people could generally be trusted while only 26% in the Japanese sample agreed (Hayashi, 1982). A more recent comparative study between Denmark and Korea revealed that the Danes had higher general trust than Koreans. In fact, Danes trusted general others to a similar extent as they trusted close ingroup members, whereas Koreans trusted close ingroup members more than general others (Delhey & Newton, 2005; Kim et al., 2004). Consistent with these findings, Buchan and colleagues (2002) found in the World Value Survey (Inglehart, Basanez, & Moreno, 1998) that Americans and Chinese do not differ in how much they trust a specific referent group. The two groups differ, however, in their trust toward strangers, with Americans having significantly higher general trust than the Chinese (50% vs. 10%). Despite these findings, there are also other seemingly contradictory results. For instance, although Japanese were found to be less trusting than Americans in past studies mentioned earlier, Japanese and American undergraduates did not differ in their trusting behaviors when participating in a one-shot trust game with strangers (Buchan et al., 2002).

The aforementioned research findings show that the trustor's culture can influence initial trust decisions. When trust toward the ingroup (family, friends, or specific relational others) and strangers were measured separately, Americans showed high general and specific referent trust while East Asians showed lower general trust but high referent trust. One possible explanation is that trustors in different cultures hold different trusting beliefs, which influence their trust decisions as well as the trust development process. Specifically, the East Asians often use the trustee's relational cues (Brewer, 1999; Yuki, Maddux, Brewer, & Takemura, 2005) and institution sanctioning and group monitoring cues (Yamagishi & Yamagishi, 1994) to infer the trustee's trustworthiness. When those cues are absent, trust is low compared to that of Americans or Western Europeans.

In short, the trustor's culture influences the preferences of which trust cues to use when making trust decisions. That is, it is not simply the trustor's traits that determine the trust decision; rather, it is the person–situation interaction, which involves both the trustor's characteristics and the trustee's cues in the situation, that determines trust decisions. The nature of the person–situation interaction differs across cultures. In the next section, we will review how different types of trustee's characteristics are used by the trustor to establish trust and how the trustor's culture might influence them in using trustee's characteristics differently.

Trustees' Characteristics and Their Effects on Cognitive Processes

Aside from trustor characteristics, cognitive processes such as categorization of a trustee's characteristics also influence trust decisions (McKnight et al., 1998). There are two ways to categorize trustee's characteristics when making trust decisions: (1) social categorization and (2) personal characteristics. In social categorization, the trustor trusts the trustee based on the group that the trustee belongs to. Specifically, as we argued before, both ingroup membership or membership of a reputable group would increase the trustee's trustworthiness (Foddy, Platow, & Yamagishi, 2009). For personal characteristics, research has shown that a trustor focuses on a trustee's benevolence, integrity, and competence to gauge trust. Although social categorization has been shown to be effective in guiding trust judgments for individuals across cultures, the studies that sought to understand a trustee's personal characteristics have mainly used participants from North America. We mentioned earlier that East Asians' trust toward a specific close referent group is higher than their trust toward strangers (Inglehart et al., 1998). Based on these findings, it is possible that the East Asians and the North Americans use social categorization and personal character to different extents when they engage in trust decisions.

Social Categorization

As social beings, humans are strongly inclined to identify the self as a part of the larger society (Brewer & Yuki, 2007; Turner, Brown, & Tajfel, 1979). Such identification provides the basis for ingroup and outgroup distinction. In the context of trust, a trustor's categorization of a trustee's group identification helps him or her determine whether the trustee can be trusted. A vast amount of research showed that social identification has important implications for trust development and intergroup relationships (Turner, Brown, & Tajfel, 1979). Studies have found the presence of intergroup bias even in minimal group settings. In one classic study, participants were divided into two groups based on trivial features such as bogus feedback on whether the participants underestimated or overestimated the number of dots briefly presented on a computer screen. The participants repeatedly exhibited ingroup favoritism, such as giving a higher monetary reward to the group to which they belonged (Tajfel, Biling, Bundy, & Flament, 1971). This effect was found even when the participants were not given a chance to interact with other members, when the participants expected no future interactions with each other, or when the participants' own benefit was not involved. All of these findings suggest that social categorization is often accompanied by favoritism toward ingroup members, including differential trust.

In one study involving trust decisions, Foddy and colleagues (2009) offered participants the choice of having either an ingroup or outgroup member to allocate monetary resources to them. When the participants were told that their ingroup (outgroup) identity is salient to the allocator, they chose the ingroup allocator over the outgroup allocator regardless of the allocator's positive or negative stereotypes. This finding suggests that the shared ingroup identity conveys the expectation of favorable behaviors among ingroup members. Interestingly, in the second part of the study, Foddy and colleagues (2009) showed that when participants were told that the allocator did not know participants' group memberships, the participants' trust decisions were guided by positive stereotypes of the allocator rather than their group membership. This finding suggests that participants use social categorization information (ingroup vs. outgroup) to infer that the trustee would favor an ingroup member when the group membership information is available, which can trump the trustee's own personal characteristics. As such, the trustor's representation of the trustee vis-à-vis social categorization is important.

Aside from using only "in" versus "out" group categorization, researchers have suggested identification can be based on additional considerations. Brewer and Gardner (1996) propose three different levels of self-identification—the individual self, the relational self, and the collective self. The collective self refers to the representation of the self as a member of a collective (group), and the individual self refers to the representation of the self as a unique entity. Both collective self and individual self are central constructs in the social identification theory (SIT; Tajfel et al., 1971; Turner et al., 1979). The main difference between the relational and the collective self, as Brewer and Gardner (1996) suggest, lies in the locus of personalized versus depersonalized attention toward their ingroup members. The relational self incorporates the self in personalized relationships with the ingroup and its network. In contrast, the collective self depersonalizes the representation of ingroup members. Specifically, in a depersonalized collective, it is not necessary for the self to have an interpersonal relationship or personal knowledge regarding others in the group. Rather, ingroup members share a symbolic relationship regardless of their levels of personal liking or affinity toward specific ingroup members.

Based on this distinction, Yuki (2003; see also Yuki & Takemura, Chapter 3, this volume) suggests that group cognition and behaviors differ across cultural contexts. Social categorization in SIT is more applicable in Western than Eastern cultures. In Eastern cultures, individuals tend to think about the self as embedded in a more relational network. Based on this framework, Yuki and colleagues (2005) propose that there are cultural differences in trust relations as a function of the relative dominance of the collective versus relational self. To test this idea, Yuki and colleagues (2005) compared Japanese and American participants in their trust responses to hypothetical scenarios and in an online game. The researchers found that the Japanese trusted a target in their relational network more than the Americans did. Specifically, the Japanese trusted an unknown target from an ingroup (a target who attended the same university as the participant) and an unknown target connected to their relational network (a target who attended the same university as an acquaintance) to a similar extent. In contrast, Americans trusted the ingroup target significantly more than the relational target. In short, the use of social categorization when making trust decisions is common in Eastern and Western cultures. Both groups trust their ingroup members more than strangers. Cross-cultural differences, however, are also present such that East Asians use the trustee's relational characteristics as the basis for making trust decisions more than Americans do.

East Asians' greater tendency to trust someone with relational characteristics is consistent with research on the impact of *guanxi*—an informal social relationship (King, 1991; Lin, 2001) on trust decisions. Literature on *guanxi* networks suggests that informal relationship can facilitate the development of a particular kind of trust—affective-based trust. Researchers have differentiated two bases of trust, namely affective- and cognitive-based trust. Affective-based trust encompasses the emotional bond between the trustor and the trustee and such emotional ties and relationships provide the basis of trust; whereas cognitive-based trust is calculated by instrumental gain and loss, and trust is often qualified by the trustee's competency and reliability (McAllister, 1995). When a trustor has high affective-based trust in the trustee, he or she is more willing to share his or her personal difficulties and hopes and dreams (Chua, Morris & Ingram, 2009). Overall, the trustor also expects the trustee to reciprocate the same care and concern (Chua & Morris, 2006).

East Asians have denser *guanxi* networks and individuals are more embedded within the social group (Chua & Morris, 2006; Su, Sirgy, & Littlefield, 2003). In addition, higher density networks are positively correlated with successful affective-based trust development (Chua & Morris, 2006). These findings indicate that East Asians are more likely to use relational cues to form the basis of trust (within their relational *guanxi* network), especially when trust is needed for personal matters (i.e., personal problems or difficulties).

Personal Characteristics

Other research has examined the trustee's trustworthiness from the perspective of whether the trustee possesses certain types of characteristics (Butler, 1991). Mayer et al. (1995) classify these characteristics into three main groups: trustee's ability, benevolence, and integrity.

First, trustors trust those who have the ability to deliver as promised. Having skills or expertise will ensure effective performance within a specific domain. For example, individuals trust a computer programmer to write a computer program using his or her technical expertise, but not to fly an airplane. A vast amount of research has linked the trustee's trustworthiness to the trustee's ability to make trust decisions within a specific domain (Barber, 1983; Butler, 1991; Butler & Cantrell, 1984; Kee & Knox, 1970; Mayer et al., 1995; Powell, 1996).

Second, benevolence of the trustee is the perception that the trustee wants to do good to the trustor. Highly benevolent trustees are expected to help the trustor beyond his or her own personal gains and external obligations. Trust research has shown that benevolent intention in leaders is important to gain subordinates' trust (Cheng, Chou, Wu, Huang, & Farh, 2004). A trustee's benevolent intentions, as well as altruistic behaviors, have been linked to positive trust decisions (Cook & Wall, 1980; Frost, Stimpson, & Maughan, 1978). Moreover, benevolence expectations of others are crucial in social group formation. For example, in the context of computer-mediated communication (CMC), researchers find that high trust among virtual group members is associated with group members' benevolence actions (through sharing of intellectual resources with others), and these groups flourish. In contrast, virtual communities where members do not show benevolence actions (measured by the frequency of information sharing by the members) have low trust among members, and these virtual communities usually crumbled (Wasko & Faraj, 2000).

Third, trustees who are perceived to have high moral integrity are expected to behave in accordance with moral norms and principles, including the norms of being honest and not taking advantage of the trustor in general terms. The relationship between integrity and trust has been demonstrated extensively in past research, with high reputational morality and integrity leading to trusting decisions (Butler & Cantrell, 1984; Gabarro, 1978; Hart, Capps, Cangemi, & Caillouet, 1986; Sitkin & Roth, 1993).

The characteristics that a trustor relies on when making trust decisions also differ across cultures. Cross-cultural studies that examine McAllister's (1995) conception of affective- versus cognitive-based trust highlight some of these differences. Whereas affective-based trust is determined mainly by one's social relationships, cognitive-based trust is determined by the trustee's abilities. The contexts of where the two types of trust take place also differ. Whereas cognitive-based trust is associated with instrumental exchanges of economic resources and task-related advice, affective-based trust is related to relationship exchanges such as friendships. Recent cross-cultural studies have found that in Chinese organizational settings, individuals' cognitive and affective trust is more intertwined compared with that of Americans (Chua et al., 2009). In Chinese organizations, it is possible that affective-based trust serves as the foundation for cognitive-based trust development; that is, trusting someone's abilities follows when *guanxi* (affective-based trust) has been developed. This is not likely for the organizational culture in America, where cognitive-based trust and affective-based trust are perceived to be two distinct concepts (cf. Sanchez-Burkes & Uhlmann, Chapter 6, this volume).

Relatedly, as mentioned earlier, while group identity cues (through *guanxi* networks) serve as the primary basis for Easterners to form both affective- and cognitive-based trust, Westerners use group identity cues as a secondary information source when making trust decisions. For example, in one study (Tanis & Postmes, 2005), University of Amsterdam students were put in an investment game where they were exposed to a trust partner with or without his or her personal identity information (either name or picture of the trustee); these trust targets were either an ingroup or outgroup member (from same or different university). Results indicated that the trustee showed more trusting behaviors when personal identity of the trustee was revealed. Only when the personal identity of the trustee was absent, ingroup membership raised reciprocity norms and elevated trust.

To summarize, the trustee's characteristics can be grouped by identity relevance or personal character relevance (ability, benevolence, and integrity). Even though individuals from across cultures use identity-relevant information to a certain extent to determine trust, they do so to different extents under different situational conditions (i.e., when social categorization information is missing or when relational group members are the target of trust). From the literature reviewed earlier, individuals in Eastern and Western cultures vary on their reliance on different trustee characteristics when making trust decisions. Easterners rely on relational network information more than Westerners do, whereas Westerners rely on the personal characteristics (for example, abilities) of the trustee more than Easterners do. We will return to this cross-cultural difference after we have discussed the third type of trust cue—institution-based trust—for initial trust development.

Institution-Based Trust Effects on Initial Trust Development

Institution-based trust is the belief that an impersonal structure is in place to assure certain outcomes, thereby reducing risk and uncertainty (McKnight et al., 1998; Shapiro, 1987; Zucker, 1986). Such structural assurances are often referred to as "safeguards" for the trustor, in the sense that the institutional structure would prevent trust transgressions via institutional sanctioning of the transgressors. The existing literature has identified two types of institution-based trust factors, namely (1) formal institutions, including law and its enforcement (e.g., the judicial system), and (2) informal institutions, including interpersonal monitoring and sanctioning.

Most trust relationships develop without prior experiences between the trustor and the trustee (McKnight et al., 1998). In these relationships, institutional structures (both formal and informal) independent of the dyadic relationship often serve as a third party providing assurance.

In the field of economics and sociology, an institution is made up of formal rules and structures, which govern an organized pattern of actions within the society (Lane & Bachmann, 1996; McKnight et al., 1998; Shapiro, 1987). The existence of strong institutions, such as state-managed certifications, escrows, laws, and regulations in the society, reduces the trustee's risk and uncertainty in a transaction as well as the transaction cost within the system; and thereby increases the likelihood of trust development. Because these formalized rules and regulations permeate the culture and are highly communicable among individuals within the culture, they are highly stable and resistant to change (Nelson & Winter, 1982; Zucker, 1977, 1983, 1987).

Consumer research has demonstrated how institutional elements can facilitate trust in economic transactions. In these studies, the buyer's trust toward the seller is conceptualized as his or her purchase intention despite the potential risk involved in the transaction (Gefen, 2002; Jarvenpaa & Tractinsky, 1999). In a study on trust in e-commerce, researchers found that institutionalized elements, including feedback mechanisms, escrow services, and credit card assurances, decrease the perceived risk in the transaction and thereby increase trust (Doney & Cannon, 1997; Stewart, 2003). Formal institutions facilitate transactions because of the economic incentive principle. Specifically, when a set of formal rules is well implemented to penalize transgressors, both the trustor (buyer) and the trustee (seller) would adhere to these institutional rules as adherence optimizes the balance between risks and gains over time.

Individuals' trust changes with the institutional environment. In one study, Bohnet and Huck (2004) showed that trust responses are learned through an incentive system within an institutional context. Specifically, this study engaged participants in a multiple-trial trust game that was divided into two phases. The researchers demonstrated that the propensity to trust (the trustor) or to be trustworthy (the trustee) in the second phase of the game could be predicted by the incentives that the participants were exposed to in the first phase. Results of this study indicated that individuals used their learned response to interact with their game partner in phase 2. More important, the effects of past experience diminished as soon as the participants realized the institutional incentive structure at phase 2 of the trust game had changed. This finding highlighted the individual's adaptability toward new institutional structures. In sum, strong institutional elements can reduce risk and uncertainty, which increases trust; and this effect is driven by learned responses to optimize one's gains given the payoff in the institutional structure.

In the aforementioned examples, institution is operationalized as a formal set of rules, focusing mainly on quantifiable institutional elements discussed in the earlier section. However, others have taken a broader perspective on the definition of institution. For example, Fukuyama (1995) defines an institution as the expectations of the community, which govern the behaviors of its members. From this perspective, an institution can be a set of formal rules or informal social norms and expectations that regulate behaviors of society members.

Research by Yamagishi and Yamagishi (1994) sought to demonstrate the strong impact of informal institution on trust. They posit that social monitoring and sanctioning facilitate trust within a community through punishing trust transgressors by other members. According to this view, for individuals living in a tightly controlled social environment, trusting behaviors are enforced by a system of mutual monitoring among members of the society. That is, in a social system where this informal institution-based trust system is shared and carried out, the exhibition of trust is a reflection of effective enforcement of such a monitoring and sanctioning system. A series of studies on informal institution-based trust showed that Japanese, compared to Americans, are more inclined to use personal relations, such as informal monitoring, as risk mitigating strategies that ensure trusting behaviors (Jin, Yamagishi, & Kiyonari, 1996; Yamagishi & Yamagishi, 1994).

Yamagishi and colleagues (Yamagishi, Jin, & Miller, 1998; Yamagishi & Yamagishi, 1994) provided an explanation for the cross-cultural difference in reliance on relational cues in initial trust decisions. Japanese use personal relationships to establish trust because the network that an individual is embedded in is also a social control mechanism that serves to monitor and sanction deviant behaviors. Hence, it reduces the perceived uncertainty in interpersonal transactions. Specifically, informal monitoring mechanisms were instituted in societies with high interdependency (e.g., tight societies) to regulate and sanction deviant actions (Yamagishi & Cook, 1993). Therefore, individuals in these societies can rely on informal monitoring and sanctioning to manage social uncertainty.

In a resource allocation study by Karp and colleagues (1993), groups of Japanese participants were asked to allocate monetary resources to two members at a time (one ingroup and one outgroup member based on their own identification). Ingroup favoritism surfaced when the participants' own monetary gain depended on other participants. However, when there was no resource allocation dependency among group members (i.e., when all players received a fixed amount of payment), the players no longer displayed ingroup favoritism (Karp et al., 1993). This study implies that ingroup favoritism can be fostered by resource interdependence.

It is possible that resource interdependency elevates the reliance members have on each other within their group and violation of members' expectations could potentially influence the welfare of the whole group. Therefore, transgression of normative expectations within a group (i.e., free riding on group's resources) could result in sanctioning actions from other group members. Indeed, Japanese are more willing to punish the free rider even at their own expense, particularly when the free rider is an ingroup member (Shinada & Yamagishi, 2007). These findings shed light on why individuals in Japanese culture trust someone when this person's social group can monitor the person's actions. Furthermore, this explanation has received consistent support from a series of experimental studies (Jin et al., 1996; Jin & Tanaka, 2009; Karp et al., 1993; Yamagishi, Kanazawa, Mashima, & Terai, 2005).

The social expectation that discourages cheating fellow ingroup members might arise from the strong informal institution-based monitoring and sanctioning system that is prevalent not only in Japanese cultures but also deeply rooted in many East Asian cultures. For example, in a tradition of kinship exterminations, tribes and relatives related to the transgressor are executed as a form of punishment in ancient China and Korea. The shared belief in East Asian cultures is that others would be benevolent to ingroup members only when the social monitoring system can be enforced. In sum, institution provides a third-party guarantee independent of the dyadic trust relationship. Such institutional-based trust can take the form of formal institutional elements or informal social monitoring and sanctioning behaviors.

Both formal and informal institution-based trust can be effective for trust development; yet the effectiveness of using different types of trust cues (i.e., different types of trustee characteristics) can differ. Because using the wrong strategies in trust engagement could be costly, it would be important to determine which cues are most effective in predicting the trustworthiness of the trustee *before* any occurrence of trust transgression. Under formal institution, formal rules and orders regulate an individual's behaviors, and the trust violator will be held responsible for his or her own actions. The blame is attributed to the transgressor solely, because we believe the transgressor committed the act of transgression out of his or her own personal volition. Along the same line, in a society where formal institution is more prevalent, it is the trustee's personal choice to behave in a trustworthy or untrustworthy way, and thus the trustee's personal characteristics such as ability, benevolence, and integrity are relevant predictors of the trustee's trustworthiness. However, in a society where informal institutions are more prevalent, people focus on how much the trustee's behaviors are constrained and regulated by the social networks within which he or she is embedded, and thus the nature of the social monitoring and sanctioning system is more useful in predicting the likelihood of transgression. For example, in a recent study conducted by the authors (Kwan & Hong, unpublished data) on trust in an e-commerce setting, Singaporean Chinese found the seller with social monitoring cues (seller that was embedded in a heavily sanctioned selling group) more trustworthy than the seller with individual integrity cues (based on the individual's past selling record). The reverse was true for Caucasian Americans.

The aforementioned research indicates a pattern where different societies tend to use one type of institution (formal or informal) over the other; the type of criteria used to determine trust may also differ. For example, cultures high in tightness (vs. looseness; Gelfand et al., 2011) should use informal (vs. formal) institution as the basis of trust. We will discuss further the implication of culture on institution-based trust after we have discussed the remaining two stages of trust: trust dissolution and trust restoration.

TRUST DISSOLUTION AND TRUST RESTORATION

We have focused our attention thus far on initial trust formation and its relation to group processes. However, trust processes also involve two other possible phases, which are trust dissolution and trust restoration (Kim, Dirks, & Cooper, 2009). Trust dissolution refers to the decline in trust after trust violation, whereas trust restoration is the process whereby the decline in trust rebounds toward stability (Fulmer & Gelfand, 2011; Kim et al., 2009; Rousseau et al., 1998).

The importance of understanding trust dissolution and restoration is two-fold. First, the three types of characteristics—characteristics of the trustor, characteristics of the trustee, and institutional characteristics—that influence trust formation are likely to influence the other stages of trust via the same psychological mechanisms. Second, anticipation of the propensity of trust dissolution and restoration may also have implications for subsequent trust formation. We will elaborate the implications of culture and group processes for these two stages of trust.

Trust Dissolution

Factors that lower one's ongoing trust in another person can be categorized into two separate processes: vigilance and idiosyncratic credits (Fulmer & Gelfand, 2011). Vigilance is the alertness toward the intention of trust violation (Fulmer & Gelfand, 2011). Individuals high on alertness are more likely to notice trust violations and lower their trust accordingly.

Even though high-vigilance trustors are more sensitive to trust violations, trustors do not necessarily react to all transgressions. The decision to react is also based on the trustee's idiosyncratic credit—the accumulation of positive impressions of the trustee. Idiosyncratic credits can be perceived as positive tokens gained from past interactions with the trustee. For example, the trustee has fewer idiosyncratic credits if he or she had a history of transgressions in the past (Doz & Hamel, 1998; Gilliland, Benson, & Schepers, 1998).

While the concepts of vigilance and idiosyncratic credits are often explored as individual variables, they are also influenced by the trustor's culture. In a study of word-deed consistency, researchers found that Indian participants are less vigilant in picking up trust violating cues when the trust violation is performed by the boss toward a subordinate than by an employee toward another same-level employee. By contrast, American participants showed the reverse pattern. These cross-cultural differences were driven in part by the higher power distance in India than in the United States (Friedman, Hong, & Simons, 2009).

Trust Restoration

The need for and the importance of trust have been repeatedly emphasized throughout this chapter. However, trusting behavior also provides a gateway for negative outcomes: trust violations. Trust violations are common, and such transgressions usually lead to both social losses (in the form of psychological betrayal) and economic losses (increased transaction cost). Given the grave impact of trust violation, understanding trust restoration, the turning point where trust stops declining and begins to bounce back to a stable level, is important.

Trust restoration affects trust within two types of relationships: (a) trust restoration within the transgressed relationship, and (b) trust outside the transgressed relationship. Past literature explained how individuals regain trust mainly through the trustee's perspective. According to attribution theory, trust restoration within the transgressed relationship is usually understood through the perceived intention of the transgressor. Specifically, if the violation is unintentional or uncontrollable, trust restoration is easier and faster to achieve (Tomlinson & Mayer, 2009). In fact, a meta-analysis by Fehr, Gelfand, and Nag (2010) showed that the perceived intent and responsibility of the transgressor are negatively related to forgiveness by the trustor.

Trust literature has also explored how the trust violator can regain trust from the trustor. For instance, Fehr and colleagues (2010) note the importance of the trustor's personality. Particularly, individuals with greater propensity to make dispositional (versus situational) attribution are more likely to resist trust restoration in comparison to those with weaker propensity.

Although different trust-building strategies can be used in restoring trust after violation, their effects on trust restoration differ. Trust restoration can mean re-establishing positive trust expectation or overcoming the negative expectations from previous violations. A handful of studies have explored the impact of apology and denial on trust restoration when the trust violator is in a leadership position (Bottom, Gibson, Daniels, & Murnighan, 2002; Ohbuchi, Kameda, & Agarie, 1989; Tomlinson, Dineen, & Lewicki, 2004). In general, verbal apology represents repentance and remorse, and aids in reinstating trust from others. However, some findings also suggested that the denial of trust-violating acts helps restore trust. For example, in a study that looked at trust restoration toward a fictitious political leader who either denied or apologized for a trust violation, the political leader who denied any trust violation received more votes than the leader who apologized for his transgression (Sigal, Hsu, Foodim, & Betman, 1988).

To understand these results better, Kim and colleagues explored the conditions that denial or apology would work better in trust restoration. Their study discovered that, depending on the type of characteristics (e.g., integrity or competency) that is perceived to be important for trust rebuilding in the specific context, different strategies are required (apology versus denial). For example, their results showed that if the violation is a concern of integrity, the trustee would have a higher chance to restore trust through apologizing. Contrarily, if the violation is a concern of competency, the trustee should deny the act of violation for a better chance of trust restoration.

There are also cross-cultural differences in trust restoration processes. In a series of studies, individuals from Eastern cultures favor leaders who have high moral character while individuals in Western cultures favor leaders who have high competency (Cheng et al., 2004). In a recent study (Kwan, Chiu, Leung, & Fu, unpublished data) that examined trust toward leaders, the authors found that compared to the Caucasian American participants, Chinese participants were less likely to forgive the leader if they committed an immoral act. Additionally, apologizing and the denial of the immoral act helped restoration of trust for the Caucasian American participants but not for the Chinese participants. No cultural differences were found when the violation was about the competency of the leader, indicating that the immoral act results were not simply a matter that Chinese people do not restore trust in general.

A seemingly opposite pattern was found in the word-deed inconsistency study that we mentioned earlier (Friedman et al., 2009). Friedman et al. (2009) have shown that Indians' trust toward a boss does not decrease as much as that toward a subordinate target when the target fails to deliver what he or she has agreed (word-deed inconsistency) because the Indian participants do not infer that word-deed inconsistency is a violation of behavioral integrity for the leader as much as for the subordinate. Strikingly, Americans show the opposite response pattern: their trust toward a leader target decreases more than that toward a subordinate target when the target displays word-deed inconsistency. The authors found that these effects are related to the perceived power distance in the two cultures. In a culture with greater power distance such as India, perceivers show deference toward leaders and thus their trust toward them is not undermined by the word-deed inconsistency. By contrast, in a culture with lower power distance such as America, perceivers demand leaders to deliver what they promised more, as they have more resources than the subordinate.

Taken together, although a moral transgression of a leader would create greater damage on the trust toward the leader in Eastern than in Western culture, leaders also enjoy more lenient evaluation when they show word-deed inconsistency. This may be because Eastern participants are less likely to see word-deed inconsistency as a serious violation of promise, and thus the morality of the leaders was not in question.

CULTURE INFLUENCE ON TRUST AND TRUSTWORTHINESS

Thus far, we have discussed how trust development, trust dissolution, and trust restoration can influence our everyday social interactions. We have also pointed out that the trustor's decision is not decided solely by his or her own traits but a combination of the trustor's characteristics and the cues that are present. What type of trusting cues the trustor uses depends, in part, on the culture the trustor belongs to. Specifically, Westerners tend to use the trustee's personal cues (e.g., the trustee's perceived ability, benevolence, and integrity, and even his or her ingroup versus outgroup status) to infer trustworthiness, whereas Easterners tend to use the nature of the trustee's social networks (e.g., whether the groups or networks the trustee's embedded in monitor its members closely for transgression). What is missing in our analysis is the understanding of what specific cultural factors/ dimensions influence one's preference for using different types of trust cues. In the current section, we will use tight versus loose culture and lay beliefs of agency as examples to explain why Easterners and Westerners prefer different cues in deciding trust.

Tight Versus Loose Cultures

Tight cultures are those with stronger norms and lower tolerance of deviant behaviors, while loose cultures are those with weaker norms and higher tolerance of deviant behaviors. In a cross-national study that covered 33 nations, the overall strength of social norms and tolerance of deviant behaviors were measured through a six-item scale that addressed the pervasiveness of social norms in the nation (Gelfand et al., 2011). Gelfand and colleagues (2011) asserted that tight versus loose nations were influenced by distal ecological and historical factors in combination with the sociopolitical institutions of the cultures. Nations that had a history of conflict, natural disaster, and scarce resources are less tolerant of deviant behaviors and they impose stricter social norms. In general, Western nations are "looser" than Eastern nations. On a unidimensional scale, in which a higher score indicates a tighter culture and a lower score a looser culture, America scored 5.1, while Japan and South Korea scored 8.6 and 10.0, respectively. This indicates that America is a relatively loose culture in comparison to Japan and South Korea.

In a loose culture where individuals are more tolerant of transgressions of social norms, social regulation of behaviors by informal monitoring via personal relationships is less prevalent. To avoid being cheated, the trustor will make his or her trust decisions based on personal characteristics of the trustee, such as integrity, morality, and competency. By contrast, in a tight culture where individuals are closely monitored and heavily sanctioned, it is easier to trust someone whose social group is reputable and efficient in monitoring and regulating the behaviors of its members. These differences may explain why Americans from a relatively "loose" culture rely on trustee's personal cues (including the trustee's perceived ability, benevolence, and integrity, and even his or her ingroup versus outgroup status), whereas Chinese and Japanese from a relatively "tight" culture rely on cues of the trustee's social networks. These different bases of trust across cultures can in turn create environments that facilitate specific trust strategies to flourish. For example, in Chinese culture, a relatively tight culture, people derive trust from closely knitted *guanxi* networks; therefore, to increase other's trust in oneself, people are willing to invest resources (time and money) in building quality *guanxi* networks.

Lay Beliefs in Individual Agency Versus Group Agency

Culture is a set of shared knowledge that gives a common frame of reference for people within the society to make sense of reality, conduct their behaviors, and coordinate actions with others (Chiu & Chen, 2004; Hong & Chiu, 2001). In any society, certain knowledge is more widely shared among individuals than in others. Moreover, some ideas are more widely distributed in some cultures than in others; there is a relative difference in individuals' prevalence of some cultural lay beliefs over others across different cultures. Because lay beliefs can influence individuals' perceptions and behaviors, to understand the way culture influences trust, it is necessary to understand the cultural lay beliefs that mediate trust perceptions. The findings that Americans prefer using the trustee's individual characteristics and Asians prefer the trustee's social network information to infer trust may imply that people from these two cultures have different agency beliefs.

Agency refers to the ability to act with an intention to produce a particular result (Soanes & Stevenson, 2008) and the capability to initiate actions that intentionally guide them toward a particular goal (Rychlak, 2008). Agentic social beings are guided by goals and are responsible for the consequences of their own actions regardless of the consequences being positive or negative (Abelson, Dasgupta,

Park, & Banaji, 1998; Hamilton, Sherman, & Lickel, 1998; Yzerbyt, Castano, Leyens, & Paladino, 2000).

People across cultures hold different lay beliefs with regard to whether the individual or group has greater agency. Menon and colleagues (1999) showed that Euro-Americans assume individuals are autonomous agents. As a result, Euro-Americans focus more on individual actors when explaining outcomes. In contrast, Chinese tend to focus more on the groups to which people belong when explaining outcomes. These differences reflect the different degrees of prevalence of the individual agency versus collective agency beliefs in Euro-American and Chinese cultures.

The conception of agency is grounded in historical practices. For example, in China, *lianzuo* was practiced between the Qin Dynasty (221–206 BCE) and the Qing dynasty (1644–1911 CE). *Lianzuo* stipulates that an illegal act of an individual would lead to punishment of not only the individual but also others with whom the actor is associated (individual's tribe and his or her family). These historical practices may have continued in modern East Asian cultures in the practices of collective responsibility attribution (Chao, Zhang, & Chiu, 2008) and monitoring (Karp et al., 1993). By contrast, American culture celebrates the value of individual rights, self-actualization, equality, and liberty. The inclination of Americans to perceive agency as residing within an individual may lead them to use trait-like individual characteristics in determining the trustee's trustworthiness. Asians, on the contrary, perceive that agentic actions are initiated and controlled by the group. Therefore, Asians tend to trust someone who is embedded in a group that can readily monitor and sanction transgressors. In a recent study on trust in e-commerce (Kwan & Hong, unpublished data), the findings revealed that Chinese Singaporeans prefer to use cues that are related to informal institution (social monitoring and sanctioning) when making trust decisions, whereas Caucasian Americans prefer to use personal characteristics (integrity) cues when making trust judgment across different purchase scenarios. Additionally, the lay beliefs of agency (group versus individual) mediate this cross-cultural difference. The results of these recent findings suggest the dynamics of how culture influences trust decisions (in using different trust cues) through individuals' endorsement of different cultural lay beliefs. Furthermore, it is possible that individuals within the culture are aware of the preferred type of character (individual characteristic or institution characteristic) in a trust relationship, which influences how they conduct themselves with social others in their own culture.

We submit that both normative control and certain cultural lay beliefs can influence trust establishment. While tight versus loose norms and cultural lay beliefs are two distinct concepts, they can work together to reinforce a culture-specific trust pattern. It is possible that the loose cultural norm reinforces an individual agency belief, whereas the tight cultural norm reinforces a group agency belief. Importantly, both of these cultural dimensions work in the same direction to support the specific trust strategies that are deemed more applicable within the cultural context.

CONCLUSION

With rapid globalization, trust across cultural boundaries is commonplace. The need to understand trust process becomes crucial in understanding everyday social behaviors. We began the chapter by proposing that trust can be understood through culture and group processes, and these three interrelated concepts reinforce each other in a mutually constituting manner. Furthermore, trust behaviors differ in the stages of formation, dissolution and restoration across cultures, and these differences have direct implications on how social relationships are formed in different cultures. We have also identified three types of characteristics that are commonly used for trust establishment: trustor's characteristics, trustee's characteristics, and the type of institution; and these three characteristics can also influence trust processes at later stages (trust dissolution and trust restoration). With respect to cross-cultural differences, North Americans prefer using individual characteristics and East Asians prefer using social relations as trust-establishing cues. These cultural differences can be related to cultural norms, for example, the looseness or tightness norms of culture; and it can also be explained by agency beliefs. Particularly, we have provided specific evidence that the relative prevalence of individual versus group agency beliefs explained why certain trust cues are more likely to be selected and used across different cultures.

REFERENCES

Abelson, R. P., Dasgupta, N., Park, J., & Banaji, M. R. (1998). Perceptions of the collective other. *Personality and Social Psychology Review*, *2*(4), 243–250.

Arrow, K. J. (1974). *The limits of organization*. New York, NY: Norton.

Barber, B. (1983). *The logic and limits of trust*. New Brunswick, NJ: Rutgers University Press.

Berscheid, E., & Graziano, W. (1979). The initiation of social relationships and interpersonal attraction. In R. L. Burgess & T. L. Huston (Eds.), *Social exchange in developing relationships* (pp. 31–60). New York, NY: Academic Press.

Bohnet, I., & Huck, S. (2004). Repetition and reputation: Implications for trust and trustworthiness when institutions change. *American Economic Review*, *94*(2), 362–366.

Bottom, W. P., Gibson K., Daniels, S. E. & Murnighan, J. K. (2002). When talk is not cheap: Substantive penance and expressions of intent in rebuilding cooperation. *Organization Science*, *13*(5), 497–513.

Brewer, M. B., (1981). Ethnocentrism and its role in interpersonal trust. In M. B. Brewer & B. E. Collins (Eds.), *Scientific inquiry in the social science* (pp. 214–231). San Francisco, CA: Jossey-Bass.

Brewer, M. B. (1999). The psychology of prejudice: Ingroup love or outgroup hate? *Journal of Social Issues*, *55*(3), 429–444.

Brewer, M. B., & Gardner, W. (1996). Who is this "we?" Levels of collective identity and self representations. *Journal of Personality and Social Psychology*, *71*(1), 83–93.

Brewer, M. B., & Yuki, M. (2007). Culture and social identity. In S. Kitayama, & D. Cohen (Eds.), *Handbook of cultural psychology* (pp. 307–322). New York, NY: Guilford Press.

Bromiley, P., & Cummings, L. L. (1995). Transactions costs in organizations with trust. *Research on negotiation in organizations, 5*, 219–250.

Buchan, N. R., Croson, R. T. A., & Dawes, R. M. (2002). Swift neighbors and persistent strangers: A cross-cultural investigation of trust and reciprocity in social exchange. *American Journal of Sociology, 108*(1), 168–206.

Butler, J. K. (1991). Toward understanding and measuring conditions of trust: Evolution of a conditions of trust inventory. *Journal of Management, 17*(3), 643–663.

Butler, J. K., & Cantrell, R. S. (1984). A behavioral decision theory approach to modeling dyadic trust in superiors and subordinates. *Psychological Reports, 55*(1), 19–28.

Chao, M., Zhang, Z., & Chiu, C-Y. (2008). Personal and collective culpability judgment: A functional analysis of East Asian-North American differences. *Journal of Cross-Cultural Psychology, 39*(6), 730–744.

Cheng, B. S., Chou, L. F., Wu, T. Y., Huang, M. P., & Farh, J. L. (2004). Paternalistic leadership and subordinate responses: Establishing a leadership model in Chinese organizations. *Asian Journal of Social Psychology, 7*(1), 89–117.

Chiu, C-Y., & Chen, J. (2004). Symbols and interactions: Application of the CCC model to culture, language, and social identity. In S-H. Ng, C. Candlin, & C-Y. Chiu (Eds.), *Language matters: Communication, culture, and social identity* (pp. 155–182). Hong Kong: City University of Hong Kong Press.

Chua, R. Y-J., & Morris, M. W. (2006). Dynamics of trust in guanxi networks. In Y-R. Chen (Ed.), *National culture and groups* (pp. 95–113). Oxford, UK: Emerald Group.

Chua, R. Y-J., Morris, M. W., & Ingram, P. (2009). Guanxi vs networking: Distinctive configurations of affect- and cognition-based trust in the networks of Chinese vs American managers. *Journal of International Business Studies, 40*, 490–508.

Cook, J., & Wall, T. (1980). New work attitude measures of trust, organizational commitment and personal need non-fulfillment. *Journal of Occupational Psychology, 53*(1), 39–52.

Delhey, J., & Newton, K. (2005). Predicting cross-national levels of social trust: Global pattern or Nordic exceptionalism? *European Sociological Review, 21*(4), 311–327.

Dirks, K. T. (2000). Trust in leadership and team performance: Evidence from NCAA basketball. *Journal of Applied Psychology, 85*(6), 1004–1012.

Doney, P. M., & Cannon., J. P. (1997). An examination of the nature of trust in buyer-seller relationships. *Journal of Marketing, 61*(2), 35–51.

Doz, Y. L., & Hamel, G. (1998). *Alliance advantage: The art of creating value through partnering*. Boston, MA: Harvard Business School Press.

Dunn, J. R., & Schweitzer, M. E. (2005). Feeling and believing: The influence of emotion on trust. *Journal of Personality and Social Psychology, 88*(5), 736–748.

Erikson, E. H. (1956). The problem of ego identity. *Journal of the American Psychoanalytic Association, 4*, 56–121.

Fahr, R., & Irlenbusch, B. (2008). Identifying personality traits to enhance trust between organisations: An experimental approach. *Managerial and Decision Economics, 29*(6), 469–487.

Fehr, R., Gelfand, M. J., & Nag, M. (2010). The road to forgiveness: A meta-analytic synthesis of its situational and dispositional correlates. *Psychological Bulletin, 136*(5), 894–914.

Ferrin, D. L., & Gillespie, N. (2010). Trust differences across national-societal cultures: Much to do, or much ado about nothing? In M. N. Saunders, D. Skinner, G.

Dietz, N. Gillespie, & R. J. Lewicki (Eds.), *Organizational trust: A cultural perspective* (pp. 42–86). Cambridge, UK: Cambridge University Press.

Foddy, M., Platow, M. J., & Yamagishi, T. (2009). Group-based trust in strangers: The role of stereotypes and expectations. *Psychological Science, 20*(4), 419–422.

Friedman, R., Simons, T. L., & Hong, Y-Y. (2009, June). *Culture's impact on behavioral integrity: When is a promise not a promise?* Paper presented at the 22nd Annual International Association for Conflict Management Conference, Kyoto, Japan.

Frost, T., Stimpson, D. V., & Maughan, M. C. (1978). Some correlates of trust. *Journal of Psychology, 99*(1), 103.

Fukuyama, F. (1995). *Trust: The social virtues and the creation of prosperity*. New York, NY: Free Press.

Fulmer, C. A., & Gelfand, M. J. (2011). How do I trust thee? Dynamic trust patterns and their individual and social contextual determinants. In K. Sycara, M. J. Gelfand, & A. Abbe (Eds.), *Modeling inter-cultural collaboration and negotiation* (pp. 97–131). New York, NY: Springer.

Gabarro, J. J. (1978). The development of trust, influence, and expectations. In A. G. Athos & J. J. Gabarro (Eds.), *Interpersonal behavior: Communication and understanding in relationships* (pp. 290–303). Englewood Cliffs, NJ: Prentice-Hall.

Gefen, D. (2002). Reflections on the dimensions of trust and trustworthiness among online consumers. *ACM SIGMIS Database, 33*(3), 38–53.

Gelfand, M. J., Raver, J.L., Nishii, L., Leslie, L. M., Lun, J., Lim, B. C., &... Yamaguchi, S. (2011). Differences between tight and loose cultures: A 33-nation study. *Science, 332*(6033), 1100–1104.

Gilliland, S. W., Benson, L., & Schepers, D. H. (1998). A rejection threshold in justice evaluations: Effects on judgment and decision-making. *Organizational Behavior and Human Decision Processes, 76*(2), 113–131.

Golembiewski, R., & McConkie, M. (1975). The centrality of interpersonal trust in group process. In C. L. Cooper (Ed.), *Theories of group processes* (pp. 131–185). New York, NY: John Wiley.

Greene, G. (1973). *The ministry of fear: An entertainment.* London, UK: Penguin Press.

Hamilton, D. L., Sherman, S. J., & Lickel, B. (1998). Perceiving social groups: The importance of the entitativity continuum. In C. Sedikides, J. Schopler, & C. A. Insko (Eds.), *Intergroup cognition and intergroup behavior* (pp. 47–74). Mahwah, NJ: Erlbaum.

Hardin, R. (2002). *Trust and trustworthiness*. New York, NY: Russell Sage Foundation.

Hart, K. M., Capps, H. R., Cangemi, J. P., & Caillouet, L. M. (1986). Exploring organizational trust and its multiple dimensions: A case study of general motors. *Organization Development Journal, 4*(2), 31–39.

Hayashi, F. (1982). Tobin's marginal q and average q: A neoclassical interpretation. *Econometrica, 50*(1), 213–224.

Hofstede, G. (1980). Culture and organizations. *International Studies of Management and Organization, 10*(4), 15–41.

Hong, Y-Y., & Chiu, C-Y. (2001). Toward a paradigm shift: From cross-cultural differences in social cognition to social-cognitive mediation of cultural differences. *Social Cognition, 19*(3), 181–196.

Inglehart, R. F., Basanez, M., & Moreno. A. (1998). *Human values and beliefs: A cross cultural sourcebook*. Ann Arbor, MI: University of Michigan Press.

Jarvenpaa, S. L., & Tractinsky, N. (1999). Consumer trust in an Internet store: A cross-cultural validation. *Journal of Computer-Mediated Communication, 5*(2), 34–57.

Jin, A., & Tanaka, T. (2009). When is trust reciprocated? *Japanese Journal of Psychology, 80*(2), 123–130.
Jin, N., Yamagishi, T., & Kiyonari, T. (1996). Bilateral dependancy and the minimal group paradigm. *Japanese Journal of Psychology, 67*(2), 77–85.
Karp, D., Jin, N., Yamagishi, T., & Shinotsuka, H. (1993). Raising the minimum in the minimal group paradigm. *Japanese Journal of Experimental Social Psychology, 32*(3), 231–240.
Kee, H. W., & Knox, R. E. (1970). Conceptual and methodological considerations in the study of trust and suspicion. *Journal of Conflict Resolution, 14*(3), 357–366.
Kim, P. H., Dirks, K. T., & Cooper, C. D. (2009). The repair of trust: A dynamic bilateral perspective and multilevel conceptualization. *Academy of Management Review, 34*(3), 401–422.
Kim, P. H., Ferrin, D. L., Cooper, C. D., & Dirks, K. T. (2004). Removing the shadow of suspicion: The effects of apology versus denial for repairing competence- versus integrity-based trust violations. *Journal of Applied Psychology, 89*(1), 104–118.
King, A. Y-C. (1991). Kuan-hsi and network building: A sociological interpretation. *Daedalus, 120*(2), 63–84.
Kosfeld, M., Heinrichs, M., Zak, P. J., Fischbacher, U., & Fehr, E. (2005). Oxytocin increases trust in humans. *Nature, 435*(7042), 673–676.
Lane, C., & Bachmann, R. (1996). The social constitution of trust: Supplier relations in Britain and Germany. *Organization Studies, 17*(3), 365–395.
Lewis, J. D., & Weigert, A. J. (1985). Trust as a social reality. *Social Forces, 63*(4), 967–85.
Lin, N. (2001). Guanxi: A conceptual analysis. In A. So, N. Lin, & D. Poston (Eds.), *The Chinese triangle of mainland, Taiwan, and Hong Kong comparative institutional analysis* (pp. 153–166). Westport, CT: Greenwood.
Mayer, R. C., Davis, J. H., & Schoorman, F. D. (1995). An integrative model of organizational trust. *Academy of Management Review, 20*(3), 709–734.
McAllister, D. J. (1995). Affection- and cognition-based trust as foundations for interpersonal trust. *Academy of Management Journal, 38*(1), 24–59.
McKnight, D. H., & Chervany, N. L. (2002). What trust means in e-commerce customer relationships: An interdisciplinary conceptual typology. *International Journal of Electronic Commerce, 62*, 35–59.
McKnight, D. H., Cummings, L. L., & Chervany, N. L. (1998). Initial trust formation in new organizational relationships. *Academy of Management Review, 23*(3), 473–490.
Menon, T., Morris, M. W., Chiu, C-Y., & Hong, Y-Y. (1999). Culture and the construal of agency: Attribution to individual versus group dispositions. *Journal of Personality and Social Psychology, 76*(5), 701–717.
Meyerson, D., Weick, K. E., & Kramer, R. M. (1996). Swift trust and temporary groups. In R. M. Kramer & T. R. Tyler (Eds.), *Trust in organizations: Frontiers of theory and research* (pp.166–195). Thousand Oaks, CA: Sage.
Nelson, R. R., & Winter, S. G. (1982). *An evolutionary theory of economic change.* Cambridge, MA: Harvard University Press.
Ohbuchi, K., Kameda, M., & Agarie, N. (1989). Apology as aggression control: Its role in mediating appraisal of and response to harm. *Journal of Personality and Social Psychology, 56*(2), 219–227.
Powell, W. W. (1996). Trust-based forms of governance. In R. M. Kramer & T. R. Tyler (Eds.), *Trust in organizations: Frontiers of theory and research* (pp. 51–67). Thousand Oaks, CA: Sage.

Rotter, J. B. (1967). A new scale for the measurement of interpersonal trust. *Journal of Personality, 35*(4), 651–665.

Rotter, J. B. (1971). Generalized expectancies for interpersonal trust. *American Psychologist, 26*(5), 443–452.

Rotter, J. B. (1980). Interpersonal trust, trustworthiness and gullibility. *American Psychologist, 35*(1), 1–7.

Rousseau, D. M., Sitkin, S. B., Burt, R. S., & Camerer, C. (1998). Not so different after all: A cross-discipline view of trust. *Academy of Management Review, 23*(3), 393–404.

Rychlak, J. (2008). *Agency: Encyclopedia of psychology*. Washington, DC: American Psychological Association.

Schlosser, A. E., White, T. B., & Lloyd, S. M. (2006). Converting website visitors into buyers: How website investment increases consumer trusting beliefs and online purchase intentions. *Journal of Marketing, 70*(2), 133–148.

Shapiro, S. P. (1987). The social control of impersonal trust. *American Journal of Sociology, 93*(3), 623–58.

Shinada, M., & Yamagishi, T. (2007). Punishing free riders: Direct and indirect promotion of cooperation. *Evolution and Human Behavior, 29*(2), 147.

Sigal, J., Hsu, L., Foodim S. & Betman, J. (1988). Factors affecting perceptions of political candidates accused of sexual and financial misconduct. *Political Psychology, 9*(2), 273–280.

Sitkin, S. B., & Roth, N. L. (1993). Explaining the limited effectiveness of legalistic remedies for trust/distrust. *Organization Science, 4*(3), 367–392.

Soanes, C., & Stevenson, A. (Eds.). (2008). *Concise Oxford English dictionary*. Oxford, UK: Oxford University Press.

Stewart, K. J. (2003). Trust transfer on the world wide web. *Organization Science, 14*(1), 5–17.

Su, C., Sirgy, M. J., & Littlefield, J. E. (2003). Is guanxi orientation bad, ethically speaking? A study of Chinese enterprises. *Journal of Business Ethics, 44*, 303–312.

Tajfel, H., Billig, M. G., Bundy, R. P., & Flament, C. (1971). Social categorization and intergroup behavior. *European Journal of Social Psychology, 1*(2), 149–178.

Tanis, M., & Postmes, T. (2005). A social identity approach to trust: Interpersonal perception, group membership and trusting behaviour. *European Journal of Social Psychology, 35*, 413–424.

Turner, J. C., Brown, R. J., & Tajfel, H. H. (1979). Social comparison and group interest ingroup favouritism. *European Journal of Social Psychology, 9*(2), 187–204.

Tomlinson, E. C., Dineen, B. R., & Lewicki, R. J. (2004). The road to reconciliation: Antecedents of victim willingness to reconcile following a broken promise. *Journal of Management, 30*(2), 165–187.

Tomlinson, E. C. & Mayer, R. C. (2009). The role of causal attribution dimensions in trust repair. *Academy of Management Review, 34*(1), 85–104.

Wasko, M. M., & Faraj, S. (2000). It is what one does: Why people participate and help others in electronic communities of practice. *Journal of Strategic Information Systems, 9*(2), 155–173.

White, T. B. (2005). Consumer trust and advice acceptance: The moderating roles of benevolence, expertise, and negative emotions. *Journal of Consumer Psychology, 15*(2), 141–148.

Yamagishi, T. (1999). Generalized reciprocity and culture of collectivism. *Organizational Science, 33*(1), 24–34.

Yamagishi, T. (2011). *Trust: The evolutionary game of mind and society*. Tokyo, Japan: Springer Press.

Yamagishi, T., & Cook, K. S. (1993). Generalized exchange and social dilemmas. *Social Psychology Quarterly, 56*(4), 235–248.

Yamagishi, T., Jin, N., & Miller, A. S. (1998). Collectivism and in-group bias. *Asian Journal of Social Psychology, 1*(3), 315–328.

Yamagishi, T., Kanazawa, S., Mashima, R., & Terai, S. (2005). Separating trust from cooperation in a dynamic relationship: Prisoner's dilemma with variable dependence. *Rationality and Society, 17*(3), 275–308.

Yamagishi, T., & Yamagishi, M. (1994). Trust and commitment in the United States and Japan. *Motivation and Emotion, 18*(2), 129–166.

Yuki, M. (2003). Intergroup comparison versus intragroup relationships: A cross-cultural examination of social identity theory in North American and East Asian cultural contexts. *Social Psychology Quarterly, 66*(2), 166–183.

Yuki, M., Maddux, W. W., Brewer, M. B., & Takemura, K. (2005). Cross-cultural differences in relationship- and group-based trust. *Personality and Social Psychology Bulletin, 31*(1), 48–62.

Yzerbyt, V., Castano, E., Leyens, J. P., & Paladino, M. P. (2000). The primacy of the ingroup: The interplay of entitativity and identification. *European Review of Social Psychology, 11*(1), 257–295.

Zucker, L. G. (1977). The role of institutionalization in cultural persistence. *American Sociological Review, 42*(5), 726–743.

Zucker, L. G. (1983). Organizations as Institutions. In S. B. Bacharach (Ed.), *Research in the sociology of organizations* (pp. 1–47). Greenwich, CT: JAI Press.

Zucker, L. G. (1986). Production of trust: Institutional sources of economic structure. In L. L. Cummings & B. M. Staw (Eds), *Research in organizational behavior* (pp. 1840–1920). Greenwich, CT: JAI Press.

Zucker, L. G. (1987). Institutional theories of organization. *Annual Review of Sociology, 13*, 443–464.

PART TWO

Culture and Intragroup Processes

6

Outlier Nation

The Cultural Psychology of American Workways

JEFFREY SANCHEZ-BURKS AND ERIC LUIS UHLMANN*

Blessed is he who has found his work; let him ask no other blessedness.

—THOMAS CARLYLE

America is an outlier nation. This is true in terms of US individualism, religious pluralism, and political organization (Greeley, 1991; Henrich, Heine, & Norenzayan, 2010; Inglehart & Welzel, 2005; Kingdon, 1999; Lipset, 1996; Schuck & Wilson, 2008; Tocqueville, 1840/1990). Of particular interest to the present chapter, America is also an outlier in terms of a unique cognitive, emotional, and behavioral approach to work and workplace interactions. This highly distinctive orientation toward work has important implications for the dynamics of cross-cultural groups.

Scholars, for over a century and from a variety of fields, have commented on America's unique work values (Lipset, 1996; Tocqueville, 1840/1990; Trompenaars & Hampden-Turner, 1997; Weber, 1904/1958). However, only in the past decade has there been rigorous experimental evidence able to support, elaborate, and articulate the boundary conditions of prior theorizing (Sanchez-Burks, 2002, 2005; Uhlmann, Poehlman, Tannenbaum, & Bargh, 2011). This chapter reviews the core themes of this experimental research and its implications for the functioning of cross-cultural work groups.

Together this research reveals three important facets of American exceptionalism that help explain how, when, and why Americans appear as an outlier vis-à-vis other cultural groups. Specifically, America is an outlier among other nations in terms of (a) its impersonal approach to work, (b) valorization of work as an end unto itself, and (c) faith in individual merit, all of which reflect the imprint left by the founding

*Author contribution was equal; author order is alphabetical.

religious communities. American norms of workplace professionalism are organized around a unique approach to workplace relations, referred to as Protestant Relational Ideology (Sanchez-Burks, 2002), that idealizes unemotional and impersonal workplace interactions. In contrast to many other cultures, where work serves a utilitarian function (e.g., earning money to support one's family), American culture valorizes working beyond material reasons (Uhlmann, Poehlman, & Bargh, 2009; Uhlmann et al., 2011). Finally, America is an outlier in its commitment to individualism and faith in meritocracy, which is manifested in both moral judgments and human resource policies (Biernat, Vescio, & Theno, 1996; Hampden-Turner & Trompenaars, 1993; McCoy & Major, 2007; Quinn & Crocker, 1999). The body of experimental evidence we review in this chapter complements findings from other fields and points to exciting directions for future research on cultural divides.

THE LEGACY OF AMERICA'S PROTESTANT HERITAGE

America's heritage as a nation founded by Calvinist Puritans has set it on a different cultural trajectory than other countries. Extremely devout Protestants, often persecuted for their beliefs in their home countries, left Europe for the New World and exerted a profound influence on the evolution of American culture (Fukuyama, 1995; Lipset, 1996; Norris & Inglehart, 2004). In Europe, the Protestant Reformation was associated with enormous economic growth that has continued to covary with the secularization of historically Protestant countries (Inglehart, 1997; Inglehart & Welzel, 2005; Norris & Inglehart, 2004). Due to the founding influence of the ascetic Protestant settlers, however, the United States remains deeply religious. Even today, seven in ten believe in the devil, and more than half are religious fundamentalists who believe that the world is at most 10,000 years old (Baker, 2005; Dawkins, 2006; Harris, 2006; Lipset, 1996; Sheler, 2006). In addition, Americans exhibit values on issues relevant to religious morality (e.g., suicide, homosexuality, and abortion) more similar to impoverished traditional societies than other developed Western democracies (Inglehart, 1997).

The unique elements of the Protestant faith as practiced and passed down by the founding communities of the United States help explain the highly distinctive aspects of the American approach to work described in this chapter. Protestant Relational Ideology stems from influential theologian John Calvin's conviction that a focus on emotions and relationships while working distracts from treating one's work as a moral calling (Sanchez-Burks, 2002). The American valorization of work done beyond material reasons stems from the notion—once explicit in Calvinist Protestantism and now implicit in contemporary American culture—that work represents a path to divine salvation (Uhlmann et al., 2011). Finally, the Protestant emphasis on one-on-one personal relationships with God and view of hard-earned success as a sign of divine favor contributed to the American ethic of individual merit (Hampden-Turner & Trompenaars, 1993; Inglehart & Welzel, 2005; Weber, 1904/1958). Cultures outside the United States do not appear to exhibit these implicit norms and values to the same degree as Americans.

One reason Protestantism had such a strong effect on the culture of the United States relative to other communities exposed to Protestantism is a lack of early ideological competition. In Europe, Protestantism had to compete with centuries of history and deeply entrenched preexisting religions. In contrast, the early American colonists were disproportionately Calvinist Protestants. Furthermore, they were comparatively likely to emigrate with their wives and children, and largely exterminated native peoples through war and disease (Zinn, 1980). In addition, the early Protestants specifically desired a psychological and ideological break from the old world, viewing themselves as founders of a "shining city on a hill" (Collins, 1999, p. 65) that would lead and inspire other nations by example (Gelertner, 2007; Morone, 2003; Uhlmann, 2012). Although these early immigrants were eventually joined by many non-Protestants who came to the future United States seeking economic opportunities, they exerted a founding influence on American culture that has yet to dissipate. Such an influence is analogous to founder effects in evolutionary biology, in which early members of a species have a disproportionate genetic influence on descendants (Mayr, 1954). However, it manifests itself at a moral and cultural level rather than a genetic one.

Importantly, the influence of America's Protestant heritage is often implicit in nature. Both cross-cultural researchers and experts on implicit social cognition have argued that cultural influences are frequently unconscious and automatic (Banaji, 2001; Cohen, 1997; Nisbett, Peng, Choi, & Norenzayan, 2001; Rudman, 2004; Sperber, 1985). This occurs because people have difficulty rejecting culturally learned associations when it comes to their spontaneous, automatic reactions (Banaji, 2001; Greenwald & Banaji, 1995). Although Americans' work morality can manifest itself in explicitly stated beliefs and values, it can also be activated implicitly and shape judgments and behaviors outside of conscious awareness. Thus, although Americans who have been raised in strong traditions of Protestant Calvinism are especially likely to evidence some of the judgments and behaviors we identify (Sanchez-Burks, 2002), even non-Protestant and less religious Americans often display an implicit orientation toward work consistent with their American heritage (Lenski, 1961; Sanchez-Burks, 2005; Uhlmann et al., 2009, 2011).

PROTESTANT RELATIONAL IDEOLOGY

Protestant Relational Ideology (PRI) refers to the explicit or implicit belief that a focus on emotions and relationships while at work is inappropriate (Sanchez-Burks, 2005). In contrast to the then prevailing sentiment that earthly work is demeaning, early Protestant theology elevated work to a moral calling with spiritual significance akin to prayer (McNeil, 1954). Rather than a debasing activity best left to one's social inferiors, work became a moral imperative done for the glory of God (Weber, 1904/1958). Consistent with this Protestant work ethic, influential theologian John Calvin argued that individuals ought to maintain an unsentimental impersonality while working. In his view, a focus on affect and relationships in work contexts "is evil because it detracts from the active performance of God's will in a calling" (Bendix, 1977, p. 62). Outside of work contexts, however, socio-emotionality was not only allowed but even encouraged in early Protestant communities (Daniels, 1995; Fischer, 1989; Weber, 1947).

Although one might expect that such seemingly quaint beliefs would have faded away by modern times, today's Americans (especially those raised in a tradition of Calvinist Protestantism) continue to implicitly uphold an ethic of impersonal work relations (Sanchez-Burks, 2005). Further consistent with traditional Protestant norms, outside of work contexts individuals with a high degree of exposure to Protestantism remain as sensitive as others to interpersonal concerns (Sanchez-Burks, 2002).

For instance, experimental studies show that PRI powerfully shapes the extent to which employees implicitly focus on and respond to emotional information while at work. One particularly insightful investigation found that Americans raised in traditions of Calvinism are less attentive to emotional cues when work, rather than nonwork, contexts are subtly primed (Sanchez-Burks, 2002). Self-identified individuals raised in a Calvinist Protestant tradition (i.e., Methodist and Presbyterian, two specifically Calvinist denominations within Protestantism well represented in the contemporary United States) or a non-Protestant tradition (e.g., Catholic, Atheist, Buddhist) were recruited for the experiment. Participants were then either primed for work contexts (by having them wear business attire and discuss a business school case) or a social context (by having them wear Hawaiian shirts and play a card game). Subsequently all participants completed an emotional Stroop task (Kitayama & Howard, 1994) assessing the extent to which they spontaneously attended to the emotional tone of words. Consistent with PRI, Calvinist Protestants were significantly less likely than non-Protestants to implicitly attend to emotional information in the work prime condition, but not in the nonwork condition.

American Calvinist Protestants' nonverbal behavior further indicates they are less relationally attentive to others at work than are members of other faiths and cultures (Sanchez-Burks, 2002). Research on behavioral mirroring and subconscious mimicry demonstrates people spontaneously adopt the body posture and mannerisms of interaction partners (Chartrand & Bargh, 1999). Sanchez-Burks (2002) primed American Calvinists (Methodists and Presbyterians) and non-Protestants with either a work context (by having them dress for a job interview) or a social context (by having them dress for the beach) and examined their nonverbal behaviors. Calvinist Protestants were less likely than non-Protestants to nonconsciously mimic the confederate's nonverbal behavior, but only when they had first been primed with a work context. When a social, nonwork context was primed, Calvinist Protestants were just as likely as non-Protestants to engage in nonverbal mimicry.

An inattention to relational and emotional cues among individuals high in exposure to PRI can lead to decrements in the job performance of coworkers raised in other cultural and religious traditions. In a field study, Latino American and Anglo American employees (the latter of whom presumably had a greater degree of prior exposure to Calvinist Protestantism) participated in a professional interview (Sanchez-Burks, Bartel, & Blount, 2009). The interviewer (actually a research confederate) either subtly mimicked the participant's nonverbal behavior or did not. In the absence of the positive relational cues provided by the nonverbal mimicry, Latino Americans suffered from anxiety and decrements in interview performance. In contrast—and consistent with their comparatively greater degree of exposure to PRI—the performance of Anglo Americans was unaffected by whether their interaction partner engaged in nonverbal mimicry.

Related research finds that Anglo Americans are less than half as likely as Mexicans and Mexican Americans to remember relationship-relevant information from a workgroup meeting (Sanchez-Burks, Nisbett, & Ybarra, 2000). In contrast, there were no cultural differences in memory for the task-relevant information the group was discussing. Consistent with their greater degree of exposure to PRI, Anglo Americans seemed to focus entirely on the task at hand and were virtually oblivious to the interpersonal cues so carefully monitored by Mexicans and Mexican Americans.

Importantly, although some subgroups within the United States conform to PRI to a greater extent than others (e.g., Calvinist Protestants vs. Catholics, Anglo-Americans vs. Mexican-Americans), PRI is also a phenomenon that characterizes American society more broadly. Thus, when comparing cross-nationally, American workplace norms are far less likely to emphasize interpersonal and relational concerns than are workplaces norms in other cultures. Uhlmann, Heaphy, Ashford, Zhu, and Sanchez-Burks (in press) asked a multicultural sample of MBA students based in the United States to describe the workspaces of a professional and unprofessional employee. "Unprofessional" workplaces were significantly more likely to include objects referencing personal relationships (e.g., family photos). Moreover, the more time participants had spent in the United States, the more likely they were to define workplace professionalism in a manner consistent with PRI.

Further experimental research demonstrates that in workplace contexts (but not in social contexts) Americans adopt a direct communication style that deemphasizes socioemotional cues such as tone of voice. In contrast, East Asian cultures are characterized by an indirect communication style both inside and outside the workplace (Sanchez-Burks et al., 2003). American, Korean, and Chinese managers were provided with negative performance feedback couched in face-saving indirect cues and asked to interpret the meaning of the message. The feedback read, "Overall the evaluation indicates your strengths are in communication skills, anticipating events, and creativity. The other areas are not as strong as these—some are poor, but it's difficult to evaluate those areas. Good job!" In one condition, participants were told the feedback came from an annual performance evaluation and in the other condition that it come from one friend giving another friend feedback on the results of the latter's personality test. Korean and Chinese managers correctly inferred the feedback was actually quite negative, regardless of whether they believed it came from a work supervisor or a friend. In the friend condition, Americans likewise inferred the communicator was trying to soften objectively harsh feedback. However, in the work evaluation condition, Americans ignored the face-saving cues and incorrectly concluded the performance evaluation was relatively positive.

In an increasingly multicultural world, many individuals are raised in more than one cultural tradition. Do bicultural Americans exhibit implicit work values and norms consistent with American culture or with the other culture to which they have been exposed? Consistent with the dynamic constructivist model of culture (Hong, Chui, & Kung, 1997; Hong, Morris, Chiu & Benet-Martinez, 2000), this appears to depend on which cultural identity is made salient. Sanchez-Burks et al. (2003) primed bicultural Thai Americans with either their Thai or American identity and then examined their tendency to rely on direct versus indirect workplace communication. Participants' attention to socioemotional cues showed remarkable plasticity, such that they relied on indirect workplace communication when primed with their Thai identity, and direct communication when primed with their American identity. This indicates the activation of different cultural identities can lead to corresponding shifts in the tendency to conform to PRI.

Another manifestation of PRI is that Americans tend to be unrealistic about the consequences of relational conflict in workgroups, believing that such interpersonal conflict is compatible with healthy team functioning (Sanchez-Burks et al., 2008). This belief is in fact inaccurate: Relational conflict is detrimental to the performance of both American and non-American work groups (see De Dreu & Weingart, 2003, for a meta-analytic review). Regardless, Americans were more than twice as willing as East Asians to join a team likely to experience relational conflict. Thus, Americans, due to a culturally specific relational ideology, may be more likely to optimistically join work teams that are destined for interpersonal conflict and failure.

Of course, there are many cases in which one has little option other than to be part of a work group fraught with relational conflict. In such circumstances, PRI may be conducive to group success. Specifically, PRI may facilitate cooperation and collaboration between individuals who dislike each other personally. When emotions and interpersonal concerns are minimized at work, individuals with a history of negative feelings can more effectively function as part of the same team. Thus, there are likely situations in which the benefits of PRI greatly outweigh its drawbacks.

The cultural imprint of PRI extends into the very fabric of Americans' social and professional lives. For example, Americans are much less likely than non-Americans to socialize outside of work with people they know from their job (Kacperczyk, Baker, & Sanchez-Burks, 2011; Mor Barak, Findler, & Wind, 2003; Morris, Podolny, & Ariel, 2000). Further evidence for the real-world relevance of the PRI construct comes from the effects of intercultural training on performance in actual cross-cultural teams. American MBA students about to be assigned to work in either China or Chile were exposed to informational instruction and experiential exercises designed to increase their awareness of cultural differences in relational sensitivity (Sanchez-Burks, Nisbett, Lee, & Ybarra, 2007). Americans exposed to cultural training based on PRI experienced less awkward interactions with their Chilean and Chinese peers and more positive affective experiences during their foreign assignment. Participants trained in PRI were also more effective at eliciting positive responses from contacts in their host company and in obtaining information necessary for success on their projects. Remarkably, training based on PRI was significantly more effective at improving cross-cultural teamwork than training using the extensively validated Cultural Assimilator (CA) approach (Bhawuk, 2001). In the CA, the most widely studied training method in intercultural awareness, participants are presented with descriptions of workplace incidents and receive feedback on whether their subjective interpretations correspond with the modal response of people from another culture. Future research should examine whether increasing awareness of cultural differences in relational sensitivity can be effectively incorporated as a standard aspect of the CA approach.

Achieving such increased awareness is an important goal, given that cultural differences in relational orientation pose a significant challenge for the functioning of cross-cultural work groups. Non-Americans may be offended by their American colleagues' seeming lack of interest in a personal relationship with them, and their work performance may suffer as a result of such negative cues. Conversely, American employees may perceive non-American coworkers as overly focused on emotions and personal issues, and even as unprofessional. Miscommunication and misunderstandings can likewise result from Americans' focus on direct workplace communication versus the more indirect communication found in East Asian, Latin American, Middle Eastern, and Mediterranean cultures. Finally, the inaccurate American belief that interpersonal conflict is not harmful to team effectiveness is problematic in the face of not only cross-cultural differences in folk theories of conflict but of human nature as well.

THE AMERICAN VALORIZATION OF WORK

As noted earlier, an important source of America's distinctive work morality is the link drawn in Protestant theology between hard work and divine salvation (McNeil, 1954; Tocqueville, 1840/1990; Weber, 1904/1958). John Calvin and other early Protestant thinkers viewed work as a spiritual calling, believing that individuals who achieved material success through productive labor enjoyed the grace of God. Although early Calvinist theological perspectives emphasized predestination, in practice American Protestant communities allowed a person to signal that he or she was likely "chosen" by virtue of his or her labor and accomplishments on Earth. Thus, for all intents and purposes Protestant cultures prescribed hard work as a moral imperative. Indeed, the early Puritans even spoke of the "Gospel of work" (Gelertner, 2007, p. 61).

Traveling through the United States in the 1800s, Alexis de Tocqueville (1840/1990) marveled at Americans' long work hours and high work productivity. Consistent with this traditional Protestant work ethic, today's Americans spend more time at work than the citizens of most other economically developed democracies (Friedman, 2008; Linstedt, 2002; Wessel, 2003). One can contrast this state of affairs with comparatively negative attitudes toward work in Western Europe, where "postmaterialist" values emphasizing the importance of leisure and quality of life are more common (Inglehart, 1997; Inglehart & Welzel, 2005).

Negative cultural attitudes toward work in France are reflected institutionally in a legally mandated 35-hour work week, 5–8 weeks of paid vacation a year, retirement between the ages of 50 and 60 years with most of one's salary, generous unemployment benefits, and frequent labor strikes (Bonoli, 2000; Nadeau & Barlow, 2004; Schludi, 2005). Indeed, France provides an excellent comparison with the United States because it is an economically developed Western democracy with only modest Protestant influence.

Why do Americans spend so much time at work, despite a level of economic development conducive to reduced work hours and increased leisure time? The Protestant ethic moralizes and valorizes work done for noninstrumental reasons. A "good person" is expected to work hard and for long hours even when he or she has no material need to do so. Other cultures that strongly value work tend to do so for more practical reasons, such as the need in poor countries to meet basic survival needs (Inglehart, 1997; Inglehart & Welzel, 2005). In contrast, Protestantism views work as something that should be pursued for its own sake. Reflecting the implicit legacy of this ideology, empirical studies show Americans intuitively valorize individuals who work for no material reasons (Uhlmann et al., 2009). For example, in one study, Americans were found to be more likely than Mexicans to praise a young postal worker who continued working after winning the lottery.

Much prior theorizing suggests the Protestant work ethic has become secularized in modern times (e.g., Fischer, 1989; Weber, 1904/1958). However, recent evidence indicates that, for contemporary Americans, work continues to be implicitly linked to religious cognition (Uhlmann et al., 2011). American, Canadian, Argentinian, German, and Italian participants completed a scrambled-sentences puzzle (Bargh, Chen, & Burrows, 1996; Srull & Wyer, 1979) containing words related to either divine salvation (e.g., heaven, saved) or neutral concepts. Reflecting the Protestant link between work and divine salvation, only American participants responded to the implicit salvation prime by working harder on a subsequent task. A multistep funneled debriefing (Bargh & Chartrand, 2000) indicated that participants were not aware their work behavior was influenced by the salvation primes.

Because work is so heavily moralized in America, and sexuality is moralized in many cultures, American work and sex attitudes are functionally intertwined (Uhlmann et al., 2009). The implicit link between work and sex morality in American cognition has its roots in basic pressures for cognitive consistency (Festinger, 1957; Greenwald et al., 2002; Heider, 1958). To the extent that work is associated with moral purity, and sexual restraint is associated with moral purity, hard work and sexual restraint should in turn be linked with one another. As a result, priming traditional work values should activate traditional sexually conservative morality and vice versa. To test this hypothesis, Uhlmann et al. (2011) primed bicultural Asian Americans with either their Asian cultural identity or their American cultural identity and then with either words related to work or with neutral concepts. As expected, bicultural Asian Americans responded to an implicit work prime by endorsing a restrictive dress code, but only when their American identity was salient.

Reflecting the implicit influence of Protestant beliefs on the judgments and actions of contemporary Americans, not only devout American Protestants but even non-Protestant and less religious Americans exhibited these effects, which we have referred to as manifestations of implicit Puritanism (Uhlmann et al., 2009, 2011). In other words, even non-Protestant Americans praised a lottery winner who kept working for no material reasons, responded to an implicit salvation prime by working harder, and implicitly linked work and sex morality. It is noteworthy that although the differences are small, American Calvinist Protestants are more likely to act in line with Protestant Relational Ideology than are American Catholics (Sanchez-Burks, 2002). However, the Sanchez-Burks (2002) studies on PRI recruited Presbyterians and Methodists, the two central Calvinist denominations among American Protestants. In contrast, research on implicit Puritanism has relied on convenience samples varying enormously in choice of faith, Protestant denomination, and level of religiosity. It seems likely that although Americans in general implicitly conform to Protestant values, individuals raised in a strong tradition of Calvinist Protestantism (e.g., devout Presbyterians and Methodists) are especially likely to do so.

Although the valorization of work in America is conducive to high productivity, it can lead to conflict with members of cultures who view work in more instrumental terms. As noted earlier, the French greatly valorize leisure and quality of life, values reflected in labor laws that mandate 5–8 weeks of paid vacation per year and norms and regulations discouraging long work hours. This can cause resentment and conflict in cross-national collaborations between American and French colleagues. The Americans tend to resent the periodic absences of French team members at seemingly critical points in the project and can even perceive them as outright lazy (Beyene & Delong, 2008). The French, in contrast, may deeply resent the higher salaries paid to counterparts in the US branch of the company based on the latter's greater number of work hours (Beyene & Delong, 2008).

THE ETHIC OF INDIVIDUAL MERIT

We now turn to a third major way in which America's Protestant heritage has shaped American work morality: the distinct emphasis placed on individual merit. One of the roots of American individualism is the Protestant emphasis on a personal relationship with God. At the same time, the Calvinist Protestant notion of earthly reward and punishment contributes to the American belief in meritocracy.

Cross-national surveys highlight American individualism, even relative to other Western cultures (Hampden-Turner & Trompenaars, 1993; Henrich et al., 2010). A history of open frontiers, and persistently high levels of geographic mobility and immigration, contribute to this exceptional individualism (Kitayama, Ishii, Imada, Takemura, & Ramaswamy, 2006; Nisbett et al., 2001; Oishi & Kisling, 2009). Another important factor is America's continued devotion to the Protestant religion. Catholicism has traditionally focused on the role of the Church in mediating between individual believers and God. In contrast, Protestantism advocates an individual relationship with God not dependent on any religious collective. Martin Luther wrote that each individual is "a perfectly free lord, subject to none" (as quoted in Sampson, 2000, p. 1427). This theological emphasis derived in part from the Protestant reformers' disgust with the corrupt selling of indulgences and other perceived heresies of the Catholic Church (Inglehart & Welzel, 2005; Weber, 1904/1958). Even today, higher levels of individualism are observed in historically Protestant countries than in historically Catholic countries (Hampden-Turner & Trompenaars, 1993; Hofstede, 1980, 2001; Trompenaars & Hampden-Turner, 1997).

The Calvinist notion of earthly reward and punishment further contributes to America's uniquely strong faith in individual merit. Catholicism promises only heavenly rewards, often consigning the virtuous to material deprivation in this world. In contrast, John Calvin argued that hard-earned success is evidence of divine favor. Thus, achieving material wealth is a sign the person is one of the select few chosen by God to go to heaven.

In keeping with traditional Protestant beliefs, 96% of Americans believe the principle that "with hard work...anyone can succeed" should be taught to children (Baker, 2005). More so than members of other wealthy countries, Americans are convinced people generally get what they deserve in life (Trompenaars & Hampden-Turner, 1997). This belief in merit is reflected in attributions for success and failure. Only a third of Americans believe that when a person fails in life it is mainly due to forces outside his or her control, but two-thirds of Germans, French, and Italians make such external attributions (Schuck & Wilson, 2008).

Americans widely view their country as a land of equal opportunity where hard work is rewarded with professional success. However, this is a shared belief unsupported by the empirical evidence. International comparisons indicate the United States actually has less income mobility than Canada and most of Western Europe (Burtless & Haskins, 2008; DeParle, 2012). Nevertheless, over half of Americans, as opposed to only one-third of Spaniards and the French, consider high levels of economic competition important in order to motivate people to work hard and achieve (Schuck & Wilson, 2008). Americans are further more likely than citizens of other countries to believe remuneration and continued employment should be based entirely on job performance (Lipset, 1996). In one international survey, 77% of American managers believed that an incompetent employee should be fired immediately (Hampden-Turner & Trompenaars, 1993). In contrast, only 42% their British counterparts favored this option. The figures were even lower for the other comparison countries: a mere 31% of German managers, 27% of Italian managers, 26% of French managers, and 19% of Korean managers considered it appropriate to terminate an unsatisfactory employee after 15 years of loyal service to the company (see also Trompenaars & Hampden-Turner, 1997).

Cultural differences in a belief in personal merit are reflected in striking discrepant regulations and practices regarding firing employees (Asselin, 2000; Nadeau & Barlow, 2004). In France and the United Kingdom, for example, terminating an employee requires an independent tribunal with the burden of proof resting on the organization. Rather than fire an incompetent or otherwise undesirable employee in this manner, many firms prefer to place the employee in show positions with little to no power or responsibility (a practice called "cupboarding" or "putting them in the cupboard"; in France, there is even a popular comedic movie by this name). In many cases, the organization's goal is simply to limit the damage caused by an ineffective employee. In others, the hope is the employee will "get the message" that he or she is not wanted and leave voluntarily.

Although it can increase the motivation to achieve positive personal and organizational outcomes, the Protestant notion that God rewards the good with earthly prosperity and punishes wrongdoers with material suffering also has the effect of promoting prejudice against those less fortunate (Jost & Banaji, 1994; Katz & Hass, 1988; Sidanius & Pratto, 1999). In experimental studies, priming Protestant work values led Americans to endorse negative stereotypes of Black Americans (Biernat et al., 1996; Katz & Hass, 1988), led obese women to feel negatively about themselves (Quinn & Crocker, 1999), and led to increased psychological rationalizations for the unfair treatment of low-status individuals (McCoy & Major, 2007).

The kind of behaviors encouraged and elicited by Protestant work values such as individualism and a belief in merit have likely contributed to the structure of the economy of the United States, which is characterized by free competition, skewed distribution of wealth, and weak social welfare. Thus, we again find American work morality is a double-edged sword. The ethic of individual merit facilitates free competition by acting against nepotism and corruption. However, it also promotes prejudice against individuals who fail to obtain employment as well as low-status groups such as the obese and racial minorities.

Different beliefs about the importance and relevance of individual merit can lead to conflict in multicultural workplaces. For example, personnel selection practices that are perceived as "efficient" from an American point of view may not be from other cultural perspectives. Indeed, removing noncontributing or otherwise unqualified group members may be perceived as disloyal and inappropriate in some cultural contexts. For example, Mexican bank employees are more likely than American bank employees to report they would include an incompetent friend in their work group (Zurcher, Meadow, & Zurcher, 1965). Tellingly, rather than perceive themselves as choosing friendship over moral principles, Mexicans saw themselves as upholding a different moral principle. When asked what the study was about, Americans perceived it as a survey about honesty. In contrast, Mexicans construed it as a survey about loyalty. Disagreements in cross-cultural teams can result when members of different cultures form such profoundly different construals of the same situation or decision.

FUTURE DIRECTIONS FOR RESEARCH ON AMERICAN WORK MORALITY

The research described in this chapter complements prior work in sociology, political science, and related disciplines by providing the first experimental evidence of the influence of Calvinist Protestantism on the judgments and behaviors of contemporary Americans and its implications for cross-cultural collaborations. At the same time, these studies raise unanswered questions that point to exciting future research directions.

Similarities and Differences Between Protestant Relational Ideology and Implicit Puritanism

PRI and implicit Puritanism can both be broadly described as ideologies, defined as a "body of doctrine, myth, belief, etc., that guides an individual, social movement, institution, class, or large group" (Ideology, n.d.; Kennedy, 1979). In addition, PRI and implicit Puritanism share deep roots in Calvinist Protestant theology (Weber, 1904/1958) and the tendency for individuals' implicit cognitions to strongly reflect traditional cultural values (Banaji, 2001; Greenwald & Banaji, 1995).

At the same time, however, there are important differences in focus and underlying psychological processes between implicit Puritanism and PRI. Research on implicit Puritanism seeks to explain why Americans valorize hard work as an end unto itself. PRI, by contrast, deals with the process of working well, prescribing impersonal and unemotional workplace relationships. Moreover, while implicit Puritanism is based in a person's sense of what is morally right versus wrong, PRI deals with notions of what is normatively appropriate and professional. Thus, while Americans view individuals who lack a strong work ethic as bad people (Uhlmann et al., 2009), employees who frequently refer to their family while at work are seen as unprofessional rather than immoral (Uhlmann et al., in press).

There are a number of means by which this theoretical distinction between norms regarding workplace professionalism and personal moral values could be tested more directly. We hypothesize that Americans high in self-monitoring (Snyder, 1974; Snyder & Gangestad, 2000) or for whom normative concerns are temporarily salient (Epley & Gilovich, 1999) should be more likely to conform to the impersonal work relations prescribed by PRI. In contrast, Americans' moral judgments of individuals who fail to uphold the traditional work ethic should be more strongly influenced by manipulations of moral outrage (Tetlock et al., 2007) than by concerns about what is normatively appropriate.

How Secular Are American Work Values?

Most prior theorizing suggests that once deeply religious Protestant ideals have, over time, become secularized in American culture (e.g., Fischer, 1989; Weber, 1904/1958). However, that implicitly priming divine salvation leads both religious and nonreligious Americans to work harder (Uhlmann et al., 2011) suggests that at least some historically Protestant beliefs remain nonsecular in that they are still linked to religious concepts. If American work morality were wholly secular, activating thoughts about salvation would have no effect on contemporary Americans' work behavior (or at the very least, it would not influence the work behavior of nonreligious Americans).

Future research should examine whether US individualism and belief in meritocracy are secularized vestiges of Calvinist Protestantism or continue to be linked to and shaped by religious ideas from American cultural history. We predict that nonconsciously priming religious concepts (e.g., God, heaven, saved) will lead Americans (but not members of comparison cultures) to behave in an individualistic manner and seek to uphold the merit principle in their decisions regarding whom to include in their work groups.

It also has yet to be examined whether PRI is a secular or nonsecular ideology. The original theory proposed by Sanchez-Burks (2002, 2005) suggests that impersonal work norms in the United States no longer have the same religious overtones they held in Puritan New England. However, the salvation prime effects on American work behavior observed by Uhlmann et al. (2011) raise the possibility that priming religious concepts can likewise influence Americans' standards for workplace professionalism. For example, nonconsciously activating words like God, heaven, and saved might reduce the extent to which Americans engage in nonwork referencing while at their job.

Exposure to, or Identification With, American Culture?

Another key question for future research is whether a person must actively self-identify as an American to be influenced by American work values or whether exposure to and knowledge of American culture is in some cases sufficient. This issue is particularly relevant given the global presence of American media. Is this sort of indirect cultural exposure implicitly Americanizing the world, or are cultures retaining their own work values and relational styles? Consider, for example, that despite generous government subsidies for French films, the average French person watches more American movies than French movies (Lange, 1998). Is a French person with a high degree of exposure to American media, but who does not self-identify with America in any way, any more likely to favor impersonal work relations and moralize work as an end unto itself? This question holds implications for the extent to which citizens of an increasingly global world are coming to implicitly adopt the norms and values present in American work groups.

Consider also the effects of cultural identity primes on the judgments and behaviors of bicultural individuals. Bicultural Thai-Americans utilize an impersonal workplace communication style when their American identity is salient, but not when their Thai identity is salient (Sanchez-Burks et al., 2003). Also, bicultural Asian Americans exhibit implicit Puritanism only when their American identity is primed (Uhlmann et al., 2011). Is it truly necessary to identify with two cultures at once to show such effects, or is mere knowledge of American work values sufficient to lead individuals to respond to primes associated with US culture in this way? For example, would a French person well aware of the influence of the Protestant work ethic on the contemporary United States respond to a subliminally flashed American flag by implicitly conforming to the norms of American work groups? This remains an open question for future empirical inquiry.

Individual Differences in Implicit Work Cognitions

Research on PRI and implicit Puritanism has relied primarily on experimental designs such as the prime-to-behavior paradigm popularized by Bargh and his colleagues (Bargh & Chartrand, 1999). This use of experimental manipulations complements scholarship from other fields (Lipset, 1996; Tocqueville, 1840/1990; Trompenaars & Hampden-Turner, 1997; Weber, 1904/1958) by allowing for confident causal inferences about the influence of Protestant work values on contemporary Americans. However, individual differences measures of implicit attitudes and beliefs have also been developed, among these the Implicit Association Test (IAT; Greenwald, McGhee, & Schwartz, 1998), evaluative priming tasks (Fazio, Sanbonmatsu, Powell, & Kardes, 1986), and Affect Misattribution Procedure (AMP; Payne, Cheng, Govorun, & Stewart, 2005). Such implicit measures could be profitably employed to assess individual differences in implicit cognitions related to work.

For example, the extent to which Americans implicitly associate work with divine salvation on the IAT may moderate the extent to which they respond to nonconsciously primed words related to salvation with improved performance on collaborative work tasks. One could additionally examine whether a person's degree of exposure to US culture predicts the extent to which he or she associates work with religious concepts, as well as potential longitudinal changes in implicit associations with work among recent immigrants to the United States. Of particular interest is whether there exists a critical period for the absorption of not only explicit (Cheung, Chudek, & Heine, 2011) but also implicit cultural values.

Implicit attitudes toward work could also be treated as an outcome measure in experimental studies. Although originally thought to be stable and difficult to change, empirical investigations indicate that automatic associations are in fact highly plastic, shifting readily in response to situational factors (Blair, 2002). For example, being deprived of nicotine causes smokers to exhibit more favorable associations with cigarettes (Sherman, Rose, Koch, Presson, & Chassin, 2003), and hungry participants exhibit more positive automatic evaluations with food-related words (Seibt, Häfner, & Deutsch, 2007). This raises the possibility that, for Americans, implicit associations with emotionality may shift between work and nonwork contexts. Consistent with PRI, Americans may automatically associate emotion words with "inappropriate" on an Implicit Association Test completed at work, but not when the IAT is completed at home (Yoshida, Peach, Zanna, & Spencer, 2012). Members of cultures not steeped in a tradition of Calvinist Protestantism should be less likely to exhibit workplace-specific negative associations with emotional expression.

Regional Variability and Subcultural Enclaves Within the United States

Empirical studies on PRI and implicit Puritanism have utilized samples of American students and lay adults collected primarily (although not exclusively) in the Midwest, New England, Los Angeles, and New York areas. Some of these studies relied on student samples at Yale University, the University of Southern California, and the University of Michigan, who come from diverse regions of the United States. However, future research should more systematically compare the extent to which the work values and norms of Americans from different regions of the United States are influenced by traditional Protestant beliefs. Southern norms of interpersonal warmth and graciousness, for example, could reflect a reduced influence of Calvinist Protestantism brought about by geographic distance from New England. Notably, significant regional differences in individualism are observed within the United States (Vandello & Cohen, 1999) as well as Japan (Kitayama et al., 2006), raising the possibility of similar regional variability in PRI and implicit Puritanism.

At the same time, subcultural enclaves within the United States may promote values and norms that counteract or even replace traditional American work morality. The extent to which individuals raised in such environments exhibit implicit workways consistent with the broader culture, with those of their local subculture, or (perhaps most interestingly) alternate between the two (Hong et al., 1997, 2000; Sanchez-Burks et al., 2003; Uhlmann et al., 2011) has yet to be fully addressed.

Workplace Relational Ideologies of Historically Protestant But Now Secular Cultures

Also worthy of further investigation is the implicit work values of historically Protestant cultures that have since secularized. Implicit Puritanism effects (e.g., the tendency to respond to an implicit salvation prime by working harder; Uhlmann et al., 2011) are readily observed in the United States, but not Germany, Canada, and the United Kingdom, suggesting that Protestant cultural roots are not sufficient to produce such effects. Although cultural uniqueness is practically impossible to establish definitively (Norenzayan & Heine, 2005), this does raise the possibility that implicit Puritanism is a uniquely American phenomenon.

To provide the most conservative test possible of the hypothesis that exposure to Calvinist Protestantism promotes impersonal work relations, the empirical studies that first established the existence of PRI compared subgroups within the United States (i.e., American Calvinist Protestants vs. American Catholics; Sanchez-Burks, 2002). Subsequent cross-national PRI studies have relied on comparisons between the United States and non-Protestant cultures (e.g., Mexico, Korea, China, and Thailand). Future cross-cultural comparisons should examine whether members of historically Protestant, but now secular cultures (e.g., Germany and the United Kingdom), endorse impersonal workplace relations. It remains an empirical question whether workgroups including both Americans and Germans will exhibit clashing or compatible relational norms.

Psychological Underpinnings of the Asian Work Ethic

Finally, future research should seek to better understand the implicit roots of Asian workways. With regard to our earlier distinction between valuing hard work and norms of workplace professionalism, Americans and East Asians most clearly differ in the latter. East Asians with exposure to US culture are less likely to approve of nonwork referencing in professional contexts (Uhlmann et al., in press), and Americans aware of cultural differences in workplace relational norms are more successful in East Asian business environments (Sanchez-Burks et al., 2007). Moreover, bicultural Asian Americans are more likely to rely on direct and decontextualized communication when their American identity is salient (Sanchez-Burks et al., 2003). Thus, individuals from the United States and East Asian countries display starkly different professional norms with regard to socio-emotional displays at work.

At the same time, many East Asian cultures are characterized by a strong work ethic. This is clear from demographic data on number of hours worked per year by the typical employee (Friedman, 2008; Linstedt, 2002; Wessel, 2003). Of particular interest, the Japanese work only slightly fewer hours per year than Americans do (Miller, 2010). Anecdotal evidence, such as the famous "sleep capsule hotels" used by exhausted businessmen to avoid the commute home, further attest to the Japanese work ethic (Tabuchi, 2010). Indeed, *karoshi*, or "death by overwork," is legally recognized as a cause of death in Japan, and 40% of all Japanese workers are concerned they might become victims of *karoshi* (Rowley, 2009).

It is very interesting to consider potential cross-cultural differences in the reasons for lengthy working hours. Suggesting noteworthy differences in implicit work values, East Asians do not exhibit the implicit link between work and sex morality so clearly evident among Americans (Uhlmann et al., 2011). We speculate that while US work morality finds its ultimate roots in America's religious heritage, Asian cultural mores regarding work find their roots in more secular concerns such as familial duty and the fear of social exclusion at one's organization. If so, then priming religious concepts should lead Americans (but not East Asians) to contribute more work to collaborative projects and praise a lottery winner who continues to work at a menial job. Conversely, activating concepts related to duty and/or concerns about social rejection should increase East Asians' commitment to hard work, but not that of Americans. In addition, bicultural Asian Americans should be more likely to exhibit an association between work and salvation on an Implicit Association Test when their American identity is salient compared to when their Asian identity is salient. These and many other as-yet-untested hypotheses have the potential to shed considerable new light on the psychological underpinnings of the cultural moralization of work.

CONCLUSION

America's exceptional cultural orientation toward work reflects the profound imprint left by the founding religious communities (Weber, 1904/1958). Unique aspects of the Protestant faith, in particular Calvinist beliefs, help account for impersonal American work norms (Sanchez-Burks, 2005), the valorization of noninstrumental work in America (Uhlmann et al., 2009, 2011), and the American ethic of individual merit (Inglehart & Welzel, 2005; McCoy & Major, 2007). The influence of traditional Protestant beliefs on the judgments and actions of contemporary Americans is often implicit in nature. As a result, Protestantism shapes the work-related behaviors not only of devout American Protestants but also of less religious and non-Protestant Americans. These highly distinctive norms, values, and behaviors related to work represent unique challenges for cross-cultural groups.

REFERENCES

Asselin, G. (2000). *Au contraire: Figuring out the French*. Boston, MA: Intercultural Press.

Baker, W. (2005). *America's crisis of values*. Princeton, NJ: Princeton University Press.

Banaji, M. R. (2001). Implicit attitudes can be measured. In H. L. Roedeger, III, J. S. Nairne, I. Neath, & A. Surprenant (Eds.), *The nature of remembering: Essays in honor of Robert G. Crowder* (pp.117–150). Washington, DC: American Psychological Association.

Bargh, J. A., & Chartrand, T. L. (1999). The unbearable automaticity of being. *American Psychologist, 54*, 462–479.

Bargh, J. A., & Chartrand, T. L. (2000). The mind in the middle: A practical guide to priming and automaticity research. In H. T. Reis, Jr., & C. M. Judd (Eds.), *Handbook of research methods in social and personality psychology* (pp. 253–285). New York, NY: Cambridge University Press.

Bargh, J. A., Chen, M., & Burrows, L. (1996). Automaticity of social behavior: Direct effects of trait construct and stereotype activation on action. *Journal of Personality and Social Psychology, 71*, 230–244.

Bendix, R. (1977). *Max Weber: An intellectual portrait.* Berkeley: University of California Press.

Beyene, T. L., & Delong, T. J. (2008). Managing a global team: Greg James at Sun Microsystems, Inc. *Harvard Business School Case 9-409-003.*

Biernat, M., Vescio, T. K., & Theno, S. A. (1996). Violating American values: A "value congruence" approach to understanding outgroup attitudes. *Journal of Experimental Social Psychology, 32*, 387–410.

Blair, I. V. (2002). The malleability of automatic stereotypes and prejudice. *Personality and Social Psychology Review, 6*, 242–261.

Bonoli, G. (2000). *The politics of pension reform: Institutions and policy change in Western Europe.* Cambridge, UK: Cambridge University Press.

Bhawuk, D. P. (2001). Evolution of culture assimilators: Toward theory-based assimilators. *International Journal of Intercultural Relations, 25*, 141–163.

Burtless G., & Haskins, R. (2008). Inequality, economic mobility, and social policy. In P, H. Schuck & J. Q. Wilson (Eds). *Understanding America: The anatomy of an exceptional nation* (pp. 495–538). New York, NY: Public Affairs.

Chartrand, T. L. & Bargh, J. A. (1999). The chameleon effect: The perception-behavior link and social interaction. *Journal of Personality and Social Psychology, 76*, 893–910.

Cheung, B. Y., Chudek, M., & Heine, S. J. (2011). Evidence for a sensitive window for acculturation. Younger immigrants report acculturating at a faster rate. *Psychological Science, 22*, 147–152.

Cohen, D. (1997). Ifs and thens in cultural psychology. In R. S. Wyer, Jr. (Ed.), *The automaticity of everyday life: Advances in social cognition* (Vol. 10, pp. 1–61). Mahwah, NJ: Erlbaum.

Collins, O. (Ed.). (1999). *Speeches that changed the world.* Louisville, KY. Westminster John Knox Press.

Daniels, B. C. (1995). *Puritans at play.* New York, NY: St. Martin's Griffin.

Dawkins, R. (2006). *The God delusion.* Boston, MA: Houghton Mifflin.

De Dreu, C. K. W., & Weingart, L. R. (2003). Task versus relationship conflict and team effectiveness: A meta-analysis. *Journal of Applied Psychology, 88*, 741–749.

DeParle, J. (2012). Harder for Americans to rise from lower rungs. New York Times. Retrieved from http://www.nytimes.com/2012/01/05/us/harder-for-americans-to-rise-from-lower-rungs.html?_r=1&hp

Epley, N., & Gilovich, T. (1999). Just going along: Nonconscious priming and conformity to social pressure. *Journal of Experimental Social Psychology, 35*, 578–589.

Fazio, R. H., Sanbonmatsu, D. M., Powell, M. C., & Kardes, F. R. (1986). On the automatic activation of attitudes. *Journal of Personality and Social Psychology, 50*, 229–238.

Festinger, L. (1957). *A theory of cognitive dissonance.* Stanford, CA: Stanford University Press.

Fischer, D. (1989). *Albion's seed: Four British folkways in America.* New York, NY: Oxford University Press.

Friedman, B. M. (2008). The economic system. In P. H. Schuck & J. Q. Wilson (Eds.), *Understanding America: The anatomy of an exceptional nation* (pp. 87–120). New York, NY: Public Affairs.

Fukuyama, F. (1995). *Trust: The social virtues and the creation of prosperity.* New York, NY: Simon & Schuster.

Gelertner, D. (2007). *Americanism: The fourth great western religion.* New York, NY: Doubleday.

Greeley, A. M. (1991). American exceptionalism: The religious phenomenon. In B. E. Scafer (Ed.), *Is America different? A new look at American exceptionalism* (pp. 94–115). New York, NY: Oxford University Press.

Greenwald, A. G., & Banaji, M. R. (1995). Implicit social cognition: Attitudes, self-esteem, and stereotypes. *Psychological Review, 102*, 4–27.

Greenwald, A. G., Banaji, M. R., Rudman, L. A., Farnham, S. D., Nosek, B. A., & Mellot, D. S. (2002). A unified theory of implicit attitudes, beliefs, self-esteem and self-concept. *Psychological Review, 109*, 3–25.

Greenwald, A. G., McGhee, D. E., & Schwartz, J. L. K. (1998). Measuring individual differences in implicit cognition: The implicit association test. *Journal of Personality and Social Psychology, 74*, 1464–1480.

Hampden-Turner, C., & Trompenaars, F. (1993). *The seven cultures of capitalism: Value systems for creating wealth in the United States, Britain, Japan, Germany, France, Sweden, and the Netherlands.* New York, NY: Doubleday.

Harris, S. (2006). *Letter to a Christian nation.* New York, NY: Knopf.

Heider, F. (1958). *The psychology of interpersonal relations.* New York, NY: Wiley.

Henrich, J., Heine, S. J., & Norenzayan, A. (2010). The weirdest people in the world? *Behavioral and Brain Sciences, 33,* 61–83.

Hofstede, G. (1980). *Culture's consequences: International differences in work-related values.* Beverly Hills, CA: Sage.

Hofstede, G. (2001). *Culture's consequences: Comparing values, behaviors, institutions, and organizations across nations.* Thousand Oaks, CA: Sage.

Hong, Y., Chiu, C., & Kung, T. (1997). Bringing culture out in front: Effects of cultural meaning system activation on social cognition. In K. Leung, Y. Kashima, U. Kim, & S. Yamaguchi (Eds.), *Progress in Asian social psychology* (pp. 135–146). New York, NY: Wiley.

Hong, Y., Morris, M., Chiu, C., & Benet-Martinez, V. (2000). Multicultural minds: A dynamic constructivist approach to culture and cognition. *American Psychologist, 55,* 709–729.

Ideology. (n.d.). In *Dictionary.com.* Retrieved from http://dictionary.reference.com/browse/ideology.

Inglehart, R. (1997). *Modernization and postmodernization: Cultural, economic, and political change in 43 societies.* Princeton, NJ: Princeton University Press.

Inglehart, R., & Welzel, C. (2005). *Modernization, cultural change, and democracy: The human development sequence.* Cambridge, MA: Cambridge University Press.

Jost, J. T., & Banaji, M. R. (1994). The role of stereotyping in system-justification and the production of false consciousness. *British Journal of Social Psychology, 33,* 1–27.

Kacperczyk, A., Baker, W., & Sanchez-Burks (2011). *Social isolation in the workplace: A Cross-cultural and longitudinal analysis.* Unpublished raw data.

Katz, I., & Hass, R.G. (1988). Racial ambivalence and American value conflict: Correlational and priming studies of dual cognitive structures. *Journal of Personality and Social Psychology, 55,* 893–905.

Kennedy, E. (1979). "Ideology" from Destutt De Tracy to Marx. *Journal of the History of Ideas, 40,* 353–368.

Kingdon, J.W. (1999). *America the unusual.* Boston, MA: Worth.

Kitayama, S., & Howard, S. (1994). Affective regulation of perception and comprehension: Amplification and semantic priming. In P. M. Niedenthal & S. Kitayama (Eds.), *The heart's eye: Emotional influences in perception and attention* (pp. 41–65). New York, NY: Academic Press.

Kitayama, S., Ishii, K., Imada, T., Takemura, K., & Ramaswamy, J. (2006). Voluntary settlement and the spirit of independence: Evidence from Japan's "northern frontier". *Journal of Personality and Social Psychology, 91,* 369–384.

Lange, A. (1998). The trends of the film market in France. *Print Publications of the European Audiovisual Observatory.* Retrieved from http://www.obs.coe.int/oea_publ/eurocine/00001439.html

Lenski, G. (1961). *The religious factor: A sociological study of religion's impact on politics, economics, and family life.* New York, NY: Doubleday Anchor.

Linstedt, S. (2002, October 14). Wonder where your time goes? You probably spent it at work. *Buffalo News,* p. B7.

Lipset, S. M. (1996). *American exceptionalism: A double edged sword.* New York, NY: W. W. Norton.

Mayr, E. (1954). Change of genetic environment and evolution. In J. Huxley, A. C. Hardy, & E. B. Ford (Eds.), *Evolution as a process* (pp. 157–180). London, UK: Allen & Unwin.

McCoy, S. K., & Major, B. (2007). Priming meritocracy and the psychological justification of inequality. *Journal of Experimental Social Psychology, 43*, 341–351.

McNeil, J. T. (1954). *The history and character of Calvinism.* New York, NY: Oxford University Press.

Miller, G. E. (2010, October 12th). The U.S. is the most overworked developed nation in the World—when do we draw the line? *20somethingfinance.com*. Retrieved from http://20somethingfinance.com/american-hours-worked-productivity-vacation/

Mor Barak, M. E., Findler, L., & Wind, L. H. (2003). Cross-cultural aspects of diversity and well-being in the workplace: An international perspective. *Journal of Social Work Research and Evaluation, 4*, 49–73.

Morone, J.A. (2003). *Hellfire nation: The politics of sin in American history.* New Haven, CT: Yale University Press.

Morris, M. W., Podolny, J. M., & Ariel, S. (2000). Missing relations: Incorporating relational constructs into models of culture. In C. P. Earley & H. Singh (Eds.), *Innovations in International and Cross-Cultural Management* (52–89). Thousand Oaks, CA, Sage.

Nadeau, J., & Barlow, J. (2004). *Sixty million Frenchmen can't be wrong: What makes the French so French?* London, UK: Robson Books.

Nisbett, R. E., Peng, K., Choi, I., & Norenzayan, A. (2001). Culture and systems of thought: Holistic vs. analytic cognition. *Psychological Review, 108*, 291–310.

Norenzayan, A., & Heine, S. J. (2005). Psychological universals: What are they and how can we know? *Psychological Bulletin, 135*, 763–784.

Norris, P., & Inglehart, R. (2004). *Sacred and secular: Religion and politics worldwide.* New York, NY: Cambridge University Press.

Oishi, S., & Kisling, J. (2009). The mutual constitution of residential mobility and individualism. In R. S. Wyer, Jr., C-Y. Chiu, Y. Y. Hong, and S. Shavitt (Eds.), *Understanding culture: Theory, research, and application* (pp. 223–238). New York, NY: Psychology Press.

Payne, B. K., Cheng, C. M., Govorun, O., & Stewart, B. (2005). An inkblot for attitudes: Affect misattribution as implicit measurement. *Journal of Personality and Social Psychology, 89*, 277–293.

Quinn, D. M., & Crocker, J. (1999). When ideology hurts: Effects of belief in the Protestant ethic and feeling overweight on the psychological well-being of women. *Journal of Personality and Social Psychology, 77*, 402–414.

Rowley, I. (2009, June 9). Anxious Japanese are working themselves to death. *Businessweek.com*. Retrieved from http://www.businessweek.com/globalbiz/content/jun2009/gb2009069_718282.htm

Rudman, L. A. (2004). Sources of implicit attitudes. *Current Directions in Psychological Science, 13*, 80–83.

Tabuchi, H. (2010, January 1). For some in Japan, home is a tiny plastic bunk. *New York Times*. Retrieved from http://www.nytimes.com/2010/01/02/business/global/02capsule.html

Sampson, E. E. (2000). Reinterpreting individualism and collectivism: Their religious roots and monologic versus dialogic person-other relationship. *American Psychologist, 55*, 1425–1432.

Sanchez-Burks, J. (2002). Protestant Relational Ideology and (in) attention to relational cues in work settings. *Journal of Personality and Social Psychology, 83*, 919–929.

Sanchez-Burks, J. (2005). Protestant Relational Ideology: The cognitive underpinnings and organizational implications of an American anomaly. *Research in Organizational Behavior, 26*, 265–305.

Sanchez-Burks, J., Bartel, C., & Blount, S. (2009). Fluidity and performance in intercultural workplace interactions: The role of behavioral mirroring and social sensitivity. *Journal of Applied Psychology, 94*, 216–223.

Sanchez-Burks, J., Lee, F., Choi, I., Nisbett, R., Zhao, S., & Jasook, K. (2003). Conversing across cultures: East-West communication styles in work and non-work contexts. *Journal of Personality and Social Psychology, 85*, 363–372.

Sanchez-Burks, J., Neuman, E., Ybarra, O., Kopelman, S., Goh, K., & Park, H. (2008). Cultural folk wisdom about relationship conflict. *Negotiation and Conflict Management Research*, 1, 55–78.

Sanchez-Burks, J., Nisbett, R., Lee, F., & Ybarra, O. (2007). Intercultural training based on a theory of relational ideology. *Basic and Applied Social Psychology, 29*, 257–268.

Sanchez-Burks, J., Nisbett, R., & Ybarra, O. (2000). Cultural styles, relational schemas and prejudice against outgroups. *Journal of Personality and Social Psychology, 79*, 174–189.

Schludi, M. (2005). *The reform of Bismarckian pension systems: A comparison of pension politics in Austria, France, Germany, Italy and Sweden.* Amsterdam, The Netherlands: Amsterdam University Press.

Schuck, P. H., & Wilson, J. Q. (2008). Looking back. In P. H. Schuck & J. Q. Wilson (Eds.), *Understanding America: The anatomy of an exceptional nation* (pp. 627–643). New York, NY: Public Affairs.

Seibt, B., Häfner, M., & Deutsch, R. (2007). Prepared to eat: How immediate affective and motivational responses to food cues are influenced by food deprivation. *European Journal of Social Psychology, 37*, 359–379.

Sheler, J. S. (2006). The lure of the prophetic world [Special issue]. *U.S. News & World Report: Mysteries of faith: The prophets*, 4–5.

Sherman, S. J., Rose, J. S., Koch, K., Presson, C. C., & Chassin, L. (2003). Implicit and explicit attitudes toward cigarette smoking: The effects of context and motivation. *Journal of Social and Clinical Psychology, 22*, 13–39.

Sidanius, J., & Pratto, F. (1999). *Social dominance: An intergroup theory of social hierarchy and oppression.* New York, NY: Cambridge University Press.

Snyder, M. (1974). Self-monitoring of expressive behavior. *Journal of Personality and Social Psychology, 30*, 526–37.

Snyder, M. & Gangestad, S. (2000). Self-monitoring: Appraisal and reappraisal. *Psychological Bulletin, 126*, 530–55.

Sperber, D. (1985). Anthropology and psychology: Towards an epidemiology of representations. *Man, 20*, 73–89.

Srull, T. K., & Wyer, R. S. (1979). The role of category accessibility in the interpretation of information about persons: Some determinants and implications. *Journal of Personality and Social Psychology, 37*, 1660–1672.

Tetlock, P. E., Visser, P., Singh, R., Polifroni, M., Elson, B., Mazzocco, P., & Rescober, P. (2007). People as intuitive prosecutors: The impact of social control motives on attributions of responsibility. *Journal of Experimental Social Psychology, 43*, 195–209.

Tocqueville, A. D. (1990). *Democracy in America.* New York, NY: Vintage Books. (original work published 1840)

Trompenaars, F., & Hampden-Turner, C. (1997). *Riding the waves of culture: Understanding diversity in global business*. New York, NY: McGraw-Hill.

Uhlmann, E. L. (2012). American psychological isolationism. *Review of General Psychology, 16*, 381–390.

Uhlmann, E.L., Heaphy, E., Ashford, S.J., Zhu, L., & Sanchez-Burks, J. (in press). Acting professional: An exploration of culturally bounded norms against non-work role referencing. *Journal of Organizational Behavior.* DOI: 10.1002/job.1874.

Uhlmann, E. L., Poehlman, T. A., & Bargh, J. A. (2009). American moral exceptionalism. In J. T. Jost, A. C. Kay, & H. Thorisdottir (Eds.), *Social and psychological bases of ideology and system justification* (pp. 27–52). New York, NY: Oxford University Press.

Uhlmann, E. L., Poehlman, T. A., Tannenbaum, D., & Bargh, J. A. (2011). Implicit Puritanism in American moral cognition. *Journal of Experimental Social Psychology, 47*, 312–320.

Vandello, J. A., & Cohen, D. (1999). Patterns of individualism and collectivism across the United States. *Journal of Personality and Social Psychology, 77*, 279–292.

Weber, M. (1947). *The theory of social and economic organization.* New York: Free Press.

Weber, M. (1958). *The Protestant ethic and the spirit of capitalism.* New York, NY: Charles Scribner's Sons. (original work published 1904)

Wessel, H. (2003, November 16). A 40-hour workweek just a dream to many. *Houston Chronicle*, Houston, Texas.

Yoshida, E., Peach, J. M., Zanna, M. P., & Spencer, S. J. (2012). Not all automatic associations are created equal: How implicit normative evaluations are distinct from implicit attitudes and uniquely predict meaningful behavior. *Journal of Experimental Social Psychology, 48*, 694–706.

Zinn, H. (1980). *A people's history of the United States.* New York, NY: Harper Perennial.

Zurcher, L. A., Meadow, A., & Zurcher, S. L. (1965). Value orientation, role conflict and alienation from work: A cross-cultural study. *American Sociological Review, 30*, 539–548.

7

Culture, Group Processes, and Creativity

CHENCHEN LI, LETTY Y-Y. KWAN, SHYHNAN LIOU, AND CHI-YUE CHIU

Creativity and culture are intricately related. Humans are not the only species capable of engaging in social learning. Other primates are also capable of copying novel use of tools from their peers (Whiten et al., 1999). What distinguishes human culture from primate culture is that human culture is cumulative; only human beings build on the inventions of others, so that once somebody had invented the wheel, others do not have to reinvent it (Tomasello, 2001). Instead, others build on it to develop new applications (e.g., the wheels of a motor vehicle). This process, which has been referred to as *ratcheting*, illustrates the reciprocal influence of culture and creativity. On the one hand, creativity is *the* process that moves the evolution of culture forward. On the other hand, culture provides inspirations for new inventions. In addition, existing knowledge in the culture serves as a benchmark for evaluating the level of creativity of the new inventions: What is creative is something that is not something already in the culture (Chiu & Kwan, 2010).

Nonetheless, what is creative does not have to be a new creation. An old idea in a certain cultural tradition may be perceived to be a creative idea in another cultural tradition (Niu & Sternberg, 2001). For example, the neurological effect of mindfulness (e.g., Zeidan et al., 2011), an "established" knowledge in Zen Buddhism, is new knowledge in contemporary psychology. In addition, what is creative to an individual may not be seen as creative to the group or the larger culture. For example, Vincent Van Gogh, whose paintings opened the doors to modern art, was way ahead of his time and was not appreciated by most of his contemporaries. Intense negotiation of what constitutes a creative idea often takes place within a cultural community before a consensus can be reached on how creative an idea is. In short, creativity is an intrinsically cultural and social process (Chiu & Kwan, 2010).

Paradoxically, in psychology, creativity is often studied as an intrapersonal cognitive process that occurs in a social and cultural vacuum. The study of creative personality as an individual difference (e.g., Helson, 1996) and the study of creative cognition as intraindividual cognitive processes (e.g., Finke, Ward, & Smith, 1992; Mumford & Gustafson, 1988) have deepened our understanding of the intrapersonal factors that underlie individual creativity performance. What is relatively less thoroughly researched is the interplay of culture and group processes in both individual and group creativity. The objective of the present chapter is to fill this gap.

In this chapter, we will review three research topics to illuminate the interplay of culture, group processes, and creativity. The first topic concerns how culture affects the group processes that underlie group creativity. Research on this topic has treated the heritage culture of the individual as an independent causal factor that shapes the creative outcomes of work teams through certain intervening group processes. The second topic concerns how exposure to foreign cultures can evoke intergroup processes that enhance or hinder creative performance of an individual. Research on this topic focuses on creative performance of the individual and seeks to explore when inflow of ideas from foreign cultures would inspire new ideas and when it will incite group centrism and increase resistance to cultural learning. The third topic concerns the positive and negative effects of working in culturally diverse work teams on the creative performance of the teams. Research on this topic focuses on when cultural diversity in a work team would evoke group processes that support or hinder group creativity.

A challenge of writing this review is the nonavailability of an integrated theoretical framework in the literature to bring these three research traditions in culture and creativity together. In this chapter, we propose a preliminary framework to fill this theoretical void. Although we have tried to constrain our theoretical propositions with available empirical data, our analysis is severely limited by the dearth of research that has examined the interplay of culture, group processes, and creativity. Nonetheless, we hope our preliminary framework would inspire more in-depth conceptual and empirical investigations into this emerging field. To provide an overarching framework to structure our discussion, we will begin this chapter with a discussion of (a) what culture is and (b) what creativity is.

WHAT IS CULTURE?

Psychological research on culture has traditionally focused on national cultures or the knowledge tradition of a national group (Lehman, Chiu, & Schaller, 2004). However, broadly speaking, a culture is any knowledge tradition that is widely shared in a community of interdependent individuals and has a history (Chiu, Leung, & Hong, 2010). By this definition, a culture can be a shared knowledge tradition of a national, religious, political, or disciplinary group (Chiu, Kwan, & Liou, 2014).

Every established human group has its culture, which serves important functions for the group and each of its individual members (Chiu & Hong, 2006). At the group level, culture prescribes desirable and acceptable behaviors or behaviors that would benefit not just the individual but also the group. Culture also proscribes behavioral expressions of selfish maximization that would hurt the welfare of the collective (Chiu & Chao, 2009; Chiu, Kim, & Chaturvedi, 2010). From this perspective, cultural prescriptions and proscriptions serve important regulatory functions of coordinating goal pursuits of multiple individuals in a complex system.

Culture also serves important functions for the individual (Chiu & Hong, 2006). First, individuals can rely on knowledge that is shared or widely accepted in a community when they need firm answers in uncertain situations (Chiu, Morris, Hong, & Menon, 2000; Kosic, Kruglanski, Pierro, & Mannetti, 2004). That is, culture confers epistemic security when individuals are confronted with decisional uncertainty. Second, the continuity of one's cultural tradition also offers existential security to individuals (Greenberg, Solomon, & Pyszczynski, 1997). Individuals, when confronted with the inevitability of one's mortality, may question the purpose of life. Knowing that one belongs to a long-lasting tradition provides the assurance that one lives on, albeit symbolically, as a contributing member of the tradition, and hence can assuage existential anxiety (Solomon, Greenberg, & Pyszczynski, 1991).

Finally, culture also addresses an individual's identity needs. The desire to be connected to others is a basic human need (Baumeister & Leary, 1995). Individuals can satisfy this need through participating in a culture. When the need to belong is activated, individuals who strongly identify with their ingroup were motivated to claim possession of the characteristic qualities of the group (Pickett, Bonner, & Coleman, 2002). Individuals who identify strongly with their culture are more motivated to adhere to and defend the perceived norms of their culture (Jetten, Postmes, & Mcauliffe, 2002).

As will be discussed later, the reliance on culture to satisfy one's identity needs and needs for epistemic and existential security is a primary driver of (a) motivated effort to protect the purity, integrity, and vitality of one's culture and (b) motivated adherence to cultural norms. These motivational processes have important implications for understanding the interplay of culture and group processes in creativity.

WHAT IS CREATIVITY?

Creativity is *the* factor that drives advances in art, science, culture, business, and the national economy. A creative product is one that embodies an original idea and has value to its users (Amabile, 1986). As noted, the originality of an idea is audience dependent; it is defined in relation to what is already known in a certain human group. Thus, a well-established idea in a certain group could be an original idea in another group, and vice versa. For example, Niu and Sternberg (2002) noted that while Chinese reviewers did not regard the film *Crouching Tiger, Hidden Dragon* as a particularly novel film, Western reviewers acclaimed the film for its stylistic innovations.

A creative product is also a valuable product to its users. A creative product is valuable if it can help its users achieve their valued goals. For example, the goal of psychological science is to explain, predict, and control human behaviors. A piece of creative research in the psychological sciences contributes to new knowledge, affording better understanding, more accurate predictions, and more effective interventions of human behaviors (Sternberg, 2003). Likewise, in commercial product design, a creative product embodies a new design idea that can increase consumer satisfaction (Liou, 2009). According to this definition, the value of a creative product is relative to the goals of the creative activity, as well as the needs and expectations of the product's consumers.

The process of producing a creative idea involves three iterative stages (Chiu & Kwan, 2010). Idea generation is the stage in which knowledge workers generate and author new ideas. Idea editing and marketing is the stage in which a subset of new ideas is selected for further development and refinement. Idea acceptance is the stage in which potential users of the new idea choose to adopt or reject the idea.

The three stages are qualitatively different stages, each with its distinct performance expectations (Chiu & Kwan, 2010). For example, at the idea generation stage, the goal is to generate *novel* ideas. A primary driver of creative activities at this stage is the intrinsic satisfaction and projected extrinsic rewards (e.g., social recognition, patents) associated with creating something new and distinctive. Reality checks gain importance at the idea editing and marketing stage. At this stage, knowledge workers need to consider the perceived preferences of the potential users, assess the acceptance potential of each candidate idea, and select ideas with high acceptance potentials for further development. At the acceptance stage, ideas compete with each other in the marketplace and those that possess the highest collective utility or match the preferences of the audience are likely to be accepted. Ideas that have received endorsement from the pertinent authorities are also likely to be accepted. Given the different performance expectations at the three stages of creative production, it is not surprising that oftentimes, the most novel idea may not be as successful in the marketplace as the minimally counterintuitive ideas (Norenzayan, Atran, Faulkner, & Schaller, 2006). Because market acceptance of creative ideas involves complex interactions between historical, sociopolitical, economic, and psychological processes that go beyond the scope of analysis in this chapter, we will focus on the cultural and group processes in the idea generation and editing stages.

Different cognitive styles and motivational predilections are associated with successful performance in the idea generation and editing stages. For example, divergent or lateral thinking (thinking that aims to find diverse answers to the same problem) improves fluency in idea generation, whereas convergent thinking (thinking that aims to find the correct answer for a problem) hinders it (Milliken, Bartel, & Kurtzberg, 2003). Broadening the attention field and an expansive mental search for nonconventional exemplars of a semantic category facilitate performance at the creative idea generation stage only (Friedman, Fishbach, Förster, & Werth, 2003; Ip, Chen, & Chiu, 2006). Whereas a self-regulatory focus on maximizing gains facilitates fluency in idea generation (Friedman & Forster, 2001; Herman & Reiter-Palmon, 2011; Ip et al., 2007), a self-regulatory focus on avoiding failures promotes persistence in idea editing (Lam & Chiu, 2002).

When individuals work in teams, performance of the teams at idea generation and editing stages are related to different group processes. For example, to generate the most novel ideas, knowledge workers need to defy the crowd and explore uncharted intellectual territories (West & Wallace, 1991). Team members are prepared to suggest new ways to achieve task goals and generate new ideas to improve performance when the team climate promotes the creative self-efficacy of the individual team members and encourages expression of dissident views. The team leaders can also play an important role in facilitating creative idea generation in teamwork by supporting mutual inspiration and intellectual stimulation (Shin, Kim, Lee, & Bian, 2012). In contrast, at the selection and editing stage, an overemphasis on conflict avoidance could lead team members to prioritize ideas that are likely to be accepted by all team members even when these ideas are not the most original and valuable ones the group has generated (Liou & Nisbett, 2011). Thus, a challenge in managing team performance is to minimize the group dynamics that would increase the likelihood of groupthink.

CULTURE → GROUP PROCESSES → GROUP CREATIVITY

How does culture affect group creativity? We seek to answer this question by examining how culture affects the group processes that are implicated in idea generation and selection in a group creativity task. Our argument, as illustrated in Figure 7.1, is that the most pronounced cultural differences in team creativity performance occur at the idea selection stage, when members of the team deliberate to select ideas for further development. To elaborate, the tendency to adhere to cultural norms is most salient in the presence of a group. During the deliberation process, the need to reach consensus with other group members motivates the individual members to assess what the perceived creativity norms in the group are and tune their decisions toward the perceived norms. Perceived creativity norms vary across cultures. For example, novelty is perceived to be more valued in Western cultures, whereas usefulness is perceived to be more valued in Asian cultures (see Morris & Leung, 2010; Paletz & Peng, 2008). Because of these cultural differences, different types of ideas tend to be selected in different cultures. Continuing with the example of East-West differences, novel ideas are more likely to be selected in Western cultures and useful ideas more likely to be selected in Asian cultures. In addition, culture also affects the relative importance of perceived norms and personal preferences in idea selection, with perceived norms being a more important consideration in cultures that emphasize group conformity.

Culture and Individual Differences in Creativity

As a straightforward answer to the question of how culture impacts group creativity, one may argue that some cultural processes support the development and expression of creativity, while others do not. For example, some writers (Nisbett, 2003) contend that people in individualist cultures are socialized to become analytical thinkers,

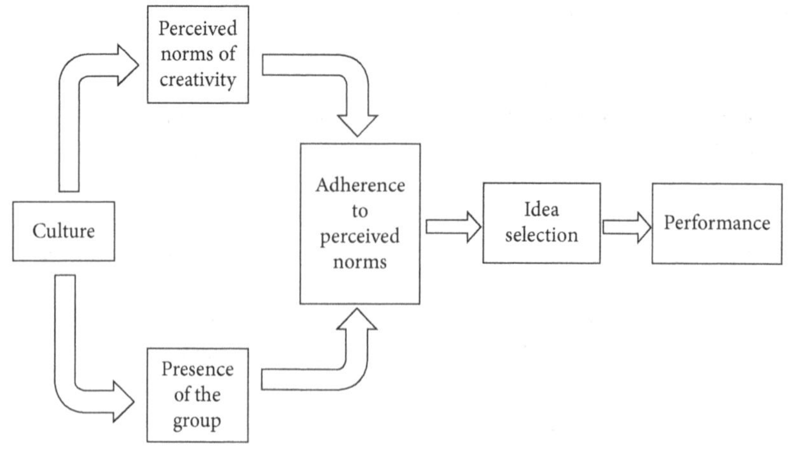

Figure 7.1. A model of cultural differences in creative idea selection and group creativity.

whereas those in collectivist cultures are socialized to become holistic thinkers. Because only analytical thinking supports creative accomplishments in science, cultural differences in the preferred thinking styles may account for the superior creative scientific accomplishments in Western, individualist cultures.

Nevertheless, the empirical support for this contention is weak. Some studies (e.g., Niu, Zhang, & Yang, 2007) found that individuals from Western cultures (the United States, Europe) outperformed individuals from Asian cultures (e.g., China, Japan) in creativity tests. These results, however, are difficult to interpret because of the lack of evidence for the measurement equivalence of the tests used in these studies. Furthermore, most standard tests of creative performance were developed in the West and sometimes administered to the Asian participants (e.g., Hong Kong Chinese) in English (Zhou & Su, 2010). The lack of culture fairness in assessment has compromised the validity of any conclusions drawn from earlier cross-cultural comparisons. Finally, other studies (Nouri, Erez, Rockstuhl, & Ang, 2008) have failed to find consistent cross-cultural differences in individual performance on creativity tasks. For example, Saeki, Fan, and Dusen (2001) compared the performance of Americans and the Japanese on the figural test of the Torrance Tests of Creative Thinking. Although Americans produced more abstract and elaborate ideas than did the Japanese, the two groups did not differ in the number of ideas generated, and the ideas generated by the two groups were equally original. Other studies (Zha, Walczyk, Griffith-Ross, Tobacyk, & Walczyk, 2006) showed that Americans outperformed Chinese on divergent thinking, but personal endorsement of individualism did not mediate the performance difference between the two cultures.

Culture and Group Differences in Creativity

Despite the lack of support for differences in individual creative performance across cultures, recent studies have found robust differences in team creativity between individualist and collectivist cultures (Bechtoldt, De Dreu, Nijstad, & Choi, 2010; Liou & Nisbett, 2011; Nouri et al., 2008). For example, one study (Goncalo & Staw, 2006) found that compared to collectivist groups, individualist groups have higher creative performance, particularly when creativity is a salient task goal (e.g., when the groups are explicitly instructed to be creative).

However, it is unclear from these results how culture and group processes interact to affect creative performance in work teams. For instance, it is unclear whether cultural differences occur at the idea generation or the idea selection stage. In addition, the mechanisms that underlie this cultural difference remain to be identified. One reason for the presence of this knowledge gap is the emphasis in past research on cultural differences in creative accomplishments rather than the group processes that give rise to cultural differences in creative performance (De Dreu, 2010).

Nonetheless, evidence from a few recent studies has suggested a possible explanation for the cultural differences in group creativity. First, a study (Liou & Nisbett, 2011) showed that cultural differences in team creativity emerged at the idea selection stage. In this study, Americans and Taiwan Chinese teams were instructed to generate new design ideas for a product. At the idea generation stage, team members were instructed to work alone. Consistent with past research that has failed to find cultural differences in individual creative performance, the ideas generated by the American and Chinese participants were equally original. Next, at the idea selection stage, team members were instructed to discuss the ideas generated by the individual team members and selected some ideas for further development. At this stage, cultural differences surfaced. The ideas selected by the American teams were more original than those selected by the Taiwanese teams, and the ideas discarded by the Taiwanese teams were more creative than those discarded by the American teams. This result shows that although both Americans and the Chinese are equally capable of generating original ideas, compared to the Chinese teams, American teams are more likely to select the relatively novel ideas for further development.

This cultural difference in idea selection seems to originate from the use of different criteria for idea selection. In a cross-cultural study, Nouri, Erez, Rockstuhl, and Ang (2008) compared Singaporeans and Israelis on their performance on a creativity test performed individually and again found that the two groups performed equally well on this test. Interestingly, when the participants were asked to perform the task in groups, the Israeli teams were more original than the Singaporean teams. In contrast, the Singaporean teams elaborated more on the appropriateness of each idea they selected. In another study (Bechtoldt et al., 2010), Dutch and Korean student teams were asked to generate new ideas to improve university teaching. When Dutch students were (vs. were not) instructed to do their best, they generated more original ideas. In contrast, when Korean student teams were asked to do their best, they generated more useful ideas. The situation-induced increase in task motivation did not impact the usefulness of the ideas generated by the Dutch teams or the originality of the ideas generated by the Korean teams. Together, these findings show that compared to Western teams,

Asian teams put greater emphasis on idea usefulness and less emphasis on idea originality at the idea selection stage.

However, these cultural differences in idea selection seem to originate from the perceived norms of creativity rather than personal preferences across cultures. In one study, Paletz and Peng (2008) compared the relative importance of novelty and usefulness in evaluating the creativity of new products among Americans, the Chinese, and the Japanese. They found that the Chinese valued novelty more than Americans, whereas Americans and Japanese valued usefulness more than the Chinese. This result suggests that the East-West difference in the relative weights assigned to novelty and usefulness in idea selection does not reflect the actual personal importance of novelty or usefulness to Asians and Westerners.

Instead, as we mentioned earlier, at the idea selection stage, individuals are inclined to consider the *perceived preferences* of the audience when choosing ideas for further development. When deliberating on the choices of ideas, team members would consider the perceived preferences of other team members. When team members assume that other members in the team value novelty, they would express greater support for novel ideas. Likewise, when team members assume that others in the team value usefulness, they would show greater support for useful ideas. This contention is consistent with the intersubjective approach to cultural influence (Chiu, Gelfand, Yamagishi, Shteynberg, & Wan, 2010, Morris & Leung, 2010; Zou et al., 2009), which posits that culture impacts decisions not necessarily through internalized personal values, but through the perceived norms in the culture. In support of this contention, Bechtoldt et al. (2010) reported that when Dutch teams were experimentally induced to perceive usefulness to be the prevalent norm of creativity in the group, motivating them to do their best in a team creativity task increased the usefulness but not the novelty of their ideas.

There are several implications of these findings. First, cross-cultural differences in team creativity do not always reflect group differences in the ability to generate novel or useful ideas, or group differences in what types of ideas are considered to be creative. Instead, cultural differences in team creativity may arise from the perceived norms of creativity in the culture, which may or may not correspond to the actual norms (Morris & Leung, 2010; Wan et al., 2007).

Although both Asian and Western teams would consider the perceived norms in the team when selecting ideas for further development, the impact of perceived norms on idea selection may be stronger in more collectivist cultures. This is because the motivation to submit the self to majority influence is stronger in collectivist versus individualist cultures (Zhang, Lowry, Zhou, & Fu, 2004). Indeed, priming the interdependent self would accentuate the influence of perceived norms in decision making, whereas priming the independent self would attenuate it (Torelli, 2006). On the one hand, when making decisions in groups, the pressure to achieve early consensus could hurt the quality of the final decision. On the other hand, voicing one's disagreements with others despite the conformity pressure could enhance the quality of decisions made through cancellation of biases from individual members (Schulz-Hardt, Brodbeck, Mojzisch, Kerschreiter, &

Frey 2006). Thus, the greater conformity pressure in collectivist groups may help these groups to reach consensus more quickly at the expense of decision quality.

Thus far, we have focused on how group processes contribute to cultural differences in idea selection. Group processes also contribute to cultural differences in idea generation, although the evidence for such contributions is still limited. As noted, a focus on gain maximization versus loss minimization is associated with greater fluency and originality in idea generation. Thus, one would expect that in cultures that emphasize gain maximization, having an incentive system that rewards novel ideas would encourage generation of original ideas. There is evidence that individualist cultures emphasize gain maximization more than do collectivist ones (Lee, Aaker, & Gardner, 2000). Accordingly, having an equitable reward system for original ideas should have greater facilitative effects on novel idea generation in individualist versus collectivist cultures. Consistent with this hypothesis, Goncalo and Kim (2010) found that after participants were primed with the independent self, an equitable reward system increases group productivity in idea generation more than an egalitarian reward system. In contrast, the reward system manipulation had no impact on idea generation following priming of the interdependent self. As another example, constructive controversy facilitates team creativity (Nemeth, Personnaz, Personnaz, & Goncalo, 2004; Reining & Mejias, 2004). Specifically, encouraging group members to debate among themselves (vs. encouraging group members to avoid criticizing others' ideas) during group brainstorming improves the fluency of idea generation. Accordingly, higher levels of team creativity are expected in cultures that promote constructive controversies (e.g., individualist cultures) rather than conflict avoidance (e.g., collectivist cultures) in teamwork.

In summary, in this section, we have reviewed recent research evidence to illustrate how culture impacts group creativity at different stages of creative production through different group processes. This analysis highlights the importance of separating idea generation from idea selection, as well as the importance of considering normative process in idea selection for understanding cultural differences in team creativity.

FOREIGN CULTURAL EXPOSURE → GROUP PROCESSES → INDIVIDUAL CREATIVITY

The discussion in the previous section focuses on how socialization into one's own culture and group processes jointly influence performance in a group creativity task. In this section, we focus on how *exposure to foreign cultures* and group processes jointly influence the creative performance of an individual. First, we will review the potential creative benefits of multicultural exposure. Next, we will discuss how evocation of certain group processes may limit the potential creative benefits of exposure to foreign cultures. Specifically, our argument, as illustrated in Figure 7.2, is that when group centrism is heightened under some circumstances, such as when individuals have strong cultural identity needs or when they experience the

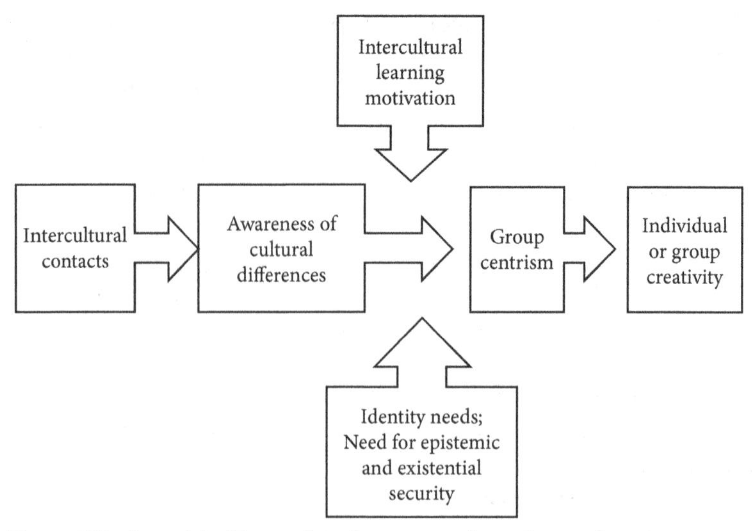

Figure 7.2. A model of intercultural contact and creative performance.

need for epistemic or existential security, people would resist influence from foreign cultures and hence miss the opportunities for intercultural learning.

The creative benefits of experiences with multiple cultures are well documented (Leung, Maddux, Galinsky, & Chiu, 2008). As individuals adapt to foreign cultures through their direct, personal experiences in these cultures, they are able to reflect critically on their own personal experiences (Chao, Okazaki, & Hong, 2011), use ideas from foreign cultures as intellectual resources in creative problem solving (Leung & Chiu, 2010), and improve their performance on various creativity tasks (Leung & Chiu, 2010; Maddux & Galinsky, 2009). The beneficial effects of multicultural experience are particularly pronounced among individuals who are sensitive to cultural differences (Leung & Chiu, 2010), are comfortable in managing their multicultural identities (Cheng, Sanchez-Burks, & Lee, 2008), and are motivated to learn from other cultures (Maddux, Adam, & Galinsky, 2010).

However, exposure to foreign culture promotes creativity only when individuals are open to new experiences (Leung & Chiu, 2008). When individuals are close minded, exposure to foreign cultures could cause culture shock and motivate rejection of foreign cultures. In this connection, recent research has identified some group processes that would incite exclusionary reactions to foreign culture and hence limit the creative benefits of multicultural experiences. We will review some of these group processes in the next sections.

Threats to Epistemic and Existential Security

As mentioned in the introductory section, cultural traditions confer epistemic and existential security to the individual (Juhl & Routledge, 2010). Individuals who desire firm answers when facing uncertainty are inclined to follow the conventionalized solutions in their cultural tradition, which are time-honored solutions with high levels of consensual validity. There is ample evidence that when individuals experience a heightened need for firm answers (either because they have a chronic need for cognitive closure, or because they face situational pressure to quickly decide on an appropriate response to an ambiguous situation), they tend to exhibit symptoms of group centrism (Chiu et al., 2000; Kruglanski, Pierro, Mannetti, & De Grada, 2006). Two symptoms of group centrism in intercultural interactions are adherence to the perceived norms of one's heritage culture and rejection of foreign cultures (Chao, Zhang, & Chiu, 2010; Fu et al., 2007). Exhibition of such symptoms would inevitably lower the motivation to learn from other cultures when performing a creativity task. Consistent with this idea, a study (Leung & Chiu, 2010) showed that when individuals are required to work on a creativity task under time pressure, they are less likely to consult ideas from foreigners than if they are not under time pressure to complete the task quickly.

Aside from being a provider of epistemic security, culture is also an existential security provider. When individuals experience an existential crisis, as when they start to question the meaning of life after being reminded of their inescapable mortality, they are particularly likely to defend their cultural worldview (Burke, Martens, & Faucher, 2010). Existentially induced cultural conformity also promotes cultural conservatism, resulting in aversion to any creative activities that would undermine the vitality and integrity of one's culture. In support of this idea, research has shown that engaging in creative expression after personal mortality has been made salient can induce feelings of guilt (Arndt, Greenberg, Solomon, Pyszczynski, & Schimel, 1999). However, consistent with the worldview defense hypothesis, the negative effect of mortality salience on creative exploration is reversed after mortality salient individuals have been reminded that creativity is culturally valued (Routledge & Arndt, 2009) or after these individuals learned that they followed the norms in their knowledge tradition (Arndt, Routledge, Greenberg, & Sheldon, 2005). Other studies showed that in intercultural interactions, rendering death thoughts salient would increase the motivation to preserve the purity of one's cultural tradition and resist culture mixing (Torelli, Chiu, Tam, Au, & Keh, 2011). When asked to expand an ordinary idea into a creative idea, mortality salient individuals also tend to avoid receiving inspirations from foreign thought leaders (Leung & Chiu, 2010).

In short, individuals can satisfy their needs for epistemic and existential security through cultural conformity. When individuals experience epistemic or existential insecurity, they display symptoms of group centrism and resist foreign cultural influence, which in turn lower the motivation to learn from other cultures and limit the creative benefits of multicultural experiences.

Identity Threats

Inflow of foreign cultures may also evoke identity concerns of individuals in local cultures. Individuals in local culture may feel that inflow of foreign cultures would contaminate or reduce the vitality of local culture (Chiu, Gries, Torelli, & Cheng, 2011). They may therefore defensively resist foreign cultural influence. Such resistance may in turn limit the creative benefits of intercultural contacts. Individuals who strongly identify with their heritage culture are particularly concerned about cultural contamination and erosion. In one study (Morris, Mok, & Mor, 2011), some Westernized Hong Kong Chinese university students were exposed to books on Asian cultures written in Western languages or books on Western cultures written in Asian languages (culture mix condition). The remaining participants were exposed to books on Asian cultures written in Asian languages or books on Western cultures written in Western languages (control condition). Following the manipulation, the participants completed the need for closure scale (Webster & Kruglanski, 1994). Participants in the culture mix condition exhibited a higher need for closure than those in the control condition, suggesting that inflow of foreign cultures could increase closed mindedness. Moreover, the effect was more pronounced among those who identified strongly with Chinese culture and not with Western cultures.

In another study (Leung & Chiu, 2010), American college students were instructed to develop an ordinary honor thesis idea into an original one. To help them complete this task, the participants were provided with ideas from well-known thought leaders from the United States or other countries (East Asia and the Middle East). Before consulting these ideas, the participants reported their level of identification with American culture and then rated how useful each idea was for the completion of the task. Stronger identification with American culture was associated with positive evaluations of ideas from American thought leaders and negative evaluations of ideas from thought leaders outside the United States.

In summary, intercultural contacts and multicultural experiences could enhance individual creativity. However, inflow of foreign cultures could also be accompanied by fear of cultural contamination and erosion and exclusionary reactions to culture mixing, limiting the potential creative benefits of intercultural contacts. Exclusionary reactions are symptoms of group centrism, motivated by cultural identity needs and the needs for epistemic and existential security. From this perspective, these exclusionary reactions are culturally motivated responses directed toward satisfying one's identity and epistemic and existential needs through preservation of one's heritage cultural tradition.

CREATIVE PERFORMANCE IN CULTURALLY DIVERSE TEAMS

We have reviewed two of the three extensively researched topics on the interactive effect of culture and group processes on creativity. The first topic concerns the creative performance of culturally homogeneous work teams. The second topic concerns the effect of exposure to foreign cultures on individual creative performance. We now turn to the last topic, which concerns the performance of multicultural work teams on group creativity tasks.

Creative Benefits of Team Diversity

The cultural and group processes involved in culturally diverse work teams are similar to those involved in psychological reactions to culture mixing. First, a culturally diverse team includes members who possess insider knowledge of different cultural traditions and hence have at their disposal a broader range of intellectual resources for creative problem solving. When members with diverse cultural expertise present ideas from their own cultural perspectives, other members become aware of the alternative approaches to solving the same problem in different cultural traditions (Han, Peng, Chiu, & Leung, 2010). Although exposure to diverse cultural perspectives could cause cognitive conflicts, successful resolution of these conflicts through considering a broader range of solutions and synthesis of seemingly incompatible ideas could result in frame-breaking innovations (Schulz-Hardt, Mojzisch, & Vogelgesang, 2007). The relationship between resolution of cognitive conflicts in culturally diverse teams and creativity has been demonstrated in several laboratory studies (De Dreu, 1997; Schulz-Hardt et al., 2006). Evidence for the role of cultural diversity in frame-breaking innovations has also been obtained in field research. For example, in one study (Dunlap-Hinkler, Kotabe, & Mudambi, 2010), the investigators analyzed the successful patent applications of pharmaceutical innovations from 98 firms filed at the Food & Drug Administration of the United States between 1992 and 2002. Patents were classified into incremental innovations and frame-breaking innovations. Frame-breaking innovations refer to innovations that start the cycle of technological change (e.g., new molecular entities), whereas incremental innovations refer to innovations in the form of new features, extensions, variations, or complements to an existing product line (e.g., generics that are bioequivalent to previously approved new drug applications). Next, the investigators examined the factors that predict the likelihood of incremental and frame-breaking innovations. The results show that companies that have an established record of making incremental innovations will continue to make incremental innovations. More interestingly, frame-breaking innovations are more likely to come from pharmaceutical companies that have recently formed an alliance with another company in a foreign country. Even more interestingly, companies that have subsidiaries in other countries are not more likely to produce frame-breaking innovations than those that do not. Together, these results show that at the organization level, the experience of working with a company with a different organizational culture in a foreign country promotes frame-breaking innovations, whereas the experience of working with a subsidiary that has the same organizational culture in a foreign country does not.

Fault Line and Relationship Conflicts

Although working in a culturally diverse group offers opportunities for intercultural cognitive stimulation, it does not always guarantee better creative outcomes. Intense cognitive conflicts can hinder consensus building within the group.

Furthermore, members from different cultures may follow different norms of social interaction, resulting in social or relationship conflicts, which in turn could cause performance impairment (De Dreu & Weingart, 2003).

To predict when culturally diverse teams will outperform culturally homogenous ones, it is important to distinguish between the presence of cultural diversity and a fault line in a team. Cultural diversity refers to the presence of team members from different cultures. There is no association between the cultural membership and other characteristics, including the beliefs, values, and preferences of the individual members. In contrast, when there is a fault line in a team, team members perceive a clear simultaneous alignment of multiple demographic (including cultural), functional, and psychological characteristics across members (Thatcher, Jehn, & Zanutto, 2003). That is, a fault line divides a culturally diverse team into relatively homogenous subgroups based on group members' alignment along the cultural category and other attributes (Lau & Murnighan, 1998).

In a culturally diverse team, if there are no associations between cultural membership and individual beliefs, values, and preferences, disagreement within the team on why and how a problem should be solved will be seen as disagreement between individuals, rather than a cultural conflict. In addition, individuals with a dissenting view would unlikely receive support from members of their own cultural group. The lack of opportunity for self-verification or social validation lowers individuals' confidence in their personal views and increases openness to alternative opinions. In contrast, once a fault line has developed in the team, individuals would likely receive support for their own opinions from members of the same culture. The opportunity for self-verification and social validation of one's personal preferences increases the individuals' confidence in the validity of their preferences and lowers receptiveness to persuasion. Under such circumstances, disagreement within the work team can easily develop into a cultural conflict within the team (Han, Peng, Chiu, & Leung 2010; Jehn, Bezrukova, & Thatcher, 2007).

Fault lines are particularly likely to develop in functionally diverse teams. Recall that a culture is a knowledge tradition that is widely shared and has a history. By this definition, most established disciplines or professions have their distinctive cultures (Chiu et al., 2014). Specifically, members of an established discipline typically agree on the set of criteria that would be applied to evaluate the validity and value of knowledge and use similar metaphors or paradigms to guide their practices. The characteristic criteria of validity, metaphors, and paradigms of a discipline are also systematically taught to or passed down to new practitioners through disciplinary socialization (Guimond, 1999; Guimond & Palmer, 1996).

When members of two disciplines need to work together in an innovation team, a cultural fault line may develop. For example, research and development (R&D) engineers and marketers often have to work together to produce marketable innovations. Research on R&D and marketing interface shows that oftentimes R&D engineers and marketers have different values. Whereas R&D engineers value scientific development, prefer a long time horizon of advanced projects, and have relatively little tolerance for ambiguity and bureaucracy, marketers focus on the market, prefer a short time horizon of incremental projects, and can accept a high degree of ambiguity and bureaucracy (Cho & Hahn, 2004; Griffin & Hauser, 1992; Song & Parry, 1997). In addition, although successful innovations often require collaboration and synergy of the two functional groups at all stages, R&D engineers prefer taking ownership of the idea generation (product design) stage and involve marketers only at the idea editing and promotion stage (Banerjee & Chiu, 2008). R&D engineers may think that the R&D perspective takes precedence in innovation projects, whereas marketers may think that their business perspective is crucial to the success of the projects. As a result, R&D and marketing often complain about each other's intellectual limitations (Workman, 1997). Not surprisingly, research on functionally diverse work teams has also revealed intense cognitive and relationship conflicts between the functional groups in innovation teams (Amason & Schweiger, 1997; Northcraft, Polzer, Neale, & Kramer, 1995). Therefore, although cultural diversity leaves room for intellectual stimulation, it is not always accompanied by better team creativity outcomes because the presence of cultural fault lines within a team could sensitize team members to deep differences between cultures, intensify relationship conflicts, and derail the creative processes. The presence of cultural fault lines could hurt creativity in both idea generation and idea selection. Creative synthesis of seemingly incompatible ideas is a useful way for generating novel ideas (Wan & Chiu, 2002). The presence of cultural fault lines discourages synthesis of ideas from dissimilar intellectual traditions and hence limits creative expansion of existing conceptual domains through interdisciplinary collaborations. The presence of cultural fault lines also promotes intellectual centrism, leading to the failure to consider perspectives from other intellectual traditions when selecting ideas for further development (Proctor et al., 2011).

Management of Cultural Diversity

Now, we are ready to return to a familiar argument. Awareness of cultural differences can promote performance in a team creativity task through cognitive stimulation or retard it through evocation of cognitive and relationship conflicts. What are the factors that can retard or improve performance in a team creativity task? Earlier, we argue that when awareness of cultural differences is accompanied by the activation of group centrism, people tend to resist inflow of foreign cultures. In contrast, when awareness of cultural differences is accompanied by activation of an intercultural learning goal, people tend to welcome foreign cultural ideas and use ideas from foreign cultures as resources to expand their intellectual horizon. We believe that these principles also apply to managing creativity in culturally diverse work teams. Specifically, when team members are aware of group differences and are motivated by their identity, epistemic, and existential needs to defend the purity and vitality of their culture, they would display symptoms of group centrism and refuse to learn from and cooperate with members from other cultures. In contrast, when team members are aware of group differences and are motivated to learn from other cultures, they would engage culturally dissimilar members differently. Specifically, they would seek stimulation from these members, understand their distinct expertise, and entrust important tasks to those members who have the distinct cultural expertise to manage these tasks (Proctor et al., 2011).

This set of principles is consistent with the existing evidence on the effect of cultural diversity on team creativity. First, in small group discussion, a higher need for closure is associated with greater conformity and lower creativity (Chirumbolo, Livi, Mannetti, Pierro, & Kruglanski, 2004; Chirumbolo, Mannetti, Pierro, Areni, & Kruglanski, 2005). Second, a culturally diverse group performs better on a creativity task when members of the group are aware of how expertise and preferences are distributed within the group (Hollingshead, Gupta, Yoon, & Brandon, 2012; Huber & Lewis, 2010). In addition, functionally diverse groups that have developed effective mechanisms to encourage individual team members to express their personal views and manage the cognitive conflicts constructively also tend to perform better on group creativity tasks (Tjosvold, 1998). In short, the same set of cognitive and motivational principles explains individuals' collaborative versus group centric reactions to foreign culture and the effect of cultural diversity on group creativity.

GENERAL CONCLUSIONS

Research on culture and creativity has focused on how cultures differ on various performance measures of individual creativity. Due to various conceptual and measurement problems, the available evidence has failed to reveal any systematic cultural differences on individual creativity. Recently, there has been a surge of interest in how multicultural experience can enhance individual creativity. This research has revealed how individual creativity is jointly influenced by an individual's cultural experiences and culturally motivated group processes. A third major topic on culture and creativity concerns the effect of cultural diversity on group creativity. Nonetheless, there has not been systematic effort to connect research on multicultural experience and individual creativity to research on cultural diversity and group creativity.

Against this backdrop, in this chapter, we attempt to bring these three research traditions together, focusing on the relevance of group processes in the link between culture and creativity. Specifically, we argue that cultural differences in creative performance may arise from adherence to perceived norms of creativity. People from different cultural groups have different shared beliefs about what constitutes creativity. Although these shared beliefs may not affect performance when individuals are required to generate new ideas by themselves, their effects on what ideas will be selected for further development are pronounced when members of the culture are required to reach consensus on idea selection. This analysis also highlights the contribution of studying creativity as a multistage process.

Exposure to foreign cultures could be an effective way to break the cultural frames that individuals through their socialization experiences would spontaneously adopt in creative problem solving. Such exposure could occur when individuals are exposed to foreign cultures in intercultural interactions, or when individuals need to work on a creativity task together with team members from diverse cultural backgrounds. Such experiences allow individuals to reflect on their cultural experiences, receive cognitive stimulation on how the same problem can be conceptualized and solved differently using intellectual tools from different cultures. Nonetheless, for individuals who are comfortable with the characteristic ways of solving problems and relating to others, awareness of marked cultural differences in problem-solving preferences and social interaction styles could cause culture shocks. The prospect of integrating "alien" ideas and practices when solving important problems may evoke fear of cultural contamination and erosion, leading to various symptoms of group centrism. In both individual responses to culture mixing and psychological reactions to cultural diversity in a work team, individuals are motivated to adhere to the perceived norms of their heritage culture when the need to preserve the purity and integrity of their heritage tradition is activated. We have argued that culture serves important psychological functions by addressing the identity, epistemic, and existential needs of the individual. Therefore, when these needs are made salient, individuals would be motivated to defend their cultural tradition by exhibiting symptoms of group centrism, which would limit the opportunities for individuals and groups to learn from dissimilar cultures and generate frame-breaking ideas.

Nonetheless, the negative effects of group centrism can be mitigated and even reversed if an intercultural learning mindset is activated, as when individuals are reminded of significant past experiences of learning from culturally dissimilar others, or when the group has developed constructive processes to encourage expressions and constructive synthesis of diverse opinions.

As we write, we are aware of the dearth of empirical evidence that directly addresses the interrelations of culture, group processes, and creativity. Nonetheless, we have made a reasonable attempt to construct a broad theoretical framework to bring together the scattered research findings from three seemingly disparate research topics on culture and creativity. We hope that our attempts will inspire new systematic research that will eventually deepen our understanding of the interplay of culture, group processes, and cognitive performance.

REFERENCES

Amabile, T. M. (1986). The social psychology of creativity: A componential conceptualization. *Journal of Personality and Social Psychology, 45*, 357–377.

Amason, A. C., & Schweiger, D. M. (1997). Resolving the paradox of conflict, strategic decision making, and organizational performance. *International Journal of Conflict Management, 5*, 340–359.

Arndt, J., Greenberg, J., Solomon, S., Pyszczynski, T., & Schimel, J. (1999). Creativity and terror management: The effects of creative activity on guilt and social projection following mortality salience. *Journal of Personality and Social Psychology, 77*, 19–32.

Arndt, J., Routledge, C., Greenberg, J., & Sheldon, K. M. (2005). Illuminating the dark side of creative expression: Assimilation needs and the consequences of creative action following mortality salience. *Personality and Social Psychology Bulletin, 31*, 327–1339.

Banerjee, P. M., & Chiu, C-Y. (2008). Professional biculturalism enculturation training: A new perspective on managing R&D and marketing interface. In M. A. Rahim (Ed.), *Current topics in management* (Vol. 13, pp. 145–159). New Brunswick, NY: Transaction.

Baumeister, R. F., & Leary, M. R. (1995). The need to belong: Desire for interpersonal attachments as a fundamental human motivation. *Psychological Bulletin, 117*, 497–529.

Bechtoldt, M. N., De Dreu, C. K. W., Nijstad, B. A., & Choi, H-S. (2010). Motivated information processing, epistemic social tuning, and group creativity. *Journal of Personality and Social Psychology, 99*, 622–637.

Burke, B. L., Martens, A., & Faucher, E. H. (2010). Two decades of terror management theory: A meta-analysis of mortality salience research. *Personality and Social Psychology Review, 14*, 155–195.

Chao, M., Okazaki, S., & Hong, Y. (2011). The quest for multicultural competence: Challenges and lessons learned from clinical and organizational research. *Social and Personality Psychology Compass, 5*, 263–274.

Chao, M. M., Zhang, Z-X., & Chiu, C-Y. (2010). Adherence to perceived norms across cultural boundaries: The role of need for cognitive closure and ingroup identification. *Group Processes and Intergroup Relations, 13*, 69–89.

Cheng, C-Y., Sanchez-Burks, J., & Lee, F. (2008) Connecting the dots within: Creative performance and identity integration. *Psychological Science, 19*, 1178–1184.

Chirumbolo, A., Livi, S., Mannetti, L., Pierro, A., & Kruglanski, A. W. (2004). Effects of need for closure on creativity in small group interactions. *European Journal of Personality, 18*, 265–278.

Chirumbolo, A., Mannetti, L., Pierro, A., Areni, A., & Kruglanski, A. W. (2005). Motivated closed-mindedness and creativity in small groups. *Small Group Research, 36*, 59–82.

Chiu, C-Y., & Chao, M. M. (2009). Society, culture, and the person: Ways to personalize and socialize cultural psychology. In R. Wyer, C-Y. Chiu, & Y. Hong (Eds.), *Understanding culture: Theory, research and application* (pp. 456–466). New York, NY: Psychology Press.

Chiu, C-Y., Gries, P., Torelli, C. J., & Cheng, S. Y-Y. (2011). Toward a social psychology of globalization. *Journal of Social Issues, 67*, 663–676.

Chiu, C-Y., & Hong, Y. (2006). *Social psychology of culture*. New York, NY: Psychology Press.

Chiu, C-Y., & Kwan, L. (2010). Culture and creativity: A process model. *Management and Organization Review, 6*, 447–461.

Chiu, C-Y., Gelfand, M., Yamagishi, T., Shteynberg, G., & Wan, C. (2010). Intersubjective culture: The role of intersubjective perceptions in cross-cultural research. *Perspectives on Psychological Science, 5*, 482–493.

Chiu, C-Y., Kim, Y-H., & Chaturvedi, A. (2010). Collective evolution: Revisiting the Donald Campbell legacy. In M. Schaller, A. Norenzayan, S. J. Heine, A., T. Yamagishi, & T. Kameda (Eds.), *Evolution, culture, and the human mind* (pp. 39–47). New York, NY: Psychology Press.

Chiu, C-Y., Kwan, L. Y-Y., & Liou, S. (2014). Professional and disciplinary cultures. In A. Cohen (Ed.), *Culture reexamined: Broadening our understanding of social and evolutionary influences* (pp. 11–30). Washington, DC: American Psychological Association.

Chiu, C-Y., Leung, K-Y., & Hong, Y-Y. (2010). Cultural processes: An overview. In A. K-Y. Leung, C-Y. Chiu, & Y-Y. Hong (Eds.), *Cultural processes: A social psychological perspective* (pp. 3–22). New York, NY: Cambridge University Press.

Chiu, C-Y., Morris, M. W., Hong, Y-Y., & Menon, T. (2000). Motivated cultural cognition: The impact of implicit cultural theories on dispositional attribution varies as a function of need for closure. *Journal of Personality and Social Psychology, 78*, 247–259.

Cho, E., & Hahn, M. (2004). Antecedents and consequences of the sociocultural differences between R&D and marketing in Korean high-tech firms. *International Journal of Technology Management, 28*, 801–819.

De Dreu, C. K. W. (1997). Productive conflict: The importance of conflict management and conflict issue. In C. K. W. & E. Van de Vliert (Eds.), *Using conflict in organizations* (pp. 9–22). London, UK: Sage.

De Dreu, C. K. W. (2010). Human creativity: Reflections on the role of culture. *Management and Organization Review, 6*, 437–446.

De Dreu, C. K. W., & Weingart, L. R. (2003). Task versus relationship conflict, team performance, and team member satisfaction: A meta-analysis. *Journal of Applied Psychology, 88*, 741–749.

Dunlap-Hinkler, D., Kotabe, M., & Mudambi, R. (2010). A story of breakthrough versus incremental innovation: Corporate entrepreneurship in the global pharmaceutical industry. *Strategic Entrepreneurship Journal, 4*, 106–127.

Finke, R. A., Ward, T. B., & Smith, S. M. (1992). *Creative cognition: Theory, research, and applications*. Bradford, MA: The MIT Press.

Friedman, R. S., & Forster, J. (2001). The effects of promotion and prevention cues on creativity. *Journal of Personality and Social Psychology, 81*, 1001–1013.

Friedman, R., Fishbach, A., Förster, J., & Werth, L. (2003). Attentional priming effects on creativity. *Creativity Research Journal, 15*, 277–286.

Fu, H-Y., Morris, M. W., Lee, S-L., Chao, M-C., Chiu, C-Y., & Hong, Y-Y. (2007). Epistemic motives and cultural conformity: Need for closure, culture, and context as determinants of conflict judgments. *Journal of Personality and Social Psychology, 92*, 191–207.

Goncalo, J. A., & Kim, S. H. (2010). Distributive justice beliefs and group idea generation: Does a belief in equity facilitate productivity? *Journal of Experimental Social Psychology, 46*, 836–840.

Goncalo, J. A., & Staw, B. M. (2006). Individualism-collectivism and group creativity. *Organizational Behavior and Human Decision Processes, 100*, 96–109.

Greenberg, J., Solomon, S., & Pyszczynski, T. (1997). Terror management theory of self-esteem and cultural worldview: Empirical assessments and conceptual refinements. In P. M. Zanna (Ed.), *Advances in experimental social psychology* (Vol. 29, pp. 61–141). San Diego, CA: Academic Press.

Griffin, A., & Hauser, J. R. (1992). Patterns of communication among marketing, engineering, and manufacturing: A comparison between two new product teams. *Management Science, 38*, 360–373.

Guimond, S. (1999). Attitude change during college: Normative or informational social influence. *Social Psychology of Education, 2*, 237–261.

Guimond, S., & Palmer, D. L. (1996). The political socialization of commerce and social science students: Epistemic authority and attitude change. *Journal of Applied Social Psychology, 26*, 1985–2013.

Han, J., Peng, S., Chiu, C-Y., & Leung, A. K-Y. (2010). Workforce diversity and creativity: A multilevel analysis. In A. K-Y. Leung, C-Y. Chiu, & Y-Y. Hong (Eds.), *Cultural processes: A social psychological perspective* (pp. 286–311). New York, NY: Cambridge University Press.

Helson, H. (1996). In search of the creative personality. *Creativity Research Journal, 9*, 295–306.

Herman, A., & Reiter-Palmon, R. (2011). The effect of regulatory focus on idea generation and idea evaluation. *Psychology of Aesthetics, Creativity, and the Arts, 5*, 13–28.

Hollingshead, A. B., Gupta, N., Yoon, K., & Brandon, D. P. (2012). Transactive memory theory and teams: Past, present and future. In E. Salas, S. M. Fore, & M. Letsky (Eds.), *Theories of team cognition: Cross-disciplinary perspectives* (pp. 421–455). New York, NY: Taylor & Francis.

Huber, G. P., & Lewis, K. (2010). Cross-understanding: Implications for group cognition and performance. *Academy of Management Review, 35*, 6–26.

Ip, G. W-M., Chen, J., & Chiu, C-Y. (2006). The relationship of promotion focus, need for cognitive closure, and categorical accessibility in American and Hong Kong Chinese university students. *Journal of Creative Behavior, 40*, 201–215

Jehn, K. A., Bezrukova, K., & Thatcher, S. (2007). Conflict diversity, and faultlines in workgroups. In C. K. W. De Drue & M. J. Gelfand (Eds.), *The psychology of conflict and conflict management in organizations* (pp. 177–208). New York, NY: Psychology Press.

Jetten, J., Postmes, T., & Mcauliffe, B. (2002). "We're all individuals": Group norms of individualism and collectivism, levels of identification and identity threat. *European Journal of Social Psychology, 32*, 189–207.

Juhl, J., & Routledge, C. (2010). Structured terror: Further exploring the effects of mortality salience and personal need for structure on worldview defense. *Journal of Personality, 78*, 969–990.

Kosic, A., Kruglanski, A. W., Pierro, A., & Mannetti, L. (2004). The social cognition of immigrants' acculturation: Effects of the need for closure and the reference group at entry. *Journal of Personality and Social Psychology, 86*, 796–813.

Kruglanski, A. W., Pierro, A., Mannetti, L., & De Grada, E. (2006). Groups as epistemic providers: Need for closure and the unfolding of group-centrism. *Psychological Review, 113*, 84–100.

Lam, T. W., & Chiu, C-Y. (2002). The motivational function of regulatory focus in creativity. *Journal of Creative Behavior, 36*, 138–150.

Lau, D., & Murnighan, J. K. (1998). Demographic diversity and faultlines: The compositional dynamics of organizational groups. *Academy of Management Review, 23*, 325–340.

Lee, A., Aaker, J., & Gardner, W. (2000). The pleasures and pains of distinct self-construals: The role of interdependence in regulatory focus. *Journal of Personality and Social Psychology, 78*, 1122–1134.

Lehman, D., Chiu, C-Y., & Schaller, M. (2004). Culture and psychology. *Annual Review of Psychology, 55*, 689–714.

Leung, A. K-Y., & Chiu, C-Y. (2008). Interactive effects of multicultural experiences and openness to experience on creativity. *Creativity Research Journal, 20*, 376–382.

Leung, A. K-Y., & Chiu, C-Y. (2010). Multicultural experiences, idea receptiveness, and creativity. *Journal of Cross-Cultural Psychology, 41*, 723–741.

Leung, A. K-Y., Maddux, W. W., Galinsky, A. D., & Chiu, C-Y. (2008). Multicultural experience enhances creativity: The when and how? *American Psychologist, 63*, 169–181.

Liou, S. (2009). Creativity, innovation, and entrepreneurship: Theory and practice of intelligent engineering. Taipei, Taiwan: Liwen.

Liou, S., & Nisbett, R. E. (2011). *Cultural difference in group creativity process*. Paper presented at the Annual Meeting of the Academy of Management, San Antonio, TX.

Maddux, W. W., Adam, H., & Galinsky, A. D. (2010). When in Rome...learn why the Romans do what they do: How multicultural learning experiences enhance creativity. *Personality and Social Psychology Bulletin, 36*, 731–741.

Maddux, W. W., & Galinsky, A. D. (2009). Cultural borders and mental barriers: The relationship between living abroad and creativity. *Journal of Personality and Social Psychology, 96, 1047–1061.*

Milliken, F. J., Bartel, C., & Kurtzberg, T. (2003). Diversity and creativity in work groups: A dynamic perspective on the affective and cognitive processes that link diversity and performance. In P. B. Paulus & B. Nijstad (Eds.), *Group creativity* (pp. 32–62). New York, NY: Oxford University Press.

Morris, M. W., & Leung, K. (2010). Creativity East and West: Perspectives and parallels. *Management and Organization Review, 6*, 313–327.

Morris, M. W., Mok, A., & Mor, S. (2011). Cultural identity threat: The role of cultural identifications in moderating closure responses to foreign cultural inflow. *Journal of Social Issues, 67*, 760–773.

Mumford, M. D., & Gustafson, S. B. (1988). Creativity syndrome: Integration, application, and innovation. *Psychological Bulletin, 103*, 27–43.

Nemeth, C., Personnaz, M., Personnaz, B., & Goncalo, J. (2004). The liberating role of conflict in group creativity: A cross-cultural study. *European Journal of Social Psychology, 34*, 365–374.

Nisbett, R. E. (2003). The geography of thought: *How Asians and Westerners think differently... and why*. New York, NY: Free Press.

Niu, W., & Sternberg, R. (2001). Cultural influence of artistic creativity and its evaluation. *International Journal of Psychology, 36*, 225–241.

Niu, W., Zhang, J., & Yang, Y. (2007). Deductive reasoning and creativity: A cross-cultural study. *Psychological Reports, 100*, 509–519.

Norenzayan, A., Atran, S., Faulkner, J., & Schaller, M. (2006). Memory and mystery: The cultural selection of minimally counterintuitive narratives. *Cognitive Science, 30*, 531–553.

Northcraft, G. B., Polzer, J. T., Neale, M. A., & Kramer, R. M. (1995). Diversity, social identity, and performance: Emergent social dynamics in cross-functional teams. In S. E. Jackson & M. N. Ruderman (Eds.), *Diversity in work teams: Research paradigms for a changing workplace* (pp. 68–96). Washington, DC: American Psychological Association.

Nouri, R., Erez, M., Rockstuhl, T., & Ang, S. (2008, August 8-13). *Creativity in multicultural teams: The effects of cultural diversity and situational strength on creativity performance*. Paper presented at the Annual Meeting of the Academy of Management, Anaheim, CA.

Paletz, S. B. F., & Peng, K. (2008). Implicit theories of creativity across cultures: Novelty and appropriateness in two product domains. *Journal of Cross-Cultural Psychology, 39*, 286–302.

Pickett, C. L., Bonner, B. L., & Coleman, J. M. (2002). Motivated self-stereotyping: Heightened assimilation and differentiation needs result in increased levels of positive and negative self-stereotyping. *Journal of Personality and Social Psychology, 82*, 543–562.

Proctor, R. W., Nof, S. Y. Yuehwern, Y., Balasubramanian, P., Busemeyer, J. R., Carayon, P., . . . Salvendy, G. (2011). Understanding and improving cross-cultural decision making in design and use of digital media: A research agenda. *International Journal of Human-Computer Interaction, 27*, 151–190.

Reining, B. A., & Mejias, R.J. (2004). The effects of national culture and anonymity on flaming and criticalness in GSS-Supported discussions. *Small Group Research, 35*, 698–723.

Routledge, C. D., & Arndt, J. (2009). Creative terror management: Creativity as a facilitator of cultural exploration after mortality salience. *Personality and Social Psychology Bulletin, 35*, 493–505.

Saeki, N., Fan, X., & Dusen, L. V. (2001). A comparative study of creative thinking of American and Japanese college students. *Journal of Creative Behavior, 35*, 24–36.

Schulz-Hardt, S., Brodbeck, F. C., Mojzisch, A., Kerschreiter, R., & Frey, D. (2006). Group decision making in hidden profile situations: Dissent as a facilitator for decision. *Journal of Personality and Social Psychology, 91*, 1080–1093.

Schulz-Hardt, S., Mojzisch, A. & Vogelgesang, F. (2007). Dissent as a facilitator: Individual and group-level effects on creativity and performance. In C. K. W. De Dreu & M. J. Gelfand (Eds.), *The psychology of conflict and conflict management in organizations* (pp. 149–177). New York, NY: Psychology Press.

Shin, S. J., Kim, T-Y., Lee, J-Y., & Bian, L. (2012). Cognitive team diversity and individual team member creativity: A cross-level interaction. *Academy of Management Journal, 55*, 197–212.

Solomon, S., Greenberg, J., & Pyszczynski, T. (1991). A terror management theory of social behavior: The psychological functions of self-esteem and cultural worldview. In L. Berkowitz (Ed.), *Advances in experimental social psychology* (Vol. 24, pp. 93–159). San Diego, CA: Academic Press.

Song, X. M., & Parry, M. E. (1997). Teamwork barriers in Japanese high-technology firms: The sociocultural differences between R&D and marketing managers. *Journal of Product Innovation Management, 14*, 356–367.

Song, X. M., & Parry, M. E. (1997). Teamwork barriers in Japanese high-technology firms: The sociocultural differences between R&D and marketing managers. *Journal of Product Innovation Management, 14*, 356–367.

Sternberg, R. (2003). *The anatomy of impact: What makes the great works of psychology great?* Washington, DC: American Psychological Association.

Thatcher, S. M., Jehn, K. A., & Zanutto, E. (2003). Cracks in diversity research: The effects of faultlines on conflict and performance. *Group Decision and Negotiation, 12*, 217–241.

Tjosvold, D. (1998). Co-operative and competitive goal approaches to conflict: Accomplishments and challenges. *Applied Psychology: An International Review, 47*, 285–342.

Tomasello, M. (2001). Cultural transmission: A view from chimpanzees and human infants. *Journal of Cross-Cultural Psychology, 32*, 135–146.

Torelli, C. J. (2006). Individuality or conformity? The effect of independent and interdependent self-concepts on public judgments. *Journal of Consumer Psychology, 16*, 238–246.

Torelli, C. J., Chiu, C-Y., Tam, K-P., Au, A. K-C., & Keh, H. T. (2011). Exclusionary reactions to foreign culture: Effects of simultaneous exposure to culture in globalized space. *Journal of Social Issues, 67*, 716–742.

Wan, C., Chiu, C-Y., Tam, K-P., Lee, S-L., Lau, I. Y-M., & Peng, S-Q. (2007). Perceived cultural importance and actual self-importance of values in cultural identification. *Journal of Personality and Social Psychology, 92*, 337–354.

Wan, W., & Chiu, C-Y. (2002). Effects of novel conceptual combination on creativity. *Journal of Creative Behavior, 36*, 227–241.

Webster, D., & Kruglanski, A. (1994) Individual differences in need for cognitive closure. *Journal of Personality and Social Psychology, 67*, 1049–1062.

West, M. A., & Wallace, M. (1991). Innovation in health care teams. *British Journal of Social Psychology, 21*, 303–315.

Whiten, A., Goodall, J., McGrew, W. C., Nishida, T., Reynolds, V., Sugiyama, Y., ...Boesch, C. (1999). Cultures in chimpanzees. *Nature, 399*, 682–685.

Workman, J. (1997). Engineering's interactions with marketing groups in an engineering-driven organization. In R. Katz (Ed.), *The human side of managing technological innovation: A collection of readings* (pp. 535–549). New York, NY: Oxford University Press.

Zeidan, F., Martucco, K. T., Kraft, R. A., Gordon, N. S., McHaffie, J. G., & Goghill, R. C. (2011). Brain mechanisms supporting the modulation of pain by mindfulness meditation. *Journal of Neuroscience, 31*, 5540–5548.

Zha, P., Walczyk, J. J., Griffith-Ross, D. A., Tobacyk, J. K., & Walczyk, D. F. (2006). The impact of culture and individualism-collectivism on the creative potential and achievement of American and Chinese adults. *Creativity Research Journal, 18*, 355–366.

Zhang, D., Lowry, P. B., Zhou, L., & Fu, X. (2004). The impact of individualism—Collectivism, social presence, and group diversity on group decision making under majority influence. *Journal of Management Information Systems, 23*, 53–80.

Zhou, J., & Su, Y. (2010). A missing piece of the puzzle: The organizational context in cultural patterns of creativity. *Management and Organization Review, 63*, 391–413.

Zou, X., Tam, K-P., Morris, M. W., Lee, S-L., Lau, Y-M., & Chiu, C-Y. (2009). Culture as common sense: Perceived consensus vs. personal beliefs as mechanisms of cultural influence. *Journal of Personality and Social Psychology, 97*, 579–597.

8

How Does Culture Matter?

A Contextual View of Intercultural Interaction in Groups

MARY E. ZELLMER-BRUHN AND CRISTINA B. GIBSON

> People are not captive recipients of cultural influence. Rather people can turn culture into an object of reflection.
>
> —Chiu, Gelfand, Yamagishi, Shteynberg, & Wan, 2010 (p. 488)

Both as a result of and in support for globalization, the study of culture and work has become a dynamic and important field of research (Tsui, Nifadkar, & Ou, 2007). An area with much research focus and attention surrounds national culture and its effects on interpersonal processes and outcomes at work. Existing research illustrates that people from different cultural backgrounds vary on many workplace norms and behaviors such as conflict resolution (e.g., Black & Mendenhall, 1993; Morris et al., 1998), seeking and providing feedback (e.g., Earley, Gibson, & Chen, 1999; Osland, 1995; Takeuchi, Imahori, & Matsumoto, 2001), participation and negotiation (e.g., Adler, Brahm, & Graham, 1992; Brett & Okumura, 1998; Francis, 1991; Tinsley, 2001), and informal social communication (e.g., Earley, 1987), to name just a few. Because people from different cultural backgrounds vary on these and other important workplace norms and behaviors, it is often argued that individuals must deviate from their intuitive, culturally ingrained behavior to act effectively in intercultural work interactions (Berry, 1997; Graves, 1967). The expectation that effective intercultural work interactions require adaptation has led scholars to focus on whether such deviation occurs and, if so, whether attempted adaptation is functional.

The majority of research examining intercultural effectiveness at work has been done in the literature on expatriate adaptation and success (e.g., Black & Gregersen, 1999; Black, Mendenhall, & Oddou, 1991; Mendenhall & Oddou, 1985). This research is placed in settings characterized by three things: (1) ongoing interaction, (2) between individuals from two cultures, (3) focused on senior managers. While research on long-term expatriate assignments continues to be important (e.g., Haslberger, 2005; Yamazaki, 2010) and expatriate phenomena continue to be an important aspect of international management (e.g., McNulty & Cieri, 2011; Werner, 2002; Yamazaki, 2010), globalization and technology development have changed the characteristics of intercultural work in important ways (Friedman, 2005; Ger, 1999).

First, intercultural work now frequently occurs among individuals who remain in their home country or are not specifically relocated to a foreign assignment. Hence, much of today's intercultural work does not involve expatriates at all. In parallel, it is now common for nonmanagerial employees to engage in intercultural work (e.g., Barinaga, 2007; Ely & Thomas, 2001). Frontline sales and service personnel respond to calls from coworkers in other overseas locations, or from globally dispersed clients and customers. Firms in many different industries, from mineral, oil, and gas extraction to automotive design and manufacturing, have remote (i.e., nonheadquarters) locations, in which diverse employees from engineers to construction teams, visit or interact with each other using technology. Global procurement and supply chain management are common strategies in most businesses, necessitating a comprehensive network of suppliers and buyers from different cultures. Even university students commonly participate with peers in global virtual projects or go to foreign countries for exchange programs or intercultural work experiences. As a result, intercultural work is becoming less and less about senior managers who have relocated for a foreign country assignment.

Second, intercultural interactions tend now to be more frequent, horizontal, unstructured, temporary, sporadic, and across global locations. Intercultural interactions also often involve multiple cultures rather than relationships representing two cultures, such as between an expatriate manager and her host country employees. One important setting where such dynamic, multicultural interactions are common is in geographically distributed work. For example, a midlevel project engineer working at a US medical device company may, within the span of a day, call a software engineer in India to resolve a programming issue on the device he is working on, then later relay that information to a plant manager in Taiwan, where the device is being manufactured, and finally, file a report on the changes with an EU regulator in Belgium.

In addition to globally distributed work, the use of globally distributed teams has become more and more common to resolve complex organizational problems. These teams likely are multicultural, but they also must, to solve complex problems, engage in significant boundary-spanning activities such as searching outside the team in different parts of the organization for knowledge and information and selling the team's ideas, activities, and products to external stakeholders (Ancona & Bresman, 2007). Consider a team of community relations staff who implement programs on behalf of their multinational firm in remote East Timor, where the firm has operations. They interact sporadically with a variety of service providers (that come and go) as they conduct their work on the ground in Timor. The multicultural team may not have formal supervisory authority over the service providers, the interactions are likely to be extemporaneous, and they often pertain to urgent matters arising dynamically in the complex task of working in remote communities, rather than in regularly held meetings. These interactions are critical in accomplishing the mission of the firm (i.e., if community infrastructure does not work effectively in the remote locations, operations cannot proceed), yet the intercultural interactions that occur in this setting do not resemble those typically in focus in the international management literature. As a result, intercultural interactions may not be long-term engagements providing time to learn and adapt to a single, foreign culture.

What this means, taken together, is that in order to keep pace with workplace developments, there is a need for research that considers the characteristics of modern intercultural workplace interaction, namely, (1) shorter term, (2) more horizontal than vertical, (3) multicultural, and (4) distributed. It will be important for scholars to develop theory and conduct empirical work considering the ways in which dynamic, shorter term intercultural interaction differs from more sustained face-to-face cultural adaptation. For instance, some view these shorter term interactions as "building blocks" to gaining the competencies necessary for longer term adaptation to single cultures (Molinsky, 2007). Yet prior research rarely has focused on interaction processes. While there is more recent attention to dynamic views of culture (e.g., Erez & Gati, 2004; Hong, 2009; Oyserman & Sorensen, 2009), these studies have yet to develop theory about the interactions themselves and to what extent characteristics of the interactions may affect the ways in which culture "matters."

In this chapter, we present some foundational work for a framework about dynamic workplace intercultural interaction, with specific attention paid to how variations in the context of the interactions may affect the responses and outcomes achieved by participants. Importantly, a central point of our conceptual development is that the context characteristics of the interaction setting affect whether culture matters, when it does, and in what ways. To do this, we first describe what we mean by intercultural interaction. We then review the literature to contrast two different perspectives on why culture matters in group interactions. In doing so, we show the necessity for an approach that addresses important boundary conditions in this prior research. We then introduce the concept of intercultural interaction spaces (IIS) to address limitations of prior research and provide a platform for future research on intercultural work. While our conceptual approach has implications for a variety of intercultural work, we conclude with some specific implications that our approach has for globally distributed teamwork.

INTERCULTURAL INTERACTION

Intercultural interaction is a process involving perception-behavior-response cycles among individuals from different cultures (Thomas & Ravlin, 1995). For the purposes of this chapter, we limit the focus to intercultural *work* interactions—or contact among individuals from different cultural contexts for the purpose of completing organizationally sanctioned tasks (as opposed to social reasons for contact). We provide this rather broad definition of work interactions to develop a wide-angle view of how culture matters.

To build a case for a fresh approach, it is important first to consider the different ways culture is construed. A complete review of culture across all the disciplines in which it is covered is beyond the scope of this chapter. Instead, we focus here on two dominant views of culture that are particularly relevant to the workplace setting: values based and constructivist. In each case, we briefly describe the perspective and how it conceptualizes culture (the substance of culture), how it suggests culture matters to individual and group behavior, and the challenges and limitations the view has for explaining short-term, horizontal, intercultural group interactions in distributed work.

Values-Based Views of Culture

Within the organizational behavior research literature, the dominant perspective on culture has been the values-based perspective. Values are socially shared conceptions of what is good (Sagiv & Schwartz, 1995) and are "cognitive, social representations of basic motivational goals that serve as guiding principles in people's lives" (Roccas, Schwartz & Amit, 2010: 394). Values-based views approach culture with the perspective that bounded social groups can be identified by, and also are expected to have, shared values. Values-based views focus on universal cultural values and identifying central tendencies within distinct societies or groups.

Values-based views of culture typically adopt a dimensional approach, focusing on the differences between nations (or sometimes other significant social groups) to describe the characteristics of people from different nations in terms of each dimension. Drawing largely from anthropology, sociology, and social psychology, values-based view researchers have either developed a series of dyadic dimensions of cultures (also called pan-cultural conceptual tools or etic approaches), such as individualism-collectivism (e.g., Triandis, 1989); tightness-looseness (e.g., Triandis, 1989); independence-interdependence (e.g., Markus & Kitayama, 1991); or values typologies (e.g., Schwartz, 1992) to account for cultural variations in social cognitive processes and behaviors.

For example, perhaps the best-known and applied culture theory in the management and organization studies literature is the classical dimensional approach developed by Hofstede (for a review of two decades of Hofstede-inspired research, see Kirkman, Lowe, & Gibson, 2006). Hofstede (1980, 2001) proposed that cultural characteristics of nations differ in terms of individualism, power distance, uncertainty avoidance, and masculinity, and short-term versus long-term orientation. Over the past several decades, other researchers have also developed a variety of dimensions to describe cultural differences in values. For example, Trompenaars's work (1994) across 28 countries provided a comprehensive framework, including five cultural dimensions: individualism/collectivism, universalism/particularism, neutral/affective, specific/diffuse, and achievement/ascription. In a more simplified model, Gelfand et al. (2011) showed the differences between cultures that are tight (having many strong norms and a low tolerance of deviant behavior) versus loose (having weak social norms and a high tolerance of deviant behavior). She and her colleagues (2011) proposed that tightness-looseness is part of a "complex, loosely integrated system that involves processes across multiple levels of analysis, including ecological, historical, and institutional factors, along with everyday situations and psychological processes" (p. 1101). Still others have highlighted time-related values, suggesting, for example, that cultures vary between preferences for sequential versus synchronous activity (e.g., Hodgetts & Luthans, 2003; Trompenaars, 1994) or preference for the use of public or private space (Feldman, 2002; Kiser, 1999).

Scholars who approach culture with the values-based view adopted the concepts of values and preferences, and use theories about values (e.g., Kluckhohn, 1951; Rokeach, 1973) to explain why and how stable sets of preferences learned by individuals socialized in a particular cultural setting (typically defined by national boundaries) ought to influence behavior.

How Culture Matters in Groups From a Values-Based Perspective

At the heart of the values-based perspective is that values are long-set in individuals through socialization within their national culture and are quite stable (Hofstede, 1980). This means that if we think about how culture causally operates in workplace interactions, it is by differences in values across people from different cultures. Much of the research considering cross-national differences in values, therefore, not surprisingly, is comparative, showing, for example, how organizational structures and practices, employee attitudes and preferences, or leadership styles (House, Hanges, Javidan, Dorfman, & Gupta, 2004) vary in predictable ways across nations.

Other scholars have extended the values-based approach to the individual level, arguing that values affect behavior by influencing whether different courses of action are viewed as attractive to individuals based on their culture (Feather, 1995). People with a given set of values will display a corresponding (and predictable) set of responses (Hong, 2009, p. 3). This branch of values-based research has demonstrated correlations between specific values and relevant outcomes such as readiness for outgroup interaction (Sagiv & Schwartz, 1995) and national identification (Roccas, Schwartz, & Amit, 2010).

Values-based approaches offer a means of characterizing the central tendencies that distinguish members of a particular cultural group. In doing so, they enable comparison and illustration of key differences in expectations and behaviors that may exist in intercultural situations such as global teams. For example, Gibson and Zellmer-Bruhn (2001) demonstrated that there are fundamental differences in the meaning of the concept of teamwork across cultures. These differences can be revealed in the metaphors people use to talk about teams, and the metaphors have implications for what is expected from team management (Gibson & Zellmer-Bruhn, 2001). Thus, they asserted that our most basic assumptions about what workers understand to be a "team" cannot be universally applied across cultures, necessitating a reassessment of theories of group behavior with special attention to cultural differences in the concepts of teamwork they hold.

Demonstrating such underlying differences in the ways people understand teamwork provides at least two major contributions to the literature. First, specifically related to research concerning teams, verifying variance in teamwork conceptualizations provides insight into the differences in preferred practices that have been noted across cultural contexts in prior empirical research. Second, doing so challenges scholars to build specific theories of teamwork that incorporate these differences, and it challenges practitioners to adapt teaming practices to become congruent with the prevailing conceptualizations in a cultural setting. Hence, coinciding with a values-based view, many argue that awareness of potential differences is a key precursor to inclusive, respectful, optimal incorporation of diversity in the workplace (Maznevski & DiStefano, 1995). This view presumes that through contact, experience, and even preinteraction training, people can learn about other people's values and then presumably adapt or (at the very least) reduce their unconscious, rapid attributions that could interfere with effective interaction at work.

Likewise our understanding of the role of culture in workplace interaction has benefited from the values-based approach, in that by empirically demonstrating that central tendencies do exist, and that they differentiate cultural groupings, researchers have been able to make some strides toward predicting behavior and performance outcomes in intercultural settings (see Gelfand, Leslie, & Keller, 2008, Gibson & McDaniel, 2010; Tsui et al., 2007; for reviews). For example, knowing that a set of values characterize a given culture but do not characterize another, and that these values have been linked to conflict when these cultures come into contact, offers at least partial explanation for why the conflict may be occurring and clues to how it can be addressed.

Shortcomings of the Values-Based View for Intercultural Interaction

Hofstede's (1980, 2001) work is focused on cross-national differences in *national* culture. This perspective limits the applicability of his values-based view to the types of interactions we are interested in in this chapter. In contrast, other values-based researchers take a distinctly individual view of values (e.g., Schwartz, 1990; Schwartz & Sagiv, 1995). So, one issue is a levels question about where cultural values lie or are held, and correspondingly how they translate to individual thoughts and action.

Also, some have argued that the values-based view of culture has failed the "causal test," meaning that it has been difficult to empirically support the idea that actions are based on outcomes (values) being sought (e.g., Swidler, 1986). Others note that culture is not a set of values but rather the meaning attached to the world around us (Earley, 2006). Earley argues for a need for theories that link culture to action, and there are several features of the values approach that make this challenging. For example, values-based approaches often fall prey to stereotypes, and the biases associated with them. More specifically, once an individual learns that there is a tendency for a certain cultural group to be characterized by a certain set of values, it is tempting to assume that everyone in that group will hold the same level of those values. Of course, this is often not the case. Furthermore, such approaches often result in individuals assuming that the typical representative of a given cultural group will consistently behave in a certain way that reflects certain cultural values, even across dramatically different situations and contexts. When these expectations are violated, the focal individual may be puzzled and confused, because interaction partners are not adhering to the anticipated "norms" of their cultural group.

Values-based approaches to culture are also often criticized because they tend to isolate a small subset of values (commonly a single value), measure whether individuals hold that value, and then assume that if a link to behavior or outcomes is demonstrated, this constitutes a "cultural explanation." The danger here is that individuals actually hold a *configuration* of value orientations, not just a single value (Chao & Moon, 2005). Adding even more complexity—which is often not reflected in values-based theory and research—is that a given individual likely participates in a variety of cultural groups, each of which is characterized by a *different* configuration of values. For example, an individual may have parents of different ethnic or cultural backgrounds; he or she may have been born in a country different to that of his or her parents; he or she may currently reside in a country different from his or her country of birth; the organization he or she works for may be headquartered in yet another country; and he or she may affiliate with a variety of social groups (Leung, Maddux, Galinsky, & Chiu, 2008). As borders become more permeable and the workforce is more mobile, this is increasingly the case. If the variety of cultural groups one affiliates with form some part of his or her identity, he or she may very well be multicultural within (i.e., hold multiple cultural values simultaneously) (Brannen & Thomas, 2010). Hence, the individual follows norms of one parent's culture in some circumstances, norms of the other parent in still others, and may take on norms of the country in which he or she resides or which characterizes his or her workplace in yet other situations (Benet-Martinez, Lee, & Leu, 2006). This makes behavior incredibly difficult (if not impossible) to predict based on knowledge about a limited set (or single) cultural value.

Conclusions About the Values-Based View of Culture

If we think about what the values-based approaches say about short-term intercultural interactions, we would expect it to go something like this: When people from different cultural backgrounds come in contact in a short-term, ad hoc intercultural interaction, if they have different intensity and direction of cultural values, they will experience culture shock. Likely they will behave in ways that clash with expected norms for their own culture, generating problems such as conflict, confusion, and uncertainty. The only thing that could perhaps explain or anticipate productive outcomes is whether the parties in the intercultural contact have experienced intercultural training or have had extensive prior international experience in the same or similar countries.

In summary, values-based approaches to culture offer a parsimonious means of capturing central tendencies in cultural groupings, which can help develop a starting point or serve as a precursor for intercultural interactions. But values-based frameworks often suffer from simplistic assumptions about stability across situations, unidimensional (rather than configurational) characterizations, and a lack of recognition of multicultural identities. From our review of the literature, we conclude that values-based views of culture focus on the substance of culture. We need to know more about the processes by which culture matters in order to understand whether and how aspects of intercultural contact situations might support or impede effective interaction outcomes.

Constructivist View of Culture

A more recently developed view of culture that stands in relatively stark contrast to the values-based view is the constructivist view. Rather than view culture as a stable set of values, the constructivist view suggests culture consists of bundles of knowledge, or a repertoire for "strategies of action" (e.g., Swidler, 1986). Still others think of culture as involving "networks of knowledge" (Hong, 2009, p. 4). Importantly in this view, culture is not seen as a stable set of these cultural components, but rather the cognitive components of culture may be combined and recombined, or drawn upon with varying degrees of frequency to produce observed behavior.

One example of a constructivist view of culture is Hong and her colleagues' dynamic constructivist approach to culture (Hong, 2009; Hong & Chiu, 2001; Hong, Morris, Chiu, & Benet-Martinez, 2000). The crux of this view is that individuals have multiple cultural-based schemata that they learn over time and through experience. Similarly, Oyserman and her colleagues (Oyserman & Markus, 1998; Oyserman & Sorensen, 2009) developed the cultural syndrome approach in which they argue that individuals hold multiple, sometimes overlapping, and even potentially contradictory networks of cultural features in their minds (syndromes). Oyserman and Sorensen (2009) go on to suggest that societies differ not in whether certain values such as individualism/collectivism exist, but in how likely each perspective is to be enacted (p. 28). In these views, culture is understood as diverse and dynamic content represented in individuals' minds.

Some of the content described in constructivist view studies is very similar to the values described in values-based approaches. Yet, rather than be dominated by a societally defined direction and intensity of a particular value as in the values-based view, in the constructivist approach to culture, individuals may hold multiple sets of ideas, values, and schema that may encompass both ends of a given dyadic value dimension. As cognitive processes are thought to be guided by just one set of knowledge structures at a time, a specific cultural knowledge structure can influence attitudes and behaviors only when it comes to the forefront of the mind. Scholars who approach cultures with the constructivist view adopt concepts of accessibility, availability, and applicability from knowledge activation theory (Higgins, 1996; Wyer & Srull, 1986, 1989) to explain what determines whether a particular piece of cultural knowledge becomes operative and comes to the forefront of the mind to subsequently influence behavior.

How Culture Matters in Groups From a Constructivist Perspective

The constructivist perspective considers that the causal potential of culture is based in the activation of shared cultural knowledge like schema or syndromes. These are cognitive structures that organize thoughts around a particular concept or idea, and when activated, help individuals make sense of observations as well as trigger cognitive and behavioral responses. Because individuals hold multiple such cognitive structures, the constructivist view stresses that cultural processes are dynamic, not deterministic (i.e., rather than assuming a person from country A will hold values B and thereby act in X way, this view suggests that a person from country A could hold B, D, F and G, etc. schema and *depending upon the circumstances*, act in accordance with any one of them).

Constructivist theories would argue that when certain shared knowledge is activated, one is more likely to display behaviors typical to that cultural schema. For example, Kitayama (2002) proposes a *system view* to understanding the dynamic nature of culture, as opposed to the *entity view* that sees culture as a static entity. This *system view* suggests that each person's psychological processes are organized through the active effort to coordinate one's behaviors with the pertinent cultural systems of practices and public meanings. Yet, concurrently, many aspects of the psychological systems develop rather flexibly as they are attuned to the surrounding sociocultural environment and are likely to be configured in different ways across different sociocultural groups. For instance, Tinsley and Brodt (2004) have provided a cognitive analysis of cultural differences in conflict behaviors: *Frames* direct attention to certain aspects of the environment; *schemas* are knowledge structures that give meaning to encoded information; and *scripts* are a special type of schema that involve a temporal sequence that are most relevant for events and actions. These constructs are dynamic in the sense that their content and salience are sensitive to environmental influences.

The constructivist view highlights the possibility that cultural differences may be easier to overcome than previously assumed, if mental processes associated with national culture are relatively fluid and can be changed and sustained by situational influences. For instance, Leung and his associates (Leung, Smith, Wang, & Sun, 1996; Leung, Wang, & Smith, 2001) found that local employees in international joint ventures in China reported more positive job attitudes working with Western expatriate managers than with overseas Chinese and Japanese expatriate managers, presumably because they were more flexible in their approaches with the former than with the latter. These findings contradict the cultural distance argument, which suggests that people from very different cultures have more problems working together than people from similar cultures (Leung, Bhagat, Buchan, Erez, & Gibson, 2005), and offer an alternative view of how culture might unfold in work teams. As another example, recent research by Gibson (2012) applies a constructivist view to better understand cultural dilemmas among bicultural Australians (with both indigenous and nonindigenous cultural origins). When such individuals work in multinational firms, they often develop very sophisticated techniques for reconciling particularized internal identity conflicts that occur within them. Acting on behalf of their firm, they may violate indigenous cultural norms in certain circumstances yet express their indigenous cultural identity quite vehemently in other circumstances. Doing so is not without its challenges, but it allows them to preserve their indigenous cultural heritage, while also maintaining gainful employment.

An important contribution of the constructivist approach is the introduction of situational contingencies. While the values-based approach tends to assume consistency across individuals from a given cultural group and across contexts, the constructivist perspective embraces inconsistency. The constructivist perspective is also sensitive to the dynamism of intercultural interaction, as well as its often impromptu and improvisational nature. Important to this approach, the expectation is that individuals do not have one predisposed cultural content based on national origin or location (e.g., individualism) but rather hold (and can apprehend) multiple contents that can be elicited and applied differentially (e.g., individualism in one situation and collectivism in another). In other words, whereas the values-based approach tends to view individuals from a single cultural background as having *one* perspective on each value, the constructivist view indicates that individuals have a toolkit or repertoire of cultural knowledge at their disposal.

Shortcomings of the Constructivist View for Intercultural Interaction

Despite its strengths, the constructivist view potentially ignores more stable central tendencies in national groups, the knowledge of which can help make intercultural interaction more efficient. As mentioned earlier, knowing something about what an individual's values *might be*, based on an understanding of typical or normative behavior in a given national culture, can serve as a starting point. If that starting point is then followed by a discovery mindset, in which knowledge about a particular individual and his or her behavior in a particular context is tested against the assumptions one might have based on research, then the assumptions can be corrected and updated to fit the person and situation. Without such a starting point, the individual begins the discovery process with a blank slate. Some may argue that this is a good thing. But anyone who has been subjected to information overload on a visit to a developing country (the vivid sights, sounds, and smells can be incredibly stimulating but also overwhelming), for example, can attest to the practical value of at least having some prior knowledge on which to build expectations for behavior and interaction plans. Moreover, it is possible that frequent moving between different cultural schemas or cultural frame switching can increase contradiction, uncertainty, and ambiguity, which may impede interaction effectiveness.

Conclusions About the Constructivist View of Culture

If we think about what the constructivist approach would say about short-term intercultural interactions in groups at work, we would expect it to go something like this: When people from different cultural backgrounds come in contact in a short-term, ad hoc intercultural interaction, whether their behavior will be culturally based is dependent on whether cultural knowledge is activated. It may be that their behavior will be similar, even if they have different cultural knowledge because what might be considered "traditional" cultural knowledge (i.e., schemas often associated with their national cultural background) may not be activated. To understand the role of culture in these interactions, we would need to know more about what cultural knowledge (if any) has been activated in the individuals and what has primed it.

COMBINING THE VIEWS: INTERCULTURAL INTERACTION SPACE

How does what we learned from our review illuminate the short-term, unstructured, relatively temporary, often technology-enabled interactions that are the focus of our chapter? All in all, we conclude that cultural content can be identified as varying between significant social groups, that there is also potentially significant within-social-group variation, that individuals can develop and hold more than one cultural meaning system/cultural knowledge structure, and that within individuals, different cultural knowledge structures can be activated through cues or priming. We also highlight recent work (e.g., Chiu et al., 2010; Molinsky, 2007) proposing that cultural behaviors can be strategic responses to opportunities and constraints, that individuals can seek culturally competent behavior, and that culturally derived behaviors are goal-directed, adaptive, and malleable. In other words, cultural knowledge activation may be automatic, but it does not have to be.

The two perspectives can stimulate each other in an approach for innovative theorizing and application of cultural knowledge in intercultural interaction. Both the values-based view and the constructivist view provide rich information about important cultural knowledge structures that likely affect meaning making and behavior in intercultural interaction in groups. In addition, the constructivist view brings into focus the idea that individuals can hold more than one cultural meaning system or sets of cultural knowledge structures. As a result, in any given intercultural interaction, a variety of cultural knowledge structures could become operative and influence the interaction. Proponents of the constructivist view further suggest that priming and accessibility of cultural knowledge both affect the likelihood that any given cultural syndrome might be activated and come to bear on the interaction partners' meaning making, thoughts, and behaviors. The central tendencies identified in the values-based view may be more accessible to members of a given national culture, and thereby more commonly or more readily activated than other, less accessible cultural knowledge.

Therefore, to integrate the values-based approach with the constructivist approach, and develop greater process understanding of when and how culture matters during intercultural interaction in work groups, requires a deeper look at the *situations* in which such interactions occur. To achieve this, we introduce the concept of *intercultural interaction space (IIS), defined as the physical, cognitive, and affective features of the situational context in which people of different cultures interact.* Explicit consideration of the interaction circumstances is a key area we found lacking in both the values-based and constructivist perspectives. Neither perspective provides explicit attention to aspects of the situations or contexts of intercultural interaction that are likely to cue or trigger the recognition of cultural differences or a need to draw on alternative cultural syndromes or knowledge to effectively complete the interaction goals. Doing so responds to calls for more attention to context (i.e., Johns, 2006) in organizational research in general, and teams research in particular (Mathieu, Maynard, Rapp, & Gilson, 2008).

A cornerstone of the ability for interaction partners to engage in culturally competent behavior begins with the recognition by the interaction partners that the interaction is, in fact, an *intercultural* interaction and that culture may be playing a role in the interaction outcomes. Scholars have referred to recognition of cultural differences as influenced by a "period of contrast" (Osland, Oddou, Bird, & Osland, 2008). More specifically, dissimilarity between self and other in some aspect of the person or the situation attracts attention. Therefore, the first process component of the IIS is recognition. This may be a momentary split-second thought or a more lengthy internal conversation, which is often referred to as sense making. Sense making involves a process of placing cues into a framework that enables people "to comprehend, understand, explain, attribute, extrapolate, and predict" (Starbuck & Milliken, 1988, p. 51). Elaborating on what this sense-making process looks like, Weick (1995, p. 43) argues that people "chop moments out of continuous flows and extract cues from those moments"; when a cue is extracted from the general flow of stimuli, it is "embellished" and linked to a more general idea, most commonly to a similar cue from one's past (Weick, 1995).

Our review revealed that missing from either view of culture is a discussion about how the social context of intercultural interactions may cue both (1) that the interaction is intercultural and, (2) as a result, prime specific cultural knowledge in interaction partners about what might be appropriate or useful behavior. For example, an interesting extension of Gibson and Zellmer-Bruhn's (2001) work on cultural variations in concepts of teamwork would be to understand whether the differences in the use of teamwork metaphors (a type of cultural knowledge) uncovered by the researchers are noticed in the context of global teams, where different metaphors are being used by different members. Recognition by team members that there is variation in the team (i.e., John says to Yuki, "Why does Pedro always seem to talk about the team as if it is a family?") would be an example of "contrast." Sense making would then unfold if John and Yuki try to understand *why* Pedro considers the team a family. If they had prior knowledge of Pedro's Puerto Rican heritage and an understanding that teams often function like an extended family in that context, they might invoke a cultural explanation for the metaphor use. By highlighting the IIS, we begin to ask, what aspects of the team's context made this contrast come to light? What aspects of the IIS encourage intercultural sense making? What features of the IIS promote a cultural explanation?

Importantly, what counts as a cue will be determined by the frame a person is using to understand events. As suggested by Klein and his associates, "the knowledge and expectancies a person has will determine what counts as a cue and whether it will be noticed" (Klein, Pliske, Crandall, &Woods, 2005, p. 17). A values-based approach informs this element of our model, as awareness of potential cultural values differences can heighten one's sensitivity to cultural interaction cues. Intercultural sense making is a result of cultural variations. It can be triggered whenever a contrast occurs—that is, whenever people notice novel cultural variations, whenever they observe unexpected behavior, or whenever they make a deliberate attempt to learn more about another culture (Osland, Bird, & Gundersen, 2007). Cultural trigger events, which are perceived differentially by individuals, can lead to intercultural sense making once they pass a certain threshold. To continue with the earlier example, the values-based approach might highlight that John is prompted to ask the "why" question because he has knowledge of the differences in central value tendencies of each member of the team; without such knowledge, he may not have noticed the metaphor as a "cue."

Once cues are recognized, individuals may or may not engage in culturally adaptive behaviors due to different levels of situational constraint. Adaptation involves "changing one's behavior, manner, communication style, appearance and customs to be similar to those of another party" (Pornpitakpan, 1999, p. 320). Therefore, a second process component of the IIS is the amount of behavior discretion provided by the situational strength. Here we mean whether individuals feel that it is acceptable to adapt their behavior to support effective interaction. If the level of perceived behavioral discretion is low, based on the IIS, then individuals would feel prompted to behavior following (their own) normative cultural patterns. An important determinant of whether interaction partners strategically adapt their behaviors in an intercultural interaction will depend on whether the interaction context constitutes a strong or weak situation. Strong situations are characterized as restricting the range of appropriate behavior, leaving little room for individual discretion (Mischel, 1977). In contrast, weak situations place few external constraints on individuals, allowing individual choice among a wider range of behaviors (Gelfand et al., 2011). When situations are strong, individuals understand that there is a narrow set of behaviors that are appropriate for the situation. Situational strength has been linked to cultural variation in behaviors, wherein strong situations limit cultural variation in behavior, because the situation dictates the behavior, rather than any given cultural value doing so (Gelfand et al., 2011). Again, continuing with the earlier example, Yuki may feel free to think about possible ways of incorporating Pedro's sense that the team is a family if the organizational context is not one that dictates highly specific and standardized teaming practices—in other words, if the "situation" is somewhat weak. On the other hand, if the organization has standardized practices, adapting the practice in the team may seem out of the realm of possibility or may not even occur to her. Interestingly, prior research (Zellmer-Bruhn & Gibson, 2006) has found that organizational contexts with a strategic emphasis on global integration reduced team learning, while those emphasizing local responsiveness and knowledge management increased team learning. Team learning, in turn, positively influences both task performance and quality of interpersonal relations.

Finally, intercultural work—particularly global, distributed teamwork—often occurs in multiple episodes. Each episode constitutes an intercultural interaction. Hence, sense making is an ongoing process involving an iterative cycle of events: framing the situation, making attributions, and selecting scripts, which are undergirded by constellations of cultural values and cultural history (Osland & Bird, 2000). It follows that intercultural interactions each have different qualities because different subsets of members may be involved, the purpose and content of the interaction vary, and the physical location and communication modes differ. The different qualities mean that for each interaction, the potential effects of culture are nuanced and may be experienced anew. As a result, it may not be the case that interaction partners from a given culture should be expected to behave in the same way in each interaction. Hence, this element of our model is informed by the constructivist view of culture. It is predicated on the assumption that culture is contextually based (Fang, 2006; Gannon, 2007; Kluckholm & Strodtbeck, 1961). In our example, we may find that whenever John, Yuki, and Pedro interact, there is a sensitivity to the differences in concepts of teamwork, adaptive behavior results, and positive outcomes follow the adaptive behavior, which then subsequently serve to reinforce the intercultural sense making and adaptation among that subset of the team; however, if John interacts with others in the team, and makes attempts at sense making and adaption that are not well received, he may be less likely to do so in future interactions with those team members.

In summary, then, our idea of the intercultural interaction space centers on the extent to which the social context of the interaction provides (1) the opportunity for recognition of cultural cues and (2) information about latitude for culturally adaptive responses provided by a particular interaction episode. We propose that there are physical, cognitive, and affective characteristics of the intercultural interaction space that influence the opportunity for cue recognition and the situational constraint placed in interaction partners. In the following sections, we provide some examples to illustrate how and why these three features of the IIS may affect both cue recognition and latitude for adaptive behaviors.

Physical Aspects of the Intercultural Interaction Space

The physical aspects of the IIS vary and may affect cue availability and situational constraints. Intercultural interactions can take place locally when individuals from a group are in the same geographic spot, or they can take place between interaction partners located at varying geographic distances from one another. Furthermore, the setting could be one subsidiary or unit's offices or a neutral space such as a hotel, client office, or conference, which could be in one or some of the team members' native country or in a third country location that is not in any team member's home country. The IIS also may range from face-to-face format for interaction to technology-mediated format, and it may be at concurrent times or across multiple time zones (Stanko & Gibson, 2009). These physical characteristics of the IIS are likely to produce different meaning and different experiences for the partners of the interaction, depending upon their own cultural history and experiences.

To illustrate how the physical aspects of the IIS might affect intercultural interaction, consider the degree of virtuality (Gibson & Gibbs, 2006). Face-to-face settings have different demand characteristics than do those with a high degree of virtuality (e.g., electronic dependence or geographic dispersion) (Kirkman, Gilbson, & Kim, 2012; Stanko & Gibson, 2009). Highly virtual contexts enable anonymity, which can dampen cultural considerations. For example, Edwards and Sridhar (2005) found virtual team members' perceptions of cultural value orientation diversity in the team to have no relationship with team members' learning, satisfaction, and performance. In contrast, face-to-face intercultural interaction provides more salient demographic information. Early in a team's experience, national differences in teams relate to lower levels of perceived similarity on work style (Zellmer-Bruhn, Maloney, Bhappu, & Salvador, 2008). When cultural diversity is high and teams launch face to face, there may be a sort of anchoring to the demographic diversity, reducing levels of perceived similarity in work style (irrespective of actual differences in such "deep-level" characteristics). Using perceptions about overt demographic differences to make initial assumptions about expected work style similarities could result in positive or negative interaction cycles, depending upon the actual coupling of national/ethnic diversity and work styles. More specifically, there will be some cases where visible demographic features such as ethnicity may actually be connected to culturally based differences in work styles (i.e., the visible and less visible are tightly coupled). In such a case, the expectations about interactions based on work style similarity or difference made by team members using the visible cues about demographics that are salient in a face-to-face interaction are accurate and could aid in formulating adaptation strategies. In contrast, there will be other cases where work styles are not related to visible demographics (i.e., the visible and less visible are loosely coupled). In such a case, the chances for violated expectations of behavior are higher, potentially negating the benefits of adaptive strategies.

Research indicates that when a psychologically safe communication climate is developed within a team, then the cultural diversity coinciding with different nationalities in a team can be leveraged to contribute to team outcomes such as innovation (Gibson & Gibbs, 2006). The authors reasoned that this is true because, in the absence of face-to-face contact, a psychologically safe communication climate assists in effectively managing social categorization processes to bridge cultural communication barriers and increase integration. Larkey (1996) has argued that the social categorization process that occurs in diverse teams often results in "divergence," defined as adherence to culturally based communication patterns. This can be contrasted with convergence, defined as adjustment of one's communication style to match one's partner. Convergence is more common when there is a psychologically safe communication climate, and it helps to counterbalance ingroup/outgroup dynamics that occur when team members are virtual (Larkey, 1996). Open and accommodating communication is an important antecedent of shared cognition (Gibson, 2001); in its absence team mental models have been found to diverge over time (Levesque, Wilson, & Wholey, 2001).

Other research has indicated that developing team identification can help overcome fault lines that form based on geographical and subgroup differences and an "us versus them" mentality (Cramton & Hinds, 2004), as it makes collaborators more likely to give others the benefit of the doubt and assign positive attributions and expectations when motives or behaviors are not readily visible (Cramton, Orvis, & Wilson, 2007). Interestingly, few prior studies have regarded the interaction of virtuality and cultural considerations as critical to our understanding of the teams, and given their research designs, cannot definitively examine these interaction effects (Kirkman et al., 2012; Stanko & Gibson, 2009). But there is some growing evidence that aspects of virtuality such as geographic dispersion interact with culture, both in terms of central tendencies and degree of variation in a team, to affect team characteristics such as shared understanding (Huang, Gibson, Kirkman, & Shapiro, 2012). Hence, it may be that the degree of virtuality, a physical aspect of the IIS, may make cue recognition more difficult, but it may provide greater leeway to alter behavior to adapt to the situation due to the sense of anonymity and identity fungibility that virtuality may provide.

Cognitive Aspects of the Intercultural Interaction Space

In addition to the physical characteristics of the IIS, cognitive aspects of the interaction space also may affect availability and salience of culture-priming cues and the sense of flexibility in acceptable responses. Among possible cognitive aspects of the IIS are the purpose of the interaction and how shared that purpose is among the interaction partners. The purpose of the interaction could be a negotiation, it could be problem solving, or it could be information sharing, to name just a few. Also, individuals may play or represent a variety of roles when engaged in an intercultural work interaction. For example, partners may be interacting in the service of the team's task, could be contacting one another for a more self-serving reason, or there could be hidden motives or agendas to represent a local subsidiary's interests over the needs of the interaction partner or team. Importantly, the same individual could play out each of these different roles in a series of interaction episodes.

Taking the example of the role expectations, we expect that the role invoked by an individual in an intercultural interaction influences his or her identity in the interaction. More specifically, the role influences which identity is salient, whether it be national cultural identity, functional (i.e., discipline-based) identity, organizational identity, or team identity. For example, when the person is acting in the role of team member, in the service of the team task, team task identity may be most salient and national cultural identity less salient. The salience of a particular role identity is likely influenced by the reason and purpose individuals are assigned to global teams (Maloney & Zellmer-Bruhn, 2006). For example, if an individual is assigned to a global team for her explicit technical knowledge, such as electrical engineering of a thermostat, not because she is Japanese, then her nationality is collateral and not task related. In other cases, team composition may be deliberately based on nationality, as would be the case if the team's task required explicit knowledge about Japanese electrical standards. In this case, the national identity of the electrical engineer would be highlighted by the global team's task environment and the reason the individual was assigned to the team.

Previous research suggests that such role identity can be tied to behavioral expectations. For example, when knowledge, communication, or identity functions of norm-consistent behavior are salient, people feel a need to provide clear and explicit responses (Chao, Zhang, & Chiu, 2010; Chiu, Morris, Hong, & Menon, 2000; Fu et al., 2007). To illustrate this, consider again the case of the Japanese electrical engineer described earlier. In the second example where she was assigned to the global team explicitly for her knowledge of Japan, the salience of her Japanese identity is likely heightened, resulting in a sense of needing to behave consistent with Japanese behavioral norms. This is also true when individuals are held responsible to an ingroup audience for their behavioral choices (Briley, Morris, & Simonson, 2000; Gelfand & Realo, 1999).

If role identity connects individuals with their cultural ingroup, this may prime culture-specific knowledge, leading to certain behaviors characteristic of a values-based view of culture. For example, Gelfand and Realo (1999) demonstrated that if individuals are held accountable to their culturally based ingroup constituents for their behavioral decisions in a negotiation setting, they behaved in a way consistent with the national cultural values of that cultural ingroup. More specifically, in cross-cultural negotiation experiments, Estonians who felt they were negotiating on behalf of Estonian constituents displayed cooperation, and Americans who felt they were negotiating on behalf of American constituents displayed increased competition. In both cases, these reactions were interpreted to be representing national culture-consistent behaviors. This example shows how the cognitive understanding of the role an individual invokes in an interaction can both prime certain cultural knowledge and also influence the extent to which an individual feels he or she can modify his or her behaviors—it is unlikely that behaviors will occur that would be inconsistent with the cultural identity invoked by the cognitive characteristics of the IIS.

Consistent with our approach to the IIS, recent research by Hajro, Pudelko, and Gibson (2012) also suggests that organizational strategy can create opportunities and constraints for cognitive processes in multicultural teams. Extending the work of Zellmer-Bruhn and Gibson (2006), Hjaro et al. (2012) have found evidence in interviews across 11 firms and 89 teams that a dual strategic focus on global integration and local responsiveness enhances a team's ability to engage in both cognitive integration and cognitive differentiation. Firms that focused on either local responsiveness or global integration were not as effective in helping the teams achieve both cognitive integration and differentiation, and, as a result, teams in these organizations performed worse than their counterparts in firms with the dual strategic focus. Part of the mechanism for these influences occurred because the firms with a dual focus created an intercultural interaction space that allowed cultural differences to flourish, but teams were also better able to identify, bridge, and integrate those cultural differences within this space.

Affective Aspects of the Intercultural Interaction Space

Organizational behavior research has paid increasing attention to emotion at work and its consequences (Brief & Weiss, 2002), and research suggests that there may be differences in the processing and experience of emotion across cultures (Mesquita & Frijda, 1992) as well as the expression of culture based on emotional state (Ashton-James, Maddux, Galinsky, & Chartrand, 2009). The two perspectives reviewed in this chapter also hint at the role of emotion in intercultural interaction. For example, the values-based view discussion of culture shock and stress has emotional undertones. Furthermore, recent research suggests that characteristics of workplaces can activate emotions (Douglas et al., 2008; Rafaeli & Vinai-Yavetz, 2004). Given these links as well as considerable research suggesting that emotions affect information processing and reasoning (i.e., Estrada, Isen, & Young, 1997; Tiedens & Linton, 2001), it stands to reason that the extent to which intercultural interactions present emotional content likely affects both cue recognition and perceived leeway for behavioral responses among interaction partners.

Models of emotion (i.e., as based on work by Frijda, 1986; Shweder, 1991; Mesquita & Frijda, 1992) suggest that how emotions are elicited and manifested in interactions follows a process that begins with antecedent events and how they are encoded. Based on this perspective, we expect that there are affective qualities of the IIS that may increase or decrease the possibility that emotions are elicited and manifested in an intercultural work interaction. To see how events and appraisals are linked, consider the example event where someone observes his or her spouse flirting with another person. This event may elicit the emotion jealousy if encoded as threatening or amusement if encoded as nonthreatening (Boucher & Brandt, 1981; Brandt & Boucher, 1985). In the context of the IIS, research suggests that some events elicit emotions similarly across cultures (Mesquita & Frijda, 1992). For example, when studying the emotion fear, research suggests that events like interacting with strangers and risk often generate fear. Similarly, insult typically elicits anger, and interacting with friends elicits happiness. But differences in events that elicit certain emotions also exist across cultures, as does the focality (noticeability) of event types. As a result, depending upon the particular affective characteristics of the IIS, interaction partners may vary in elicited emotions. This could result in individuals from different countries displaying different emotional responses to the same context experiences.

Other research suggests that even when the same emotion is experienced, cultural differences exist in what response behaviors are displayed (Gullekson &

Vancouver, 2010). For either situation—some partners in an intercultural interaction experience an emotion and react to it while others do not, or partners experience the same emotion but display markedly different reactions—culture cue recognition may be heightened. For example, consider a team with members from two cultures, where one individual is from a high power distance culture and the other is from a low power distance culture. If the team holds a high-profile meeting to conduct a sales pitch to a major client, and the client sends a very junior manager to hear the presentation and make the decision, the team members from the high power distance culture may feel insulted while the individuals from the low power distance culture may pay little attention to this detail. If the appraisal of insult results in display of emotional behavior such as anger, this may be surprising to the low power distance members of the team, elevating attention and cue recognition.

In addition to affecting the possibility that cultural cues are recognized in an intercultural interaction, if the IIS involves emotional events, the emotions elicited as a result may affect the potential adaptation available. On a general level, emotional responses can interfere with cognitive processing, thereby limiting strategic adaptation. More specifically, research suggests that people have asymmetric reactions to positive versus negative events (Taylor, 1991). More precisely, research shows that negative events often have a stronger and more enduring influence on individuals than do positive events (Baumeister, Bratslavsky, Finkernauer, & Vohs, 2001). Therefore, if negative emotions are more powerful than positive, if the IIS involves bad news, failure, blame, risk, or other negative events, individuals are likely to react strongly and negatively. Emotions like shame, disgust, or anger may put individuals in a defensive position, reducing the likelihood they will engage in culturally adaptive behaviors. Research suggests, for example, that when individuals are threatened or fearful, stress and arousal increase, information processing is narrowed and limited, and people revert to dominant responses and well-learned behaviors (Gladstein & Reilly, 1985; Staw, Sandelands, & Dutton, 1981). Under negative affect, individuals tend to engage in familiar or normative behaviors (cf., Gable & Harmon-Jones, 2008). Alternatively, if emotional events in the IIS elicit positive emotions, individuals engage in more positive evaluations, more creative thought, and more novelty-seeking behavior.

Evidence for the importance of the affective features of the IIS more specifically related to intercultural work is also being gathered in recent empirical evidence. Ashton-James and her colleagues presented experimental evidence that the values expressed and behaviors exhibited by individuals were less consistent with their culture's norms when they were experiencing positive affect (Ashton-James et al., 2009). Consistent with other prior theory about reactions to positive versus negative emotion (Fredrickson, 2001), they concluded that positive emotion allowed individuals to explore thoughts and behaviors that diverged from their normal cultural constraints. These findings suggest that if the IIS supports positive emotional reactions, individuals may engage in more culturally adaptive behaviors.

Further evidence comes from field research by Gibson (2012) in the context of bicultural Australians (mentioned earlier). Prior research has documented that biculturals can feel torn in a struggle, trying to either merge or decide between their two identities, as if trying to reconcile dichotomous aspects of self in a state of "cultural homelessness" (Vivero & Jenkins, 1999; Benet-Martinez, Leu, Lee, & Morris, 2002). Gibson (2012) has found that the conflict between these facets of one's multiple identities is deeply emotional for indigenous Australians, and that they have little support in determining how to navigate that emotional divide. While working for a multinational company that may be violating indigenous cultural norms, they may hold feelings of abandonment, disloyalty, and perjury to their culture, particularly when put into a situation where their allegiance to the company must be explicit. But in attempting to uphold their spiritual connection to their cultural heritage (e.g., by expressing reservations about corporate policy or operations), they experience the same feelings of disloyalty and perjury toward their employer, which is also contributing to the economic progress of their people (and others in their community). We have yet to see these deep-seated spiritual and emotional remnants made visible in prior work on this topic, but our approach to the IIS highlights such affect features. It is likely that threat of social consequences from the intercultural interaction triggers affective responses and these responses influence how interaction will unfold.

Using the examples of cultural psychology research on social threat clearly reveals how affective characteristics of the IIS can affect the priming of certain cultural response as well as the perceived need to comply to cultural norms or discretion to part from cultural norms.

DISCUSSION

The process of reviewing the values-based and the constructivist views of culture led us to introduce the new concept of the intercultural interaction space (IIS) to better understand how culture matters in short-term, horizontal, ad hoc intercultural interactions as often occur in distributed multicultural teams. The IIS serves as a linchpin between these views of culture and helps illuminate the conditions under which cultural content is likely identified and noticed as potentially impactful to an interaction. Only through this process can interaction partners be enabled to approach cultural adaptation strategically to support effective interaction outcomes. Without the concept of the IIS, existing theory cannot explain why in some intercultural interactions, culture will be noticed and in others it will not be, or even more important, why in some intercultural interactions, participants are able to more deliberately contemplate alternative cultural responses while in others, cultural responses are more or less constrained or even automatic.

This introduction of the IIS helps bring to the fore a clearer understanding of why different intercultural interactions may produce different adaptive responses and opportunities for adaptive responses. We introduced and defined the IIS, and we also identified, based on existing conceptual and empirical work in the constructivist view of culture, some potentially relevant features of an IIS that likely affect the likelihood of cultural knowledge being primed and subsequently acted on or adapted from. Our expectation is that the context of intercultural interaction matters, as it shapes two aspects: (1) the opportunity for recognition of cultural cues and (2) information about latitude for culturally adaptive responses provided by a particular interaction episode. A key insight from this expectation is that these two aspects importantly affect whether and in which ways cultural differences "matter" in an intercultural work interaction.

Importantly, depending upon the specific set of features, the IIS may result in *either* an *increase or decrease* in cultural difference effects. The opportunity for cue recognition likely affects the use of automatic mental processes. Automaticity reduces full experience of the moment (Bargh, 1994) and increases the chances that engrained brain states influence cognitive processing and behavior (Siegel, 2007). Automatic processing thus precludes the opportunity for adaptation. When cues are available via the IIS, attention is drawn to contrasting characteristics of individuals and the situation prompting more mindful processing of the situation. This opens a "window of opportunity" for adaptation (Tyre & Orlikowski, 1994). Yet our framework would suggest that beyond their influence on cue recognition, features of the IIS may also support or inhibit adaptive responses, thus illustrating the complex ways "culture matters" in intercultural work.

To illustrate how this might work, consider an example. A large US manufacturer of recreational vehicles has been rapidly expanding internationally. As a result, personnel at headquarters have increasing intercultural interactions. A typical interaction occurs between a US engineer and an Indian sales representative because India is one of the most rapidly growing international markets for this firm. Individuals in the US headquarters are known to say things like "We 'get' India because there is no language issue." (This is often said in contrast to similar experiences with interaction partners in China or Brazil.) The engineer has a planned phone call to address a routine question the Indian sales representative has regarding a feature in a new model being introduced. In this case, the IIS has the physical feature of technology (phone) mediation with two parties highly fluent in English, the cognitive features of clear roles (engineer and sales representative, headquarters and subsidiary, helper and helped) and a routine task (communicating explicit information about a product specification), and affective feature of planned interaction (no surprise) and little expectation for confrontation. In this case, our framework would suggest that the opportunity for cultural cue recognition would be low, making it less likely that the parties (particularly the US engineer) would think culture should matter in the outcomes of this interaction. As a result, we would expect that there would be little conscious adaptive behavior taking place.

In contrast, consider an example we opened with in the introduction. A team of community relations staff implementing programs in East Timor flies from headquarters in Australia to the remote township they are helping to develop near a mine operation. Before going, they are briefed on cultural differences that exist between Australia and Timor, and hence certain (potentially stereotypical) norms are salient in their minds as the plane touches down. Given that they lack formal supervisory authority over the service providers, and the providers frequently change, there is no routine and no established roles or reporting structure. Problems have occurred on a particular program, and tempers have flared, with both sides feeling defensive about the need to protect their own best interests. In this case the IIS has physical features that make cultural differences salient (i.e., the remote location, flying in to meet face to face). The cognitive features of the IIS include uncertainty and unpredictability but also with high stakes for an important, high-profile outcome. The team members are met with surprises in everything from who will actually attend the meeting, who will lead the discussion, and what the outcome might be. The firm may have provided little guidance, wishing to allow for "local responsiveness" and intercultural flexibility. The team members have a lot at stake as the location development and programs are critical for both sides; hence, emotions run high, identity and ego may be engaged, and even the affective characteristics of the IIS are extreme. All of these features suggest that culture will play a large role in the interactions, and adaptive behavior will be cued because the project outcome is highly valued by all parties.

These examples indicate the potential benefit of developing a dynamic process view including the context of interaction to enhance research on intercultural work. In terms of future research, next steps include further fleshing out the features of the IIS. We anticipate that the three dimensions we highlighted (physical, cognitive, and affective) are comprised of subdimensions, and that they likely interact in interesting ways. For instance, there is some evidence that physical characteristics of the work environment provide stimuli that may trigger emotion (e.g., Rafaeli & Vilnai-Yavetz, 2004). In this way, subfeatures of the three dimensions may interact in important ways to affect culture-related perceptions and behaviors. Research that identifies the subdimensions, and tests their interactions in influencing cue recognition and adaptive responses, would be important for developing the concept of and IIS and how it unfolds in practice. Ethnographic research that compares and contrasts IIS across industries, regions, or tasks would help to further our knowledge of what comprises an IIS and which features are most salient.

Subsequently, we can envision research that examines contingency approaches to intercultural interaction, incorporating the concept of IIS. Certain strategies for interaction are likely to be more or less effective, depending on the features of the IIS. For example, in a highly virtual team, developing behavioral responses based on cultural assumptions may be more effective than in a team that operates primarily face to face, providing more cues about emotion and identity. We also anticipate that the influence of the IIS may differ depending on team composition, particularly the distribution of cultural backgrounds and languages (Henderson, 2005). The concept of the IIS may be particularly helpful in understanding how and why the dynamics of interacting subsets of multinational teams may differ because aspects of the cognitive, affective, and physical experiences vary widely depending upon things like the participants, languages, purposes, and expectations for a given interaction. Experimental designs or comparative case studies may be excellent means to understanding further the implications of different IIS for the performance of multicultural teams.

In conclusion, like Leung, Chiu, and Hong (2010), we advocate multiple-paradigm approaches and encourage international management researchers to take advantage of the different vantage points offered by diverse perspectives on culture, highlighting the importance of context and the intercultural interaction space in understanding multicultural interaction.

ACKNOWLEDGMENTS

We thank Dana McDaniel and Lingtao Yu for their help in identifying literature and providing comments as we developed this chapter.

REFERENCES

Adler, N. J., Brahm, R., & Graham, J. L. (1992). Strategy implementation: A comparison of face-to-face negotiations in the People's Republic of China and the United States. *Strategic Management Journal, 13*, 449–466.

Ancona, D. G., & Bresman, H. (2007). *X-teams: How to build teams that lead, innovate, and succeed.* Cambridge, MA: Harvard Business Press.

Ashton-James, C. E., Maddux, W. W., Galinsky, A. D., & Chartrand, T. L. (2009). Who I am depends on how I feel: The role of affect in the expression of culture. *Psychological Science, 20*, 340–346.

Bargh, J. A. (1994). The four horsemen of automaticity: Awareness, efficiency, intention, and control in social cognition. In R. S. Wyer, Jr., & T. K. Srull (Eds.), *Handbook of social cognition* (2nd ed., pp. 1–40). Hillsdale, NJ: Erlbaum.

Barinaga, E. (2007). Cultural diversity at work: "National culture" as a discourse organizing an international project group. *Human Relations, 60*, 315–340.

Baumeister, R. F., Bratslavsky, E., Finkernauer, C., & Vohs, K. D. (2001). Bad is stronger than the good. *Review of General Psychology, 4*, 323–370.

Benet-Martinez, V., Lee, F., & Leu, J. (2006). Biculturalism and cognitive complexity: Expertise in cultural representations. *Journal of Cross-Cultural Psychology, 37*, 386–407.

Benet-Martínez, V., Leu, J., Lee, F., & Morris, M. W. (2002). Negotiating biculturalism cultural frame switching in biculturals with oppositIonal versus compatible cultural identities. *Journal of Cross-Cultural Psychology, 33*(5), 492–516.

Berry, J. W. (1997). Immigration, acculturation and adaptation. *Applied Psychology: An International Review, 46*, 5–68.

Black, J. S., & Gregersen, H. B. (1999, March/April). The right way to manage expats. *Harvard Business Review*, 52–62.

Black, J. S., & Mendenhall, M. (1993). Resolving conflicts with the Japanese: Mission impossible? *Sloan Management Review, 34*, 49–59.

Black, J. S., Mendenhall, M. E., & Oddou, G. (1991). Toward a comprehensive model of international adjustment: An integration of multiple theoretical perspectives. *Academy of Management Review, 16*, 291–317.

Boucher, J. D., & Brandt, M. E. (1981). Judgment of emotion: American and Malay antecedents. *Journal of Cross-Cultural Psychology, 12*, 272–283.

Brandt, M. E., & Boucher, J. D. (1985). Judgments of emotions from the antecedent situation in three cultures. In I. R. Lagunes & Y. H. Poortinga (Eds.), *From a different perspective: Studies of behavior across cultures* (pp. 348–362). Lisse, The Netherlands: Swets & Zeitlinger.

Brannen, M. Y., & Thomas, D. C. (2010). Bicultural individuals in organizations: Implications and opportunity. *International Journal of Cross Cultural Management, 10*, 5–16.

Brett, J. M., & Okumura, T. (1998). Inter-and intracultural negotiation: U.S. and Japanese negotiators. *Academy of Management Journal, 41*, 495–510.

Brief, A. P., & Weiss, H. M. (2002). Organizational behavior: Affect in the workplace. *Annual Review of Psychology, 53*, 279–307.

Briley, D. A., Morris, M. W., & Simonson, I. (2000). Reasons as carriers of culture: Dynamic versus dispositional models of cultural influence on decision-making. *Journal of Consumer Research, 27*, 157–178.

Chao, G. T., & Moon, H. (2005). The cultural mosaic: A metatheory for understanding the complexity of culture. *Journal of Applied Psychology, 90*, 1128–1140.

Chao, M. M., Zhang, Z. X., & Chiu, C. Y. (2010). Adherence to perceived norms across cultural boundaries: The role of need for cognitive closure and ingroup identification. *Group Process and Intergroup Relations, 13*, 69–89.

Chiu, C. Y., Morris, M., Hong, Y., & Menon, T. (2000). Motivated cultural cognition: The impact of implicit cultural theories on dispositional attribution varies as a function of need for closure. *Journal of Personality and Social Psychology, 78*, 247–259.

Cramton, C. D., & Hinds, P. (2004). Subgroup dynamics in internationally distributed teams: Ethnocentrism or cross-national learning? In B. M. Staw & R. M. Kramer (Eds.), *Research in Organizational Behavior* (Vol. 26, pp. 231–263). Greenwich, CT: JAI Press.

Cramton, C. D., Orvis, K. L., & Wilson, J. M. (2007). Situation invisibility and attribution in distributed collaborations. *Journal of Management, 33*, 525–546.

Douglas, S. C., Kiewitz, C., Martinko, M., Harvey, P., Kim, Y., & Chun, J. U. (2008). Cognitions, emotions, and evaluations: An elaboration likelihood model for workplace aggression. *Academy of Management Review, 33*, 425–451.

Earley, P. C. (1987). Intercultural training for managers: A comparison of documentary and interpersonal methods. *Academy of Management Journal, 30*, 685–698.

Earley, P. C. (2006). Leading cultural research in the future: A matter of paradigms and taste. *Journal of International Business Studies, 37*, 922–931.

Earley, P. C., Gibson, C. B., & Chen, C. C. (1999). "How did I do?" versus "How did we do?" Cultural contrasts of performance feedback use and self-efficacy. *Journal of Cross-Cultural Psychology, 30*, 594–619.

Edwards, H. K., & Sridhar, V. (2005). Analysis of software requirements engineering exercises in a global virtual team setup. *Journal of Global Information Management, 13*, 21–41.

Ely, R. J., & Thomas, D. A. (2001). Cultural diversity at work: The effect of diversity perspectives on work group processes and outcomes. *Administrative Science Quarterly, 46*, 229–273.

Erez, M., & Gati, E. (2004). A dynamic multi-level model of culture: From the micro level of the individual to the macro level of a global culture. *Applied Psychology: An International Review, 53*, 583–598.

Estrada, C. A., Isen, A. M., & Young, M. J. (1997). Positive affect facilitates integration of information and decreases anchoring in reasoning among physicians. *Organizational Behavior and Human Decision Processes, 72*, 117–135.

Fang, T. (2006). From "onion" to "ocean": Paradox and change in national cultures. *International Studies of Management and Organization, 35*, 71–90.

Feather, N. T. (1995). Values, valences, and choice: The influence of values on the perceived attractiveness and choice of alternatives. *Journal of Personality and Social Psychology, 68*, 1135–1151.

Feldman, D. A. (2002). Distance coaching: Out of sight, but not out of mind. *Training and Development Journal, 1*, 54–57.

Francis, N. P. (1991). When in Rome? The effects of cultural adaptation on intercultural business negotiations. *Journal of International Business Studies, 22*, 403–428.

Fredrickson, B. L. (2001). The role of positive emotions in positive psychology: The broaden-and-build theory of positive emotions. *American Psychologist, 56*, 218–226.

Friedman, T. L. (2005). *The world is flat: A brief history of the twenty-first century.* New York, NY: Farrar, Straus, and Giroux.

Frijda, N. (1986). *The emotions.* Cambridge, UK: Cambridge University Press.

Fu, H. Y., Morris, M. W., Lee, S. L., Chao, M., Chiu, C. Y., & Hong, Y. (2007). Epistemic motives and cultural conformity: Need for closure, culture, and context as determinants of conflict judgments. *Journal of Personality and Social Psychology, 92*, 191–207.

Gable, P. A., & Harmon-Jones, E. (2008). Approach-motivated positive effect reduces breadth of attention. *Psychological Science, 19*, 476–482.

Gannon, M. J. (2007). *Paradoxes of culture and globalization.* Thousand Oaks, CA: Sage.

Gelfand, M. J., Leslie, L., & Keller, K. (2008). On the etiology of conflict cultures in organizations. *Research in Organizational Behavior, 28*, 137–166.

Gelfand, M. J., Raver, J. L., Nishii, L., Leslie, L. M., Lun, J., Lim, B. C., . . . Yamaguchi, S. (2011). Differences between tight and loose cultures: A 33-nation study. *Science, 332*, 1100–1104.

Gelfand, M. J., & Realo, A. (1999). Individualism-collectivism and accountability in intergroup negotiations. *Journal of Applied Psychology, 84*, 721–736.

Ger, G. (1999). Localizing in the global village: Local firms competing in global markets, *California Management Review, 41*, 64–83.

Gibson, C. B. (2001) From accumulation to accommodation: The chemistry of collective cognition in work groups. *Journal of Organizational Behavior, 22*, 121–134.

Gibson, C. B. (2012, July 20). *Heartsick for country: The role of indigenous identity integration in developing sustainable communities.* Paper presented at the International Association of Cross-Cultural Psychology, Stellenbosch, South Africa.

Gibson, C. B., & Gibbs, J. L. (2006). Unpacking the concept of virtuality: The effects of geographic dispersion, electronic dependence, dynamic structure, and national diversity on team innovation. *Administrative Science Quarterly, 51*, 451–495.

Gibson, C. B., & McDaniel, D. (2010). Moving beyond conventional wisdom: Advancements in cross-cultural theories of leadership, conflict, and teams. *Perspective on Psychological Science, 5*, 450–462.

Gibson, C. B., & Zellmer-Bruhn, M. (2001). Metaphor and meaning: An intercultural analysis of the concept of teamwork. *Administrative Science Quarterly, 46*, 274–303.

Gladstein, D. L., & Reilly, N. P. (1985). Group decision making under threat: The tycoon game. *Academy of Management Journal, 28*, 613–627.

Graves, T. (1967). Psychological acculturation in a tri-ethnic community. *South-Western Journal of Anthropology, 23*, 337–350.

Gullekson, N. L., & Vancouver, J. B. (2010). To conform or not to conform? An examination of perceived emotional display norms among international soujourners. *International Journal of Intercultural Relations, 34*, 315–325.

Hajro, A., Pudelko, M., & Gibson, C. B. (2012, June 30–July 3). *A theory of multicultural team interaction: Linking cultural configurations, cognitive integration-differentiation and organization context to team performance.* Paper presented at the Academy of International Business Meeting, Washington, DC.

Haslberger, A. (2005). The complexities of expatriate adaptation. *Human Resource Management Review, 15*, 160–180.

Henderson, J. K. (2005). Language diversity in international management team. *International Studies of Management and Organization, 35*, 66–80.

Higgins, E. T. (1996). Knowledge activation: Accessibility, applicability, and salience. In E. T. Higgins & A. Kruglanski (Eds.), *Social psychology: Handbook of basic principles* (pp. 133–168). New York, NY: Guilford Press.

Hodgetts, R. M., & Luthans, F. (2003). *International management* (5th ed.). New York, NY: McGraw-Hill/Irwin.

Hofstede, G. (1980). *Culture's consequences: International differences in work-related values.* Beverly Hills, CA: Sage.

Hofstede, G. (2001). *Culture's consequences: Comparing values, behaviors, institutions, and organizations across nations* (2nd ed.). Thousand Oaks, CA: Sage.

Hong, Y-Y. (2009). A dynamic constructivist approach to culture: Moving from describing culture to explaining culture. In R. S. Wyer, Jr., C. Chiu, & Y. Hong (Eds.), *Understanding culture: theory, research and application* (pp. 3–23). New York, NY: Psychology Press.

Hong, Y-Y., & Chiu, C-Y. (2001). Toward a paradigm shift: From cross-cultural differences in social cognition to social-cognitive mediation of cultural differences. *Social Cognition, 19*, 181–196.

Hong, Y-Y., Morris, M. W., Chiu, C-Y., & Benet-Martinez, V. (2000). Multicultural minds: A dynamic constructivist approach to culture and cognition. *American Psychologist, 55*, 709–720.

House, R. J., Hanges, P. J., Javidan, M., Dorfman, P. W., & Gupta, V. (2004). *Leadership, culture, and organizations: The GLOBE Study of 62 societies.* Thousand Oaks, CA: Sage.

Huang, L., Gibson, C. B., Kirkman, B. L, & Shapiro, D. (2012). *The impact of cultural diversity and virtuality on teams.* Working paper, Wharton Business School, University of Pennsylvania, Philadelphia.

Johns, G. (2006). The essential impact of context on organizational behavior. *Academy of Management Review, 31*, 386–408.

Kirkman, B. L., Gibson, C. B., & Kim, K. (2012). Across borders and technologies: Advancements in virtual teams research. In S.W. Kozlowski (Ed.), *Oxford handbook of industrial and organizational psychology* (pp. 789–858). Cambridge, UK: Oxford University Press.

Kirkman, B. L., Lowe, K. B., & Gibson, C. B. (2006). A quarter century of culture's consequences: A review of empirical research incorporating Hofstede's cultural values framework. *Journal of International Business Studies, 37*, 285–320.

Kiser, K. (1999). Working on world time. *Training, 36*, 28–34.

Kitayama, S. (2002). Cultural and basic psychological processes-Toward a system view of culture: Comment on Oyserman et al. (2002). *Psychological Bulletin, 128*, 189–196.

Klein, G., Pliske, R., Crandall, B., & Woods, D. (2005). Problem detection. *Cognition, Technology and Work*, *7*, 14–28.

Kluckhohn, F. (1951). Values and value orientations in the theory of action. In T. Parson & E. Shils (Eds.), *Toward a general theory of action* (pp. 391–436). Cambridge, MA: Harvard University Press.

Larkey, L. K. (1996). Toward a theory of communicative interactions in culturally diverse workgroups. *Academy of Management Review*, *21*, 463–491.

Leung, K., Bhagat, R., Buchan, N., Erez, M., & Gibson, C. B. (2005). Culture and international business: recent advances and their implications for future research. *Journal of International Business Studies*, *36*, 357–378.

Leung, K., Chiu, C. Y., Hong, Y. Y. (2010). *Cultural processes: A social psychological perspective*. New York, NY: Cambridge University Press.

Leung, K., Maddux, W. W., Galinsky, A. D., & Chiu, C-Y. (2008). Multicultural experience enhances creativity: The when and how. *American Psychologist*, *3*, 169–181.

Leung, K., Smith, P. B., Wang, Z., & Sun, H. (1996). Job satisfaction in joint venture hotels in China: An organizational justice analysis. *Journal of International Business Studies*, *27*, 947–962.

Leung, K., Wang, Z. M., & Smith, P. B. (2001). Job attitudes and organizational justice in joint venture hotels in China: The role of expatriate managers. *International Journal of Human Resource Management*, *12*, 926–945.

Levesque, L. L., Wilson, J. M., & Wholey, D. R. (2001). Cognitive divergence and shared mental models in software development project teams. *Journal of Organizational Behavior*, *22*, 135–144.

Maloney, M. M., & Zellmer-Bruhn, M. (2006). Building bridges, windows, and cultures: Mediating mechanisms between heterogeneity and performance in global teams. *Management International Review*, *46*, 697–720.

Markus, H. R., & Kitayama, S. (1991). Culture and the self: Implications for cognition, emotion, and motivation. *Psychological Review*, *98*, 224–253.

Mathieu, J., Maynard, M., Rapp, T., & Gilson, L. (2008). Team effectiveness 1997-2007: A review of recent advancements and a glimpse into the future. *Journal of Management*, *34*, 410–476.

Maznevski, M. L., & DiStefano, J. J. (1995). *Measuring culture in international management: The cultural perspectives questionnaire*. The University of Western Ontario Working Paper Series. Richard Ivey School of Business, London, Ontario, Canada. Working paper 95-20.

McNulty, Y., & Cieri, H. (2011). Global mobility in the 21st century. *Management International Review*, *51*, 897–919.

Mendenhall, M. E., & Oddou, G. (1985). The dimensions of expatriate acculturation: A review. *Academy of Management Review*, *10*, 39–47.

Mesquita, B., & Frijda, N. (1992). Cultural variations in emotions: A review. *Psychological Bulletin*, *112*, 179–204.

Mischel, W. (1977). The interaction of person and situation. In D. Magnusson & N. S. Endler (Eds.), *Personality at the crossroads* (pp. 333–352). Hillsdale, NJ: Erlbaum.

Molinsky, A. (2007). Cross-cultural coding-switching: The psychological challenges of adapting behavior in foreign cultural interactions. *Academy of Management Review*, *32*, 622–640.

Morris, M. W., Williams, K. Y., Leung, K., Larrick, R., Mendoza, M. T., Bhatnagar, D., ... Hu, J. C. (1998). Conflict management style: Accounting for cross-national differences. *Journal of International Business Studies*, *29*, 729–747.

Osland, J. S. (1995). *The adventures of working abroad: Hero tales from the global frontier.* San Friancisco, CA: Jossey-Bass.
Osland, J. S., & Bird, A. (2000). Beyond sophisticated stereotyping: Cross-cultural sense-making in context. *Academy of Management Executive, 14,* 1–12.
Osland, J. S., Bird, A., & Gundersen, A. (2007). *Trigger events in intercultural sensemaking.* Paper presented at the Annual Meeting of the Academy of Management, August 3–8, Philadelphia, PA.
Osland, J. S., Oddou, G., Bird, A., & Osland, A. (2008). *Global leadership in context.* Working Paper, San José State University, San Jose, CA.
Oyserman, D., & Markus, H. (1998). Self as social representation. In S. U. Flick (Ed.), *The psychology of the social* (pp.107–125). New York, NY: Cambridge University Press.
Oyserman, D., & Sorensen, N. (2009). Understanding cultural syndrome effects on what and how we think: A situated cognition model. In C. Y. Chiu, R. Wyer, & Y. Y. Hong (Eds.), *Problems and solutions in cross-cultural theory, research and application* (pp. 25–52). New York, NY: Psychology Press.
Pornpitakpan, C. (1999). The effects of cultural adaptation on business relationships: Americans selling to Japanese and Thais. *Journal of International Business Studies, 30,* 317–337.
Rafaeli, A., & Vilnai-Yavetz, I. (2004). Emotion as a connection of physical artifacts and organizations. *Organization Science, 15,* 671–686.
Roccas, S., Schwartz, S. H., & Amit, A. (2010). Personal value priorities and national identification. *Political Psychology, 31,* 393–419.
Rohan, M. J. (2000). A rose by any name? The values construct. *Personality and Social Psychology Review, 4,* 255–277.
Rokeach, M. (1973). *The nature of human values.* New York, NY: Free Press.
Sagiv, L., & Schwartz, S. H. (1995). Value priorities and readiness for out-group social contact. *Journal of Personality and Social Psychology, 69,* 437–448.
Schwartz, S. H. (1990). Toward a theory of the universal content and structure of values: Extensions and cross-cultural replications. *Journal of Personality and Social Psychology, 58,* 878–891.
Schwartz, S, H. (1992). Universals in the content and structure of values: Theoretical advances and empirical tests in 20 countries. In M. P. Zanna (Ed.), *Advances in experimental social psychology* (pp. 1–65). San Diego, CA: Academic Press.
Schwartz, S., & Sagiv, L. (1995). Identifying culture specifics in the content and structure of values. *Journal of Cross Cultural Psychology, 32,* 269–290.
Shweder, R. A. (1991). *Thinking through cultures.* Cambridge, MA: Harvard University Press.
Siegel, D. J. (2007). *The mindful brain: Reflection and attunement n the cultivation of well-being.* New York, NY: Norton.
Stanko, T. L., & Gibson, C. B. (2009). Virtuality here and now: The role of cultural elements in virtual teams. In R. S. Bhagat, & R. M. Steers (Eds.), *Cambridge handbook of culture, organization, and work* (pp. 272–304). Cambridge, UK: Cambridge University Press.
Starbuck, W. H., & Milliken, F. J. (1988). Executives' perceptual filters: What they notice and how they make sense. In D. C. Hambrick (Ed.), *The executive effect: Concepts and methods for studying top managers* (pp. 35–65). Greenwich, CT: JAI Press.
Staw, B. M., Sandelands, L. E., & Dutton, J. E. (1981). Threat rigidity effects in organizational behavior: A multilevel analysis. *Administrative Science Quarterly, 26,* 501–524.

Swidler, A. (1986). Culture in action: Symbols and strategies. *American Sociological Review, 51*, 273–286.

Takeuchi, S., Imahori, T., & Matsumoto, D. (2001). Adjustment of criticism styles in Japanese returnees to Japan. *International Journal of Intercultural Relations, 25*, 315–327.

Taylor, S. E. (1991). Asymmetrical effects of positive and negative events: The mobilization- minimization hypothesis. *Psychological Bulletin, 110*, 67–85.

Tiedens, L. Z., & Linton, S. (2001). Judgment under emotional certainty and uncertainty: The effects of specific emotions on information processing. *Journal of Personality and Social Psychology, 81*, 973–988.

Tinsley, C. H. (2001). How negotiators get to yes: Predicting the constellation of strategies used across cultures to negotiate conflict. *Journal of Applied Psychology, 86*, 583–593.

Tinsley, C. H., & Brodt, S. E. (2004). Conflict management in Asia: A dynamic framework and future directions. In K. Leung & S. White (Eds.), *Handbook of Asian management* (pp. 439–458). New York, NY: Kluwer.

Thomas, D. C., & Ravlin, E. C. (1995). Responses of employees to cultural adaptation by a foreign manager. *Journal of Applied Psychology, 1*, 133–146.

Triandis, H. C. (1989). The self and social behavior in differing cultural contexts. *Psychological Review, 96*, 506–520.

Trompenaars, F. (1994). *Riding the waves of culture: Understanding diversity in global business*. Burr Ridge, IL: Irwin.

Tsui, A. S., Nifadkar, S. S., & Ou, A. Y. (2007). Cross-national, cross-cultural organizational behavior research: Advances, gaps, and recommendations. *Journal of Management, 33*, 426–478.

Tyre, M. J., & Orlikowski, W. J. (1994). Windows of opportunity: Temporal patterns of technological adaptation in organizations. *Organizational Science, 5*, 98–118.

Vivero, V. N., & Jenkins, S. R. (1999). The existential hazards of the multicultural individual: Defining and understanding "cultural homelessness". *Cultural Diversity and Ethnic Minority Psychology, 5*, 6–26.

Weick, K. E. (1995). *Sensemaking in organizations*. Thousand Oaks, CA: Sage.

Werner, S. (2002). Recent developments in international management research: A review of 20 top management journals. *Journal of Management, 28*, 277–305.

Wyer, R. S., & Srull, T. K. (1986). Human cognition in its social context. *Psychological Review, 93*, 322–359.

Wyer, R. S., & Srull, T. K. (1989). *Memory and cognition in its social context*. Hillsdale, NJ: Erlbaum.

Yamazaki, Y. (2010). Expatriate adaptation. *Management International Review. 50*, 81–108.

Zellmer-Bruhn, M., & Gibson, C. B. (2006). Multinational organizational context: Implication for team learning and performance. *Academy of Management Journal, 49*, 501–518.

Zellmer-Bruhn, M., Maloney, M. M., Bhappu, A. D., & Salvador, R. (2008). When and how do differences matter? An exploration of perceived similarity in teams. *Organizational Behavior and Human Decision Processes, 107*, 41–59.

9

Unpacking Four Forms of Emergent Third Culture in Multicultural Teams

WENDI L. ADAIR AND OMAR GANAI

Multicultural teams are defined as groups of three or more people with distinct cultural identities (Earley & Gibson, 2002). The last two decades of the 20th century saw enormous growth in immigration, international trade, and workforce mobility, transforming many formerly homogeneous towns and cities into diverse, multicultural societies. In many countries around the world, it is now commonplace to encounter multicultural teams in a variety of everyday settings such as universities, hospitals, and technology companies. Between 1990 and 2010, psychological and organizational researchers have identified many potential challenges as well as benefits of working in culturally diverse teams (see Stahl, Maznevski, Voigt, & Jonsen, 2010, for a review). For example, whereas cultural diversity in teams tends to increase creativity and team member satisfaction, it also tends to increase conflict and reduce the chances of team members developing a strong team identity (Van Knippenberg & Schippers, 2007). Moving forward in the next decade, researchers have been called on to specifically tackle more issues of multicultural team processes and identity (Halverson, 2008). This chapter reports on theorizing and research developing the construct of third culture as a way to measure multicultural teams' shared cognition and identity.

The term "third culture" originally appeared in the anthropology and development literatures describing the mixed cultural identity of children of internationally mobile diplomats, missionaries, or businesspeople (Bochner, 1986). A "third culture kid" is someone whose identity is shaped by multiple cultural influences. However, contemporary psychological researchers have moved away from this term, referring instead to multiple cultural identities residing within the individual as biculturalism or multicultural identity (Nguyen & Benet-Martinez, 2010; Phinney, 1999; Tadmor & Tetlock, 2006; Tsai, Ying, & Lee, 2000).

Organizational researchers have to some extent stayed with the term "third culture" and "hybrid culture" (Earley & Mosakowski, 2000) or "synergy" (Adler, 1991) to describe multicultural teams and multinational organizations that have developed shared mental models, values, and communication systems that are a composite of the organizational members' distinct cultures (Casmir, 1992; Hambrick, Davison, Snell, & Snow, 1998; Useem, Useem, & Donoghue, 1963). Building on this prior literature, Adair, Tinsley, and Taylor (2006) proposed a model of third culture in multicultural teams (MCTs), a construct which they defined as "a multicultural team's shared schema that contains not only team and task knowledge, but also a shared set of beliefs, values, and norms grounded in the national culture of team members" (p. 205). While it is true that our conceptualization of third culture may apply to other types of culture (e.g., ethnic, regional, gender, age, and so on), we focus on national culture in particular as a common source of team diversity that predicts distinct values and norms that are relevant to teamwork. In contrast to other existing conceptualizations of team mental models (e.g., Klimoski & Mohammed, 1994; Mohammed & Dumville, 2001, Earley & Mosakowski, 2000), the third culture construct is notable for the explicit inclusion of culture-based beliefs, values, and norms.

> That cross-cultural teams develop shared and simplified sets of strategies and behaviors may be evidence of third culture at the visible tip of the iceberg. Yet, our tendency to... measure it primarily in behaviours has limited our understanding of the underlying cognitive side of third culture, the merging and melding of values, norms, and beliefs often deeply embedded in an individual's national culture identity. (Adair, Tinsley, & Taylor, 2006, p. 209)

In other words, third culture in MCTs should include a team's shared understanding of teamwork, task work, and cultural guiding principles. The authors propose a framework defining four types of third culture in MCTs that vary in terms of mental model strength and mental model content. Recently, we have been refining this framework and examining preferences and expectations for these four types of third culture with respect to a team's guiding values and norms. Team motivational values provide guiding principles for how team members "should" and "ought" to behave (Adair, Hideg, & Spence, in press; Klein, Knight, Ziegert, Lim, & Saltz, 2011). Our research over the past few years has focused specifically on MCT shared values because whereas shared teamwork and taskwork mental models are largely influenced by a team's specific task and routines, shared values are rooted in and emergent from team members' cultural value system. Thus, we expect to capture an MCT's shared value system by examining the shared motivational values and norms guiding individual team members when they work in their team.

In this chapter, we discuss recent psychological and organizational literature that helps inform and contextualize our work on third culture. Then, we review the definition and operationalization of the four-quadrant model of third culture in MCTs. Next we summarize findings from our empirical research, which begins to examine the nomological net of antecedents and consequences of the four third culture forms. This work leads us to offer predictions for several cognitive and behavioral moderators that should predict the formation and consequences of MCT third culture. In conclusion, we discuss issues of measurement and conceptualization for third culture researchers and avenues for future research.

THIRD CULTURE PROCESSES: THE NEGOTIATION OF VALUES AND SHARED MENTAL MODELS

Third culture is a shared, team-level schema. Multicultural teams face several pressures that push them toward merging individual team member schemas into a shared schema. First, research has demonstrated that teams are naturally inclined to move toward consensus, which should prompt team members to merge their individual schemas into a shared team schema (Brandon & Hollingshead, 2004; Levine & Moreland, 1991). Second, the development of a shared schema is more efficient for teamwork than a set of unrelated individual schemas (Fiske & Taylor, 1991). Shared schemas help improve information processing (Levine & Moreland, 1991; Rentsch & Hall, 1994), adaptation to changing task demands (Cannon-Bowers, Salas, & Converse, 1993), sense making and the determination and prediction of future events (Rouse & Morris, 1986), and team performance (Mathieu, Heffner, Goodwin, Salas, & Canon-Bowers, 2000; Walsh & Fahey, 1986; Walsh, Henderson, & Deighton, 1988). Assuming team members have some implicit notion of the advantages of a shared understanding, they should be motivated to develop a third culture.

Third Culture Emerges When Conflicting Values and Norms Are Resolved in Multicultural Teams

Prior research has found many ways that cultures differ in motivational values that affect work schemas and norms (Adair, Okumura, & Brett, 2001; Adair, Taylor, & Tinsley, 2009; Brett & Okumura, 1998; Gibson & Zellmer-Bruhn, 2001). Cultural values can account for unique cultural behavioral repertoires that clash and make interpersonal interactions in multicultural teams difficult (Earley & Mosakowski, 2000; Ravlin, Thomas, & Ilsev, 2000). As a result, many scholars have attempted to elucidate the importance of understanding cultural differences and how to manage the intercultural interface through mutual adaptation and/or adjustment (Adler, 1991; Brett, 2007; Graham & Sano, 1989; Salacuse, 1991; Trompenaars & Hampden-Turner, 1998). Third culture is one lens to examine emergent shared cognition and motivation in multicultural teams. For example, in a longitudinal study of 78 four-person teams, a cluster analysis revealed that almost 50% of teams that were fully heterogeneous with respect to national culture had developed a shared set of team motivational values that was distinct from the values shared in homogeneous North American, homogeneous East Asian, or moderately heterogeneous teams (with two North Americans and two East Asians) (Adair, Wang, Soraggi, & Hideg, 2008). This unique, emergent set of shared values is an example of third culture.

Research on cultural diversity in work groups has uncovered many challenges for multicultural teams. Cultural diversity is defined as the distribution of differences among members of a team with respect to cultural attributes (Harrison & Klein, 2007). Cultural diversity has been labeled a "double-edged sword" because it may lead to both positive and negative outcomes for teams and organizations (Van Knippenberg & Schippers, 2007). Researchers arguing for the benefits of cultural diversity have taken an information processing perspective, showing that cultural diversity can increase the knowledge, skills, and abilities that teams have at their disposal to reach their creative potential (Cox & Blake, 1991; Robinson & Dechant, 1997). Other researchers, taking a social-categorization perspective, have pointed out that the variety of values and attitudes in culturally diverse teams may lead to the formation of culture-based subgroups and prevent cooperative performance (Lau & Murnighan, 1998, 2005). The complexity of these processes becomes apparent when considering that a team member may manage the intercultural interface by adapting his or her ways and beliefs to those of the other parties, by pushing the other parties to adopt his or her ways and beliefs, or by meeting somewhere in the middle (Adair et al., 2001, 2009; Adair & Brett, 2005; Weiss, 1994). Our work on MCT third culture informs this prior research by identifying how team members develop shared values that allow them to overcome negative social categorization effects and capitalize on shared information processing benefits.

Third Culture as Shared Cognition: Shared Mental Models in Multicultural Teams

Third culture in MCTs is a shared mental model, and research has shown the importance of developing shared schemas for performance in a variety of work contexts, for example, military teams and production teams (Matieu, Heffner, Goodwin, Salas, & Canon-Bowers, 2000; Marks, Sabella, Burke, & Zaccaro, 2002; Mohammed & Dumville, 2001). Teams whose members share and organize their task and team-related knowledge in similar ways are likely to find it easier to coordinate their activities compared to teams whose members do not. Shared team mental models are important for performance, particularly in contexts where teams have very little time for explicit coordination. For example, a shared understanding of an emerging situation helps military action teams take appropriate, efficient collective action (Lim & Klein, 2006). Shared mental models are also important in contexts where team members have to collaborate on a complex task, such as strategic decision making in top management teams (Ensley & Pearce, 2001). Our research on third culture in MCTs extends this prior work by modeling an MCT's shared schema specifically with respect to motivational values and norms.

Recently, psychological researchers have also found that experience with different cultures improves cognitive complexity. For example, individuals with multicultural identities, or attachments and loyalties to more than one cultural group, develop the ability to detect, process, and organize everyday cultural meaning in more complex ways than monocultural individuals (Benet-Martinez, Lee, &, Leu, 2006; Tadmor & Tetlock, 2006). Likewise, exposure to different cultures by living abroad can enhance creativity by improving individuals' ability to make connections between different cultural ideas (Leung, Maddux, Galinksy, & Chiu, 2008). This prior work suggests that teams and organizations can benefit from putting individuals in a multicultural environment that will broaden perspectives and enhance creativity.

In sum, it is clear from past research that multicultural teams have the diverse cognitive ingredients (e.g., different cultural values and norms) necessary to generate cognitive complexity and creativity. At the same time, multicultural teams are vulnerable to social-categorization processes that can lead to culture-based subgroups. We propose that MCTs that develop a third culture, that is, a shared understanding of the values and norms that guide team members when working together, should be able to perform more effectively because that shared understanding should facilitate synergistic processes and stifle divisive processes.

THIRD CULTURE IN MULTICULTURAL TEAMS: CLASSIFICATIONS, PREDICTORS, AND CONSEQUENCES

As noted previously, the two dimensions of MCT third culture are strength and content (Adair et al., 2006). These two dimensions are derived directly from Klimoski and Mohammed's (1994) work on team mental models, and they refer to the amount of individual schema overlap or commonly shared information in a team's third culture. In other words, third culture strength is defined by the amount of motivational values and norms shared within a multicultural team. The strength dimension is distinguished by the degree to which team members share all values and norms (representing a stronger team identity) versus maintain some distinct individual values and norms (representing a weaker team identity). Teams in which all members fully share their understanding of the team's guiding values are labeled Identical, whereas teams in which members only partially share their understanding of the team's motivational values (i.e., team members maintain some distinct, individual values not shared by the team) are termed Overlapping (Adair et al., 2006).

Third culture content addresses the novelty of constructs within the team's third culture schema. This dimension captures whether the team's guiding principles were brought to the team by individual team members (a less novel third culture) versus whether they emerged during the team interactions (a more novel third culture). A MCT third culture comprised only of values and norms brought to

Table 9.1. 2 × 2 Model of Third Culture in Multicultural Teams

		Third Culture Strength	
		Identical (All values shared)	**Overlapping (Some unique values)**
Third Culture Content	Fixed (Only preexisting values)	Assimilation	Fusion
	Emergent (Some emergent values)	Melting Pot	Mosaic

the team by individual members is a Fixed third culture (note, previously termed "Intersection" by Adair et al., 2006). In contrast, an Emergent third culture contains some values and norms that members did not bring to the group, but rather emerged as a function of team processes.

The Strength and Content dimensions presented as a 2 × 2 framework result in four kinds of MCT third culture: Identical/Fixed (Assimilation), Overlapping/Fixed (Fusion), Identical/Emergent (Melting Pot), and Overlapping/Emergent (Mosaic) (see Table 9.1).

To make the model more concrete, it may be useful to consider the following scenarios we developed for purposes of field research. Imagine a multicultural team being formed at a large corporation. This team is to be composed of three members, with one member each from the United States, France, and Brazil. As such, these individuals differ in terms of their cultural value preferences for time management, project leadership, teamwork goals, and communication styles (see Table 9.2). Over time (e.g., a period of 6 months), as team members interact and learn how to work effectively with each other, they adapt and adjust some of their cultural values to their team context. If the multicultural team develops fully shared preferences for all values, and if these values came from preexisting cultural values of team members, that is, if these values did not emerge as a function of the team interaction, the team would have an Assimilation third culture (see Table 9.3). If they develop preferences that are shared on two out of four values (i.e., they are partially shared), and if the values that they endorse are not emergent, the team would have a Fusion third culture (see Table 9.4). If the team develops fully shared preferences for all values, and if some of these preferences emerged as a result of the team interacting (e.g., the members see that having a transformational leadership style is best suited for their team), the team would have a Melting Pot third culture (see Table 9.5). Finally, if they develop preferences that are partially shared on some preference dimensions and some of these preferences are emergent as a result of the team interaction, the team would have a Mosaic third culture (see Table 9.6).

An MCT may take on one of these four types of third culture, depending on team members' motivation to adapt or adjust, organizational diversity principles, national multicultural policies, and the type of team task and interactions. We have

Table 9.2. Team at Inception

Cultural Background	Time Management	Leadership	Teamwork Goals	Communication Style
American team member	Likes schedules and deadlines	Likes leaders to empower and involve subordinates in decisions	Values personal outcomes	Likes explicit and direct communication
French team member	Likes schedules and deadlines	Likes leaders to give direction to subordinates	Values group outcomes	Likes implicit and direct communication
Brazilian team member	Dislikes schedules and deadlines	Likes leaders to give direction to subordinates	Values group outcomes	Likes implicit and indirect communication

NOTE: The team is composed of three individuals, with one member each from the United States, France, and Brazil. However, individuals in the team differ in terms of their preferences for time management, project leadership, teamwork goals, and communication style.

begun investigating some individual-level predictors of preferences and .expectations for the four third culture types. In our research, we survey full-time employees who have experience working in teams. We present them with a description of a hypothetical MCT in an organization, using verbal or visual representations to describe each team member's culture-based motivational values at team inception, and adapted motivational values when working in their team after 6 months have passed. We have used both within-subject and between-subject designs to examine employee preferences and expectations for the four third culture forms in our model.

Table 9.3. Assimilation Third Culture

Cultural Background	Time Management	Leadership	Teamwork	Communication
American team member French team member Brazilian team member	Like schedules and deadlines	Like leader to give direction to subordinates	Value group outcomes	Like implicit and indirect communication

NOTE: Team members have developed *fully shared preferences* for time management, leadership, teamwork, and communication. These preferences come from the *preexisting cultural practices* of team members.

Table 9.4. Fusion Third Culture

Cultural Background	**Time Management**	**Leadership**	**Teamwork**	**Communication**
All team members		Like followers to take initiative	Value group outcomes	
American team member	Likes schedules and deadlines			Likes explicit and direct communication
French team member	Likes schedules and deadlines			Likes implicit and direct communication
Brazilian team member	Dislikes schedules and deadlines			Likes explicit and direct communication

NOTE: Team members have developed *fully shared* preferences for leadership and teamwork. Preferences for leadership and teamwork come from the *preexisting* cultural practices of team members. Team members have partially shared preferences for time management and communication.

Third Culture Predictors

Diversity Beliefs and Ideology

In recent years, researchers have looked at several cognitive variables related to how people manage cultural diversity and behave in intercultural situations, which have implications as moderators of third culture formation. These

Table 9.5. Melting Pot Third Culture

Cultural Background	**Time Management**	**Leadership**	**Teamwork**	**Communication**
American team member French team member Brazilian team member	Like schedules and deadlines	Like leader to inspire followers to become leaders	Value group outcomes	Like explicit and direct communication

NOTE: Team members have developed *fully shared* preferences for time management, leadership, teamwork, and communication. Preferences for time management, teamwork, and communication come from the *preexisting cultural practices* of team members. Team members have also developed a *fully shared and new hybrid preference* for leadership that *fuses together aspects* of leadership preferences from all three cultural groups.

Table 9.6. Mosaic Third Culture

Cultural Background	Time Management	Leadership	Teamwork	Communication
All team members		Like leader to inspire followers to become leaders	Value group outcomes	
American team member	Likes schedules and deadlines			Likes explicit and direct communication
French team member	Likes schedules and deadlines			Likes implicit and direct communication
Brazilian team member	Dislikes schedules and deadlines			Likes explicit and direct communication

NOTE: Team members have developed *fully shared* preference for leadership and teamwork. Preference for teamwork comes from the *preexisting cultural practices* of team members. Team members have also developed a *fully shared* preference for leadership that *fuses together aspects* of leadership preferences from all three cultural groups. Team members have *partially shared* preferences for time management and communication.

variables include diversity beliefs, intercultural ideology, individual cognitive style, and team and task type. Diversity beliefs refer to beliefs individuals hold about whether diversity is beneficial or detrimental for multicultural team performance (Van Dick, Van Knippenberg, Hägele, Guillaume, & Brodbeck, 2008). Intercultural ideology is a shared set of beliefs that (1) guides societies' interpretation of cultural diversity present in them and (2) prescribes norms about how to manage that cultural diversity toward an ideal state (Wolsko, Park, Judd, & Wittenbrink, 2000).

Diversity beliefs and intercultural ideologies influence how people perceive cultural diversity. As a result, diversity beliefs and intercultural ideologies should influence how multicultural teams go about creating third cultures. For example, individual team members who hold a belief that cultural diversity is useful for the attainment of team goals may be more willing to consider Fusion and Mosaic third cultures as appropriate in a multicultural team, whereas individuals that view cultural diversity as a source of interpersonal tension may be more likely to support Assimilation or Melting Pot third culture forms (Ely & Thomas, 2001).

Our empirical research to date has shown that indeed individual values for multiculturalism lead to preferences for Mosaic forms of third culture. In contrast, employees with low values for multiculturalism are more likely to prefer Assimilation forms of third culture in MCTs.

Individual Cognitive Style

Individuals high in need for cognition (NFCog) enjoy spending time and energy on cognitively taxing efforts, such as accurately understanding their environment (Cacioppo, Petty, Feinstein, & Jarvis, 1996). Presumably, the process of perceiving, interpreting, and adapting to cultural values in multicultural teams is a cognitively complex task that individuals high in NFCog would enjoy. Thus, we should expect teams composed of individuals with high need for cognition to have more complex forms of third culture (e.g., Melting Pot and Mosaic), as individuals in these teams should prefer creating third cultures with dynamic and emergent characteristics. While no research to date has directly found evidence for a link between high need for cognition and the development of third culture, there is some corollary evidence in the literature that suggests our thinking may be correct. For example, teams that have high need for cognition as well as high age or education diversity engaged in greater task-relevant information elaboration and exchange (Kearney, Gebert, & Voelpel, 2009). Similarly, teams that have high team reflexivity (the degree to which a team discusses the group's task and goals and the way in which those goals can be reached) engage in more information elaboration and exchange, which increases the degree to which team members understand task requirements (Van Ginkel, Tindale, & Van Knippenberg, 2009). Taken as a whole, these two studies suggest that spending time and energy thinking in order to come to an accurate understanding of the team environment results in greater communication between team members, and this increase in communication improves the sharedness of team mental models.

Past research indicates that individuals high in need for closure (NFCl) respond to ambiguous cultural events by increasing reliance on implicit theories of culture acquired through acculturation (Chiu, Morris, Hong, & Menon, 2000). Thus, NFCl moderates the influence of culture, whereby individuals high in NFCl resort to chronically accessible cultural knowledge. Such individuals' low tolerance for ambiguity should lead them to prefer MCTs in which team members develop fixed, fully shared values and norms (e.g., Assimilation or Melting Pot). This argument is supported by research showing that individuals with high NFCl contribute to group centrism, which is characterized by pressures for conformity and stable group norms (Kruglanski, Pierro, Mannetti, & De Grada, 2006). Other studies show that groups high in NFCl are limited in their ability to perform complex cognition actions. For example, groups composed of individuals high in NFCl display lower ideational fluidity and creativity compared with groups that are composed of individuals with low NFCl (Chirumbolo, Livi, Mannetti, Pierro, & Kruglanski, 2004). This suggests that groups that are high in NFCl would be unable to create more complex forms of third culture that require creativity and cognitive flexibility. Instead, groups high in NFCl may prefer simpler forms of third culture that do not require much cognitive processing (e.g., Assimilation or Melting Pot).

Our preliminary research suggests that individual cognitive style does relate to employee preferences for different third culture forms. Employees who have a high need for cognition report preferences for MCTs with a Mosaic or Melting Pot third culture form for a wide range of factors such as psychological safety and creativity. Need for closure is less widely related, influencing only preferences for working in an MCT with an Assimilation third culture.

Team and Task Type

Team and task type may further influence third culture formation in multicultural teams. For example, prior team research suggests that product assembly teams are primarily engaged in a clear and well-defined process and final product with little interaction among team members, whereas product design teams are primarily engaged with conceptual tasks that do not have clearly defined processes or final products and require team members to interact with each other in novel ways (Stewart & Barrick, 2000). Thus, we expect MCTs responsible for product assembly will prefer an Assimilation third culture because it requires team members to be on the "same page" with respect to a clearly defined set of tasks and goals. On such a team, members are not expected to collaboratively develop innovative processes or creative products, so there will be no need to combine and adjust their cultural values or norms. In contrast, we expect MCTs to indicate a preference for a Melting Pot third culture when they are responsible for product design because such a Melting Pot third culture requires participants to spend a substantial amount of time interacting with each other so that they can combine any potential cultural value differences in synergistic and creative ways.

To date, we have not found consistent preferences for third culture forms when participants imagine working in product assembly versus creative design teams. However, we expect additional field research that surveys employees who are actually working in assembly versus design teams to clarify our understanding of how team tasks can influence preferences for third culture forms. For example, we expect the strongest third cultures to form in MCTs that engage in information elaboration (Van Knippenberg, De Dreu, & Homan, 2004). For an MCT to have a strong third culture, team members must have a highly shared understanding of the cultural values and norms found within the team. Intuitively then, it makes sense why we expect greater information elaboration to lead to stronger third cultures: MCTs in which team members share information with each other regarding their own cultural values or ask each other to share their unique cultural perspectives will increase the chances of them realizing that they share similar cultural values, or the chances of them learning about and adopting new cultural values. As far as we are aware, no study has directly examined the relationship between information elaboration and third culture. However, a long line of research studies demonstrate that groups in which members make explicit attempts to share unique information with each other make better decisions because they understand the environment and their task better (Stasser, 1999).

Third Culture Consequences

The four forms of third culture vary in the amount and origin of shared team values, two composition variables that should have implications for team processes and team outcomes. The content dimension distinguishes whether team shared values were all brought to the team by its members or developed partially as a function of the team interaction. We know from prior research that when people face uncertainty in cross-cultural settings, they tend to rely on comfortable, implicit values to guide their behavior (Chi et al., 2000). Thus, when team shared values are all brought to the team by its members, they should experience greater psychological safety than when the team endorses new, unfamiliar values.

The strength dimension distinguishes whether team members share all values or maintain some unique individual values when working in the team. Fusion and Mosaic third cultures allow team members to maintain some unique, individual values that are not shared by their MCT. According to optimal distinctiveness theory (Brewer, 1991), people strive for both belongingness and uniqueness in social identity. Thus, employees may predict the greatest personal satisfaction and inspiration working in teams when they can maintain some distinct individual values that are not shared by the team.

Our preliminary research suggests that employees predict the greatest psychological safety in MCTs with a Fusion third culture and the greatest personal satisfaction in MCTs with a Fusion or Mosaic third culture form. These findings suggest that team members recognize important psychological consequences of various forms of MCT identity. Much of the research on team identity has focused on performance- or productivity-based outcomes (Earley & Mosakowski, 2000; Van Dick et al., 2008). We suggest that an important avenue for future research is to consider team member motivation, commitment, safety, and satisfaction as important consequences of team identity.

Additional Predictors, Moderators, and Consequences

Just as individual diversity values can predict preferences for third culture forms in MCTs, organizational diversity policies may also influence third culture formation by providing appropriate norms for diversity and inclusivity. For example, Cisco, a multinational high-tech company based in the United States, has an organizational intercultural ideology that explicitly embraces multiculturalism that should lead to the formation of Fusion or Mosaic third cultures. Similarly, national multicultural policies provide the appropriate norms for managing cultural diversity at the societal level. For example, in comparison to other countries such as India, it can be argued that Canada has a multicultural ideology (Moghaddam & Solliday, 1991), which emphasizes the importance of cultural diversity, as well as a strong, shared national culture. Thus, perhaps teams in Canadian organizations are likely to favor Fusion or Mosaic third culture forms.

Recent research on individualism-collectivism and cooperation in workgroups also suggests the value in testing both organizational- and societal-level variables as moderators of the relationship between third culture form and team processes (Nguyen, Le, & Boles, 2010). Our research comparing preferences for third culture forms in India versus the United States supports comparative cross-cultural effects to be developed in future research. As we expected, in the United States, which is characterized by strong values for individualism, independence, and self-interest (Brett, 2007; Hofstede, 1980; Schwartz, 1994), people tend to prefer MCT third cultures that allow team members to maintain unique, individual values, that is, the Fusion and Mosaic forms. However, in India, where there are strong values for collectivism, harmony, face saving, and conflict avoidance (Hofstede, 1980; Schwartz, 1994), people tend to prefer MCT third cultures in which all team members fully share values, that is, the Assimilation or Melting Pot forms.

Furthermore, we expect communication quality and quantity to play a role in the development of third culture in MCTs. In terms of communication quality, the construct of Quality of Communication Experience (QCE) may help guide future research. QCE encompasses the clarity, responsiveness, and comfort that communicators experience during a communication episode (Liu, Chua, & Stahl, 2010). Clarity refers to the degree of comprehension of the meaning being communicated. Responsiveness refers to how coordinated or synchronized speech patterns are in a social situation, as well as responses to informational inquiries and expressions of empathy toward emotions expressed by another person. Finally, comfort refers to the emotional sense of satisfaction that communicators feel when interacting. We predict strong and emergent third cultures to form in MCTs in which team members fully understand the meaning behind each other's words and actions (high clarity), answer questions in an empathetic way (high responsiveness), and feel at ease while communicating (high comfort).

We expect quantity of communication and information elaboration to play a role in the formation of third culture in MCTs. Information elaboration in groups refers to the exchange, discussion, and integration of task-relevant information and perspectives (Van Knippenberg, De Dreu, & Homan, 2004). Previously we discussed how teams that spend more time discussing their tasks and goals understand their task requirements better than teams that do not (Van Ginkel et al., 2009). Besides a better understanding of task requirements, greater information elaboration and exchange should also place team members in a better position to understand the cultural frame that each team member brings, and thus lead to the formation of a strong third culture.

Finally, we think team tenure and the stage of team development will influence third culture formation. In general, teams go through five stages of development: forming, storming, norming, performing, and adjourning (Tuckman & Jensen, 1977). Each stage of team development provides a different context, and thus different types of third culture may be present. In the forming stage, individuals first meet each other and try to gather information about each other as well as their task. In the forming stage, team members may assume they have shared values when in fact team members may all have unique cultural values that they bring with them from their cultural heritage. A lack of shared values and understanding in highly culturally diverse teams helps explain why they underperform culturally homogenous teams in the beginning stages of team development (Earley & Mosakowski, 2000).

In the storming stage, team members realize that there are differences and engage in conflict to reconcile these differences. The form of third culture the MCT ultimately develops may depend upon how they emerge from this stage. A team in which some members are dominant and others quickly concede may develop an Assimilation third culture, fully sharing cultural values brought to the table by a few powerful team members. A team that develops consensus through QCE and information elaboration should develop some unique, emergent team values that are all shared in a Melting Pot third culture. If the team is unable to form a consensus and instead breaks up into small coalitions, it will adopt the Fusion or Mosaic form, depending on the quality and quantity of communication and understanding. By the penultimate team stage of performing, MCT third cultures should be relatively stable, although they could shift with changes in team membership, leadership, or tasks.

CONCEPTUAL CONCERNS, MEASUREMENT ISSUES, AND CONCLUDING THOUGHTS

Our 2 x 2 model of third culture in MCTs is not exhaustive or without limitations. In future work, we hope to conceptualize and measure additional forms of MCT third culture. For example, current work on color blindness (e.g., Richeson & Nussbaum, 2004) could be incorporated to suggest multiple forms of an Assimilation third culture, depending on whether it represents the host nation culture, a hybrid of team members' native cultures, or something entirely culture-free.

We propose MCT third culture as a rather static form of team identity. This is in contrast to models such as fusion teamwork, according to which multicultural teams dynamically adjust the degree to which team member cultural uniqueness is accessed depending on the team task at hand (Crotty & Brett, in press). We suggest that whereas fusion teamwork is a process construct because it describes the conditions under which multicultural teams may enact teamwork effectively, MCT third culture is an identity construct, in that it focuses upon how adaptation of cultural values and norms within a team come to define the identity of a team. Thus, future research can examine to what degree the four forms of MCT third culture are likely to generate fusion teamwork.

We also recognize the challenge of studying and measuring MCT third cultures. Much research on team shared mental models employs data collection methods that are quite cumbersome and unrealistic in a real-world work setting, such as paired similarity judgments. But establishing an MCT third culture is not something quick and easy. We do not suggest it can be developed in an hour in a laboratory. Thus, many challenges exist for future empirical study of third cultures in MCTs.

Our current empirical research aims to flesh out the nomological net of third culture in MCTs, identifying individual-level predictors as well as expected consequences of the four third culture forms. To date, our preference data support theories such as optimal distinctiveness (Brewer, 1991) that emphasize our desire to balance needs for individuality along with needs for social identity, and previous findings that employees' acculturation preferences involve both preserving one's native cultural identity while still adopting a strong team identity (Luijters, Van der Zee, & Otten, 2008). Our data also suggest that psychological variables associated with openness to culture and experience (multiculturalism ideology and need for cognition) are related to preferences for emergent third culture forms, whereas variables associated with a more wary approach to culture and newness (low multiculturalism ideology and need for closure) are related to preferences for fixed third culture forms. Next steps are to investigate consequences of the distinct MCT third culture forms in intact teams, such as individual satisfaction and commitment to the team as well as team performance, learning, and longevity.

REFERENCES

Adair, W. L., & Brett, J. M. (2005). The negotiation dance: Time, culture, and behavioral sequences in negotiation. *Organization Science, 5*, 33–51.

Adair, W. L., Hideg, I., & Spence, J. R. (2013). The culturally intelligent team: The impact of team cultural intelligence and cultural heterogeneity on team shared values. *Journal of Cross-Cultural Psychology, 44*, 941–962.

Adair, W. L., Okumura, T., & Brett, J. M. (2001). Negotiation behavior when cultures collide: The United States and Japan. *Journal of Applied Psychology, 86*, 371–385.

Adair, W. L., Taylor, M. S., & Tinsley, C. H. (2009). Starting out on the right foot: Negotiation schemas when cultures collide. *Negotiation and Conflict Management Research, 2*, 138–163.

Adair, W. L., Tinsley, C. H., & Taylor, M. (2006). Managing the intercultural interface: Third cultures, antecedents, and consequences. *Research on Managing Groups and Teams, 9*, 205–232.

Adair, W.L., Wang, Z. Soraggi, M., & Hideg, I. (2008, August 8–13). *Third culture in multicultural teams*. Paper presented at the Annual Meeting of the Academy of Management, Organizational Behavior Division. Anaheim, CA.

Adler, N. J. (1991). *International dimensions of organizational behavior*. Boston, MA: Kent.

Benet-Martínez, V., Lee, F., & Leu, J. (2006). Biculturalism and cognitive complexity. *Journal of Cross-Cultural Psychology, 37*, 386–407.

Bochner, S. (1986). Coping with unfamiliar cultures: Adjustment or culture learning? *Australian Journal of Psychology, 38*, 347–358.

Brandon, D. P., & Hollingshead, A. B. (2004). Transactive memory systems in organizations: Matching tasks, expertise, and people. *Organization Science, 15*, 633–644.

Brett, J. M. (2007). *Negotiating globally: How to negotiate deals, resolve disputes, and make decisions across cultural boundaries*. Hoboken: NJ: Jossey-Bass.

Brett, J. M., & Okumura, T. (1998). Inter-and intracultural negotiation: US and Japanese negotiators. *Academy of Management Journal, 5*, 495–510.

Brewer, M. B. (1991). The social self: On being the same and different at the same time. *Personality and Social Psychology Bulletin, 17*, 475–484.

Cacioppo, J. T., Petty, R. E., Feinstein, J. A., & Jarvis, W. B. G. (1996). Dispositional differences in cognitive motivation: The life and times of individuals varying in need for cognition. *Psychological Bulletin, 119*, 197–253.

Cannon-Bowers, J. E., Salas, E., & Converse, S. (1993). Shared mental models in expert team decision making. In N. J. Castellan, Jr. (Ed.), *Individual and group decision making: Current issues* (pp. 221–247). Hillsdale, NJ: Erlbaum.

Casmir, F. L. (1992). Third-culture building: A paradigm shift for international and intercultural communication. *Communication Yearbook, 16*, 407–428.

Chirumbolo, A., Livi, S., Mannetti, L., Pierro, A., & Kruglanski, A. W. (2004). Effects of need for closure on creativity in small group interactions. *European Journal of Personality, 18*, 265–278.

Chiu, C., Morris, M. W., Hong, Y., & Menon, T. (2000). Motivated cultural cognition: The impact of implicit cultural theories on dispositional attribution varies as a function of need for closure. *Journal of Personality and Social Psychology, 78*, 247–259.

Cox, T. H., & Blake, S. (1991). Managing cultural diversity: Implications for organizational competitiveness. *The Executive, 5*, 45–56.

Crotty, S., & Brett, J. (2012). Fusion, metacognition, and creativity in multicultural teams. *Negotiation and Conflict Management Research, 5*, 210–234.

Earley, P. C., & Gibson, C. B. (2002). *Multinational work teams: A new perspective.* Mahwah, NJ: Erlbaum.

Earley, P. C., & Mosakowski, E. (2000). Creating hybrid team cultures: An empirical test of transnational team functioning. *Academy of Management Journal, 43*, 26–49.

Ely, R. J., & Thomas, D. A. (2001). Cultural diversity at work: The effects of diversity perspectives on work group processes and outcomes. *Administrative Science Quarterly, 46*, 229–273.

Ensley, M. D., & Pearce, C. L. (2001). Shared cognition in top management teams: Implications for new venture performance. *Journal of Organizational Behavior, 22*, 145–160.

Fiske, S. T., & Taylor, S. E. (1991). *Social cognition* (2nd ed.). New York, NY: Mcgraw-Hill.

Gibson, C. B., & Zellmer-Bruhn, M. E. (2001). Metaphors and meaning: An intercultural analysis of the concept of teamwork. *Administrative Science Quarterly, 46*, 274–303.

Graham, J. L., & Sano, Y. (1989). *Smart bargaining: Doing business with the Japanese.* Pensacola, FL: Ballinger.

Halverson, C. B. (2008). Team development. In P.C. Earley & H. Singh (Eds.), *Advances in group decision and negotiation* (pp. 81–110). Vienna, Austria: Springer Verlag.

Hambrick, D. C., Davison, S. C., Snell, S. A., & Snow, C. C. (1998). When groups consist of multiple nationalities: Towards a new understanding of the implications. *Organization Studies, 19*, 181–205.

Harrison, D. A., & Klein, K. J. (2007). What's the difference? Diversity constructs as separation, variety, or disparity in organizations. *Academy of Management Review, 32*, 1199–1228.

Hofstede, G. (1980). *Culture's consequences: International differences in work-related values.* Beverly Hills, CA: Sage.

Kearney, E., Gebert, D., & Voelpel, S. C. (2009). When and how diversity benefits teams: The importance of team members' need for cognition. *Academy of Management Journal, 52*, 581–598.

Klein, K. J., Knight, A. P., Ziegert, J. C., Lim, B. C., & Saltz, J. L. (2011). When team members' values differ: The moderating role of team leadership. *Organizational Behavior and Human Decision Processes, 114*, 25–36.

Klimoski, R., & Mohammed, S. (1994). Team mental model: Construct or metaphor? *Journal of Management, 20*, 403–437.

Kruglanski, A.W., Pierro, A., Mannetti, L. & De Grada, E. (2006). Groups as epistemic providers: Need for closure and the unfolding of group-centrism. *Psychological Review, 113*, 84–100.

Lau, D. C., & Murnighan, J. K. (1998). Demographic diversity and faultlines: The compositional dynamics of organizational groups. *Academy of Management Review, 23*, 325–340.

Lau, D. C., & Murnighan, J. K. (2005). Interactions within groups and subgroups: The effects of demographic faultlines. *Academy of Management Journal, 48*, 645–659.

Liu, L. A., Chua, C. H., & Stahl, G. K. (2010). Quality of communication experience: Definition, measurement, and implications for intercultural negotiations. *Journal of Applied Psychology, 95*, 469–487.

Levine, J. M., & Moreland, R. L. (1991). Culture and socialization in work groups. In L. B. Resnick, J. M. Levine, & S. D. Teasley (Eds.), *Perspectives on socially shared cognition* (pp. 257–279). Washington, DC: American Psychological Association.

Leung, A. K., Maddux, W. W., Galinsky, A. D., & Chiu, C. (2008). Multicultural experience enhances creativity: The when and how. *American Psychologist, 63*, 169–181.

Lim, B. C., & Klein, K. J. (2006). Team mental models and team performance: A field study of the effects of team mental model similarity and accuracy. *Journal of Organizational Behavior, 27*, 403–418.

Luijters, K., Van der Zee, K. I., Otten, S. (2008). Cultural diversity in organizations: Enhancing identification by valuing differences. *International Journal of Intercultural Relations, 32*, 154–163.

Marks, M. A., Sabella, M. J., Burke, C. S., & Zaccaro, S. J. (2002). The impact of cross-training on team effectiveness. *Journal of Applied Psychology, 87*, 3–13.

Mathieu, J. E., Heffner, T. S., Goodwin, G. F., Salas, E., & Cannon-Bowers, J. A. (2000). The influence of shared mental models on team process and performance. *Journal of Applied Psychology, 85*, 273–283.

Moghaddam, F. M., & Solliday, E. A. (1991). Balanced multiculturalism and the challenge of peaceful coexistence in pluralistic societies. *Psychology and Developing Societies, 3*, 51–72.

Mohammed, S., & Dumville, B. C. (2001). Team mental models in a team knowledge framework: Expanding theory and measurement across disciplinary boundaries. *Journal of Organizational Behavior, 22*, 89–106.

Nguyen, A. M. T. D., & Benet-Martínez, V. (2010). Multicultural identity: What it is and why it matters. In R. J. Crisp (Ed.), *The psychology of social and cultural diversity* (pp. 87–114). Malden, MA: Blackwell.

Nguyen, H-H. D., Le, H., & Boles, T. (2010). Individualism-collectivism and co-operation: A cross-society and cross-level examination. *Negotiation and Conflict Management Research, 3*, 179–204.

Phinney, J. (1999). An intercultural approach in psychology: Cultural contact and identity. *Cross Cultural Psychology Bulletin, 33*, 24–30.

Ravlin, E. C., Thomas, D. C., & Ilsev, A. (2000). Beliefs about values, status, and legitimacy in Multicultural Groups. In P. C. Earley & H. Singh (Eds.), *Innovations in international and cross-cultural management* (pp. 17–51). Thousands Oaks, CA: Sage.

Rentsch, J. R., & Hall, R. J. (1994). Members of great teams think alike: A model of team effectiveness and schema similarity among team members. *Advances in Interdisciplinary Studies of Work Teams, 1*, 223–261.

Richeson, J. A., & Nussbaum, R. J. (2004). The impact of multiculturalism versus color-blindness on racial bias. *Journal of Experimental Social Psychology, 40*, 417–423.

Robinson, G., & Dechant, K. (1997). Building a business case for diversity. *Academy of Management Executive, 11*, 21–31.

Rouse, W. B., & Morris, N. M. (1986). On looking into the black box: Prospects and limits in the search for mental models. *Psychological Bulletin, 3*, 349–363.

Salacuse, J. W. (1991). *Making global deals: What every executive should know about negotiating abroad.* New York, NY: Random House.

Schwartz, S. H. (1994). Universals in the content and structure of values: Theoretical advances and empirical tests in 20 countries. In M. P. Zanna (Ed.), *Advances in experimental social psychology* (Vol. 25, pp. 1–65). San Diego, CA: Academic Press.

Stahl, G. K., Maznevski, M. L., Voigt, A., & Jonsen, K. (2010). Unraveling the effects of cultural diversity in teams: A meta-analysis of research on multicultural work groups. *Journal of International Business Studies, 41*, 690–709.

Stasser, G. (1999). A primer of social decision scheme theory: Models of group influence, competitive model-testing, and prospective modeling. *Organizational Behavior and Human Decision Processes, 80*, 3–20.

Stewart, G. L., & Barrick, M. R. (2000). Team structure and performance: Assessing the mediating role of intrateam process and the moderating role of task type. *Academy of Management Journal, 43*, 135–148.

Tadmor, C. T., & Tetlock, P. E. (2006). Biculturalism. *Journal of Cross-Cultural Psychology, 37*, 173–190.

Trompenaars, A., & Hampden-Turner, C. (1998). *Riding the waves of culture: Understanding cultural diversity in global business.* New York, NY: McGraw Hill.

Tsai, J. L., Ying, Y. W., & Lee, P. A. (2000). The meaning of "being Chinese" and "being American": Variation among Chinese American young adults. *Journal of Cross-Cultural Psychology, 31*, 302–332.

Tuckman, B. W., & Jensen, M. A. C. (1977). Stages of small-group development revisited. *Group and Organization Management, 2*, 419–427.

Useem, J., Useem, R., & Donoghue, J. (1963). Men in the middle of the third culture: The roles of American and non-Western people in cross-cultural administration. *Human Organization, 22*, 169–179.

Van Dick, R., Van Knippenberg, D., Hägele, S., Guillaume, Y. R. F., & Brodbeck, F. C. (2008). Group diversity and group identification: The moderating role of diversity beliefs. *Human Relations, 61*, 1463–1492.

Van Ginkel, W., Tindale, R. S., & Van Knippenberg, D. (2009). Team reflexivity, development of shared task representations, and the use of distributed information in group decision making. *Group Dynamics: Theory, Research, and Practice, 13*, 265–280.

Van Knippenberg, D., De Dreu, C. K. W., & Homan, A. C. (2004). Work group diversity and group performance: An integrative model and research agenda. *Journal of Applied Psychology, 89*, 1008–1022.

Van Knippenberg, D., & Schippers, M. C. (2007). Work group diversity. *Annual Review of Psychology, 58*, 515–541.

Walsh, J. P., & Fahey, L. (1986). The role of negotiated belief structures in strategy making. *Journal of Management, 12*, 325–338.

Walsh, J. P., Henderson, C. M., & Deighton, J. (1988). Negotiated belief structures and decision performance: An empirical investigation. *Organization Behavior and Human Decision Processes, 42*, 194–216.

Weiss, S. E. (1994). Negotiating with Romans. *Sloan Management Review, 35*, 51–61.

Wolsko, C., Park, B., Judd, C. M., & Wittenbrink, B. (2000). Framing interethnic ideology: Effects of multicultural and color-blind perspectives on judgments of groups and individuals. *Journal of Personality and Social Psychology, 78*, 635.

PART THREE

Culture and Intergroup Processes

10

Culture and Intergroup Communication

KIMBERLY A. NOELS

Culture is communication and communication is culture.

—Edward T. Hall, *1973 (p. 186)*

For many social and cultural theorists, the relation between culture and communication is posited to be a close one; some, such as Hall (1973), have suggested that they are virtually synonymous. In this chapter, we will examine this relationship as it pertains to intergroup relations and explore ways in which the understanding of the psychology of culture and of intergroup communication can be mutually enhanced by integrating these two areas of research. Until very recently, researchers have not extensively examined the role of culture in intergroup communication, either in terms of how culture affects intergroup communication or how intergroup communication influences cultural dynamics (but see Fortman & Giles, 2006; Carbaugh, Lie, Locmele, & Sotirova, 2012). Referring to research traditions in intercultural communication, Hecht, Jackson, and Pitts (2005) comment that "the construct of culture is itself undernourished within the intergroup perspective" (p. 23). A reader might find this surprising, given that a great deal of the work in intergroup communication has focused on relations between ethnolinguistic groups, and there would seem to be an obvious connection between ethnicity and culture.

This chapter, then, will consider some ways in which culture and intergroup communication are interwoven. For the present purpose, "culture" is defined as the dynamic systems of meanings (e.g., beliefs, attitudes, and other such representations) that are shared within a community in the sense that they are co-constructed between individuals and they become the conventions and mores distributed within a social group. Culture is, in a sense, the consensual reality of a social group. "Communication" is defined similarly to Carey (1975), such that it refers not simply to the transmission of information between sender and receiver (cf. Shannon & Weaver, 1949), but more fully to the "symbolic process[es] whereby reality is produced, maintained, repaired and transformed" (p. 23). It has both an informational and a relational aspect to it (among other functional aspects; cf. Watzlawick, Beavin, & Jackson, 1967; Kashima, 2008). Communication constitutes the practices by which culture is constructed and maintained, transmitted, and transformed. Language is recognized to have special status as a communicative and cognitive tool that is particularly well adapted to orienting interlocutors' mutual attention to important aspects of their common physical and psychological environments (cf. Tomasello, 2011); however, meaning is also carried by communicative acts through paralinguistic and nonlinguistic moves.

Although intergroup communication research has examined groups defined in numerous ways (e.g., gender, sexual orientation, age, police-civilian, organizational, etc.; see Harwood & Giles, 2005, and Giles, 2012, for analyses across various intergroup communication contexts), the present chapter will focus on groups defined in ethnolinguistic terms because communication across groups with clearly different cultural and communication systems highlights complexities that may not be as evident in other intergroup contexts. I begin with a description of a well-known intergroup communication framework, and in the subsequent two sections I describe ways in which culture might be overlaid on such a model, highlighting issues of identity and status dynamics that complicate the understanding of the relation between culture and intergroup communication. In the final section I argue that a perspective that emphasizes the situatedness of identity and communication processes for people living in multicultural contexts can facilitate understanding of cultural change. Consistent with Hecht and his colleagues (2005), I maintain that the themes of social identity and the groups' relative sociostructural status that are highlighted in intergroup theory are critical to understanding cultural dynamics. Moreover, I suggest that this perspective can contribute to a dynamic perspective on culture, including cultural changes in ethnolinguistic identity.

AN INTERGROUP PERSPECTIVE ON COMMUNICATION

Several communication frameworks draw from the principles laid down by social identity theory (SIT) and/or self-categorization theories (SCTs; Tajfel, 1978; Tajfel & Turner, 1986; Turner, Hogg, Oakes, Reicher, & Wetherell, 1987), and thus they can be described as theories of intergroup communication (e.g., Gudykunst, 2004; Hecht, Warren, Jung, & Krieger, 2004). Here I describe the framework forwarded by Howard Giles and his colleagues, as articulated in communication accommodation theory (CAT) and ethnolinguistic identity theory (ELIT; see Giles & Noels, 2002, and Gallois, Ogay, & Giles, 2004, for overviews). Because it was formulated in close association with social identity and self-categorization theories, it perhaps most thoroughly encapsulates intergroup processes as they relate to communication.

One of the many purposes of CAT is to elucidate the manner in which people use communication styles, including languages, dialects, accents, and other communication characteristics, to index social groups, statuses, locales, and a variety of other socially relevant dimensions (Coupland, 2007). CAT maintains that interlocutors generally shift their communication styles in response to one another and their social context. In many circumstances, this involves adapting verbal and nonverbal features to become more similar to one's interlocutor. In others, however, an interlocutor might refuse to converge or even diverge away from his or her partner's communication style. These shifts might be used to accomplish a number of potentially simultaneous goals, including not only the effective transmission of information but also the management of relational concerns (e.g., power, face management), which is closely associated with the establishment of identities and the achievement of intergroup comparisons (Harwood, Giles, & Palomares, 2005). More particularly, patterns of communicative convergence are argued to increase a psychological sense of similarity and interpersonal attraction, whereas patterns of divergence emphasize the distinctiveness of each interlocutor, strategically characterizing a situation as involving complementarity or intergroup differentiation, and highlighting social status, roles, and identities.

Importantly, actual patterns of accommodation are not necessarily synonymous with the intentions of speakers or the interpretations of listeners. Speakers might not be aware of their own shifts (Thakerar, Giles, & Cheshire, 1982), or their communication moves might belie their actual intent (e.g., they might converge to their listener objectively but the intent behind this convergence might not be to indicate affiliation but rather indifference or exclusion from the speaker's ingroup;see Woolard, 1989). In a complementary fashion, the listener might not perceive shifts in the speaker's communication style, and even if so, such changes might not be interpreted as the speaker intended (e.g., a convergence in accent might be seen as mimicry or condescension). Moreover, interlocutors appear to have a sense of optimal levels of convergence: Giles and Smith (1979) varied convergence on pronunciation, speech rate, and message content, and found that although convergence on any one of these linguistic characteristics was perceived positively, convergence on all three levels was perceived negatively. This potential mismatch between objective accommodation, the speaker's psychological intention, and the subjective interpretation by the listener implies that interlocutors have some more or less shared beliefs and expectations which serve as standards for what is appropriate and acceptable accommodation behavior. Two such guidelines, that we will discuss later, are stereotypes regarding ingroups and outgroups and norms regarding appropriate language use.

Whereas CAT outlines the social psychological dynamics of communication shifts, "ELIT…discusses the socio-psychological processes underlying specific language strategies adopted by ethnolinguistic group members in a social interaction" (Harwood et al., 2005, p. 9). Following social identity theory (Tajfel, 1978; Tajfel & Turner, 1986), ELIT maintains that social categorization involves knowledge of our own membership in certain social categories, including ethnolinguistic groups when language is a salient marker of group membership (Giles & Johnson, 1987). This knowledge, along with the positive and negative values attached to it, constitutes ethnolinguistic identity. ELIT assumes that we strive to maintain a positive, distinct identity from other ethnolinguistic groups, and this can, at least partially, be accomplished through our speech and nonverbal actions.

If the comparison process favors our own group, particularly on status dimensions, then there is no cause to adopt another communication style. However, if one has a relatively negative identity as a result of this comparison process, several strategies to overcome this uncomfortable position are possible. One might disidentify with the lower status group and attempt to shift to the more positively valued group (e.g., by adopting the language of the other group). Alternatively, one might redefine different dimensions of comparison between groups (e.g., redefine one's lower status language as more "friendly"). Third, one might compete with the higher status group to change the status quo (e.g., by maintaining a conversation in a minority language despite the presence of speakers of the higher status language). The strategy chosen depends on several aspects of the intergroup situation, including the strength of ethnolinguistic identity, the perceived permeability of group boundaries, the number of alternative social categories with which one can identify, and, perhaps most important for the present discussion, the perceived "ethnolinguistic vitality"[1] of the ingroup relative to the outgroup. Ethnolinguistic vitality is defined in terms of the social status and prestige, demographic representation, and institutional support received by a language group (Giles, Bourhis, & Taylor, 1977), and it can be used to characterize a group's sociostructural status relative to other ethnolinguistic groups.

In sum, CAT and ELIT provide a communication perspective on intergroup dynamics that describes how people use language and other communication devices to create a sense of psychological distance or closeness with another person, and emphasizes that aspects of the intergroup contact context, particularly the perceived relative ethnolinguistic vitality of groups, might explain these moves (at least in part). These theories explain communicative moves in immediate social situations, as well as the strategies that individuals can employ to change their intergroup situation or at least their evaluation of it. Moreover, these social psychological processes have implications for explaining intergroup relations on a larger scale, including societal-level phenomena such as culture and language maintenance and shift. It is a powerful paradigm to consider communication processes between members of different groups, but as we noted earlier, little work has considered how culture relates to communication between groups (but see Fortman & Giles, 2006; Giles, Bonilla, & Speer, 2012). Thus, we turn to consider some potentially complementary ways in which culture may be overlaid on this intergroup communication theory, and how it might inform understanding of cultural change.

Culture Influences Intergroup Communication

One way to conceptualize the relation between culture and intergroup communication processes is in terms of how psychological dimensions found to differentiate cultural groups (often operationally defined on the basis of nationality or ethnicity) are linked to communication within and between groups. Cultural psychologists commonly differentiate between groups that emphasize independent self-construals, individualistic values, and an analytic cognitive style (often represented by North American samples), and those that emphasize interdependent self-construals, collectivistic values, and a holistic cognitive style (often represented by East Asian samples; see Triandis, 1988, 1989; Markus & Kitayama, 1991; Nisbett, 2003). These dimensions of individualism-collectivism or independence-interdependence have been associated with a variety of communication differences across ethnolinguistic groups (cf., Ting-Toomey, 2010, for a discussion of how Hofstede's, 1980, dimensions relate to aspects of communication). For instance, a particularly prominent topic concerns how these psychological dimensions relate to the extent to which interlocutors use direct or indirect communication styles, that is, the degree to which communicators habitually use contextual cues to carry meaning, including nonverbal acts, relationship and conversational history, situational cues, social roles, and so on. A growing body of research on verbal and nonverbal aspects of communication, including pronoun use (e.g., Kashima & Kashima, 1998, 2003), verb choice (e.g., Maass, Karasawa, Politi, & Suga, 2006), vocal tone (e.g., Ishii, Reyes, & Kitayama, 2003), and use of contextual cues, including the interlocutor's point of view (e.g., Singelis & Brown, 1995; Haberstroh, Oyserman, Schwarz, Kühnend, & Ji 2002), shows that interdependently oriented persons tend to attend more to the context and use a more indirect communication style than independently oriented persons.

More germane to the present discussion is the idea that the extent to which one is chronically focused on independence or interdependence impacts the extent to which one differentiates between ingroups and outgroups in their communication style (for an early review, see Gudykunst & Bond, 1997).[2] More specifically, some evidence supports the claim that people with a strong interdependent orientation are more likely to differentiate between ingroups and outgroups than those with a more independent orientation. For instance, Hoyle, Pinkley, and Insko (1989) found that interactions with ingroup members are considered less abrasive and less unpredictable than interactions with outgroup members, and this pattern was more evident for the (presumably more interdependent) Japanese than the (more independent) American participants. Gudykunst and Nishida (1986) found that collectivists (i.e., Japanese) perceive ingroup communication (i.e., interactions with a classmate) as more intimate than outgroup communication (i.e., interactions with a stranger), but they found no significant differences across these contexts for individualists (i.e., Americans). Moreover, communication uncertainty was lower for communication with members of ingroups than with members of outgroups in Japan and Hong Kong, but there was no difference in Australia and the United States. East Asians also used greater personalization (intimacy and synchronization) with ingroup than outgroup members, whereas Americans did not make such a distinction. Oetzel and Ting-Toomey (2003) demonstrated that collectivists express greater other-face concerns with ingroup members and greater self-face maintenance concerns with outgroup members in intergroup conflict situations, whereas individualists express greater self-face maintenance concerns and less other-face maintenance concerns in dealing with both ingroup and outgroup conflict situations.

A variety of related explanations have been proffered to explain why interdependently oriented people differentiate between ingroups and outgroups more readily than independently oriented people: Persons with strong interdependent self-construals place greater importance on social networks within the ingroup and have stronger, more durable ingroup identities (Chen, Brockner, & Katz, 1998); they entertain multiple-group identities (Gudykunst, 1989); and/or they draw sharper boundaries between ingroups and outgroups (Triandis, 1988). Brewer and Chen (2007) offer an alternative explanation that draws from Brewer and Gardner's (1996; see also Brewer & Yuki, 2007) distinction between groups that define their ingroup in terms of relational networks (more common in East Asia) and those that define them on the basis of a common group identity (more typical in Europe and America). They suggest that in an intragroup context the former might be more likely than the latter to use an indirect speech style to maintain relationships within the social network, but in an intergroup context such concerns might be less important, and both cultural groups might use a more direct communication style.

This line of comparative research provides insight into whether and how groups from different cultural backgrounds are likely to shift their language styles in response to the presence of ingroup and outgroup members. It suggests that intergroup interactions across cultural lines might be fraught because interlocutors are not familiar with each other's communication styles, their ways of defining ingroups and outgroups, and/or norms for ingroup and outgroup communication. Such explanations might elucidate miscommunication in some intercultural interactions, particularly those where groups have not established their relative status (as is the case of many experimental settings, and, arguably, temporary sojourners, such as tourists or international students). They may not, however, provide a sufficient account of the dynamics of communication between ethnolinguistic groups in more permanent situations of intercultural contact. Because many of these comparative studies have contrasted interactions using relatively "status-free" comparisons, such as interactions between a classmate versus a stranger, they do not explicitly address how sociostructural status and power relations between groups might affect intergroup communication (cf. Giles & Watson, 2008; Gallois, 2010). Thus, although an understanding of cultural norms regarding appropriate communication practices for ingroups and outgroups is necessary for understanding intergroup communication, the relative sociostructural positioning of ethnolinguistic groups must also be considered. With this in mind we now consider how these aspects of intergroup communication processes might be implicated in the construction of culture in groups of different sociostructural status.

Communication Processes Construct (Inter)Group Culture

A complementary perspective on the relation between culture and intergroup communication examines how intergroup communication processes contribute to the construction of culture. Discursive psychologists and ethnographers such as Potter and Wetherall (1987), van Dijk (1987), and Carbaugh (e.g., Carbaugh, Lie, Locmele, & Sotirova, 2012) have long emphasized that "communication plays an important role in constructing the nature of group memberships and group categories" (Harwood et al., 2005, p. 6) and, we would argue, group culture. To elucidate the process by which communication "carries" culture, we begin with a discussion of Kashima and his colleagues' recently proposed "situated functionalist" model (e.g., Clark & Kashima, 2007; Kashima, 2008). Building on the work of Herbert Clark (1996), Kashima maintains that communication happens through a process of "grounding," whereby interlocutors cooperatively work to establish and maintain some common ground or understanding. This mutual understanding draws from a variety of sources, including the information exchanged, what participants know about each other from previous experience, and from conventionalized knowledge. Establishing common ground has been shown to be fundamental to the effective exchange of information in both same- and mixed-ethnic dyads (Li, 1999). Once interlocutors' create a common understanding, they can introduce new information into the discussion, and as their mutual understanding grows, this information can potentially be exchanged with new interlocutors. According to Kashima (2008), this conventionalized information (in contrast with novel information) is more readily communicated and thus more widely distributed within a group. This shared knowledge, then, can be construed as the cultural knowledge that defines a group's characteristic beliefs (Schaller, Conway, & Tanchuk, 2002).

Drawing on the distinction between content and relational aspects of messages, Kashima (2008) argues that the exchange of conventionalized knowledge serves a relational function, such that greater social cohesion among people is fostered when they believe that they share a common understanding. This is particularly the case if the sender believes that the recipient endorses that normative/conventional perspective (Clark & Kashima, 2007). To examine this possibility, Kashima and his colleagues (Clark & Kashima, 2007; Lyons & Kashima, 2003;) focused on one type of conventionalized information: stereotypes. They found that as information was communicated across individuals in a communication chain, the stereotyped information was more readily communicated and became more stereotypical, especially when the communicators believed that their listeners and community members shared the stereotypes. Moreover, although stereotyped information is perceived to be less novel than inconsistent information (and hence of less informational value), it did function to enhance social connectivity among interlocutors.

Extending this paradigm further, it would seem reasonable to think that stereotypes regarding the outgroup and the ingroup might be similarly communicable between members of the ingroup. Given the pervasiveness of the ingroup bias (Brewer, 2007) and people's tendency to act in accordance with an ingroup prototype when their social identity is salient (Reid & Anderson, 2010), we might expect that the positive stereotypes of the ingroup would be readily communicated but negative stereotypes less so. The converse would be true for outgroup stereotypes, especially under conditions of threat. Consistent with Kashima's situated functional model, the exchange of this information would facilitate ingroup cohesion. An example of how stereotyping is accomplished communicatively comes from examinations of the linguistic intergroup bias (Maass, Salvi, Arcuri, & Semin, 1989), which shows that people describe ingroup members' positive actions using abstract language (e.g., adjectives), and their negative actions with concrete language (e.g., verbs), and the converse is true for outgroup members. The bias in communication leads to attributions that present the ingroup favorably and the outgroup unfavorably.

Research on language attitudes, however, illustrates how status differences might complicate the stereotyping process for ingroups and outgroups (see Garrett, 2010, and Giles & Watson, in press, for recent reviews). Lambert, Hodgson, Gardner, and Fillenbaum's (1960) seminal study of Anglophones and Francophones in the predominantly French-speaking city of Montréal use the matched-guise technique in which bilingual speakers of French and English read a content-neutral text to Anglophone and Francophone participants who rated the speakers across a variety of traits (e.g., intelligence, ambition, kindness, dependability). The results showed, perhaps not unexpectedly, that Anglophones rated the English-speaking guises more positively than the French guises. More surprising, however, was that Francophones did likewise-rating the English-speaking guises more positively than their ingroup guises. These results were interpreted to mean that both dominant and subordinate groups have more positive attitudes toward the language of the higher status group (at the time, Anglophones enjoyed greater social status than Francophones). Later studies have refined the dimensions of comparison by differentiating between "status" (e.g., intelligence, ambition, etc.) and "solidarity" (e.g., kindness, dependability, etc.),[3] and some research suggests that higher status groups are rated higher on "status" traits by both dominant and subordinate groups, and that lower status groups may be rated higher on "solidarity" traits (e.g., Ryan, Giles, & Sebastian, 1985; Stewart, Ryan, & Giles, 1985; for reviews, see Giles & Billings, 2005; Giles & Marlow, 2011; Dragojevic, Giles & Watson, 2012).

A mechanism to explain status differences in the patterns of ingroup and outgroup evaluations, not unrelated to Kashima's (2008) situated functional model, might be derived from Latrofa, Vaes, Pastore, and Cadinu's (2009) self-stereotyping study. Latrofa and her colleagues found that, although perceived discrimination was associated with lower levels of well-being, these members of a stigmatized group effectively coped with the effects of discrimination by ascribing the ingroup's stereotypical features, both positive and negative, to their self-image. They argue that people who belong to a subordinate group are likely to assume stereotypical personality traits associated with their ingroup because this practice is linked with increased identification with the ingroup and greater social cohesion, which offsets the negative effects of prejudice on well-being. Correspondingly, minority members might use their less valued language, even if it is associated with negative social stereotypes and discrimination because the language also connotes identification and solidarity with other ingroup members.

Such a disadvantageous situation is not without the possibility of change, however; subordinate groups might not long be satisfied with an ambivalent social identity or convinced of the justification for the relative status of the groups (cf. Taylor, King, & Usborne, 2010). Drawing from the earlier discussion of ELIT, under particular circumstances, minority group members might strive to change their unfavorable position by using communication strategies that enable them to move individually into the higher status group, to seek creative alternatives to the existing power structure, or to challenge the intergroup status quo. An example of challenges to the existing hierarchy come from the work of Bourhis and Giles (1977; see also Bourhis, Giles, & Tajfel, 1973), who found that Welsh speakers emphasized their Welsh accents when confronted by an arrogant speaker of English (i.e., the higher status language). Similar patterns of communicative divergence and ethnic affirmation in the face of identity threat (with evidence of convergence under situations of no threat) have been found by Bond and his colleagues in Hong Kong (e.g., Bond & Yang, 1982; Bond, 1984, 1985; Chen & Bond, 2007).

In sum, we readily communicate conventionalized knowledge, such as stereotypes, with like-minded (ingroup) members, and the exchange of this kind of information may enhance social cohesion. For higher status groups, this knowledge favors the ingroup, and this communication dynamic would not seem likely to threaten their collective self-esteem. For lower status minority groups, although this conventionalized knowledge might negatively impact self-esteem and contribute to an ambivalent social identity, the exchange of this knowledge might enhance social cohesion. Thus, an intergroup perspective highlights how groups of different statuses may communicate in ways that create different cultural meaning systems (in this example, stereotypes regarding ingroups and outgroups). It also underscores the strategic possibilities that people can adopt in order to resist and change existing power structures and their related cultures.

Intergroup Relations, Communication, and Cultural Change

One could argue that there have been important transformations in intergroup relations in many areas in the world, partly due to changes in the rates and patterns of intra- and international migration. This increased contact between more diverse cultural groups has raised new issues with regard to ethnolinguistic identity. As described earlier, much intergroup research would seem to emphasize the ease with which people categorize themselves and others into "us vs. them" dichotomies and the negative consequences of such social categorization processes. In contrast, researchers from other areas of psychology, notably acculturation and ethnic minority psychology (e.g. Berry, 1990; Lafromboise,

Coleman, & Gerton, 1993; Phinney, 1990), have long argued that contact with other ethnocultural groups does not necessarily result in exclusive identification with one or another group, but rather persons can identify to a greater or lesser extent with each of the reference groups that are relevant to them. This possibility of assuming multiple ethnic identities has been taken up more recently by researchers interested in biculturality and social identity complexity (e.g., No, Wan, Chao, Rosner, & Hong, 2011; Benet-Martinez & Haritatos, 2005; Brewer, 2010).

The "situated ethnic identity" perspective on ethnolinguistic identity is likewise open to the possibility that persons living in multicultural contexts might assume multiple identities, and that the specific pattern of identity depends upon the situational and societal context (Clément & Noels, 1992; Noels et al., 2004, 2010). Drawing from discussions of ethnolinguistic identity in CAT and ELIT, along with social psychological theories of second language learning and bilingualism (Lambert, 1978; Clément, 1980), this framework maintains that interlocutors adjust their communication style to correspond with the style of those with whom they interact in order to achieve a variety of goals, including exchange of referential information and the negotiation of relationships and identities (cf. Watzlawick et al., 1967). In many everyday interactions where identities are not contested, communicative convergence generally involves a parallel shift in identity, such that a person's identity tends to complement that of his or her interlocutor.

Because we encounter different people in different situations, language use and identities change depending upon the characteristics of the situation. Following the work of scholars who emphasize the socially situated nature of communicative behavior (e.g., Hymes, 1972; Brown & Fraser, 1979), we argue that people hold more or less consensual expectations for commonly experienced situations, not unlike scripts or interaction episodes (e.g., Abelson, 1981; Forgas & Bond, 1985). These normative situations are defined primarily in terms of the setting (e.g., home, school), the relationship between interlocutors (e.g., family, friends, bosses), and the purpose of the interaction (i.e., the activity or topic of conversation engaged in). With regard to communication, situational norms have both a descriptive and an injunctive aspect, such that not only do they describe what is typically or normally done within a group but they can also have a moral force relating to what ought to be done (cf. Cialdini, Reno, & Kallgren, 1990; Jacobsen, Mortensen, & Cialdini, 2011). They are generally implicit, but they can be made explicit, and indeed formalized in institutional policies, as reflected in official language legislation, codes of conduct for religious, political, or other ceremonies, and so on. This consensual understanding of what is appropriate language behavior across different everyday interactions eases communication within and between groups. For instance, the use of a higher status, outgroup speech style might be viewed as the standard form in more formal situations (e.g., a meeting at work with one's boss) but considered inappropriate in less formal situations (e.g., a conversation at home with one's mother), where the lower status, ingroup speech style is appropriate. Situational norms, however, are neither static nor uncontestable determiners of language acts or other types of behavior. Rather, depending on a person's motivation and/or the contextual affordances and constraints, these norms can be respected, revised, and/or resisted.

Situated Ethnic Identity and Acculturation

Situational domains vary in their level of intimacy,[4] and this variation has important implications for patterns of cultural change in language use and identity. Noels, Clément, and Gaudet (2004; see also Clément & Noels, 1992) posit that in multicultural contexts, facets of ethnicity expressed in less intimate situational domains (such as the workplace) are assimilated more quickly than aspects of ethnicity restricted to more intimate domains (e.g., with friends and family) because the former domains are more likely to involve interethnic contact than the latter. Stated otherwise, identity in intimate domains is hypothesized to be relatively sheltered from the acculturative pressures of intergroup contact and communication.

A growing body of evidence supports this premise (e.g., Clément & Noels, 1992; Clément, Singh, & Gaudet, 2006; Noels et al., 2004; Noels, Leavitt, & Clément, 2010; Zhang & Noels, 2012). For instance, Noels and her colleagues (2010) examined situational variations in the identity of Chinese Canadians by using an adapted version of Clément and Noels's (1992) Situated Ethnic Identity Scale, which presents 16 hypothetical scenarios across four situational domains that varied in the relative level of intimacy (e.g., friends, family, university, community). For each of the scenarios participants indicated the extent to which they identified with members of the Chinese community and, on a separate scale, the extent to which they identified with members of the (Anglo-) Canadian community. As can be seen in Figure 10.1, for the first-generation (G1) Chinese Canadians, Chinese identity was considerably stronger than Canadian identity in the family situation, but Canadian identity was stronger than Chinese identity in the university and community domains. In the friendship domain Chinese identity was weaker and Canadian identity was stronger than in the family domains, such that both identities were equivalent, a pattern that is consistent with the possibility that these young university students have interethnic friendships. These findings support the idea that acculturative shifts in identity would be evident first in less intimate situations and that intimate domains would be relatively sheltered from acculturative pressures. Friendship interactions, although intimate, possibly involve interethnic contact and hence lie between these extremes.

Further evidence that acculturative change eventually penetrates into more intimate domains comes from a consideration of second-generation (G2) Chinese Canadians. Like the G1 group, the G2 group endorsed greater identification with Canadians and lower identification with Chinese in less intimate situations (see Fig. 10.1). Also like the G1 group, the G2 group felt more Chinese than Canadian in the family situation, although the G2 group felt more Canadian in this situation than the G1 group. In the friendship domain, whereas the G1 group felt their two identities were relatively equivalent, the G2 group felt their Canadian identity was stronger than their Chinese identity. Assuming that the G2 group has greater interethnic contact across more situational domains, this pattern further supports the idea that acculturation is a situated process, such that acculturative

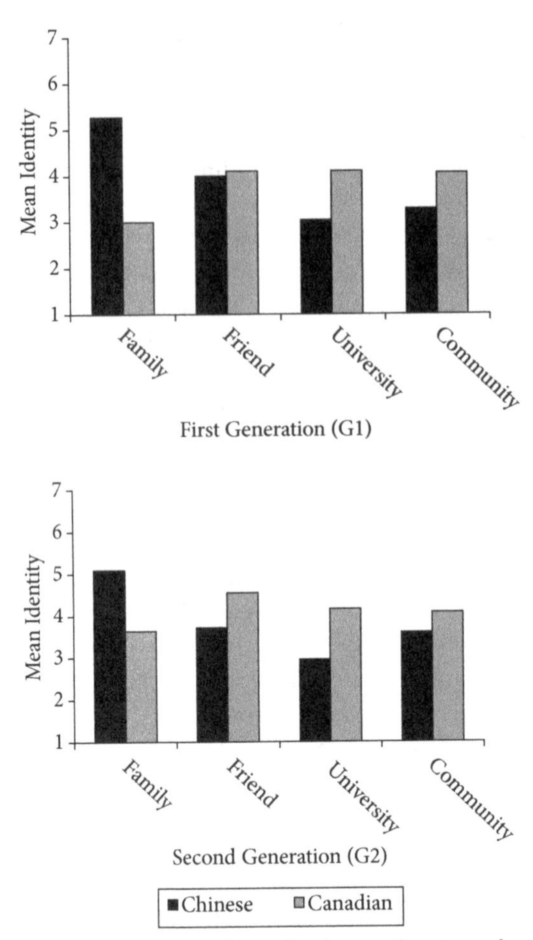

Figure 10.1. Mean ethnic identity as a function of reference group, situation, and generation group (adapted from Noels et al., 2010).

effects of intercultural contact are first evident in more public spheres of life and eventually penetrate more intimate domains. Moreover, it is noteworthy that these findings from studies involving hypothetical scenarios are consistent with experiential-sampling and diary studies that show that heritage ethnic identity becomes more salient when the ethnic composition of the situation favors the heritage group, when one is with family members, and when the heritage language is used (Yip & Fuligni, 2002; Yip, 2005).

Identity Negotiation and Identity Gaps

The success of an identity claim depends on the acceptability of identity claims to both interlocutors (Schlenker, 1985), and in part acceptability is based on consistency with normative expectations. In intergroup contexts, the failure to respect these norms might not only predict unsatisfactory communication in the immediate social interaction but also precipitate intergroup conflict on a broader scale (DeRidder & Tripathi, 1992). As pointed out by Bourhis and his colleagues in their Interactive Acculturation Model (e.g., Bourhis, Moïse, Perreault, & Senecal, 1997; Bourhis, Montreuil, Barrette, Montaruli, 2009), across multicultural contexts, the dominant group in receiving societies may have expectations, often inscribed in public policy, regarding the form of relationship and type of identity that newly arriving minority group members should assume in relation to established members of that society. Mismatches between the newcomers' and the receiving society's acculturation orientations might well lie at the heart of intergroup conflict and poor adaptation outcomes for the newcomers.

With regard to mismatches in identity during face-to-face interactions, Noels and her colleagues (2010) found both G1 and G2 Chinese Canadians reported gaps between their actual Chinese and (Anglo-) Canadian identities and the identities reflected on them by Chinese and English Canadian interlocutors across the four situational domains noted earlier. In general, with both groups of interlocutors, while there was a weak tendency to perceive a gap between actual and reflected Canadian identities across domains, there was a stronger tendency for a gap between actual and reflected Chinese identities. The smallest gaps were in interactions with friends (indeed, they were nonexistent with Anglo Canadian friends), which is consistent with the idea that close intimates focus on personal rather than stereotypical knowledge in their interactions.

Interestingly, although family members might also be considered close intimates, identity gaps were also found in family interactions, although in a manner quite different than in the other social situations. Participants felt that family members saw them as less Chinese and more Canadian than they saw themselves, and for the G2 group, family members' reflected profile was completely incongruent with the participants' own appraisal: Whereas G2 individuals felt more Chinese than Canadian when with family members, they felt their family members saw them as more Canadian than Chinese. This inconsistency, experienced with others who might be presumed to know the participant very well, might flag a context where there is misunderstanding and tension between parents/grandparents and their young adult offspring. In the G2 group, such identity gaps were associated with perceived discrimination from both ingroup and outgroup members across most situations (see also Clément, Noels, & Deneault, 2001; Jung & Hecht, 2008). Given that these discrepancies might arise in part because of interlocutors' capacity to claim identities, we turn now to explore the role of status and communication competence in these negotiations.

Ethnolinguistic Vitality, Situated Ethnic Identity, and Communication

The situated identity patterns described earlier are complicated by a consideration of ethnolinguistic vitality. According to Clément (1980; Clément & Noels, 1992; Noels & Clément, 1996), when ethnolinguistic groups learn and use a second language and acquire a new cultural identity, they might evidence a pattern of identification that reflects integration of the two identities or the assimilation of the original identity into the other cultural group. When a group has high vitality, members are likely to remain secure in their original language and cultural identity. However, when a group has low vitality, there is a tendency to lose the original language and cultural identity (cf. Lambert's, 1978, discussion of additive and subtractive bilingualism).

Much of the previous research on situational variations in ethnic identity is limited in its capacity to examine the impact of vitality on patterns of ethnic identity because it was conducted on immigrant groups, who generally are a minority group within a receiving society. The case of French Canadians, however, provides a useful example of how the relative vitality of ethnolinguistic groups can affect patterns of identity. French has an official language status equal to English, and in some parts of Canada, Francophones are a numerical majority. Noels and her colleagues (Noels et al., 2004) examined the identity of French Canadians who originated from regions of Canada where French enjoys greater or lesser vitality. The university at which this study took place is an officially bilingual institution situated in Ottawa, Canada, which is a city that lies on the border of Ontario (a predominantly English-speaking province) and Québec (a predominately French-speaking province). Thus, these Francophone students could originate from a provincial context in which they represent a minority (i.e., Ontario) or a majority (i.e., Québec) ethnolinguistic group. As with the study of Chinese Canadians reported earlier, participants from minority and majority backgrounds completed an instrument that assessed their feelings of identity as an Anglophone and as a Francophone in relatively intimate (e.g., with friends in personal settings) and nonintimate hypothetical situational domains (e.g., with fellow students in the university and people in the community; adapted from Clément & Noels, 1992). For a third of the participants, the interlocutor was specified to be a Francophone, for another third an Anglophone, and for the remaining third the interlocutor's identity was not specified.

The results indicated that the ethnicity of the interlocutor had a significant impact on patterns of ethnic identity, and this effect was not moderated by the situation or the status background. When the ethnicity of the interlocutor was not specified, Francophone identity was stronger than Anglophone identity. A similar pattern was evident when the interlocutor was designated as Francophone, although Anglophone identity was weaker and Francophone identity was marginally stronger than in the ethnicity-neutral condition. With Anglophone interlocutors, Francophone identity was lower and Anglophone identity was higher than in the neutral and Francophone conditions, such that both identities were equivalent. This pattern of findings suggests that ethnolinguistic identification tends to converge to the ethnicity of the interlocutor. Such a pattern is consistent with experimental studies of cultural framing, which underscore the ease with which bilingual people shift their thoughts, feelings, and identities in response to cultural primes such as language (Hong, Morris, Chiu, & Benet-Martinez, 2000; Ross, Xun, & Wilson, 2002).

Independently of the ethnicity of the interlocutor, however, the ethnolinguistic vitality of the participant's group and the intimacy of the situation affected patterns of identification, a finding that underscores the importance of group status and situational norms independently of the ethnicity of the interlocutor. This effect was further modified by the participants' degree of confidence in using English, operationalized in this study as low levels of anxiety using English. More specifically, for participants who were comfortable using English, there were clear differences in the identity patterns of the higher and lower status groups. For the higher vitality group, a distinction between identities was evident, such that Francophone identity was stronger than Anglophone identity in both situations, and Francophone identity was stronger in intimate situations than in nonintimate situations (see Fig. 10.2a). This finding is consistent with the idea that the heritage identity is sheltered from acculturative influences in more intimate situational domains. For the lower vitality group, Francophone identity was lower and Anglophone identity was higher across both situational domains (see Fig. 10.2b).

HIGH ENGLISH CONFIDENCE

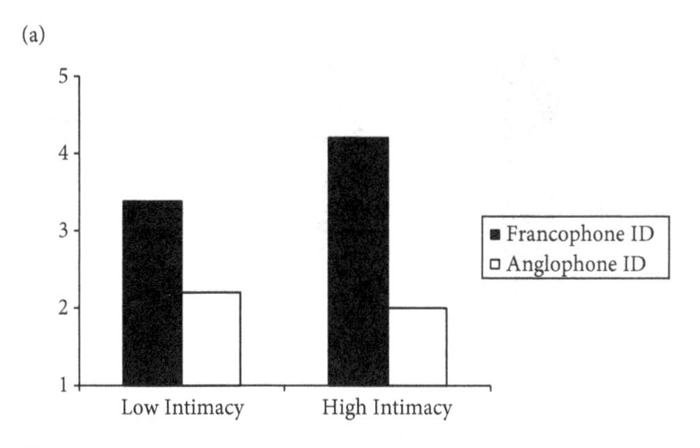

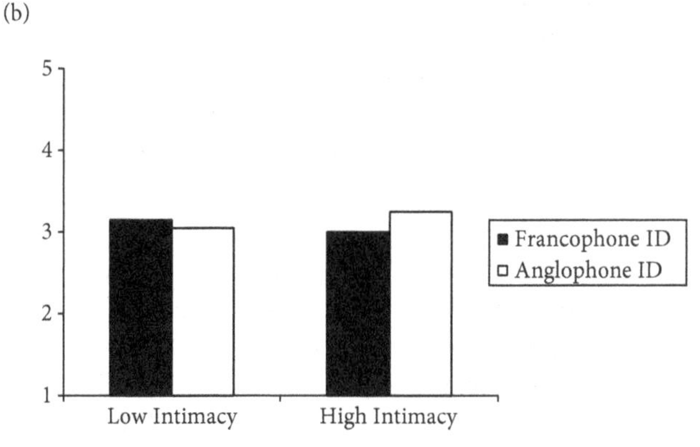

Figure 10.2. Mean identity as a function of reference group, situation, ethnolinguistic vitality, and anxiety using English (adapted from Noels et al., 2004). (*a*) High ethnolinguistic vitality; (*b*) low ethnolinguistic vitality; (*c*) high ethnolinguistic vitality; and (*d*) low ethnolinguistic vitality.

LOW ENGLISH CONFIDENCE

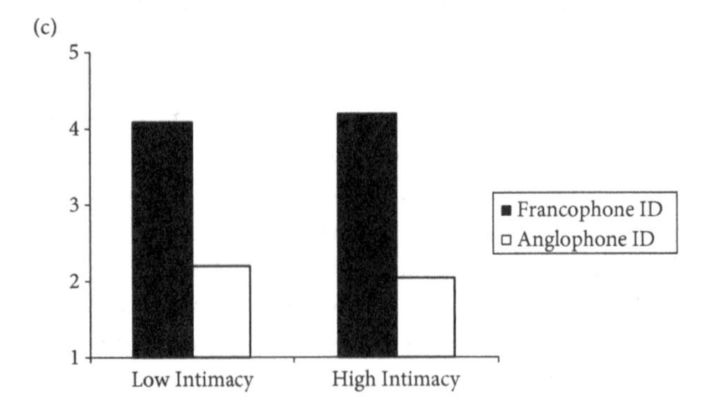

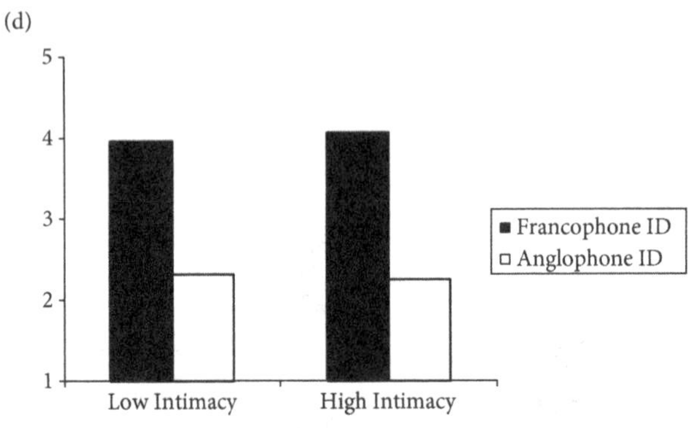

Figure 10.2. (Continued)

Moreover, there was no difference between the two identities in either situation. This finding suggests that lower vitality group members who are comfortable speaking English are more likely to experience a lessened sense of Francophone identity and an increased sense of identity with Anglophones, suggestive of a shift from one group to the other. The similarity of identity patterns across domains suggests that they do not maintain their ethnolinguistic heritage even in relatively sheltered intimate situations.

For participants who were anxious using English, however, Francophone identity was higher than Anglophone identity in both intimate and nonintimate situations, and there were no differences in the levels of each identity across situations or across minority and majority groups (see Figs. 10.2c and 10.2d). Thus, these Francophones who lacked the confidence to use English showed no variation in identity, even when they were from a lower status group or in a situation with the potential for interethnic contact. These findings are important because they suggest a mechanism by which acculturative change takes place, such that facility in communicating with people from other ethnic groups is critical to the effective negotiation of ethnic identities. Without this communicative capacity, the kind of linguistic convergence that facilitates social interaction across groups is limited, and correspondingly the kinds of identity shifts that might correspond with language shifts are also constrained.

However, communicative competence and confidence are not sufficient to explain identity shifts. Communication is a motivated process, influenced by the various goals that people strive to achieve in everyday social interactions. It is also a normative process, such that the kinds of goals and the manner in which they can be achieved are constrained by the expectations of others (both significant others and the "generalized other"). In intergroup contexts the norms and expectations of both ingroup and outgroup members can constrain and lend affordances to the achievement of these goals. This situated ethnic identity perspective, thus, responds to calls for more communication-oriented models of acculturation (e.g., Giles, Bonilla, & Speer, 2012).

Although we argue for the centrality of language for ethnic identity, we recognize that for some groups, language is not central concern and other characteristics besides language, including physical characteristics and/or religious affiliation, can support a sense of ethnic identity (cf. Rosenthal & Hrynevich, 1985), and it is possible that the kind of identity patterns shown here are restricted to ethnic groups for which language serves as an important symbolic marker of identity (but see Clément, Sylvestre, & Noels, 1991). Nonetheless, if the definition of language is broadened to include other aspects of communication style, such as differences in accent, vocabulary, and jargon, or even the directness of the speech style, these more subtle communication features may be likewise associated with group identity, identity negotiation, and acculturative change. It might simply be easier to document shifts in communicative practice across ethnolinguistic groups than across groups that share a common language.

CONCLUSION

The purpose of this chapter was to elucidate several ways in which culture relates to intergroup communication processes. This review suggests a bidirectional relation between culture and (intergroup) communication, as we reviewed research that investigated how culture influences intergroup communication processes (including the definition of ingroups and outgroups), and studies that examined how communication processes might contribute to the construction of group culture. We have also argued that understanding communication dynamics is important for understanding acculturative changes in identity for groups in intercultural contact. We maintain that a more complete account of the relation between culture and intergroup communication requires explicit attention to the relative sociostructural status, or ethnolinguistic vitality, of groups in contact, the normative expectations for communication across situations and groups of different status, as well as the communicative competence of interlocutors. In a world where it is estimated that there are approximately 6,000 languages across 200 countries, many people regularly interact with people from other ethnolinguistic groups. Indeed, Tucker (1999) argues that for the majority of people in the world, bilingualism is an everyday experience. In light of this contemporary situation, we echo the call of Fortman and Giles (2006) and Hecht et al. (2005) for further examination of the relation between culture and intergroup communication. Such efforts might not only benefit many people in multilingual and multicultural contexts but perhaps also respond to Taylor et al.'s (2010) call for greater diversity in theories of intergroup communication.

ACKNOWLEDGMENTS

The author would like to thank Richard Clément, Howard Giles, and Donald Taylor for their insightful comments on an earlier draft of this chapter.

NOTES

1. In this chapter, the terms "ethnolinguistic vitality" and "(sociostructural) status" will be used synonymously.
2. See Gudykunst (1987, 1988) and Gallois, Giles, Jones, Cargile, and Ota (1995) for detailed discussions of the relations between Hofstede's (1980) cultural dimensions and key intergroup constructs.
3. These findings parallel recent discussions of the Stereotype Content Model, which differentiates dimensions of "competence" and "warmth" in person perception (see Fiske, Cuddy, & Glick, 2006).
4. Intimacy is negatively related to a second, independent dimension termed "task-focus," which represents task-oriented situations where there is greater attention to formal, elaborated language (see Côté & Clément, 1994).

REFERENCES

Abelson, R. P. (1981). Psychological status of the script concept. *American Psychologist, 36*, 715–729.

Benet-Martinez, V., & Haritatos, J. (2005). Bicultural identity integration (BII): Components and psychosocial antecedents. *Journal of Personality, 73*, 492–516.

Berry, J. W. (1990). Psychology of acculturation. In J. J. Berman (Ed.), *Nebraska Symposium on Motivation, 1989: Cross-cultural perspectives* (pp. 201–234). Lincoln: University of Nebraska Press.

Bond, M. H. (1984). Experimenter language choice and ethnic affirmation by Chinese trilinguals in Hong Kong. *International Journal of Intercultural Relations, 8*(4), 347–356. doi:10.1016/0147-1767(84)90014-2.

Bond, M. H. (1985). Language as a carrier of ethnic stereotypes in Hong Kong. *Journal of Social Psychology, 125*(1), 53–62. doi:10.1080/00224545.1985.9713508.

Bond, M. H., & Yang, K-S. (1982). Ethnic affirmation versus cross-cultural accommodation: The variable impact of questionnaire language on Chinese bilinguals from Hong Kong. *Journal of Cross-Cultural Psychology, 13*(2), 169–185. doi:10.1177/0022002182013002003.

Bourhis, R. Y., & Giles, H. (1977). The language of intergroup distinctiveness. In H. Giles (Ed.), *Language, ethnicity and intergroup relations* (pp. 119–135). London, UK: Academic Press.

Bourhis, R. Y., Giles, H., & Tajfel, H. (1973). Language as a determinant of Welsh identity. *European Journal of Social Psychology, 3*, 447–460.

Bourhis, R. Y., Moïse, L. C., Perreault, S., & Senecal, S. (1997). Towards an interactive acculturation model: A social psychological approach. *International Journal of Psychology, 32*, 369–386.

Bourhis, R. Y., Montreuil, A., Barrette, G., & Montaruli, E. (2009). Acculturation and immigrant/host community relations in multicultural settings. In S. Demoulin, J. P. Leyens & J. Dovidio (Eds.), *Intergroup misunderstanding: Impact of divergent social realities* (pp.39–61). New York, NY: Psychology Press.

Brewer, M. (2007). The importance of being "we": Human nature and intergroup relations. *American Psychologist, 62*(8), 728–738. doi:10.1037/0003-066X.62.8.728.

Brewer, M. (2010). Social identity complexity and acceptance of diversity. In R. J. Crisp (Ed.), *The psychology of social and cultural diversity* (pp. 11–33). Hoboken, NJ: Wiley-Blackwell.

Brewer, M., & Chen, Y-R. (2007). Where (who) are collectives in collectivism? Toward conceptual clarification of individualism and collectivism. *Psychological Review, 114*(1), 133–151. doi:10.1037/0033-295X.114.1.133.

Brewer, M., & Yuki, M. (2007). Culture and social identity. In S. Kitayama & D. Cohen (Eds.), *Handbook of cultural psychology* (pp. 307–322). New York: Guilford Press.

Brown, P., & Fraser, C. (1979). Speech as a marker of situation In K. R. Scherer & H. Giles (Eds.), *Social markers in speech* (pp. 33–62). Cambridge, UK: Cambridge University Press.

Carbaugh, D., Lie, S., Locmele, L., & Sotirova, N. (2012). Ethnographic studies of intergroup communication. In H. Giles (Ed.), *The handbook of intergroup communication* (pp. 44–57). New York, NY: Routledge.

Carey, J. (1975). *Communication as culture: Essays on media and society.* Boston, MA: Unwin Hyman.

Chen, S. X., & Bond, M. H. (2007). Explaining language priming effects: Further evidence for ethnic affirmation among Chinese-English bilinguals. *Journal of Language and Social Psychology, 26*(4), 398–406. doi:10.1177/0261927X07306984.

Chen, Y., Brockner, J., & Katz, T. (1998). Towards an explanation of cultural differences in ingroup favoritism: The role of individual vs. collective primacy. *Journal of Personality and Social Psychology, 75*, 1490–1502.

Cialdini, R. B., Reno, R. R., & Kallgren, C. A. (1990). A focus theory of normative conduct: Recycling the concept of norms to reduce littering in public places. *Journal of Personality and Social Psychology, 58*, 1015–1026.

Clark, A. E., & Kashima, Y. (2007). Stereotypes help people connect with others in the community: A situated functional analysis of the stereotype consistency bias in communication. *Journal of Personality and Social Psychology, 93*(6), 1028–1039.

Clark, H. H. (1996). *Using language.* Cambridge, UK: Cambridge University Press.

Clément, R. (1980). Ethnicity, contact and communicative competence in a second language. In H. Giles, W. P. Robinson, & P. M. Smith (Eds.), *Language: Social psychological perspectives* (pp. 147–154). Oxford, UK: Pergamon,

Clément, R., & Noels, K. A. (1992). Towards a situated approach to ethnolinguistic identity: The effects of status on individuals and groups. *Journal of Language and Social Psychology, 11*, 203–232.

Clément, R., Noels, K. A., & Deneault, B. (2001). Interethnic contact, identity, and psychological adjustment: The mediating and moderating roles of communication. *Journal of Social Issues, 57*(3), 559–577. doi:10.1111/0022-4537.00229.

Clément, R., Singh, S. S., & Gaudet, S. (2006). Generational status, gender, reference group and situation as factors in identity and adjustment among minority Indo-Guyanese. *Group Processes and Intergroup Relations, 9*, 289–304.

Clément, R., Sylvestre, A., & Noels, K. A. (1991). Modes d'acculturation et identité située: Le cas des immigrants haïtiens de Montréal [Modes of acculturation and situated identity: The case of Haitian immigrants in Montreal] *Canadian Ethnic Studies, 33*, 81–94.

Côté, P., & Clément, R. (1994). Language attitudes: An interactive situated approach. *Language and Communication, 14*, 237–251.

Coupland, N. (2007). *Style: Language variation and identity.* Cambridge, UK: Cambridge University Press.

DeRidder, R., & Tripathi, R. C. (1992). *Norm violation and intergroup relations.* Oxford, UK: Claredon/Oxford University Press.

Dragojevic, M., Giles, H., & Watson, B. M. (2015). Language ideologies and language attitude principles. In H. Giles & B. Watson (Eds.), *The social meanings of accent and dialect: International perspectives* (pp. 1–25). New York: Peter Lang.

Fiske, S. T., Cuddy, A. J. C., & Glick, P. (2006). Universal dimensions of social cognition: Warmth and competence. *Trends in Cognitive Sciences, 11*, 77–83. doi:10.1016/j.tics.2006.11.005.

Forgas, J. P., & Bond, M. H. (1985). Cultural influences on the perception of interaction episodes. *Personality and Social Psychology Bulletin, 11*(1), 75–88. doi:10.1177/0146167285111007.

Fortman, J., & Giles, H. (2006). Communicating culture. In J. R. Baldwin, S. L. Faulkner, & M. L. Hecht (Eds.), *Redefining cultures: Perspectives across the disciplines* (pp. 91–102). Mahwah, NJ: Erlbaum.

Gallois, C., Giles, H., Jones, C., Cargile, A., & Ota, H. (1995). Accommodating intercultural encounters: Elaborations and extensions. In R. Wiseman (Ed.), *Theories of intercultural communication* (pp. 115–147). Thousand Oaks, CA: Sage.

Gallois, C. (2010). Communication and intercultural/intergroup relationships. In S. Allan (Ed.), *Rethinking communication: Keywords in communication research* (pp. 5–7). Cresskill, NJ: Hampton.

Gallois, C., Ogay, T., & Giles, H. (2004). Communication accommodation theory: A look back and a look ahead. In W. Gudykunst (Ed.), *Theorizing about intercultural communication* (pp. 121–148). Thousand Oaks, CA: Sage.

Garrett, P. (2010). *Attitudes to language.* Cambridge, UK: Cambridge University Press.

Giles, H. (Ed.). (2012). *Handbook of intergroup communication.* New York, NY: Routledge.

Giles, H., & Billings, A.C. (2005). Assessing language attitudes: Speaker evaluation studies. In A. Davies & C. Elder (Eds.), *The handbook of applied linguistics* (pp. 187–209). Oxford, UK: Blackwell.

Giles, H., Bonilla, D., & Speer, R. B. (2012). Acculturating intergroup vitalities, accommodation and contact. In J. Jackson (Ed.), *The Routledge handbook of language, and intercultural communication* (pp. 244–259). New York, NY: Taylor & Francis.

Giles, H., Bourhis, R. Y., & Taylor, D. M. (1977). Towards a theory of language in ethnic group relations. In H. Giles (Ed.), *Language, ethnicity and intergroup relations* (pp. 307–348). London, UK: Academic Press.

Giles, H., & Johnson, P. (1987). Ethnolinguistic identity theory: A social psychological approach to language maintenance. *International Journal of the Sociology of Language, 68*, 69–100, doi: 10.1515/ijsl.1987.68.69.

Giles, H., & Marlow, M. L. (2011). Theorizing language attitudes: Existing frameworks, an integrative model, and new directions. *Communication Yearbook, 35*, 161–197.

Giles, H., & Noels, K.A. (2002). Communication accommodation in intercultural encounters. In J. N. Martin, T. K. Nakayama, & L. A. Flores (Eds.), *Readings in intercultural communication: Experiences and contexts* (2nd ed., pp. 117–126). Boston, MA: McGraw-Hill.

Giles, H., & Smith, P. M. (1979) Accommodation theory: Optimal levels of convergence. In H. Giles & R. St. Clair (Eds.), *Language and social psychology* (pp. 45–65). Oxford, UK: Blackwell.

Giles, H., & Watson, B. (2008). Intergroup and intercultural communication. In W. Donsbach (Ed.), *The international encyclopedia of communication* (pp. 2337–2348). Hoboken, NJ: Wiley-Blackwell.

Giles, H., & Watson, B. (2012). *The social meanings of accent and dialect: International perspectives.* New York: Peter Lang.

Gudykunst, W. B. (1987). The influence of individualism-collectivism on perceptions of communication in ingroup and outgroup relationships. *Communication Monographs, 54*(3), 295–306. doi:10.1080/03637758709390234.

Gudykunst, W. B. (1988). Culture and intergroup processes. In M. H. Bond (Ed.), *The cross-cultural challenge to social psychology* (pp.153–181). Newbury Park, CA: Sage.

Gudykunst, W. B. (1989). Cultural variability in ethnolinguistic identity. In S. Ting-Toomey & F. Korzenny (Eds.), *Language, communication and culture: Current directions* (pp. 222–243). Newbury Park, CA: Sage.

Gudykunst, W. B. (2004). *Bridging differences: Effective intergroup communication.* Thousand Oaks, CA: Sage.

Gudykunst, W. B., & Bond, M. H. (1997). Intergroup relations across cultures. In J. W. Berry, M. H. Segall, & C. Kâgitçibasi (Eds.), *Handbook of cross-cultural psychology: Social behavior and applications* (2nd ed., Vol. 3, pp. 119–162). Boston, MA: Allyn & Bacon.

Gudykunst, W. B., & Nishida, T. (1986). Attributional confidence in low- and high-context cultures. *Human Communication Research, 12*, 525–549.

Haberstroh, S., Oyserman, D., Schwarz, N., Kühnen, U., & Ji, L-J. (2002). Is the interdependent self more sensitive to question context than the independent self? Self-construal and the observation of conversational norms. *Journal of Experimental Social Psychology, 38*, 323–329.

Hall, E.T. (1973). *The silent language.* Oxford, UK: Anchor.

Harwood, J., & Giles, H. (2005). *Intergroup communication: multiple perspectives.* New York, NY: Peter Lang.

Harwood, J., Giles, H., & Palomares, N. A. (2005). Intergroup theory and communication processes. In J. Harwood & H. Giles (Eds.), *Intergroup communication: Multiple perspectives* (pp. 1–17). New York, NY: Peter Lang.

Hecht, M. L., Jackson, R., & Pitts, M. (2005). Culture: Intersections of intergroup and identity theories. In J. Harwood & H. Giles (Eds.), *Intergroup communication: Multiple perspectives* (pp. 21–42). New York, NY: Peter Lang.

Hecht, M. L., Warren, J., Jung, J., & Krieger, J. (2004). Communication theory of identity. In W. B. Gudykunst (Ed.), *Theorizing about intercultural communication* (pp. 257–278). Newbury Park, CA: Sage.

Hofstede, G. (1980). *Culture's consequences: International differences in work-related values*. Beverly Hills, CA: Sage.

Hong, Y. Y., Morris, M. W., Chiu, C. Y., & Benet-Martínez, V. (2000). Multicultural minds: A dynamic constructivist approach to culture and cognition. *American Psychologist, 55*(7), 709–720.

Hoyle, R. H., Pinkley, R. L., & Insko, C. A. (1989). Perceptions of social behavior: Evidence of differing expectations for interpersonal and intergroup interaction. *Personality and Social Psychology Bulletin, 15*(3), 365–376. doi:10.1177/0146167289153007.

Hymes, D. (1972). Models of the interaction of language and social life. In J. J. Gumperz & D. Hymes (Eds.), *Directions in sociolinguistics* (pp. 30–47) New York, NY: Holt, Rinehart & Winston.

Ishii, K., Reyes, J. A., & Kitayama, S. (2003). Spontaneous attention to word content versus emotional tone: Differences among three cultures. *Psychological Science, 14*(1), 39–46.

Jacobson, R. P., Mortenen, C. R., & Cialdini, R. B. (2011). Bodies obliged and unbound: Differentiated response for injunctive and descriptive social norms. *Journal of Personality and Social Psychology, 100*, 433–448.

Jung, E., & Hecht, M. L. (2008). Identity gaps and level of depression among Korean immigrants. *Health Communication, 23*, 313–325.

Kashima, Y. (2008). A social psychology of cultural dynamics: Examining how cultures are formed, maintained, and transformed. *Social and Personality Psychology Compass, 2*(1), 107–120. doi:10.1111/j.1751-9004.2007.00063.x.

Kashima, E. S., & Kashima, Y. (1998). Culture and language: The case of cultural dimensions and personal pronoun use. *Journal of Cross-Cultural Psychology, 29*(3), 461–486. doi:10.1177/0022022198293005.

Kashima, Y., & Kashima, E. S. (2003). Individualism, GNP, climate, and pronoun drop: Is individualism determined by affluence and climate, or does language use play a role? *Journal of Cross-Cultural Psychology, 34*(1), 125–134. doi:10.1177/0022022102239159.

LaFromboise, T., Coleman, H. L., & Gerton, J. (1993). Psychological impact of biculturalism: Evidence and theory. *Psychological Bulletin, 114*(3), 395–412.

Lambert, W. E. (1978). Cognitive and socio-cultural consequences of bilingualism. *Canadian Modern Language Review, 34*, 537–547.

Lambert, W. E., Hodgson, R., Gardner, R., & Fillenbaum, S. (1960). Evaluational reactions to spoken languages. *Journal of Abnormal and Social Psychology, 2*, 84–90.

Latrofa, M., Vaes, J., Pastore, M., & Cadinu, M. (2009). United we stand, divided we fall! The protective function of self-stereotyping for stigmatised members' psychological well-being. *Applied Psychology, 58*(1), 84–104. doi:10.1111/j.1464-0597.2008.00383.x.

Li, H. (1999). Grounding and information communication in intercultural and intracultural dyadic discourse. *Discourse Processes, 28*, 195–215.

Lyons, A., & Kashima, Y. (2003). How are stereotypes maintained through communication? The influence of stereotype sharedness. *Journal of Personality and Social Psychology, 85*(6), 989–1005.

Maass, A., Karasawa, M., Politi, F., & Suga, S. (2006). Do verbs and adjectives play different roles in different cultures? A cross-linguistic analysis of person representation. *Journal of Personality and Social Psychology*, *90*(5), 734–750.

Maass, A., Salvi, D., Arcuri, L., & Semin, G. R. (1989). Language use in intergroup contexts: The linguistic intergroup bias. *Journal of Personality and Social Psychology*, *57*, 981–993.

Markus, H. R., & Kitayama, S. (1991). Culture and self: Implications for cognition, emotion and motivation. *Psychological Review*, *98*, 224–253.

Nisbett, R. (2003). *The geography of thought: Why we think the way we do*. New York, NY: Free Press.

No, S., Wan, C., Chao, M. M., Rosner, J. L., & Hong, Y. (2011). Bicultural identity negotiation. In A. K-Y. Leung, C-Y. Chiu, & Y-Y. Hong (Eds.), *Cultural processes: A social psychological perspective* (pp. 213–240). New York, NY: Cambridge University Press.

Noels, K. A., & Clément, R. (1996). Communicating across cultures: Social determinants and acculturative consequences. *Canadian Journal of Behavioural Science/Revue canadienne des sciences du comportement*, *28*(3), 214–228. doi:10.1037/0008-400X.28.3.214.

Noels, K. A., Clément, R., & Gaudet, S. (2004). Language and the situated nature of ethnic identity. In S. H. Ng, C. N. Candlin, & C. Y. Chiu (Eds.), *Language matters: Culture, identity and communication* (pp. 245–266). Hong Kong: Hong Kong City University Press.

Noels, K. A., Leavitt, P. A., & Clément, R. (2010). "To see ourselves as others see us": On the implications of reflected appraisals for ethnic identity and discrimination. *Journal of Social Issues*, *66*(4), 740–758.

Oetzel, J. G., & Ting-Toomey, S. (2003). Face concerns in interpersonal conflict: A cross-cultural empirical test of the face negotiation theory. *Communication Research*, *30*(6), 599–624. doi:10.1177/0093650203257841.

Phinney, J. S. (1990). Ethnic identity in adolescents and adults: Review of research. *Psychological Bulletin*, *108*, 299–514.

Potter, J., & Wetherell, M. (1987). *Discourse and social psychology: Beyond attitudes and behaviour*. Thousand Oaks, CA: Sage.

Reid, S. A., & Anderson, G. L. (2010). Language, social identity, and stereotyping. In H. Giles, S. Reid & J. Harwood (Eds.), *The dynamics of intergroup communication*. (pp. 91–104). New York, NY: Peter Lang.

Ross, M., Xun, W. Q. E., & Wilson, A. E. (2002). Language and the bicultural self. *Personality and Social Psychology Bulletin*, *28*, 1040–1050.

Rosenthal, D., & Hrynevich, C. (1985). Ethnicity and ethnic identity: A comparative study of Greek-, Italian- and Anglo-Australian adolescents. *International Journal of Psychology*, *20*, 723–742.

Ryan, E. B., Giles, H., & Sebastian, R. (1985). The effects of speech style and social class background on social judgments of speakers. *British Journal of Social and Clinical Psychology*, *19*, 229–233.

Schaller, M., Conway, L. G., & Tanchuk, T. L. (2002). Selective pressures on the once and future contents of ethnic stereotypes: Effects of the communicability of traits. *Journal of Personality and Social Psychology*, *82*, 861–877.

Schlenker, B. R. (1985). Identity and self-identification. In B. Schlenker (Ed.), *The self and social life* (pp 65–99). New York, NY: McGraw-Hill.

Shannon, C. E., & Weaver, W. (1949). *A mathematical model of communication*. Urbana: University of Illinois Press.

Singelis, T. M., & Brown, W. J. (1995). Culture, self, and collectivist communication. *Human Communication Research, 21*, 354–389.

Stewart, M. A., Ryan, E. B., & Giles, H. (1985). Accent and social class effects on status and solidarity. *Personality and Social Psychology Bulletin, 11*, 98–105.

Tajfel, H. (1978). *Differentiation between social groups: Studies in the social psychology of intergroup relations.* London, UK: Academic Press.

Tajfel, H., & Turner, J. C. (1986). The social identity theory of intergroup behavior. In S. Worchel & W. Austin (Eds.), *Psychology of intergroup relations* (pp. 7–24). Chicago, IL: Nelson-Hall.

Taylor, D. M., King, M., & Usborne, E. (2010). Towards theoretical diversity in intergroup communication. In H. Giles, S. A. Reid, & J. Harwood (Eds.), *The dynamics of intergroup communication* (pp. 263–276). New York, NY: Peter Lang.

Thakerar, J. N., Giles, H., & Cheshire, J. (1982). Psychological and linguistic parameters of speech accommodation theory. In C. Fraser & K. R. Scherer (Eds.), *Advances in the social psychology of language* (pp. 205–255). Cambridge, UK: Cambridge University Press.

Ting-Toomey, S. (2010). Applying dimensional values in understanding intercultural communication. *Communication Monographs, 77*(2), 169–180. doi:10.1080/03637751003790428.

Tomasello, M. (2011). Human culture in evolutionary perspective. In M. Gelfand, Y-Y. Hong, & C. Y. Chiu (Eds.), *Advances in cultural psychology* (pp. 5–51). Oxford, UK: Oxford University Press.

Triandis, H. C. (1988). Collectivism and individualism: A reconceptualization of a basic concept in cross-cultural psychology. In G. K. Verma & C. Bagley (Eds.), *Personality, attitudes, and cognitions* (pp. 60–95). London, UK: MacMillan.

Triandis, H. C. (1989). The self and social behavior in differing cultural contexts. *Psychological Review, 96*, 506–520.

Tucker, G. R. (1999). *A global perspective on bilingualism and bilingual education.* Retrieved November 2011, from http://www.cal.org/resources/digest/digestglobal.html

Turner, J. C., Hogg, M. A., Oakes, P. J., Reicher, S. D. & Wetherell, M. S. (1987). *Rediscovering the social group: A self-categorization theory.* Oxford, UK: Blackwell

van Dijk, T.A. (1987). *Communicating racism: Ethnic prejudice in thought and talk.* Newbury Park, CA: Sage.

Watzlawick, P., Beavin, J. H., & Jackson, D. D. (1967). *Pragmatics of human communications : A study of interactional patterns, pathologies and paradoxes.* New York, NY: Norton.

Woolard, K. A. (1989). *Double talk: Bilingualism and the politics of ethnicity in Catalonia.* Stanford, CA: Stanford University Press.

Yip, T. (2005). Sources of situational variation in ethnic identity and psychological well-being: A palm pilot study of Chinese American students. *Personality and Social Psychology Bulletin, 31*, 1603–1616.

Yip, T., & Fuligni, A. (2002). Daily variation in ethnic identity, ethnic behaviors, and psychological well-being among adolescents of Chinese descent. *Child Development, 73*, 1557–1572.

Zhang, R., & Noels, K.A. (2012). When ethnic identities vary: Cross-situation and within-situation variation, authenticity and well-being. *Journal of Cross-Cultural Psychology, 44*, 552–573.

11

Culture and the Contagion of Conflict

TIANE L. LEE, MICHELE J. GELFAND, AND GARRIY SHTEYNBERG ■

> In 1964, Jedu'a Abu-Sulb, a member of a Negev Bedouin tribe, became involved in a dispute during which he killed a man from the Tawara group in self-defense. For several years after this, he lived in fear of revenge from the Tawara group. During this time, he married and had a son, Ayub. When Jedu'a died, the blood dispute between Jedu'a and the Tawara group transferred to his son, who now bears the burden of retaliation from a group harmed by this father.
>
> —Ginat, 1987

The case of Jedu'a Abu-Sulb clearly illustrates the process of conflict contagion wherein conflicts between two disputants rapidly spread across networks and time. In this case, the original dispute between Abu-Sulb and one Tawara member spread to other Tawara members via the effect that the harm had on other individuals in the group. Then, it spread further to involve any member of Abu-Sulb's group, including future generations such as Abu-Sulb's son. Conflict contagion episodes like this can be seen worldwide, from the highly publicized incident that occurred when the Danish daily newspaper *Jyllands-Postan* published an article entitled "Muhammeds ansigt," which led to hundreds of protests and an escalation of violence across the Muslim world in 2006, to the spread of conflict that transpired in Rwanda in 1994 wherein 800,000 Rwandans were killed, approximately 20% of the nation's population (Grant, 2010). Understanding the mechanisms that produce these contagion processes is critical for both psychological theory (which tends to look at conflict in isolated episodes; Gelfand et al., 2012), as well as practice, in order to develop interventions to reduce the spread of disputes with such catastrophic consequences.

Toward this end, in this chapter we advance a model of conflict contagion that seeks to explain why and when these processes occur in groups. As detailed later, we theorize that these processes occur most frequently in groups which emphasize the collective self—wherein group members are perceptually undifferentiated from each other and are depersonalized entities—which is found more in vertical collectivistic (VC) cultures than other cultural groups (Triandis, 1995; Triandis & Gelfand, 1998). After differentiating different types of individualism and collectivism, we discuss the implications of VC for entitativity processes both within and across groups, and detail the implications they have for the spread of conflict. We present a model and advance specific propositions describing these effects and discuss some initial qualitative and experimental data that show some support for our suppositions. We conclude with implications for the study of culture and conflict.

INDIVIDUALISM AND COLLECTIVISM

The relationship between the individual and the group has long been of interest to social science theorists. Approaches to study this relationship include such contrasts as *self-emphasis* and *collectivity* (Parsons, 1949), *Gesellschaft* and *Gemeinschaft* (Toennies, 1957), *individualism* and *collaterality* (Kluckhohn & Strodtbeck, 1961), *agency* and *communion* (Bakan, 1966), *independence* and *interdependence* (Markus & Kitayama, 1991), among others. Across several disciplines, these theories all explore the extent to which an individual is autonomous or embedded in the group (Schwartz, 1994) or what has been commonly referred to as *individualism* versus *collectivism* (IC) (Hofstede, 1980; Triandis, 1989, 1995). Research over the last few decades has shown that IC has important implications for a range of psychological processes, including cognition, motivation, and emotion (see Gelfand, Erez, & Aycan, 2007, for a review; Markus & Kitayama, 1991; Triandis, 1989), as well as for interpersonal-, organizational-, and national-level processes (for reviews, see Gelfand et al., 2007; Gelfand, Bhawuk, Nishii, & Bechtold, 2004).

Generally speaking, individualistic cultures have their historical roots in the Enlightenment and the Kantian notions of individual reason and free will (Markus, Kitayama, & Heiman, 1997). In such cultures, the independent self-construal is highly developed (Markus & Kitayama, 1991; Triandis, 1989), and the self is defined in terms of specific accomplishments, attitudes, and abilities and is perceived as detached from collectives. The cultural ideal is to be separate from others, to express one's uniqueness, and to feel "good" about oneself (Markus & Kitayama, 1991; Shweder & Bourne, 1982). In individualistic cultures, the individual is a being whose actions are self-determined and self-actualizing (Triandis, McCusker, & Hui, 1990) and, most of all, reflects the self as a free agent that is entitled to do what it wishes (Landrine, 1995).

By contrast, collectivism has its historical roots in Confucius' moral-political philosophy as well as Buddhist teachings of sacrifice and the submerged self, in

East Asia, and has its historical roots in Islamic traditions and practices in the Middle East (Markus et al., 1997). In such cultures, the self is largely defined in terms of the groups to which one belongs and is conceived of as fundamentally embedded in the larger social context (Markus & Kitayama, 1991; Triandis, 1989). As Markus and Kitayama (1991) explain, "experiencing interdependence entails seeing oneself as part of an encompassing social relationship and recognizing that one's behavior is determined, contingent on, and to a large extent, organized by what the actor perceives to be the thoughts, feelings and actions of *others* in the relationship" (p. 226). Consequently, there is a pervasive attentiveness to relevant others in the social environment (i.e., increased social awareness), and meeting social responsibilities and obligations to others in the group is a moral imperative (Miller, Bersoff, & Harwood, 1990). An examination of the ecology of collectivism and individualism reveals that collectivistic societies tend to have lower affluence (Hofstede, 1980; Triandis, 1995) and lower social mobility (e.g., residential, jobs), making it rather difficult to enter and willingly "exit" one's group (Oishi, 2010; Schug, Yuki, Horikawa, & Takemura, 2009; Schug, Yuki, & Maddux, 2010; Yamagishi & Suzuki, 2010; see also Yuki & Takemura, Chapter 3, this volume).

Notwithstanding these general differences across individualistic and collectivistic cultures, it is critical to point out that not all individualistic or collectivistic cultures are alike. Research has shown that the individualism-collectivism dimension needs to be further differentiated along both vertical and horizontal dimensions (see Singelis, Triandis, Bhawuk, & Gelfand, 1995; Triandis, Chen, & Chan, 1998; Triandis & Gelfand, 1998). In *vertical individualist* (VI) *cultures* people emphasize hierarchical relationships, focusing on their *individual* status, obtained through achievement and competition. In *horizontal individualist* (HI) *cultures* there is a focus on people's uniqueness and self-reliance and individuals' status differences are minimized. Similarly, like individualism, the collectivism dimension can be further differentiated into vertical and horizontal varieties. Members of *vertical collectivist* (VC) *cultures* emphasize deference to authority and sacrificing one's own goals for the group. The advancement of one's group's status and reputation, and the protection of the group from other outgroups, are of supreme importance (Ho, 1973; Kim, 1994). Members of *horizontal collectivistic* (HC) *cultures*, by contrast, emphasize sociability and harmony within groups and are less attentive to status differences within or across groups (for a review of the vertical and horizontal dimensions, see Shavitt, Torelli, & Riemer, 2011; Triandis & Gelfand, 1998).

Differentiating vertical and horizontal individualism and collectivism is critical, we believe, for understanding and predicting conflict contagion. As we will expand upon in the next section, the emphasis on prioritizing group goals and group standing in VC cultures is theorized to lead to a focus on one's collective identity (Brewer & Chen, 2007; Brewer & Gardner, 1996; Kashima et al., 1995; Triandis, 1989), which results in perceptions that group members are undifferentiated from each other. These processes, we argue, provide greater motivation to seek revenge on behalf of *any* harmed ingroup member against *any* outgroup member. Conversely, given that harmony and sociability are the primary concern in HC cultures, we expect there to be more of a focus on relational identity

(Brewer & Gardner, 1996; Kashima et al., 1995; Yuki, 2003) in such groups, and the motivation to seek revenge on behalf of an ingroup member will depend more on the strength of the specific relationship with the harmed party (as compared to when the ingroup is perceived as an undifferentiated whole). Finally, we expect the least conflict contagion in both vertical and horizontal individualistic cultures wherein the independent self is cultivated and the self is seen as detached from the group. We next discuss these mediating mechanisms—namely different forms of identity and how they relate to group entitativity processes—and their implications for differences in conflict contagion between VC and other cultural groups.

CULTURE, IDENTITY, ENTITATIVITY, AND CONFLICT

A core process that underlies the escalation of conflict is *group entitativity*, or the degree to which groups are perceived to be bonded together in a coherent unit wherein members are thought to be substitutable (Campbell, 1958; Kashima et al., 2005; Lickel, Hamilton, & Sherman, 2001; Yzerbyt, Corneille, & Estrada, 2001). Next, we outline the cultural dimensions VC, HC, HI, and VI and their implications for entitativity and conflict contagion.

Vertical Collectivism and the Collective Self

As noted earlier, vertical collectivistic cultures are characterized by deference to authority, sacrificing one's own goals for the group, and the importance of upholding the reputation and status of the group vis-à-vis outgroups. We theorize that in such contexts, the collective self (Brewer & Chen, 2007; Brewer & Gardner, 1996; Brewer & Yuki, 2007; Kashima et al., 1995; Triandis, 1989) is highly accessible. In the representation of a collective self, the basis for group entitativity is a strong *shared social identity*, and group members are perceptually undifferentiated from each other and constitute depersonalized entities (Kim, 1994; Yuki, 2003). Moreover, when the collective self is defined according to one's group membership, a sharp distinction is made between one's ingroup and all outgroups, thereby directing collective selves toward an intergroup orientation. Indeed, a clear boundary between one's ingroup and the outgroup, or "us" versus "them" mentality, also serves to create the belief that the outgroup is one cohesive entity comprised of undifferentiated members, thereby reinforcing both ingroup and outgroup identity-based entitativity. Furthermore, when people's identities are defined by their group, an intergroup incident implicates a wide range of people and creates the potential for large escalation of conflict. Accordingly, we predict that in contexts or groups in which the *collective self* is activated, there is a greater likelihood of conflict contagion. This is due to the fact that group members are undifferentiated from each other (leading to ingroup entitativity) coupled with the strong ingroup-outgroup distinctions that characterize these groups (leading to an intergroup attentional outlook wherein outgroup members are also undifferentiated; i.e., outgroup entitativity). Put simply, when the collective self is activated, harm to anyone in one's group is felt as *harm to all* and motivates the defense of the group through harming an (undifferentiated) outgroup member.

Horizontal Collectivism and the Relational Self

As noted, horizontal collectivistic cultures are characterized by an emphasis on sociability and harmony within groups. Thus, while horizontally collectivistic cultures also cultivate a focus on the group, unlike vertical collectivists, they focus on intragroup relations rather than relative group status. Here, each individual is not a representative embodiment of the group as a whole based on a shared group identity, but rather is conceptualized within a network of relations within a group (Brewer & Chen, 2007; Brewer & Yuki, 2007; Yuki, 2003). In this respect, in horizontal collectivistic groups, the *relational self* (i.e., defined by a network of close relationships) is theorized to be more accessible. For example, while Japan has been categorized as a collectivist culture, Brewer and colleagues further clarify that Japanese are focused on relationality within the context of groups, in which people are defined according to their roles and their relationships, and group members are interdependent, yet distinguished from each other (Brewer & Chen, 2007; Brewer & Yuki, 2007; Yuki, 2003). Although we expect that vicarious revenge—and by extension, conflict escalation—can also happen when the relational self is activated, we expect it to be of much lower severity. This is because relational selves make up common bond groups (Prentice, Miller, & Lightdale, 1994), in which members are attached to *specific* members of the group and their source of ingroup loyalty is the maintenance of reciprocal relationships with those individuals. Consequently, the basis for group entitativity among relational selves is the level of organization and structure among the members (Hamilton, Sherman, & Lickel, 1998). Accordingly, to the extent that a relational self is motivated to exact revenge on behalf of a harmed person, we expect conflict escalation to be moderated by the closeness between the two individuals and the importance of the harmed party to overall group functioning. Thus, we would expect vicarious revenge from a relational self only if she or he has a connection to the harmed person, either directly and personally or via a network (e.g., Guanxi). Moreover, because relational selves emphasize the connections between people and are intragroup versus intergroup in their orientation, conflicts are not likely to escalate beyond the original perpetrator as the target of revenge may be limited to only the perpetrator or a few close others (i.e., low outgroup entitativity).

Horizontal and Vertical Individualism and the Independent Self

In contrast to collectivistic cultures, people in vertical and horizontal individualistic cultures experience themselves as free agents who are entitled to do what they wish (Landrine, 1995; Markus & Kitayama, 1991). Generally speaking, they are afforded high mobility such that people can enter new groups and choose to exit their groups with relative ease and frequency (Oishi, 2010; Schug et al., 2009, 2010; Yamagishi & Suzuki, 2010). Because the self is an independent self whose outcomes are not dependent on others as compared to the self in vertical or horizontal collectivist cultures, it is not implicated to nearly the same degree when it witnesses an interpersonal conflict between two other individuals. Furthermore, the independent self is represented as its own entity, with little emphasis on its group membership(s) as a defining characteristic of one's identity. These differences in self-representation and motivational concerns make it less likely that people in vertically and horizontally individualistic cultures would engage in vicarious revenge. Importantly, however, we believe that if the collective self is activated even in individualistic cultures, it can produce conflict escalation processes as well, a point to which we will return later in the chapter.

In the next section, we focus our attention on the groups in which we expect the most conflict contagion—vertical collectivistic groups—and present our specific predictions. We then present some initial evidence through an examination of the contagion of harm in an experimental context where we measured vertical collectivism based on qualitative interviews among Middle Eastern cultures.

MODEL OF VERTICAL COLLECTIVISM AND CONFLICT CONTAGION

We theorize that vertical collectivism is a key driver of conflict contagion across social networks and across time due to the activation of the collective self. More specifically, three different types of entitativity are relevant for our theory of conflict contagion: (1) ingroup entitativity, (2) outgroup entitativity, and (3) transgenerational entitativity. When the collective self is activated, it results in higher *ingroup entitativity*, wherein group members are depersonalized undifferentiated entities; higher *outgroup entitativity*, wherein the outgroup is perceived as a unified whole, whose members are perceptually undifferentiated from each other and are depersonalized entities (Kashima et al., 2005); and higher *transgenerational entitativity*, wherein one's ingroup transcends past and future generations. Transgenerational entitativity can be thought of as perceptions of ingroup entitativity or interchangeability *across generations* (Kahn, 2010). Next, we set forth propositions regarding vertical collectivism and these three forms of entitativity and their implications for the contagion of conflict. Figure 11.1 summarizes our discussion.

Propositions

Line 1 first illustrates the implication of vertical collectivism and *ingroup entitativity* for the spread of disputes. An offense against *any* ingroup member is

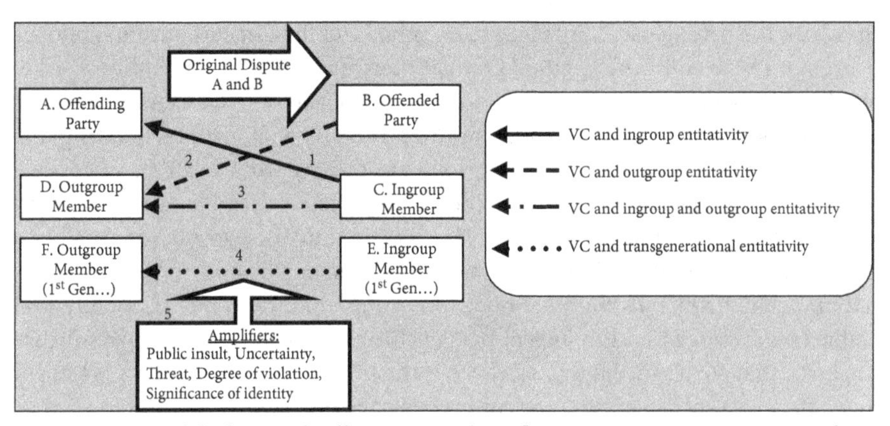

Figure 11.1. Model of vertical collectivism and conflict contagion across groups and generations.

experienced as personally relevant (i.e., as if it had happened to oneself) and emotionally distressing (Lickel, Miller, Stenstrom, Denson, & Schmader, 2006; Stenstrom, Lickel, Denson, & Miller, 2008; Yzerbyt, Dumont, Wigboldus, & Gordijn, 2003). Moreover, high ingroup entitativity based on shared identity drives ingroup observers to retaliate (Lickel et al., 2006) and punish an outgroup perpetrator to regain personal and group honor. Such retaliatory behavior is not only a personal desire but also institutionalized as an appropriate response to protect the group (e.g., is endorsed collectively as a descriptive norm; Chiu, Gelfand, Yamagishi, Shteynberg, & Wan, 2010; Shteynberg, Gelfand, & Kim, 2009; Vandello, Cohen, & Ransom, 2008). Furthermore, due to such strong group norms in vertical collectivistic cultures, altruistic behavior toward ingroup members is particularly critical for maintaining one's reputation as a good group member and for maintaining the safety of the ingroup and warding off future attacks from other groups (Bernhard, Fischbacher, & Fehr, 2006). Importantly, according to this perspective, an interpersonal offense develops into a system of back-and-forth intergroup revenge because people not only personally believe it is important to vicariously punish but also perceive that others in the group expect them to do so.

Line 2 illustrates the implication of vertical collectivism and *outgroup entitativity* for the spread of disputes. Outgroup entitativity plays a central role in collective blame and responsibility (Denson, Lickel, Curtis, Stenstrom, & Ames, 2006; Lickel et al., 2006; Lickel, Schmader, & Hamilton, 2003). Due to perceptions of outgroup entitativity, the original victim of a conflict in vertical collectivism may render *any* outgroup member (even if he or she did not commit the offense) to be responsible for the offense and, consequently, to become a justifiable target of retaliation.

Moreover, Line 3 illustrates the interactive effects of vertical collectivism and both *ingroup* and *outgroup entitativity* for the spread of disputes and, in particular, how vertical collectivism allows for the continuation of conflict even in cases in which the revenge-seeking ingroup member and the target outgroup member were not involved in the original conflict. During vicarious retribution (Lickel et al., 2006; Stenstrom et al., 2008), in which neither the person exacting revenge nor the outgroup target of revenge was directly involved in the precipitating dispute, ingroup identification and outgroup entitativity work together in concert to motivate revenge by a previously uninvolved ingroup member against a previously uninvolved outgroup member. Harm caused to one's group becomes one's own (ingroup entitativity) and avenging one's own and group's honor with retaliation against *any* outgroup member (outgroup entitativity) is personally and collectively valued and is a logical part of this cultural system. Importantly, we theorize that such processes occur even if the innocence of bystanders is known (e.g., they were not involved, nor could they have prevented the original act; i.e., sins of omission or commission; Lickel et al., 2003). Put differently, contagion to restore individual and group honor is blind to guilt or innocence of outgroup bystanders in this process.

Line 4 illustrates the dynamics of contagion of conflicts across generations in vertical collectivistic cultures. Due to greater *transgenerational entitativity* (TGE; i.e., the belief that one's ingroup transcends past and future generations) vertical collectivism makes it more likely that future generations of ingroup members, who did not witness the original act, will have biased memories of conflicts that occurred in previous generations and will feel obligated to retaliate on behalf of previous ingroup generations. In addition, because one's ingroup transcends future generations, TGE may relate to self-sacrificial behaviors for the benefit of restoring the group's honor for previous and future group members. We note that such behavior is not only fueled by a personal desire but is also institutionalized as an appropriate response to protect the group (e.g., is endorsed collectively as a descriptive norm).

An interesting potential dynamic that is derived from the model relates to the case when *one's own group member* has committed an offense against an outgroup that is dishonorable to one's group. When witnessing another's wrongdoing, people can feel vicariously guilty or shameful (Lickel, Schmader, Curtis, Scarnier, & Ames, 2005). Given greater social identity-based ingroup entitativity among vertical collectivists, when any ingroup member commits an offense, the threat to the group image may become contagious across the group (e.g., shame will transmit across group members). Accordingly, vertical collectivists may be more likely to exhibit greater *blacksheep effects* by punishing ingroup members who commit an offense that damages their group honor in order to (a) restore group identity and (b) avoid outgroup retribution now and in future generations given that there is an acute awareness that they are also the targets of bystander retribution from the other group.

Finally, it is worth noting that the very processes that account for conflict contagion may also promote the *spread of forgiveness*. In vertical collectivistic cultures, responsibility to apologize reaches a far greater web of actors and includes the collective as a whole (Maddux & Yuki, 2006). Representative group members (e.g., senior leadership) who have no personal guilt, or even involvement, often apologize on behalf of the group (Greenberg & Elliot, 2009), and these indirect apologies are especially common in collectivistic cultures (Chiu & Hong, 1992; Zemba, Young, & Morris, 2006). There may be a greater expectation, and willingness, to apologize on behalf of ingroup members (i.e., ingroup entitativity, Line 2) to outgroup victims and outgroup bystanders (i.e., outgroup entitativity, Line 3) in vertical collectivistic groups when one's ingroup member has offended the outgroup. Furthermore, there may be a greater willingness to accept apologies that are given by outgroup perpetrators and bystanders who are contemporaneous and distal to the conflict in vertical collectivistic cultures. We expect that acceptance of apologies on behalf of a harmed group member (Brown, Wohl, & Exline, 2008) may be more prevalent among vertical collectivistic group members due to ingroup entitativity.

Moderators That Amplify and Reduce Conflict Contagion

Earlier we discussed general tendencies of vertical collectivism and conflict contagion. However, there are likely numerous situational factors that moderate the extent to which conflict escalates. Put simply, conflict contagion is dynamic and subject to situational effects. Line 5 illustrates several factors that might amplify cultural differences in conflict contagion. First, situations that cause people to engage in automatic processing and rely on well-learned cultural tendencies are theorized to exacerbate conflict contagion in collectivistic groups. For example, situations that increase *the salience of cultural values and norms* may cause conflicts to be more contagious in vertical collectivistic groups. To the extent that cultural values and group norms are reinforced through peer expectations (Chiu et al., 2010; Shteynberg et al., 2009), they are made more salient when conflicts are in public wherein harm to one's ingroup is being observed by others, as compared to when they happen in private. Accordingly, we would expect that conflict contagion processes are exacerbated in contexts where offenses are public and less so when they are private.

Situations in which there is high threat and uncertainty activate strong epistemic needs for individuals to identify with groups as epistemic authorities and conform to group norms (Webster & Kruglanski, 1994). Accordingly, we would expect that such factors will amplify cultural differences in these processes. That is, when people face a high degree of threat they strongly hold on to their cultural identities in order to reduce anxiety (Greenberg, Solomon, & Pyszczynski, 1997). Therefore, we expect that individuals facing uncertainty and group threat—be it situational (Hogg, Meehan, & Farquharson, 2010) or an individual difference (e.g., need for closure, Webster & Kruglanski, 1994; self-concept uncertainty, Mullin & Hogg, 1998)—should show stronger reliance on entitativity and play a more pronounced role in the transmission of conflict across networks and time.

However, other factors may reduce or buffer against conflict contagion by mitigating both outgroup and ingroup revenge. It is important to note that one's perception of a transgression depends largely on how much it violates a group's cultural values. For example, US Southern institutions (high on "culture of honor") were more forgiving of honor-related violence than were institutions in the North (Cohen & Nisbett, 1997). That is, job application responses and media portrayals of honor violence were more sympathetic in the South, where they are considered more understandable and less egregious, as compared to in the North. In addition, people are likely to be less invested in seeking revenge if the shared group identity with the victim is one of low significance versus of high significance. It is often the case that people go to extreme lengths, often self-sacrificing, to fight on behalf of one's ethnicity, religion, and nationality. In comparison, these behaviors are found to a lesser extent, and to a lesser degree, in intergroup conflict involving group identities of comparably lower significance (e.g., school affiliation or sports rivalries).

Initial Evidence: Experimental and Qualitative Studies of Conflict Contagion

We have theorized that the rate and nature of conflict contagion have potential to be more escalatory and contagious in vertical collectivistic cultures. Although there is no direct evidence for the propositions advanced, there is indirect evidence that lends support for them. For example, several researchers examined this issue in the context of honor, which signifies a person's worth in society that people strive to gain and protect (Abou-Zeid, 1966; Nisbett & Cohen, 1996; Pitt-Rivers, 1966). The stronger sense of entitativity within ingroups, outgroups, and across generations among vertical collectivists should be related to a stronger interconnection between one's honor and the honor of others and greater contagion from honor loss. Indeed several studies have shown that honor violations provoke psychological and behavioral reactions of retaliation against the transgressor (Cohen, Nisbett, Bowdle, & Schwarz, 1996) and that they can spread to uninvolved individuals and across generations (Aase, 2002; Tewfiq, 1977).

Emerging data from our lab provide more direct evidence of conflict contagion among those that emphasize vertical collectivism. Gelfand et al. (2012) used a modified dictator game to investigate how individuals seek revenge and punish others upon observing harm to their ingroup members. In this study, participants believed they were playing with three other players: a proposer, an ingroup member, and a neutral third party. Before the game, participants were asked to select an avatar to represent them during the game. The avatar choices were either significant identities (political party, religious affiliation) or not significant identities (favorite color). After selecting their own avatar, players were shown the avatars of all other players in the game. During the game, participants first observed the proposer take away an endowment from the participant's ingroup member (indicated by a common avatar), and then they had their own turn in which to take away an endowment from any of the other three players. The results showed that when people shared a significant identity with the victim, those who were high on vertical collectivism, measured by the Triandis and

Gelfand (1998) scale, were much more likely to punish the outgroup proposer by taking away his or her tokens. These effects were not found for horizontal collectivism or horizontal or vertical individualism. We are now replicating and expanding these findings.

We have also conducted qualitative interviews across eight nations (Gelfand et al., 2012) to examine whether there is, in fact, evidence for greater contagion of harm in vertical collectivistic groups. In this study, structured interviews were conducted in Egypt, Iraq, Jordan, Lebanon, Pakistan, Turkey, the United Arab Emirates, and the United States. The Pakistani and Middle Eastern samples were of particular interest because they constitute a type of vertical collectivism in which group members are expected to sacrifice self-interests for the group, and there is a sharp demarcation between the ingroup and outgroups. A total of 184 participants—composed of community members varying in age, gender, socioeconomic status, and rural-urban residency—were interviewed across all countries. The researchers asked interviewees to talk about the interrelationship between their honor and honor loss and others' honor and honor loss. These questions included the following: (1) Is your honor (*sharaf*) related to the honor (*sharaf*) of other people, and whom? How does something affecting your *sharaf* affect the *sharaf* of others? (2) Likewise, does the loss of honor of others affect your honor? (3) Whose honor is most important to you? (4) How does it affect you?

We conducted both qualitative and quantitative analyses of responses to these questions. Using analyses of word frequency (LIWC; Pennebaker, Francis, & Booth, 2001), we examined the extent to which people discussed a wide range of social entities that are involved in the contagion of honor loss. An overall *Social Index* was calculated for each interviewee as a percentage of the total word count of the interviewee's responses to all questions. This *Social Index* included family members, with both social entities in the nuclear family (e.g., spouse, parents, children, siblings) and social entities in the extended family (e.g., aunts, uncles, cousins, relatives, ancestors); nonfamily relationships such as friends, coworkers, classmates, neighbors, and groups that comprise an extended network of social ties (e.g., neighborhood, village, tribe, company, and university); and large-scale social identity groups, such as one's nationality, ethnicity, religion, and abstracted groups, including civilization, society, and culture.

Findings from this study illustrated a clear and reoccurring theme of the interchangeability of honor and contagious effect of honor harm across the Middle East and Pakistan as compared to the US Middle Eastern participants as a group mentioned more social entities than did Americans, showing that the "web" of people to whom one's honor is related is much wider in these countries compared to the United States. On average, Americans mentioned social entities in 3.34% of their responses, while the Middle Eastern and Pakistan countries mentioned social entities 7.53%, with interviewees from Jordan and Iraq scoring as high as 11.67% and 10.14%, respectively.

Qualitative examination provided a richer account of cultural differences in the degree to which one's honor gain and loss is interrelated to the gain and loss of others' honor. Responses from US respondents tended to differentiate one person's honor from another's. Overall, Americans respondents did not think that their honor loss would affect the honor of those around them. One respondent stated: "People might look at my wife a little less friendly. But yet they shouldn't really. I mean, if it's my issue, not hers." Another American interviewee explained "The fact that I know them? Um it shouldn't. I would hope it wouldn't... I believe honor is each person, you gotta look at each person individually." In rare cases where a person's honor was related to another's, American respondents included a small circle of people to whom their honor is related: "My values and honor was probably established by my upbringing with my parents. My mom um, but it's not related to anybody else." Furthermore, American respondents discussed being less impacted personally by others' honor loss, noting in particular that it would not impact their own honor: "it would affect me... but it wouldn't affect my honor, no." Another interviewee stated, "[I would] probably feel bad for them, I would be upset, but I wouldn't lose my mind over that." Others noted that they would want to help others in honor loss situations (e.g., "If they go through a hard time where they don't have honor at school anymore, I'm going to try and fix it"); yet others' honor loss would be much less contagious to one's own sense of honor among American interviewees.

The high entitativity among vertical collectivistic group members would suggest that the honor of an ingroup member is interchangeable with that of another member. As predicted, ME and Pakistani respondents frequently discussed the interchangeability of honor. One UAE interviewee explained, "[Yes], members of my family, my extended family, my people... their honor is related to mine because they are members of my family. What touches me touches them and what touches them touches me." An interviewee from Egypt similarly commented that "Of course my honor is my husband's honor, my children's honor. All of us are one; the honor of any one of us is the honor of the other." A Lebanese interviewee echoed this sentiment by explaining, "The word *honor* in and of itself carries a non-individualist meaning... its effects are interchangeable among family members in what is related to honor." The contagion of honor loss can extend to larger social identity groups, including one's religion, gender, and other generations of one's family. For example, a Jordanian interviewee commented on the different spheres of honor loss: "Firstly his personal honor, then his children's honor and his country's honor." A Turkish interviewee likewise stated that his honor extended beyond the closest circle to "the society in which I belong." One UAE interviewee summed it up, "We all live in one boat and one society; therefore, a drowning person will affect the whole of social ties."

The interchangeability between related others' honor suggests that when a person is harmed, other individuals in the group would be similarly harmed. Indeed, responses from the Middle Eastern region and Pakistan frequently alluded to the ripple effect of honor loss to other group members. Commenting on the contagion of insults, an Egyptian interviewee explained, "I am a Qadwa, from my parents, their name would be shaken, my husband's name as well if something causes my honor to be insulted." Beyond the immediate family, ripple effects from honor loss extend *widely* ("close relatives, brothers and cousins, and tribe those who relate to his honor then people who live nearby, for example the district where he resides, neighbors, his honor, and his reputation" [Iraq]) and *quickly* ("If [the honor attack] is not confronted, it spreads like an infection and I become ashamed" [Lebanon]). And finally, honor loss is permanent: "Honor is never forgotten and if it is harmed it can never be erased" [Jordan].

Overall, the interview data from Gelfand et al. (2012) revealed that for vertical collectivists, honor is interchangeable, especially among one's family and extended networks; and it is contagious—when an ingroup member is harmed, people are much more affected by it and such effects spread through a much wider network of people. These findings suggest that group members are more entitative in vertical collectivistic groups as compared to individualistic groups, and entitativity, in turn, affects how people react to instances of a group member being harmed.

IMPLICATIONS AND FUTURE DIRECTIONS

Returning to the beginning of this chapter, it is clear that in the situation involving Jedu'a Abu-Sulb, one precipitating event set off a string of retaliations that came to involve originally uninvolved others. The case of Jedu'a is a particularly strong example of various forms of entitativity motivating revenge: The group members of his original victim felt the harm as their own (ingroup entitativity) and targeted him and, later, his son for retaliation (outgroup entitativity, transgenerational entitativity). An examination of the intersection between the group and culture literatures highlights the intricate relationship between vertical collectivism, collective identity, and entitativity based on shared identity that illustrate the underlying mechanisms that drive conflict and facilitate escalation in this situation and others where contagion takes effect.

In support for the theory, our recent experimental evidence has implicated vertical collectivism in the contagion of disputes. Moreover, recent qualitative interview data support the contention that among individuals from the Middle East, ingroup harm is more strongly felt as one's own and affects a larger web of others. To be sure, much research needs to be done to test the propositions advanced in this chapter on the intersection of vertical collectivism and conflict contagion. And, moreover, looking into the future, research is needed to examine the situational moderators that amplify or reduce conflict contagion, as well as to examine the counterintuitive notion that the very same mechanisms that account for collective blame and revenge might translate into collective responsibility (to apologize) and forgiveness in vertical collectivistic cultures.

While we have focused on vertical collectivism and presented some initial evidence for its involvement in conflict contagion, future research needs to directly examine conflict contagion processes among horizontal collectivists who emphasize the relational self and vertical and horizontal individualists who emphasize the independent self. As noted, we expect that conflict contagion is less likely in HC, VI, and HI. Among horizontal collectivists, group members are seen as connected via a network, and most important for conflict contagion, differentiated from each other, and varying in degrees of closeness to the self. When an ingroup member is harmed, horizontal collectivists may experience vicarious pain and insult to varying degrees corresponding to the dyadic closeness between the self and the victim. Yet, in horizontal collectivistic cultures, we expect the relational self to be motivated to engage in revenge only if the victim is a close, significant other. That is, ingroup entitativity is determined dyadically, not based on a shared group membership wherein members are undifferentiated. With respect to revenge against outgroups, we expect that the spread of conflict to other outgroup members is similarly moderated by the perceived closeness between the original perpetrator and his or her group members. Thus, conflict contagion in horizontal collectivistic cultures should be dampened as compared to vertical collectivistic cultures given the aforementioned processes.

In vertical and horizontal individualistic cultures, where the self is detached from others, where individuals are responsible for their own actions and not others, and where groups are seen as less entitative, we expect harm to ingroup members to be less likely to be felt personally and to engender revenge among observers on victims' behalf. Given the lower interdependence between group members, defending an ingroup member is not as critical for one's success and standing in the group. Likewise, in these cultural systems, this (lack of) response to act on another's behalf is collectively perceived as appropriate and institutionalized.

Finally, with respect to the contagion of forgiveness, in much the same way as the independent self is detached from the collective and absolved from taking revenge on its behalf, we expect that it is also absolved from seeking resolution and apologizing on its behalf in vertical and horizontal individualistic cultures. In these cultures, guilt and apology are exchanges circumscribed between a specific victim and the offender. We expect rare exceptions to be made when the apologizer is a representative (e.g., parent) of the offender. Likewise, in horizontal collectivistic cultures, vicarious apologies are similarly restricted to close others of the offender.

Future research should use qualitative, survey, archival, and experimental methods to test the suppositions in this chapter. For example, it is possible that even in individualistic cultures, if the collective self is activated (Yuki & Takemura, Chapter 3, this volume), conflict contagion would indeed occur. Particular situations are especially likely to make salient these collective self identities in individualistic cultures. For example, partisan affiliations and sports rivalries are two contexts that often produce an us versus them mentality among strident identifiers, who conceptualize both ingroup and outgroup members not as individual entities but as deindividuated members that subscribe to one side or the other. Even in individualistic cultures such as the United States, ethnic riots provide testament that it is not uncommon to see the effects of an activated collective self on conflict contagion.

In conclusion, this chapter has been devoted to our theorizing about how particular cultural norms and group dynamics may contribute to conflict escalation, but we believe that equally fruitful potential lies in how they may contribute to vicarious apologies, de-escalation, forgiveness, and resolution. That vertical collectivistic cultures promote conflict is a tempting and easy but misguided takeaway. This chapter has outlined the avenues and mechanisms by which disputes escalate in the hopes that they also highlight what may constitute adequate restoration of honor and face loss, and provide commensurate restitution for victims. In this respect, the defining features of a culture are also its best asset: the very word *collectivism* seems to presage the means by which one's group can help heal. The prioritization of group goals can promote a process that emulates escalation, one that elicits a vicarious apology on behalf of a wrong-doing ingroup member, as well as accepting a vicarious apology from a bystander outgroup member, regardless of actual involvement or guilt of the apologizer.

AUTHORS' NOTE

This research reported in this chapter was based on work supported in part by US Air Force grant FA9550-12-1-0021 and the US Army Research Laboratory and the US Army Research Office under grant W911NF-08-1-0144.

REFERENCES

Abou-Zeid, A. M. (1966). Honour and shame among the Bedouins of Egypt. In J. G. Peristiany (Ed.), *Honour and shame: The values of Mediterranean society* (pp. 245–259). Chicago, IL: University of Chicago Press.

Aase, T. (2002). The prototypical blood feud: Tangir in the Hindu Kush Mountains. In T. Aase (Ed.), *Tournaments of power: Honor and revenge in the contemporary world* (pp. 79–100). Hants, UK: Ashgate.

Bakan, D. (1966). *The duality of human existence: Isolation and communion in Western man.* Chicago, IL: Rand McNally.

Bernhard, H., Fischbacher, U., & Fehr, E. (2006). Parochial altruism in humans. *Nature, 442*, 912–915.

Brewer, M. B., & Chen, Y. (2007). Where (who) are collectives in collectivism: Toward a conceptual clarification of individualism and collectivism. *Psychological Review, 114*, 133–151.

Brewer, M. B., & Gardner, W. (1996). Who is this "we?" Levels of collective identity and self representation. *Journal of Personality and Social Psychology, 71*, 83–93.

Brewer, M. B., & Yuki, M. (2007). Culture and social identity. In S. Kitayama & D. Cohen (Eds.), *Handbook of cultural psychology* (pp. 307–322). New York, NY: Guilford Press.

Brown, R. P., Wohl, M. J. A., & Exline, J. J. (2008). Taking up offenses: Secondhand forgiveness and group identification. *Personality and Social Psychology Bulletin, 34*, 1406–1419.

Campbell, D. T. (1958). Common fate, similarity, and other indices of the status of aggregates of persons as social entities. *Behavioral Science, 3*, 14–25.

Chiu, C-Y., Gelfand, M. J., Yamagishi, T., Shteynberg, G., & Wan, C. (2010). Intersubjective culture: The role of intersubjective perceptions in cross-cultural research. *Perspectives on Psychological Science, 5*, 482–493.

Chiu, C-Y., & Hong, Y-Y. (1992). The effects of intentionality and validation on individual and collective responsibility attribution among Hong Kong Chinese. *Journal of Psychology: Interdisciplinary and Applied, 126*, 291–300.

Cohen, D., & Nisbett, R. E. (1997). Field experiments examining the culture of honor: The role of institutions in perpetuating norms about violence. *Personality and Social Psychology Bulletin, 23*, 1188–1199.

Cohen, D., Nisbett, R. E., Bowdle, B. F., & Schwarz, N. (1996). Insult, aggression, and the Southern culture of honor: An "experimental ethnography." *Journal of Personality and Social Psychology, 70*, 945–960.

Denson, T. F., Lickel, B., Curtis, M., Stenstrom, D. M., & Ames, D. R. (2006). The roles of entitativity and essentiality in judgments of collective responsibility. *Group Processes and Intergroup Relations, 9*, 43–61.

Gelfand, M. J., Bhawuk, D. P., Nishii, L., & Bechtold, D. (2004). Individualism and collectivism. In R. J. House, P. J. Hanges, M. Javidan, P.W. Dorfman, & V. Gupta (Eds.), *Culture, leadership, and organizations: The GLOBE study of 62 cultures* (pp. 437–512). Thousand Oaks, CA: Sage.

Gelfand, M. J., Erez, M., & Aycan, Z. (2007). Cross-cultural organizational behavior. *Annual Review of Psychology, 58*, 479–514.

Gelfand, M. J., Shteynberg, G., Lee, T. L., Lun, J., Lyons, S., Bell, C.,... Soomro, N. (2012). The cultural transmission of intergroup conflict. *Philosophical Transactions of the Royal Society B, Biological Sciences, 367*, 692–703.

Ginat, J. (1987). *Blood disputes among Bedouin and rural Arabs in Israel: Revenge, mediation, outcasting and family honor.* Pittsburgh, PA: University of Pittsburg Press.

Grant, R. (2010, July 22). Paul Kagame: Rwanda's redeemer or ruthless dictator? *The Telegraph*, http://www.telegraph.co.uk/news/worldnews/africaandindianocean/rwanda/7900680/Paul-Kagame-Rwandas-redeemer-or-ruthless-dictator.html.

Greenberg, J., & Elliot, C. (2009). A cold cut crisis: Listeriosis, maple leaf foods, and the politics of apology. *Canadian Journal of Communication, 34*, 189–2004.

Greenberg, J., Solomon, S., & Pyszczynski, T. (1997). Terror management theory of self-esteem and cultural worldviews: Empirical assessments and conceptual refinements. *Advances in Experimental Social Psychology, 29*, 61–139.

Hamilton, D. L., Sherman, S. J., & Lickel, B. (1998). Perceiving social groups: The importance of the entitativity continuum. In C. Sedikides, J. Schopler, & C. Insko (Eds.), *Intergroup cognition and intergroup behavior* (pp. 47–74). Mahwah, NJ: Erlbaum.

Ho, D. Y. F. (1973). Changing interpersonal relationships in Chinese families. In H. E. White (Ed.), *An anthology of seminar papers: The changing family. East and West* (pp. 103–118). Hong Kong: Hong Kong Baptist College.

Hofstede, G. (1980). *Culture's consequences: International differences in work related values.* Beverly Hills, CA: Sage.

Hogg, M. A., Meehan, C., & Farquharson, J. (2010). The solace of radicalism: Self uncertainty and group identification in the face of threat. *Journal of Experimental Psychology, 46*, 1061–1066.

Kashima, Y., Kashima, E., Chui, C. Y., Farsides, M., Gelfand, M. J., Hong, Y. Y.,... Yzerbyt, V. (2005). Culture, essentialism, and agency. Are individuals universally believed to be more real entities than groups? *European Journal of Social Psychology, 35*, 147–269.

Kashima, Y., Yamaguchi, S., Kim, U., Choi, S., Gelfand, M. J., & Yuki, M. (1995). Culture, gender, and self: A perspective from individualism-collectivism research. *Journal of Personality and Social Psychology, 69*, 925–937.

Kahn, D. (2010). *For the sake of the eternal group: Perceiving the group as a trans-generational entity and willingness to endure ingroup suffering and sacrifice.* Unpublished Ph.D. dissertation, Tel Aviv University, Israel.

Kim, U. (1994). Individualism and collectivism: Conceptual clarification and elaboration. In U. Kim, H. C. Triandis, C. Kagitcibasi, S. C. Choi, & G. Yoon (Eds.), *Individualism and collectivism: Theory, method, and applications* (pp. 19–40). Thousand Oaks, CA: Sage.

Kluckhohn, F. R., & Strodtbeck, F. L. (1961). *Variations in value orientations.* Evanston, IL: Row, Peterson.

Landrine, H. (1995). Clinical implications of cultural differences: The referential versus the indexical self. In N. R. Goldberger & J. B. Veroff (Eds.), *The culture and psychology reader* (pp. 744–766). New York, NY: New York University Press.

Lickel, B., Hamilton, D. L., & Sherman, S. J. (2001). Elements of a lay theory of groups: Types of groups, relational styles, and the perception of group entitativity. *Personality and Social Psychology Review, 5*, 129–140.

Lickel, B., Miller, N., Stenstrom, D. M., Denson, T. F., Schmader, T. (2006). Vicarious retribution: The role of collective blame in intergroup aggression. *Personality and Social Psychology Review, 10*, 372–390.

Lickel, B., Schmader, T., Curtis, M., Scarnier, M., & Ames, D. R. (2005). Vicarious shame and guilt. *Group Processes and Intergroup Relations, 8*, 145–147.

Lickel, B., Schmader, T., & Hamilton, D. L. (2003). A case of collective responsibility: Who else was to blame for the Columbine High School shootings? *Personality and Social Psychology Bulletin, 29*, 194–204.

Maddux, W. W., & Yuki, M. (2006). The "ripple effect": Cultural differences in perceptions of the consequences of events. *Personality and Social Psychology Bulletin, 32*, 669–683.

Markus, H. R., & Kitayama, S. (1991). Culture and the self: Implications for cognition, emotion, and motivation. *Psychological Review, 98*, 224–253.

Markus, H. R., Kitayama, S., & Heiman, R. J. (1997). Culture and "basic" psychological principles. In E. T. Higgins & A. W. Kruglanski (Eds.), *Social psychology: Handbook of basic principles* (pp. 857–913). New York, NY: Guilford Press.

Miller, J. G., Bersoff, D. M., & Harwood, R. L. (1990). Perceptions of social responsibilities in India and the United States: Moral imperatives or personal decisions? *Journal of Personality and Social Psychology, 58*, 33–47.

Mullin, B-A., & Hogg, M. A. (1998). Dimensions of subjective uncertainty in social identification and minimal intergroup discrimination. *British Journal of Social Psychology, 37*, 345–365.

Nisbett, R. E., & Cohen, D. (1996). *Culture of honor: The psychology of violence in the South.* Boulder, CO: Westview.

Oishi, S. (2010). The psychology of residential mobility: Implications for the self, social relationships, and well-being. *Perspectives on Psychological Science, 5*, 5–21.

Parsons, T. (1949). Social classes and class conflict in the light of recent sociological theory. *American Economic Review, 39*, 16–26.

Pennebaker J. W., Francis M. E., & Booth R. J. (2001). *Linguistic inquiry and word count.* Mahwah, NJ: Erlbaum.

Pitt-Rivers, J. (1966). Honour and social status. In J. G. Peristiany (Ed.), *Honour and shame: The values of Mediterranean society* (pp.19–77). Chicago, IL: University of Chicago Press.

Prentice, D. A., Miller, D. T., & Lightdale, J. R. (1994). Asymmetries in attachments to groups and to their members: Distinguishing between common-identity and common-bond groups. *Personality and Social Psychology Bulletin, 20*, 484–493.

Schug, J., Yuki, M., Horikawa, H., Takemura, K. (2009). Similarity attraction and actually selecting similar others: How cross-societal differences in relational mobility affect interpersonal similarity in Japan and the United States. *Asian Journal of Social Psychology, 12*, 95–103.

Schug, J., Yuki, M., & Maddux, W. W. (2010) Relational mobility explains between- and within-culture differences in self-disclosure toward close friends. *Psychological Science, 21*, 1471–1478.

Schwartz, S. H. (1994). Beyond individualism/collectivism: New cultural dimensions of values. In U. Kim, H. C. Triandis, C. Kagitcibasi, S. C. Choi, & G. Yoon (Eds.), *Individualism and collectivism: Theory, method, and applications* (pp. 85–122). Thousand Oaks, CA: Sage.

Shavitt, S., Torelli, C., & Riemer, H. (2011). Horizontal and vertical individualism and collectivism: Implications for understanding psychological processes. In M. Gelfand, C-Y. Chiu, & Y-Y. Hong (Eds.), *Advances in culture and psychology* (Vol. 1, pp. 309–350). Oxford, UK: Oxford University Press.

Shteynberg, G., Gelfand, M. J., & Kim, K. (2009). Peering into the "magnum mysterium" of culture: The explanatory power of descriptive norms. *Journal of Cross-Cultural Psychology, 40*, 46–69.

Shweder, R. A., & Bourne, E. J. (1982). Does the concept of the person vary cross-culturally? In A. J. Marsella & G. M. White (Eds.), *Cultural conceptions of mental health and therapy* (pp. 97–137). London, UK: Reidel.

Singelis, T. M., Triandis, H. C., Bhawuk, D., & Gelfand, M. J. (1995). Horizontal and vertical dimensions of individualism and collectivism: A theoretical and measurement refinement. *Cross-Cultural Research: The Journal of Comparative Social Science, 29*, 240–275.

Stenstrom, D. M., Lickel, B., Denson, T. F., & Miller, N. (2008). The roles of ingroup identification and outgroup entitativity in outgroup retribution. *Personality and Social Psychology Bulletin, 34*, 1570–1582.

Tewfiq, A-H. (1977). Song of death. In M. Manzalaoui (Ed.) & M. M. Badawi (Trans.), *Arabic writing today: Drama* (pp. 65–184). Cairo, Egypt: AUC Press.

Toennies, F. (1957). *Community and society* (C. P. Loomis, Ed. & Trans.). East Lansing: Michigan State University Press.

Triandis, H. C. (1989). The self and social behavior in differing cultural contexts. *Psychological Review, 96*, 506–520.

Triandis, H. C. (1995). *Individualism and collectivism*. New York, NY: Simon & Schuster.

Triandis, H. C., Chen, X. P., & Chan, D. K. (1998). Scenarios for the measurement of collectivism and individualism. *Journal of Cross-Cultural Psychology, 29*, 275–289.

Triandis, H. C. & Gelfand, M. J. (1998). Converging measurement of horizontal and vertical individualism and collectivism. *Journal of Personality and Social Psychology, 74*, 118–128.

Triandis, H. C., McCusker, C., & Hui, C. H. (1990). Multimethod probes of individualism and collectivism. *Journal of Personality and Social Psychology, 59*, 1006–1020.
Vandello, J. A., Cohen, D., & Ransom, S. (2008). U.S. Southern and Northern differences in perceptions of norms about aggression: Mechanisms for the perpetuation of a culture of honor. *Journal of Cross-Cultural Psychology, 39*, 162–177.
Webster, D. M., & Kruglanski, A. W. (1994). Individual differences in need for cognitive closure. *Journal of Personality and Social Psychology, 67*, 1049–1062.
Yamagishi, T., & Suzuki, N. (2010). An institutional approach to culture. In M. Schaller, A. Norenzayan, S. J. Heine, T. Yamagishi, & T. Kameda (Eds.), *Evolution, culture, and the human mind* (pp. 185–203). New York, NY: Psychology Press.
Yuki, M. (2003). Intergroup comparison versus intragroup relationships: A cross-cultural examination of social identity theory in North American and East Asian cultural contexts. *Social Psychology Quarterly, 66*, 166–183.
Yzerbyt, V., Corneille, O., & Estrada, C. (2001). The interplay of subjective essentialism and entitativity in the formation of stereotypes. *Personality and Social Psychology Bulletin, 5*, 141–155.
Yzerbyt, V., Dumont, M., Wigboldus, D., & Gordijn, E. (2003). I feel for us: The impact of categorization and identification on emotions and action tendencies. *British Journal of Social Psychology, 42*, 533–549.
Zemba, Y., Young, M. J., & Morris, M. W. (2006). Blaming leaders for organizational accidents: Proxy logic in collective- versus individual-agency cultures. *Organizational Behavior and Human Decision Processes, 101*, 36–51.

INDEX